INSTANT POT
ELECTRIC PRESSURE COOKER
COOKBOOK

Top 500 Chef-Proved Super Quick, Easy And Delicious Instant Pot Recipes For Weight Loss and Overall Health

Melissa Leory

© Copyright 2018 -Melissa Leory -All rights reserved.

In no way is it legal to reproduce, duplicate, or transmit any part of this document by either electronic means or in printed format. Recording of this publication is strictly prohibited, and any storage of this material is not allowed unless with written permission from the publisher. All rights reserved.

The information provided herein is stated to be truthful and consistent, in that any liability, regarding inattention or otherwise, by any usage or abuse of any policies, processes, or directions contained within is the solitary and complete responsibility of the recipient reader. Under no circumstances will any legal liability or blame be held against the publisher for any reparation, damages, or monetary loss due to the information herein, either directly or indirectly.

Respective authors own all copyrights not held by the publisher.

Legal Notice:
This book is copyright protected. This is only for personal use. You cannot amend, distribute, sell, use, quote or paraphrase any part or the content within this book without the consent of the author or copyright owner. Legal action will be pursued if this is breached.

Disclaimer Notice:
Please note the information contained within this document is for educational and entertainment purposes only. Every attempt has been made to provide accurate, up to date and reliable, complete information. No warranties of any kind are expressed or implied. Readers acknowledge that the author is not engaging in the rendering of legal, financial, medical or professional advice.

By reading this document, the reader agrees that under no circumstances are we responsible for any losses, direct or indirect, which are incurred as a result of the use of information contained within this document, including, but not limited to, —errors, omissions, or inaccuracies.

Table of Contents

Introduction 26

Chapter 1. Everything About The Instant Pot 28

What is an Instant Pot? 28

    The instant pot will retain minerals and vitamins 28

    The instant pot cooks faster 28

    The instant pot is very easy to use 28

    The instant pot does not need anything else 29

How an Instant Pot Works(Scientific Mechanism) 29

Instant Pot Control Panel 29

Choosing a Good Instant Pot 30

    IP-DUO60 31

    IP-DUO Plus60 31

    IP-DUO50 31

    IP-DUO80 31

    IP-LUX60 V3 31

    IP-Smart Bluetooth 31

Do's and Don'ts of Instant Pot 31

    Be aware of cooking times 32

    Make sure and read all the instructions carefully 32

    Inspect your instant pot carefully 32

    Do not overfill your instant pot 32

    Do not press the timer button to set the cooking time 32

    Make sure not to add ingredients into your instant pot without the inner pot 32

    Don't use the quick release if your instant pot is overfilled or has foamy foods in it 32

Chapter 2. Collection of Beef-Based Instant Pot Recipes 33

1. Cabbage Beef Soup 33

2. Beef & Squash Stew 33
3. Beef & Mixed Vegetable Stew 34
4. Baby Back Beef Ribs 34
5. Instant Pot Keto Brisket 35
6. Keto Thai Beef 35
7. Keto Beef & Tomato Stuffed Squash 36
8. Keto Meatloaf 36
9. Ginger Beef & Kale 37
10. Salisbury Steak 37
11. Keto Corned Beef 38
12. Beef Bourguignon 38
13. Beef Curry 39
14. Beef Stroganoff 39
15. Keto Beef Chili 40
16. Keto Chili Con Carne 40
17. Beef Pot Roast 41
18. Beef & Vegetables 41
19. Veal with Mushrooms 42
20. Beef & Kale Casserole 42
21. Korean Beef 43
22. Beef & Broccoli 43
23. Beef and Cabbage 44
24. Instant Pot Beef Cabbage Rolls 44
25. Beef & Mushroom Soup 45
26. Spicy Beef & Cashew Curry 46
27. BBQ Pot Roast with Garlic Sauce 46
28. Cheesesteak Casserole 47
29. Cabbage Stew and Beef Shank 47

30. Shredded Beef with Avocado Salsa 48

31. Cheeseburger Soup 48

32. Beef Sirloin Lettuce Wraps 49

33. Ropa Vieja 49

34. Italian-style Beef 50

35. Asian Shredded Beef 50

36. Instant Pot Beef Ragu with Herbs 50

37. Hot Roast Machaca 51

38. Korean-style Beef Tacos 51

39. Instant Pot Beef Stew 52

40. Caribbean Ginger Oxtails 52

Chapter 3. Collection of Pork-Based Instant Pot Recipes 53

41. Apple Cider Pork 53

42. Pork Sausages & Sweet Potatoes 53

43. Sausage & Red Beans 54

44. Kalua Pork 54

45. Pork with Hominy 55

46. Pork Tostadas 55

47. Pork Tamales 56

48. Pork Carnitas 56

49. Instant Pot Balsamic Pork Tenderloin 57

50. Asian Pork Short Ribs 57

51. Ribs & Coleslaw 58

52. Country-style Ribs 59

53. Pork Chops & Spinach Salad 60

54. Pork Chops & Brown Rice 60

55. Braised Pork 61

56. Chinese Barbecue Pork 61

57. Pork Roast with Fennel...61
58. Pulled Pork...62
59. Creamy Pork Chops..63
60. Pork Chops and Onion...63
61. Apple Cider Pork..64
62. Bacon and Egg Omelette..64
63. Ham Hock Soup...65
64. Bacon, Spinach & Mozzarella Bundles...65
65. Keto Carbonara with Bacon & Cream..65
66. Chorizo Sausage with Feta, Spicy Tomatoes & Spinach................66
67. Sautéed Asparagus with Bacon..66
68. Instant Pot Scrambled Egg & Sausage..66
69. Instant Pot Split Pea & Ham Soup..67
70. Instant Pot Pork Feet & Soy Bean Soup..67

Chapter 4. Collection of Lamb-Based Instant Pot Recipes.................68
71. Instant Pot Lamb Curry...68
72. Instant Pot Lamb Curry with Yogurt..68
73. Instant Pot Mediterranean Lamb Roast..69
74. Instant Pot Middle Eastern Lamb Stew...69
75. Instant Pot Lamb Rogan Josh..70
76. Instant Pot Leg of Lamb Stew with Dates & Cinnamon................70
77. Lavender Lamb Chops..71
78. Leg of Lamb & Spinach Salad..71
79. Lamb Shanks & Carrots...72
80. Lamb & Coconut Curry with Cauliflower Rice..................................72
81. Instant Pot Lamb Chops with Creamed Cauliflower......................73
82. Instant Pot Cooked Lamb Tagine..74
83. Lamb, Butternut Squash & Chickpea Tagine....................................74

84. Lamb Tagine with Orange & Prunes 75
85. Lamb, Vegetable & Lentil Soup 75
86. Tuscan Lamb with White Beans 76
87. Moroccan Lamb Stew 76
88. Instant Pot Rack of Lamb 77
89. Garlic Rosemary Lamb 78
90. Lamb Shanks with Garlic & Port Wine 78
91. Instant Pot Irish Lamb Stew 78
92. Instant Pot Lamb Stew Provencal 79
93. Guinness Lamb Stew with Vegetables 80
94. Mushroom, Potato Lamb Stew 80
95. Greek Lamb Stew with Green Beans 81
96. Ground Lamb with Zucchini Pasta 81
97. Greek Lamb Shanks with Tomatoes 82
98. Lamb & White Bean Stew 82
99. Lamb Trotters with Tomato & Thyme 83
100. Mensaf (Jordanian Lamb Stew) 83

Chapter 5. Collection of Poultry-Based Instant Pot Recipes 84

101. Garlic Chicken 84
102. Ground Turkey & Basil Meatballs 84
103. Creamy Mushroom, Rosemary Chicken 85
104. Heavy Cream Chicken Stew 85
105. Ginger Spinach Chicken 86
106. Ginger Coconut Chicken Wings 86
107. Spicy, Creamy, Coconut Chicken 87
108. Jalapeno, Curry, Garlic Chicken Meatballs 87
109. Chicken Breasts & Spicy Sauce 88
110. Chicken & Spaghetti Squash 88

111. Chicken & Cauliflower Rice 88
112. Chicken Curry 89
113. Chicken and Mushrooms 90
114. Chicken and Salsa 90
115. Chicken, Walnuts, and Pomegranate 91
116. Turkey Instant Pot Stew 91
117. Lemongrass Chicken 91
118. Chicken and Cabbage 92
119. Chicken and Corn 92
120. Duck Chili 93
121. Chicken Gumbo 94
122. Chicken Delight 94
123. Party Chicken Wings 95
124. Roasted Chicken 95
125. Braised Turkey Wings 96
126. Braised Quail 96
127. Crispy Chicken 97
128. Chicken Salad 98
129. Stuffed Chicken Breasts 98
130. Turkey Mix and Mashed Potatoes 99
131. Duck & Vegetables 99
132. Braised Duck and Potatoes 100
133. Chicken in Tomatillo Sauce 100
134. Filipino Chicken 101
135. Instant Pot Keto Chicken Stew 101
136. Chicken Romano 102
137. Turkey Chili 102
138. Sweet & Tangy Chicken 103

139. Honey Barbecue Chicken Wings..103
140. Sticky Chicken Drumsticks..104
141. Chicken, Broccoli, & Cheese...104
142. Instant Pot Cream Chicken & Sausage..105
143. Instant Pot Chicken Hash..105
144. Instant Pot Chicken Bean Chili...106
145. Instant Pot Herbal Chicken...106
146. Instant Pot Chicken Fillets..107
147. Buttery Chicken with Macadamia..107
148. Mushroom & Chicken Hash..108
149. Cheesy Spinach Stuffed Chicken Breasts..108

Chapter 6. Collection of Seafood-Based Instant Pot Recipes....................... 109

150. Spicy Lemon Salmon...109
151. Coconut Shrimp Curry..109
152. Mediterranean Fish...110
153. Ginger, Sesame Glaze Salmon..110
154. Cauliflower Risotto and Salmon...111
155. Chili, Lime Cod..111
156. Instant Pot Halibut Fillets...112
157. Fish Fillets & Orange Sauce...112
158. Calamari & Tomatoes...113
159. Red Snapper & Chili Sauce..113
160. Baked Red Snapper..114
161. Red Snapper & Tomato Sauce...114
162. Thai Red Snapper...115
163. Lobster & Sweet Potatoes..115
164. Steamed Lobster...116
165. Simple Instant Pot Lobster..116

166. Spicy Sardines...117
167. Tasty Sardines...117
168. Teriyaki Salmon..118
169. Simple Salmon & Onion..118
170. Simple Instant Pot Salmon..119
171. Salmon Fillets with Sauce...119
172. Tuna Steaks..120
173. Tuna Casserole...120
174. Zucchini Pasta with Capers...121
175. Beans & Clams...121
176. Instant Pot Squid..122
177. Italian Braised Squid..122
178. Stuffed Squid..123
179. Seafood Masala...123
180. Mediterranean Octopus Dish..123
181. Portuguese Seafood Stew..124
182. Instant Pot Gumbo...124
183. Easy to Prepare Octopus...125
184. Shrimp Risotto...126
185. Flounder & Shrimp..126
186. Italian Shrimp Scampi...127
187. Spicy Shrimp..127
188. Special Shrimp Dish...127
189. Creole Shrimp..128
190. Shrimp Stew...128

Chapter 7. Collection of Soup Instant Pot Recipes........................129

191. Sweet Potato & Broccoli Soup...129
192. Squash & Potato Soup..129

193. Parsnip Soup...129

194. Turkey & Carrot Soup..130

195. Fish Soup..130

196. Asparagus & Sour Cream Soup..131

197. Turkey & Black Bean Soup..131

198. Brussels Sprouts Soup..131

199. Chicken & Spinach Soup...132

200. Tomato Soup...132

201. Chicken Soup with Noodles..132

202. Creamy Sausage & Kale Soup..133

203. Lentils & Tomato Soup..133

204. Mixed Veggie Soup...134

205. Pork Soup...134

206. Sweet Potato, Carrot & Turmeric Soup..134

207. Creamy Bean Soup...135

208. Cauliflower Soup..135

209. Garlicky Leek & Potato Soup...136

210. Bean Soup with Chili..136

211. Instant Pot Vegan Soup..137

212. Chicken Soup with Eggs..137

213. Smoky Ham Hock & Pinto Bean Soup...138

214. Potato Soup...138

215. Chicken, Ranch & Rice Soup...139

216. Bean Soup with Pork...139

217. Hamburger Barley Vegetable Soup..140

218. Black-Eyed Pea Soup...140

219. Curried Coconut Chicken Soup...141

220. Split-Pea & Ham Soup...141

Chapter 8. Collection of Keto-Friendly Grain-Based Recipes 142

221. Chicken & Wild Rice Soup 142
222. Quinoa Beef Pot 142
223. Keto Clam Chowder 143
224. Stuffed Cuttlefish 143
225. Saffron Chicken 144
226. Sesame Meatball Stew 144
227. Burrito with Chili Colorado 145
228. Sour Dumplings 146
229. Sausage Radish Cakes 146
230. Seafood Jambalaya 147
231. Shredded Pork Fajitas 148
232. Sausage Gumbo 149
233. Pork Fried Whole Grain Rice 149
234. Bacon Wrapped Jalapenos 149
235. Shredded Beef Tacos 150
236. Beef Stuffed Eggplant 150
237. Spicy Fire Chicken with Rice 151
238. Spiced Apple & Walnut Chicken 151
239. Pulled Chicken in Soft Whole Wheat Tacos 151
240. Pesto Chicken & Whole Wheat Pasta 152
241. Pasta & Brown Turkey Sauce 152
242. Orange Chicken Drumsticks & Rice 153
243. Mediterranean Mint & Basil Chicken & Rice 153
244. Mango Citrus Chicken & Rice 153
245. Lemon, Capers, Chicken & Chinese Black Rice 154
246. Jerk Chicken Strips & Wild Rice 154
247. Greek Chicken & Sprouted Rice 155

248. Chicken Fried Wild Rice 155
249. Stuffed Bell Peppers 155
250. Chipotle Tacos 156
251. Breakfast Burritos 156
252. Wild Mushroom Rice 157
253. Spiach Casserole 157
254. Mexican Rice 158
255. Rice Pilaf 158
256. Red Beans Over Sprouted Brown Rice 159
257. Israeli Couscous 159
258. Wild Rice & Black Beans 159
259. Perfect Brown Rice 160
260. Lentil & Wild Rice Pilaf 160

Chapter 9. Collection of Keto-Friendly Egg-Based Instant Pot Recipes 161

261. Eggs En Cocotte 161
262. Spinach & Tomato Crustless Quiche 161
263. Bacon & Cheese Egg Muffins 162
264. Meaty Crustless Quiche 162
265. Breakfast in a Jar 163
266. Bread Pudding 163
267. Boiled Eggs 164
268. Turkey Meatballs with Mushroom Gravy 164
269. Cheese-Stuffed Mini Turkey Meatloaves & Mushroom Gravy 165
270. Mushroom Stroganoff 166
271. Korean Style Steamed Eggs 166
272. Eggs De Provence 167
273. Instant Pot Poached Eggs Over Spicy Potato Hash 167
274. Instant Pot Ham & Egg Casserole 168

275. Instant Pot Aromatic Egg 168
276. Instant Pot Western Omelette Quiche 169
277. Instant Pot French Baked Eggs 169
278. Instant Pot Mexican Egg Casserole 170
279. Eggs Papin Poached Eggs in Bell Pepper Cup 170
280. Egg Bake 171
281. Bacon and Egg Risotto 171
282. Instant Pot Sausage & Egg Breakfast Burritos 171
283. Poached Tomato Eggs 172
284. Instant Pot Scrambled Eggs 173
285. Instant Pot Soft Eggs 173
286. Instant Pot Soft-Boiled Eggs 173
287. Mushroom & Spinach Crustless Quiche 174
288. Instant Pot Scotch Eggs 174
289. Instant Pot Banana French Toast 175
290. Potato Egg Frittata, Quiche 175
291. Instant Pot Cheesy, Bacon & Potato Egg Bake 176
292. Instant Pot Eggs Ketogenic Style 177
293. Breakfast Egg Bread Spread 177
294. Cocoa & Bacon Muffins 177
295. Keto Style Sunny Side Up Eggs 178
296. Mug Cake with Berries & Cream 178
297. Cauliflower & Cheesy Muffins 179
298. Ketogenic Grilled Toast 179
299. Sausage, Pepper, & Cheese Rings 179
300. Egg, Beef & Bacon Fest 180

Chapter 10. Collection of Bean & Lentil-Based Instant Pot Recipes 181

301. Mung Bean Dahl 181

302. Red Bean & Lentil Chili 181

303. Falafel 182

304. Chickpea Curry 182

305. Lentil Sloppy Joe's 183

306. Lentil and Wild Rice Pilaf 183

307. Instant Pot Hummus 184

308. Stewed Chickpeas 184

309. Rainbow Beans 185

310. Northern White Bean Dip 185

311. Greek-Style Gigantes Beans with Feta 186

312. Chili Con Carne 186

313. Smokey Sweet Black-Eyed Peas & Greens 187

314. Tex Mex Pinto Beans 187

315. Instant Pot Charros 188

316. Three Bean Salad 188

317. Beans Stew 189

318. Not Re-Fried Beans 190

319. Baked Beans 190

320. Stewed Tomatoes & Green Beans 191

321. White Beans with Greens & Lemon 191

322. White Bean Dip with Tomatoes 192

323. Bacon & Black Beans 192

324. Black Bean & Sweet Potato Hash 193

325. Refried Bean Nachos 193

326. Green Bean Casserole 194

327. Green Bean, Sweet Potato & Spinach Risotto 194

328. Steamed Green Beans 195

329. Spicy Green Beans 195

330. Italian Cannellini Beans & Mint Salad 196
331. Refried Pinto Beans 196
332. Spice Black Bean & Brown Rice Salad 197
333. Quick-Soaking Dry Beans 197
334. Black-Eyed Pea Chili 197
335. Moroccan Chicken 198
336. Baked Bean Mix 198
337. Bean Counter's Medley 199
338. Tomato Lima Bean Parmigiana 199
339. Curried Cauliflower & Beans 200
340. Black Beans & Black Chinese Rice 200

Chapter 11. Collection of Vegetable Instant Pot Recipes 201

341. Sweet Potato, Red Lentil, Hemp Burgers 201
342. Creamy Kidney Beans & Lentils 201
343. Sweet Potato, Lentil & Coconut Curry 202
344. Millet & Lentils with Vegetables & Mushrooms 202
345. Basmati Rice 203
346. Vegan Butter Chickpeas 203
347. Potatoes & Peas 204
348. Spicy Veggie Mix 204
349. Vegetable Masala Mix 205
350. Masala Eggplant 205
351. Mushroom Matar Masala 206
352. Curried Potato Eggplant 206
353. Coconut Tofu Curry 207
354. Tomato Stewed Green Bean 207
355. Sesame Tofu 208
356. Lentil & Spinach Dal 208

357. *Spinach Chana Masala* 209

358. *Lentil Bolognese* 210

359. *Coconut Quinoa Curry* 210

360. *Garlic Mashed Potatoes* 210

361. *Marinara Sauce* 211

362. *Cauliflower Rice* 211

363. *Delicious Dumplings* 212

364. *Sweet Potato Pie* 212

365. *Tasty Tofu* 213

366. *Instant Pot Broccoli & Tomato Pasta* 213

367. *Refried Beans* 214

368. *Peanut & Sweet Potato Stew* 214

369. *White Bean Stew with Kale & Winter Squash* 215

370. *Lasagna Soup* 215

371. *Chickpea & Rice Soup* 216

372. *Veggie Stew* 216

373. *Mung Bean Stew* 217

374. *Curried Butternut Squash Soup* 218

375. *Split Pea Soup with Navy Beans & Sweet Potatoes* 218

376. *Lentil Red Curry & Coconut Milk Soup* 218

377. *Lentil Risotto* 219

378. *Mushroom Risotto* 219

379. *Garlic Mushrooms with White Beans* 220

380. *Potato Risotto* 220

381. *Pumpkin, Chicken, Corn Chowder* 220

382. *Sweet Summer Corn Chowder* 221

383. *Winter Minestrone* 222

384. *Potato Soup* 222

385. Bean Soup with Pork 222
386. Vegetable Barley Soup 223
387. Maple Bacon Acorn Squash 224
388. Sweet Potato Soup 224
389. Tomato, Basil & Beef Soup 225
390. African Chickpea, Coconut Soup 225
391. Lentil Vegetable Soup 226
392. Creamy Tomato Soup 226
393. Taco Soup 227
394. Mango Dal 227
395. Tuscan Chicken Stew 228
396. Butternut Squash & Spinach Lasagna Rolls 228
397. Summer Garden Boiled Peanut Salad 229
398. Wheat Berry Salad 229
399. Green Bean Casserole 230
400. Red, White & Green Brussels Sprouts 230

Chapter 12. Collection of Desserts & Appetizer Instant Pot Recipes 231

401. Chocolate Almond Fudge Cake 231
402. Pumpkin Chocolate Chip Bundt Cake 231
403. Tapioca Pudding 232
404. Carrot Cake 232
405. Brownies 233
406. Apple Crisp 233
407. Vanilla Fruit Cake 233
408. Creamy Chocolate Cheesecake 234
409. Apple Crumb Cake 235
410. Raspberry Cream Cheesecake 235
411. Crema Catalana 236

412. Cranberry Cake...237
413. Chocoflan..238
414. Cheese Flan Cake...239
415. Raspberry Curd..239
416. Fruit Clafoutis Cake...240
417. Yams Citrus..240
418. Chocolate Custard...241
419. Bread Pudding...241
420. Blueberry Custard...242
421. Purple Pudding..242
422. Mango & Cashew Cake..243
423. Corn Pudding...243
424. Pumpkin Pie...243
425. Instant Pot Chocolate Fondue..244
426. Samoa Cheesecake...245
427. Salted Caramel Cheesecake..246
428. Pumpkin Crème Brulee...247
429. Peanut Buttercup Cheesecake...247
430. Oreo Cheesecake..248
431. Orange Marble Cheesecake...249
432. Key Lime Pie..250
433. Hazelnut Flan...250
434. Custard Cream Cheesecake...251
435. Cranberry Baked French Toast..252
436. Cinnamon Raisin Bread Pudding with a Caramel Pecan Sauce.........252
437. Chocolate Cake..253
438. Borlotti Bean Brownie Cake..254
439. Chocolate Fudge Cake..254

440. Turtle Pull-Apart Biscuits 255
441. Lemon Cheesecake 255
442. Caramel Macchiato Cake 256
443. Apple Peach Cobbler 256
444. Messy Coconut Cake 257
445. Vanilla Butterscotch 257
446. Sticky Caramel Cake 258
447. Cherry Pie 258
448. Classic Coconut Pudding 259
449. Buttermilk Banana Bake 259
450. Lemongrass Pudding 260

Chapter 13. Collection of Marinades & Sauces Instant Pot Recipes 261

Sweet Sauces for Hot and Cold Desserts 261
451. Cherry Cranberry Sauce 261
452. Sweet Blackberry and Brandy Sauce 261
453. Strawberry Sauce 261
454. Lemon Dessert Sauce 262
455. Brandy Sauce 262
456. Chocolate Sauce 262
457. Cherry Sauce 263
458. Hot Fudge Sauce 263
459. Classic Caramel Sauce 263

Sauces & Marinades that Compliment Vegetarian Dishes 264
460. Chicken & Blueberry Pasta Sauce 264
461. Sweet Chocolate Pasta Sauce 264
462. Strawberry Sauce for Spaghetti 264
463. Yogurt Sauce 265
464. Wasabi with Maple Marinade 265

Marinades & Sauces that Compliment Meat & Chicken Dishes 266

465. Garlic with Lemon Marinade 266

466. Bourbon Marinade 266

467. Asian-Inspired Marinade 266

468. Spicy Orange Marinade 266

469. Olive & Lemon Moroccan Sauce 267

470. Spicy Peanut Sauce 267

471. Spicy Orange Sauce 268

472. Classic Stir-Fry Sauce 268

473. Sorghum Steak Wet Rub 268

474. Orange & Nutmeg Poultry Rub 269

475. Creole Rub 269

476. Ketchup with Cola Marinade 269

477. Spicy Beer Wings Marinade 270

478. Coffee Steak Marinade 270

479. Blue Cheese Sauce 271

480. Classic Pepper Sauce 271

481. Chili Sauce with Tomato 271

482. Classic Cream & Garlic Sauce 272

483. Marinara Sauce 272

484. Brown Sauce 272

485. Veloute Sauce 273

486. Tuscan Style Meat Sauce 273

487. Indonesian Soy Sauce 274

488. Sweet Coney Island Sauce 274

489. Wine Sauce 274

490. Mustard Cream Sauce 275

491. Green Pea Sauce 275

492. Mexican Mole Sauce 275
493. Thai-Style Peanut Sauce with Honey 276
494. Ginger-Tamarind Sauce 276
495. Enchilada Sauce 277
496. Creamy White Wine Sauce 277
497. Sweet & Sour Sauce 277
498. Mustard Sauce 278
499. Cranberry Sauce 278
500. Rum Sauce 278

Conclusion 280

Introduction

I would like to thank and congratulate you for choosing this book *"INSTANT POT ELECTRIC PRESSURE COOKER COOKBOOK- Top 500 Chef-Proved Super Quick, Easy And Delicious Instant Pot Recipes."*

This book is suitable for people of all shapes and sizes! My hope is that this collection of healthy instant pot recipes is going to help lead you and your loved ones to healthier lifestyle. All of these recipes are easy to make and delicious. Most of them are suit for people in Ketogenic Die, Low carb Diet, Atkins Diet, Paleo Diet, Vegan & Vegetarian Diet. They are all healthy and will do good to your weight loss goal! You will like them!

I know that it can be hard to lose weight, but when you find a way to do it that you will enjoy you are much more likely to succeed in your weight loss goals. I am sure you want to be healthy, avoid illness, and be a healthy weight, while getting to enjoy delicious foods. Well the good news is you can get healthy and enjoy your meals at the same time when you use this collection of weight loss instant pot recipes.

Are you like many of us and find yourself so busy with work and other things in life that you often have no time to cook? With the wonderful instant pot, you will be able to toss the ingredients into your instant pot, allow the cooking process to work its magic and before you know it you will have a delicious healthy meal to enjoy! I hope you will have plenty of healthy meals using this book as an easy guide on using the instant pot!

Chapter 1. Everything About The Instant Pot

What is an Instant Pot?

The Instant Pot is a wonderful kitchen aide, it is a multi-cooker which was designed to prepare various meals quickly and deliciously. Using an Instant Pot, you will be able to slow cook, pressure cook, sauté, make rice, yogurt and much more, all of these can be done just by pressing a few buttons and letting your instant pot do the rest. Most models come with an automatic shut-off button, so your food will not overcook once it is ready. There is plenty of benefits connected to the instant pot, including:

The instant pot will retain minerals and vitamins

Pressure cooking will allow you to retain more minerals and vitamins, opposed to other cooking methods such as steaming or boiling. The longer you cook your foods, the more nutrition will be lost out of your food, especially when cooking vegetables. Using the instant pot that only takes minutes to cook, it will retain most of its minerals and vitamins needed to help fuel your body.
Pressure cooking can also make foods easier to digest, such as lentils and beans. In a word, cook foods in your instant pot without worrying about upsetting your stomach.

The instant pot cooks faster

With an instant pot it uses pressure and heat to cook your foods; it will take much less time to cook foods. If for example it takes you one hour to cook chicken in a conventional oven it may only take 20 minutes or less to do the same job with your instant pot.

The instant pot is very easy to use

When you are preparing your meals using the conventional oven or stovetop you need to pay full attention to make sure you do not burn or ruin your meal. With the instant pot you just need to place the ingredients into it and allow it to do the rest. No need any cooking skills, no need to stand before it when cooking. The instant pot is also very easy to clean. All you have to do is to remove the gasket from the cover and wash it with warm water.

The instant pot does not need anything else

The only kitchen appliance you will need is the instant pot. You can prepare breakfast, lunch, dinner and dessert, all with the instant pot. In this cookbook you will have 500 easy and delicious instant pot recipes to try out!

How an Instant Pot Works(Scientific Mechanism)

The instant pot is a great kitchen appliance to help you to prepare meals through pressure cooking. With pressure cooking steam is used and sealed in the pressure cooker, it is an airtight cooking pot. If you add some water, the pressure will trap the vapor that rises from the liquid. Thus, it causes the pressure to raise within the cooker, along with the temperature of the water. With the increased temperature in both water and pressure, cooking time is accelerated.

The instant pot is easy to use, all you have to do is to add your ingredients into the pot and adjust the settings. You will learn what and how to use the various buttons on your instant pot.

Instant Pot Control Panel

Below is an explanation about the different controls and settings on the instant pot:

Manual: This is the main button on your instant pot. With this button you can manually set the pressure and cooking time.

Keep Warm/Cancel: This button will cancel any functions and will turn your instant pot off. If your cooking is completed, the instant pot will automatically enter the *keep warm* mode and will stay there for 10 hours. You can cancel the function at any time.

Pressure: When you cook in manual button, this button will adjust your settings of pressure to low, medium, or high.

Slow Cook: By pressing this button you will turn your instant pot into a slow cooker.

Timer: This is the button you would use for delayed cooking. You first would select a cooking function and make any required adjustments. Then you can adjust the timer button using the +/- buttons.

Sauté: With this button it will allow you to sauté and brown your foods. When you are cooking using this button you will have the lid off, this will enable you to stir your ingredients. You can adjust the heat from sauté by pressing the normal setting, more, or less. Normal is for regular browning, more is for stir-frying, and less is for simmering.

Meat/Stew: With this button you can set your instant pot to high pressure for 35 minutes.

Poultry: This button will automatically set your instant pot to high pressure for 15 minutes.

Steam: This button will automatically place your instant pot on high for 10 minutes.

Porridge: This button will automatically set your instant pot to high pressure for 20 minutes.

Multi-Grain: This button will automatically set your instant pot at high pressure for 40 minutes.

Bean/Chili: This button will automatically set your instant pot to high pressure for 30 minutes.

Soup: This button automatically will set your instant pot to high pressure for 30 minutes.

Yogurt: Pressing this button will allow you to make yogurt using your instant pot.

You need to know how to release pressure with a pressure cooker. With the instant pot there are two ways either through natural release or quick release. Using the natural release allows the pressure to release on it own naturally. With the quick release you turn the valve on top from the 'sealing' setting to the 'venting' setting.

Choosing a Good Instant Pot

There are diverse types of instant pots available on the market. You will have to decide which is the best one for you and your needs. One of the most popular is a 6-quart version to larger and more advanced models. Below are some options you might want to consider when choosing your instant pot:

IP-DUO60
This model of instant pot is the most popular. It offers a 7-in-1 multifunctional countertop appliance; which combines a slow cooker, pressure cooker, rice cooker, yogurt maker, steamer, sauté/browning functionality and a warmer.

IP-DUO Plus60
This model is an upgrade to the regular IP-DUO60. This upgraded version includes settings such as Egg, Cake, and Sterilize buttons. The alarm clock on this model is a blue LCD screen. The inner bowl also offers more comprehensive max/min fill lines.

IP-DUO50
This model of instant pot holds five quarts.

IP-DUO80
This model of instant pot has a capacity of eight quarts. It is more expensive than others, but the extra space might be useful.

IP-LUX60 V3
This model of instant pot has egg and cake settings on the control panel. However, it does not have poultry, yogurt or beans/chili settings, nor an option to cook on low pressure. It also does not come with some of the accessories that other models have.

IP-Smart Bluetooth
This model of instant pot holds six quarts with all the basic functions, and can connect via Bluetooth to your phone; so, you are able to program and monitor cooking from anywhere using the Instant Pot Smart Cooker App.

Choosing the right instant pot for yourself should not be too complicated. It is best to purchase new appliances not used, as they could have broken buttons and complications.

Do's and Don'ts of Instant Pot

If you are new to using an instant pot it would be a clever idea to become familiar with what you should and should not do with your instant pot. Below are some helpful tips for cooking with an instant pot:

Be aware of cooking times
Cooking times are a great indicator to give you an idea when your food should be cooked, but the actual cooking time can vary. This is largely due to different ingredients being used and done in different situations. For instance, different meats will take different amounts of time to soften up. Make sure to be mindful of your cooking by inspecting the result to make sure it is cooked through. You can test a small piece from your meal that you are preparing to see that it is cooked through before removing it from the instant pot.

Make sure and read all the instructions carefully
When you get your new instant pot, read all the instructions carefully to avoid any mishaps or damaging your instant pot.

Inspect your instant pot carefully
To keep your instant pot as a reliable appliance you need to make sure that you keep it clean. If parts on your instant pot begin to wear out then they need to be replaced by original parts, or you could run the risk of permanently damaging your instant pot.

Do not overfill your instant pot
If you fill your instant pot with too much food and liquid this could cause the venting knob to become clogged. There is a max line on the inner pot make sure that you do not go past this, so you won't overfill your instant pot.

Do not press the timer button to set the cooking time
People often mistake the 'timer' button for the button to set the cook time, and then wonder why their instant pot is not working. Make sure to check that the 'timer' button is not lit before you leave.

Make sure not to add ingredients into your instant pot without the inner pot
You do not want to pour ingredients into your instant pot without its inner pot being in place, believe me this happens a lot. This can cause damage and will be time consuming to clean.

Don't use the quick release if your instant pot is overfilled or has foamy foods in it
Inexperienced users of instant pots often get the Quick Pressure Release and Natural Pressure Release confused. If you use the Quick Release when you are cooking foamy foods, such as applesauce, beans, or grains, it could splatter everywhere. To prevent this from occurring use the natural release or release the pressure gradually.

Chapter 2. Collection of Beef-Based Instant Pot Recipes

1. *Cabbage Beef Soup*

Cook Time: 40 minutes **Servings: 6**

Ingredients:
- 1 head green cabbage, chopped
- 1 lb. lean ground beef
- 1 head red cabbage, chopped
- 1 can (28-ounce) tomatoes, diced
- 1 celery stalk, chopped
- 3 cups water
- 1 teaspoon fresh ground black pepper
- 1 teaspoon salt
- 1 tablespoon fresh parsley, chopped

Directions:
First press the sauté button on your instant pot. Add in the ground beef. Sauté your beef until it is no longer pink; drain. Press the keep warm/cancel setting to stop sauté mode. Return your ground beef to your instant pot. Add in the cabbage, diced tomatoes, celery, parsley, water, salt and pepper. Stir well. Close and seal the lid. Press the meat/stew button. Cook on high pressure for 20 minutes. Once completed the instant pot will automatically switch to 'keep warm' mode. Allow it to 'keep warm' mode for 10 minutes. Use the 'quick-release' when done. Open the lid carefully. Stir the ingredients, serve and garnish with fresh parsley.

Nutritional Information per serving:
Calories: 115   Fat: 4.4g   Carbohydrates: 11g   Dietary Fiber: 3g   Protein: 11g

2. *Beef & Squash Stew*

Cook Time: 50 minutes **Servings: 4**

Ingredients:
- 2 lbs. butternut squash, peeled, chopped into chunks
- 1 lb. lean ground beef
- 1 (6-ounce) can sliced mushrooms
- 2 garlic cloves
- 1 red onion, diced
- 4 cups beef broth
- 2 tablespoons butter
- 1 teaspoon fresh rosemary, chopped
- 1 teaspoon black pepper
- 1 teaspoon salt
- 2 teaspoons paprika

Directions:
Press the sauté button on your instant pot. Melt the butter. Sauté the garlic and onions for 1 minute. Add the ground beef, mushrooms, and butternut squash. Sauté until the beef is no longer pink and the vegetables have softened. Press the keep warm/cancel button to stop the sauté mode. Add in beef stock, paprika, salt, black pepper and rosemary, mix well. Close and seal the lid. Press the soup button. Cook on high pressure for 30 minutes. After the 30 minutes is up your instant pot will automatically switch to the 'keep warm' mode and remain in 'keep warm' for 10 minutes. Use the 'quick-release' when done and open the lid carefully, stir ingredients and serve.

Nutritional Information per serving:
Calories: 245   Fat: 7g   Protein: 25g   Carbohydrates: 15g   Dietary Fiber: 8g

3. Beef & Mixed Vegetable Stew

Cook Time: 45 minutes
Ingredients:
- 4 zucchinis, chopped
- 1 ½ lbs. stewing beef chunks
- 4 cups vegetable broth
- 2 cups frozen peas
- 2 carrots, chopped
- 1 tablespoon coconut oil
- ½ cup ghee

Servings: 4

- 4 cloves garlic, minced
- 1 red onion, chopped
- 2 tomatoes, chopped
- 1 tablespoon ginger
- 2 tablespoons cumin
- Salt and pepper to taste

Directions:
Press the sauté button on instant pot. Heat your coconut oil. Add onions and garlic and sweat for 1 minute. Add in your stewing beef and brown all sides. Add the zucchini, peas and carrots. Press the keep warm/cancel setting to stop the sauté mode. Add your ghee and stir well. Now add the vegetable stock, tomatoes, ginger, cumin, salt and pepper. Stir well. Close and seal lid of pot and press the meat/stew button. Cook for 35 minutes. When your instant pot timer beeps, quick-release or naturally release pressure. Open the pot lid carefully. Stir and spoon into serving bowls.

Nutritional Information per serving:
Calories: 200   Protein: 31g   Fat: 40g   Carbohydrates: 13g   Dietary Fiber: 4g

4. Baby Back Beef Ribs

Cook Time: 45 minutes
Ingredients:
- 1 rack of baby back beef ribs
- 2 cups beef broth
- 2 tablespoons granulated Splenda
- 2 tablespoons soy sauce
- 2 tablespoons coconut oil
- 4 garlic cloves, minced
- 3 tablespoons ginger, grated

Servings: 4

- 1 teaspoon onion powder
- 1 teaspoon cayenne pepper
- 1 teaspoon low-carb brown sugar
- 1 teaspoon ground mustard
- 1 tablespoon paprika
- 1 tablespoon chili powder
- Salt and pepper to taste

Directions:
In a small bowl mix together chili powder, ginger, ground mustard, paprika, cayenne pepper, onion powder, salt and pepper and stir well. Add in brown sugar and Splenda. Rinse your ribs, you will want the ribs to be a bit damp, so the seasoning will cling to them. Rub seasoning mix on both sides of ribs. Place the ribs on a flat baking sheet. Preheat your oven to broil. Place the baking sheet under the broiler for 5 minutes per side. Press the sauté mode on your instant pot. Heat the coconut oil. Add ginger and garlic. Cook for 1 minute.

Add soy sauce and beef broth. Boil for 15 seconds. Stir well. Press keep warm/cancel setting to end the sauté mode. Slice the rack of ribs up into chunks of 4-5 ribs and place them into your instant pot. Close and seal the lid and press manual button. Cook on high-pressure for 35 minutes. When done release the pressure quickly or naturally. Open lid carefully and serve.

Nutritional Information per serving:
Calories: 500   Fat: 40g   Carbohydrates: 1.5g   Dietary Fiber: 0.9g   Protein: 55g

---

5. *Instant Pot Keto Brisket*
Cook Time: 50 minutes   ***Servings:*** 5
Ingredients:
- 2 lbs. of beef brisket
- 2 tablespoons coconut oil
- 2 shallots, thinly sliced
- 3 tablespoons tomato paste
- 1 tablespoon dry mustard
- 2 tablespoons Worcestershire sauce
- 2 tablespoons soy sauce
- 8-ounces low-carb beer
- Salt and pepper to taste

Directions:
Add all the ingredients to a large Ziploc bag and massage the ingredients. Allow them to marinate for 2 hours. When ready to cook, transfer the ingredients into your instant pot. Close the lid and press the manual setting. Cook on high-pressure for 40 minutes. Once done, quick-release or naturally release the pressure. Open the instant pot lid carefully. Press the sauté mode. Cook until all the liquids evaporate. Remove the brisket. Let rest for 15 minutes before slicing. Serve and enjoy!

Nutritional Information per serving:
Calories: 400   Fat: 20g   Carbohydrates: 3.5g   Dietary Fiber: 0.5g   Protein: 45g

---

6. *Keto Thai Beef*
Cook Time: 30 minutes   ***Servings:*** 6
Ingredients:
- 1 lb. of beef, cut into strips
- 2 tablespoons coconut oil
- 4 garlic cloves, minced
- 2 teaspoons ginger, grated
- 2 cups beef broth
- Zest and juice of 1 lemon
- 1 red bell pepper, chopped
- 1 green bell pepper, chopped
- 1 tablespoon coconut amino
- 1 cup roasted pecans
- Salt and pepper to taste

Directions:
Press the sauté button on your instant pot. Heat the coconut oil. Sauté ginger and garlic for 1 minute. Add in the beef strips. Sear them for 2 minutes per side. Add bell peppers, salt and pepper. Continue to cook until meat is no longer pink. Add the coconut amino, zest and juice of lemon, pecans, and beef broth. Stir well. Close and seal lid. Press the manual setting and cook on high-pressure for 15 minutes. When done, naturally release the pressure. Open lid carefully and let sit for 10 minutes. Serve.

Nutritional Information per serving:
Calories: 225   Fat: 15g   Dietary Fiber: 1g   Carbohydrates: 20g   Protein: 20g

7. Keto Beef & Tomato Stuffed Squash

Cook Time: 30 minutes **Servings:** 4

Ingredients:
- 1 lb. of beef chopped into chunks
- 1 yellow bell pepper
- 1 green bell pepper
- 2 tablespoons ghee, melted
- 2 tablespoons coconut oil
- 1 lb. butternut squash, peeled and chopped
- 2 (14-ounce) cans of diced tomatoes
- 4 garlic cloves, minced
- 1 teaspoon cayenne pepper
- 2 tablespoons fresh parsley, chopped
- 1 tablespoon fresh rosemary, chopped
- 1 tablespoon fresh thyme, chopped
- 1 yellow or red onion, chopped
- Salt and pepper to taste

Directions:
Press sauté button on your instant pot. Heat the coconut oil. Add the onion and garlic and sweat for 2 minutes. Add the beef chunks, bell peppers, and butternut squash. Sauté until the meat is no longer pink and veggies have softened. Press keep warm/cancel to end the sauté mode. Add in the melted ghee, tomatoes, parsley, rosemary, cayenne, salt and pepper. Stir well. Close the lid and seal. Press the manual button and cook on high-pressure for 20 minutes. Quick-release the pressure when done and open lid carefully. Serve.

Nutritional Information per serving:
Calories: 250   Fat: 7g   Dietary Fiber: 2g   Carbohydrates: 4g   Protein: 10g

8. Keto Meatloaf

Cook Time: 35 minutes **Servings:** 4

Ingredients:
- 3 lbs. lean ground beef
- 4 garlic cloves, minced
- 1 yellow onion, chopped
- 1 cup mushrooms, chopped
- 3 large eggs
- ¼ cup parsley, fresh, chopped
- ¼ cup mozzarella cheese, grated
- ¼ cup parmesan cheese, grated
- ½ cup almond flour
- 2 cups water
- 2 tablespoons coconut oil
- 2 tablespoons sugar-free ketchup
- Salt and pepper to taste

Instructions:
Cover trivet with aluminum foil. In a large bowl, add ingredients (excluding the water) until well combined. Form into a meatloaf. Pour water in your instant pot. Place trivet inside. Place the meatloaf on trivet. Close and seal lid. Press manual button and cook on high-pressure for 25 minutes. When done, natural release the pressure. Allow meatloaf to rest for 5 minutes before slicing. Serve.

Nutritional Information per serving:
Calories: 250   Fat: 15g   Dietary Fiber: 3g   Carbohydrates: 5g   Protein: 25g

9. Ginger Beef & Kale
Cook Time: 35 minutes **Servings:** 4
Ingredients:
- 1 lb. beef cut into chunks
- 1 bunch of kale, stemmed, chopped
- 2 tablespoons coconut oil
- 2 tablespoons ginger, fresh, grated
- 4 garlic cloves, minced
- 1 red onion, chopped
- 2 cups beef broth
- 1 teaspoon paprika
- ½ lb. mushrooms, sliced
- Salt and pepper to taste
- Sesame seeds for garnish
- 2 spring onions, chopped, for garnish

Directions:
Press sauté button on your instant pot. Heat your coconut oil. Add in the onions and garlic and sweat for 1 minute. Add the beef chunks and sauté until the meat is no longer pink. Press the keep warm/cancel setting to end the sauté mode. Add in the remaining ingredients. Stir well. Close and seal the lid. Press manual button and cook at high-pressure for 25 minutes. When the timer beeps, quick-release or naturally release pressure. Open the lid and stir ingredients. Divide into serving plates, garnish with sesame seeds and chopped spring onion. Serve.

Nutritional Information per serving:
Calories: 325   Fat: 15g   Carbohydrates: 20g   Dietary Fiber: 2.5g   Protein: 30g

10. Salisbury Steak
Cook Time: 35 minutes **Servings:** 4
Ingredients:
- 2 lbs. lean ground beef
- 1 tablespoon coconut oil
- ½ yellow onion, diced
- 1 tablespoon Worcestershire sauce
- ¼ cup beef broth
- ¼ cup coconut flour
- 1 egg
- 1 tablespoon bread crumbs
- 2 garlic cloves, minced
- 1 tablespoon parsley, fresh, chopped
- Salt and pepper to taste

Gravy Ingredients:
- 2 cups mushrooms, sliced
- 2 tablespoons ghee, melted
- 1 onion, sliced
- 2 tablespoons parsley, fresh, chopped
- ¼ cup sour cream
- 1 tablespoon tomato paste
- 1 teaspoon Worcestershire sauce
- Salt and pepper to taste

Directions:
In a large mixing bowl, steak ingredients, except coconut oil. Shape into round patties, ¼ inch thick. Set aside. Press your sauté button on your instant pot. Heat the coconut oil. Cook the patties 2 minutes per side, until they are golden brown. Remove the patties and set aside. Heat the ghee and add gravy ingredients. Stir well. Press the keep warm/cancel button to end sauté mode. Return patties to your instant pot. Close and seal the lid. Press

manual switch and cook at high-pressure for 25 minutes. When done quick-release pressure. Open lid carefully. Serve.
Nutritional Information per serving:
Calories: 425   Fat: 35g   Carbohydrates: 5g   Protein: 32g   Dietary Fiber: 1g

---

11. *Keto Corned Beef*
Cook Time: 60 minutes
Servings: 6
Ingredients:
- 4 lbs. beef brisket
- 2 oranges, sliced
- 2 garlic cloves, minced
- 3 bay leaves
- 1 tablespoon dried dill
- 11 ounces celery, sliced thin
- 2 yellow onions, sliced thin
- 4 cinnamon sticks, cut in half
- 17 ounces of water
- Salt and pepper to taste

Directions:
Place your beef in a bowl, and cover with some water, set aside to soak for a few hours, drain and transfer to your instant pot. Add in orange slices, celery, bay leaves, onions, garlic, dill, cinnamon, salt and pepper. Stir and cover instant pot and cook on the meat/stew setting for 50 minutes. Release using quick-release or natural release of pressure, set the beef aside for 5 minutes. Transfer meat to cutting board, slice and place onto serving plates. Drizzle the juice and vegetables from instant pot over the beef. Serve.
Nutritional Information per serving:
Calories: 251   Fat: 3.14g   Fiber: 1g   Carbs: 11g   Protein: 17g

---

12. *Beef Bourguignon*
Cook Time: 30 minutes
Servings: 6
Ingredients:
- 10 lbs. round steak, cut into small cubes
- 2 tablespoons white flour
- 8 ounces mushrooms, cut into quarters
- 3 bacon slices, chopped
- 1 cup dry red wine
- ½ cup beef stock
- 2 carrots, peeled and sliced
- 12 pearl onions
- 2 garlic cloves, minced
- ¼ teaspoon basil, dried
- Salt and pepper to taste

Directions:
Set the instant pot on sauté mode, add the bacon, and brown it for two minutes. Add the beef pieces, stir and brown for 5 minutes. Add the flour and stir. Add wine, basil, garlic, onions, salt and pepper, cover and cook on the meat/stew setting for 20 minutes. Release the pressure, naturally, uncover the instant pot and add in the mushrooms and carrots. Cover the instant pot again and cook on manual setting for 5 minutes. Release the pressure again naturally, divide the beef bourguignon among serving plates. Serve.
Nutritional Information per serving:
Calories: 442   Fat: 17.2g   Fiber: 3g   Carbs: 16g   Protein: 39g

13. Beef Curry
Cook Time: 20 minutes
Servings: 4
Ingredients:

- 2 lbs. beef steak, cubed
- 3 potatoes, diced
- 2 tablespoons virgin olive oil
- 1 tablespoon Dijon mustard
- 2 garlic cloves, minced
- 2 yellow onions, chopped
- 2 ½ tablespoons curry powder
- 10 ounces canned coconut milk
- 2 tablespoons tomato sauce
- Salt and pepper to taste

Directions:
Set your instant pot to sauté mode, add oil, and heat. Add the garlic and onions and cook for 4 minutes. Add the potatoes and mustard, stir, cook for 1 minute. Add the beef and brown on all sides. Add the curry powder, salt and pepper and cook for 2 minutes. Add the coconut milk and tomato sauce, stir and cover your instant pot. Cook on the meat/stew setting for 10 minutes. Release the pressure with quick-release and then uncover pot. Divide the curry onto serving plates. Serve.

Nutritional Information per serving:
Calories: 434   Fat: 20g   Fiber: 2.9g   Carbs: 14g   Protein: 27.5g

14. Beef Stroganoff
Cook Time: 25 minutes
Servings: 4
Ingredients:

- 10 lbs. beef, cut into small cubes
- 2 ½ tablespoons almond flour
- 2 garlic cloves, minced
- 2 ½ tablespoons olive oil
- 4 ounces mushrooms, sliced
- 1 ½ tablespoon tomato paste
- 3 tablespoons Worcestershire sauce
- 13 ounces beef stock
- 8 ounces sour cream
- Egg noodles, already cooked, for serving
- Salt and pepper to taste

Directions:
Put all the beef, flour, salt and pepper in a bowl and toss to coat. Set your instant pot on sauté mode, add olive oil, and heat. Add in the meat and brown on all sides. Add the garlic, mushrooms, onion, Worcestershire sauce, stock and tomato paste and mix well. Cover instant pot and cook on the meat/stew setting for 20 minutes. Use quick-release to release the pressure. Remove the top of pot and add in the sour cream, salt and pepper. Divide among serving plates. Serve.

Nutritional Information per serving:
Calories: 335   Fat: 18.4g   Fiber: 1.3g   Carbs: 22.5g   Protein: 20.1g

15. Keto Beef Chili
Cook Time: 40 minutes
Servings: 6
Ingredients:
- 1 ½ lbs. ground beef
- 17 ounces beef stock
- 16 ounces mixed beans, soaked overnight and drained
- 1 sweet onion, chopped
- 28 ounces canned diced tomatoes
- 6 garlic cloves, chopped
- 1 teaspoon chili powder
- 1 bay leaf
- 3 tablespoons chili powder
- 4 carrots, chopped
- 2 tablespoons olive oil
- 7 jalapeno peppers, diced

Directions:
Set your instant pot on sauté mode and add half of the olive oil and heat it up. Add in the beef and brown for 8 minutes, then transfer to a bowl. Add the rest of the oil to the instant pot and heat up. Add in the jalapenos, onion, carrots and garlic, stir and sauté for 4 minutes. Add tomatoes and stir. Add beans, stock, chili powder, bay leaf, beef, salt and pepper. Cover and cook on the bean/chilli setting for 25 minutes. Release the pressure naturally, uncover your instant pot, stir chili and transfer into serving bowls. Serve.

Nutritional Information per serving:
Calories: 272   Fat: 5g   Fiber: 1g   Carbs: 32g   Protein: 25g

16. Keto Chili Con Carne
Cook Time: 30 minutes
Servings: 4
Ingredients:
- 1 lb. of ground beef
- 4 tablespoons coconut oil
- 1 yellow onion, chopped
- 2 garlic cloves, minced
- 4 ounces kidney beans, soaked overnight and drained
- 8 ounces tomatoes, canned, diced
- 1 tablespoon chili powder
- ½ teaspoon cumin
- 5 ounces water
- 1 teaspoon tomato paste

Directions:
Set your instant pot to sauté mode, add 1 tablespoon coconut oil and heat it up. Add in the meat and brown for a few minutes then transfer to a bowl. Add the rest of the coconut oil to the instant pot and heat it up. Add in the garlic, and onion and cook for 3 minutes. Return the beef to pot, beans, tomato paste, chili powder, tomatoes, cumin, salt, pepper and water. Cover pot and cook on the bean/chili setting for 18 minutes. Release the pressure naturally. Uncover the instant pot and divide the chili into serving bowls. Serve.

Nutritional Information per serving:
Calories: 256   Fat: 8g   Fiber: 1g   Carbs: 22g   Protein: 35g

17. Beef Pot Roast
Cook Time: 1 hour **Servings:** 6
Ingredients:
- 3 lbs. beef roast
- 17 ounces beef stock
- 3 ounces red wine
- 1 yellow onion, chopped
- 4 garlic cloves, minced
- 3 carrots, chopped
- 5 potatoes, chopped
- ½ teaspoon smoked paprika
- Salt and pepper to taste

Directions:
In a bowl mix the salt, pepper and paprika and rub on beef and place it into the instant pot. Add the garlic, stock, wine, onion, and toss to coat. Cover the instant pot and cook on meat/stew setting for 50 minutes. Release the pressure naturally. Uncover the instant pot and add in the potatoes and carrots and cover it again. Cook on the steam setting for 10 minutes. Release the pressure naturally again, uncover and transfer the roast to a serving platter. Drizzle roast with cooking juices and serve with the veggies on the side.

Nutritional Information per serving:
Calories: 290 Fat: 20g Fiber: 1g Carbs: 2g Protein: 35g

18. Beef & Vegetables
Cook Time: 30 minutes **Servings:** 4
Ingredients:
- 1 ½ lbs. beef chuck roast, cubed
- 2 tablespoons of coconut oil
- 4 tablespoons almond flour
- 1 yellow onion, chopped
- 2 cups water
- 2 garlic cloves, minced
- 2 tablespoons red wine
- ½ bunch parsley, chopped
- 4 potatoes, chopped
- 2 carrots, chopped
- 2 celery stalks, chopped
- ½ teaspoon thyme, dried
- 2 cups beef stock
- Salt and pepper to taste

Directions:
Mix the salt and pepper with half of almond flour and season the beef with it. Set the instant pot on sauté mode, add the coconut oil and heat it up. Add the beef and brown it for 2 minutes. Once meat is browned transfer to bowl. Add the onion to the instant pot and cook for 3 minutes. Add the garlic, stir and cook for 1 minute. Add the wine, stir and cook for 15 seconds. Add the rest of the almond flour and stir for 2 minutes.
Return the meat to the instant pot, add water, thyme, stock and cover and cook on meat/stew setting for 12 minutes. Release the pressure naturally. Remove the lid of instant pot and add potatoes and carrots into pot. Cover pot and cook on steam setting for 5 minutes. Release the pressure naturally. Uncover the instant pot, divide among serving plates, serve with parsley sprinkled on top.

Nutritional Information per serving:
Calories: 221 Fat: 5.3g Fiber: 1g Carbs: 20.2g Protein: 32.7g

19. Veal with Mushrooms

Cook Time: 35 minutes　　　　　　**Servings:** 4

Ingredients:
- 3.5 ounces button mushrooms, sliced
- 3.5 ounces shiitake mushrooms, sliced
- 9 ounces beef stock
- 16 ounces shallots, chopped
- 17 ounces potatoes, chopped
- 2 lbs. veal shoulder, cut into medium chunks
- 3 ½ tablespoons coconut oil
- 1/8 teaspoon thyme, dried
- 1 teaspoon sage, dried
- 2 tablespoons chives, chopped
- 2 garlic cloves, minced
- 1 tablespoon almond flour
- 2 ounces white wine
- Salt and pepper to taste

Directions:
Set your instant pot to sauté mode and add 1 1/2 tablespoons of coconut oil and heat it up. Add the veal, season with salt and pepper, brown for 5 minutes and transfer to bowl. Add the rest of coconut oil into instant pot and heat it up. Add the mushrooms and stir and cook for 3 minutes. Add the garlic and cook for 1 minute, transfer to bowl.
Add the almond flour and wine to the instant pot and cook for 1 minute. Add the stock, thyme and sage to instant pot and return the meat to pot. Stir, cover and cook on the meat/stew setting for 20 minutes. Release the pressure naturally. Uncover the pot, return the garlic and mushrooms, add the potatoes, shallots stir and cover. Cook on the manual setting for 4 minutes. Release the pressure again and uncover the pot, add salt and pepper, chives and stir. Divide among serving bowls. Serve.

Nutritional Information per serving:
Calories: 395　Fat: 18g　Fiber: 1.4g　Carbs: 7.1g　Protein: 47.8g

20. Beef & Kale Casserole

Cook Time: 20 minutes　　　　　　**Servings:** 4

Ingredients:
- 2 cups of kale, fresh, chopped
- 1 lb. ground beef
- 13 ounces mozzarella cheese, shredded
- 16 ounces tomato puree
- 1 celery stalk
- 1 carrot, chopped
- 1 yellow onion, chopped
- 2 tablespoons butter
- 1 tablespoons red wine
- Salt and pepper to taste

Directions:
Set your instant pot on sauté mode, add the butter and melt it. Add the onion, carrot, stir and cook for 5 minutes. Add the beef, salt, pepper and cook for 10 minutes. Add the wine and stir and cook for 1 minute. Add the kale, tomato puree, cover with water and stir set on manual setting for 6 minutes. Release the pressure naturally. Uncover the pot and add the cheese and stir. Divide into serving bowls. Serve.

Nutritional Information per serving:
Calories: 182　Fat: 11g　Fiber: 1.4g　Carbs: 31g　Protein: 22g

21. Korean Beef

Cook Time: 25 minutes **Servings: 6**

Ingredients:
- 1 cup beef stock
- ¼ cup soybean paste
- 2 lbs. beefsteak, cut into strips
- 1 yellow onion, sliced thin
- 1-ounce shiitake mushroom caps, cut into quarters
- 1 zucchini, cubed
- ¼ teaspoon red pepper flakes
- 1 scallion, chopped
- 1 chili pepper, sliced
- 12 ounces extra firm tofu, cubed
- Salt and pepper to taste

Directions:
Set the instant pot on sauté mode and add the stock and soybean paste, stir and simmer for 2 minutes. Add the beef, pepper flakes, salt and pepper. Cover the instant pot and cook on the meat/stew setting for 15 minutes. Release the pressure naturally. Add the zucchini, onion, tofu, and mushrooms, stir and bring to a boil. Cover the instant pot and cook on manual setting for 4 minutes. Release the pressure naturally again, uncover the instant pot, add more salt and pepper, add the chili pepper and scallion. Stir. Divide into serving bowls. Serve.

Nutritional Information per serving:
Calories: 310   Fat: 9.3g   Fiber: 0.2g   Carbs: 18.4g   Protein: 35.3g

22. Beef & Broccoli

Cook Time: 10 minutes **Servings: 4**

Ingredients:
- 3 lbs. beef chuck roast, cut into thin strips
- 1 tablespoon peanut oil
- 2 tablespoons almond flour

For the marinade:
- 1 tablespoon sesame oil
- 2 tablespoons fish sauce
- 1 cup soy sauce
- 5 garlic cloves, minced
- 2 teaspoons toasted sesame oil
- 1 lb. broccoli florets
- 1 yellow onion, chopped
- ½ cup beef stock
- 3 red peppers, crushed, dried
- ½ teaspoon Chinese five spice powder
- Toasted sesame seeds for serving

Directions:
Mix the soy sauce, with the fish sauce and 1 tablespoon of sesame oil in a bowl. Add in garlic and five spice powder along with crushed red peppers and stir well. Add the beef strips and toss to coat. Set the instant pot to sauté mode, adding peanut oil and heat it up. Add the onions and cook for 4 minutes. Add the beef and marinade and cook for 2 minutes. Add the stock and stir, cover the instant pot. Cook on the meat/stew setting in 5 minutes. Release the pressure naturally for 10 minutes.
Uncover the instant pot and add the almond flour with ¼ cup liquid from the instant pot, add the broccoli to the steamer basket, cover the instant pot again and cook for 3 minutes

on manual mode. Release the pressure and uncover the instant pot and divide the beef into serving bowls add the broccoli on top and drizzle with toasted sesame seeds. Serve.

Nutritional Information per serving:
Calories: 338   Fat: 18g   Fiber: 5g   Carbs: 50g   Protein: 40g

---

23. Beef and Cabbage
Cook Time: 1 hour and 20 minutes   ***Servings: 6***
Ingredients:
- 2 ½ lbs. beef brisket
- 6 potatoes, cut into quarters
- 1 cabbage head, cut into wedges
- 4 carrots, peeled and chopped
- 3 cloves garlic, peeled, chopped
- 2 bay leaves
- 4 cups water
- 1 turnip cut into quarters
- Horseradish sauce, for serving
- Salt and pepper to taste

Directions:
Add the beef brisket and water into your instant pot, add garlic, bay leaves, salt and pepper, cover the instant pot. Set on the meat/stew setting for 1 hour and 15 minutes. Release the pressure with quick-release. Add to instant pot carrots, potatoes, cabbage, and turnip, stir and cover. Cook on the manual setting for 6 minutes. Release the pressure naturally, and uncover your instant pot. Divide among serving plates. Serve with horseradish sauce on top.

Nutritional Information per serving:
Calories: 340   Fat: 24g   Fiber: 1g   Carbs: 14g   Protein: 46g

---

24. Instant Pot Beef Cabbage Rolls
Cook Time: 38 minutes   ***Servings: 6***
Ingredients:
- 2 lbs. lean ground beef
- ½ teaspoon, freshly ground black pepper
- 4 cloves garlic, minced, finely
- 1 cup green onion
- 1 large egg
- 1 large head of cabbage
- 1 cup brown rice
- 1 teaspoon sea salt

For the sauce:
- 1 cup onion, finely chopped
- 2 tablespoons butter
- 3 cloves of garlic, finely minced
- Chopped, fresh parsley for garnish
- 2 tablespoons cold water
- 1 tablespoon cornstarch
- 4 dashes Worcestershire sauce
- ½ teaspoon freshly ground black pepper
- 1 teaspoon onion powder
- ½ teaspoon garlic powder
- ¼ cup white vinegar
- 2 teaspoons low-sodium instant beef bouillon
- 1 (8-ounce can) tomato sauce
- 2 (14-ounce cans) tomatoes, diced with their juice

Directions:

Cook the brown rice according to package directions. Fluff with fork and set aside. Fill a deep large pot half full of water, and bring to a boil over high heat. Remove the core from the cabbage, and place the cabbage core side down into the pot of water. Cover and allow the head of cabbage to boil for 10 minutes. Keep checking and removing the outer leaves as they soften on the cabbage, removing them to a plate to cool. Once you have removed all the large leaves to make rolls, cook the smaller leaves until they are crisp-tender. When done remove them from heat and coarsely chop them and set aside.

For your sauce take a large saucepan and melt the butter in it, add the onion, and cook over medium heat for 2 minutes, add the garlic and stir for another minute. Add in the tomatoes, bouillon, vinegar, garlic powder, Worcestershire sauce, onion powder, salt and pepper, mix well. Remove from heat and stir in some of the chopped cabbage and set aside.

For your cabbage roll filling add to a large bowl, beaten egg, onion, cooked rice, garlic, salt, pepper, ground beef and mix with your hands until ingredients are well combined.

Take a cabbage leaf and lay it flat on a work surface with the stem end facing you. Take to tablespoonfuls of filling and place it at the bottom of the cabbage leaf. Fold in the sides of the leaf and roll away from you. Repeat this with the remaining cabbage leaves and filling, on average you should get about 15 rolls.

Place a layer of sauce in your instant pot then a layer of cabbage rolls, repeat this, layer, do not fill too much, you might have to do two batches. Secure the lid so that it is sealed and set to the Meat/Stew setting for 20 minutes. When the cooking is completed, release the pressure naturally for 15 minutes, then use quick-release to get rid of any remaining steam. Remove cabbage rolls to a platter. Set instant pot to sauté mode and bring sauce to a boil. In small bowl whisk the cornstarch and cold water, then add into sauce to thicken. Divide rolls into serving bowls, pour sauce over rolls. Serve hot!

Nutritional Information per serving:
Calories: 389   Fat: 25g   Fiber: 1g   Carbs: 23g   Protein: 37g

---

25. Beef & Mushroom Soup

Cook Time: 25 minutes   **Servings: 4**

Ingredients:

- 1 ½ lbs. steak, thinly sliced
- 32 ounces beef stock
- 10 ounces Cremini mushrooms, thinly sliced
- 3 tablespoons butter
- 3 tablespoons garlic, minced
- 1 medium onion, diced
- 1 cup heavy cream
- 1 cup sour cream
- 2 tablespoons beef bouillon granules
- 2 tablespoons Dijon mustard
- 2 tablespoons Italian parsley, chopped
- 1 ½ teaspoons onion powder
- 1 ½ teaspoons garlic powder
- 1 teaspoon Oregano, dried
- 1 teaspoon sea salt
- Black pepper to taste

Directions:
Set your instant pot onto sauté mode and add the butter and heat. Add in the onions and garlic. Add in the beef strips, mushrooms and beef stock. Sauté for a few minutes or until

beef is no longer pink. Press the keep warm/cancel button to stop sauté mode. Add in rest of ingredients and press the meat/stew button on instant and set for 20 minutes. Release pressure naturally. Remove lid and divide into serving bowls. Serve.

Nutritional Information per serving:
Calories: 310   Fat: 18.4g   Fiber: 1.3g   Carbs: 22.5g   Protein: 30.1g

26. *Spicy Beef & Cashew Curry*
Cook Time: 20 minutes   **Servings: 4**
Ingredients:
- 2lbs chuck roast
- 6 tablespoons coconut milk
- 2 tablespoons Thai fish sauce
- 2 red chilis, fresh, chopped
- 1 tablespoon onion flakes
- 1 tablespoon cumin, ground
- 5 cardamom pods, cracked
- 3 tablespoons red curry paste
- 2 cups water
- 1 tablespoon coriander, ground
- 1 tablespoon ginger, ground
- ¼ cup cashews, roughly chopped, for garnish when serving
- ¼ cup cilantro, fresh, chopped, top when serving
- 2 tablespoons coconut oil

Directions:
Set your instant pot on sauté mode and add coconut oil and heat. Add in the beef and brown on all sides for a few minutes. Press the keep warm/cancel button to cancel sauté mode once meat is browned. Set instant pot to meat/stew setting for 20 minutes. Add remaining ingredients to instant pot except the cashews and cilantro. Release pressure naturally. Open the lid and divide into serving dishes. Serve.

Nutritional Information per serving:
Calories: 374   Fat: 20g   Fiber: 2.6g   Carbs: 14g   Protein: 35.5g

27. *BBQ Pot Roast with Garlic Sauce*
Cook Time: 1 hour   **Servings: 4**
Ingredients:
- 4 lbs. chuck shoulder roast
- 5 teaspoons garlic, minced
- 1 yellow onion, chopped
- 2 tablespoons Worcestershire sauce
- 3 tablespoons butter
- 4 tablespoons vinegar
- 1 tablespoon mustard
- 1 teaspoon liquid smoke
- Salt and pepper to taste

Directions:
Rub the roast with salt and pepper. Set instant pot to sauté and add butter, then add the roast and brown meat on all sides. Press keep warm/cancel button to cancel the sauté mode. Add all other ingredients into the instant pot and set on meat/stew setting for 1 hour. Release the pressure naturally. Open the lid of pot and stir. Divide into serving dishes. Serve with choice of veggies.

Nutritional Information per serving:
Calories: 270   Fat: 20g   Fiber: 1g   Carbs: 2g   Protein: 23g

28. Cheesesteak Casserole

Cook Time: 1 hour **Servings:** 6

Ingredients:
- 2 lbs cube steak, cut into strips
- 1 red pepper, cut into strips
- 1 green pepper, cut into strips
- ½ lb. mushroom, sliced
- ¼ lb. pepperoni, thinly sliced
- 8 ounces provolone cheese, thinly sliced
- 1 tablespoon coconut oil
- 1 onion, thinly sliced
- Salt and pepper to taste

Directions:
Set your instant pot to sauté mode, and add in the coconut oil. Add the mushrooms and steak and saute until meat is no longer pink. Add in remaining ingredients except the cheese, and press the keep warm/cancel button to cancel sauté mode. Set your instant pot to the meat/stew setting for 50 minutes. Release pressure naturally. Remove the lid and stir. Divide into serving dishes. Top each dish with cheese, allow cheese to melt and then serve.

Nutritional Information per serving:
Calories: 296   Fat: 18.4g   Fiber: 1.3g   Carbs: 20.5g   Protein: 30.1g

29. Cabbage Stew and Beef Shank

Cook Time: 50 minutes **Servings:** 4

Ingredients:
- 2 center-cut beef shanks
- 4 cloves garlic, minced
- ½ lb. baby carrots
- 2 medium onions, chopped
- 1 small cabbage, cut into wedges
- 15-ounce can tomato, diced, drained
- 1 cup beef stock
- Salt and pepper to taste
- 2 tablespoons coconut oil

Directions:
Set your instant pot to sauté mode, and add in coconut oil. Add in the beef shanks and sauté until the meat is no longer pink. Press the keep warm/cancel button to stop sauté mode. Open lid of instant pot and add rest of ingredients. Set on meat/stew setting for 50 minutes. Release pressure naturally. Open lid and stir. Remove the meat and shred with fork. Divide into serving dishes. Serve.

Nutritional Information per serving:
Calories: 310   Fat: 22g   Fiber: 1g   Carbs: 14g   Protein: 42g

30. Shredded Beef with Avocado Salsa
Cook Time: 1 hour and 10 minutes   **Servings:** 6
Ingredients:
- 2 lbs. beef chuck roast, cut into strips
- 1 tablespoon taco seasoning

Cabbage Slaw & Dressing Ingredients:
- ½ a small head of cabbage
- 1 small green cabbage
- ½ cup thinly sliced green onion

Avocado Salsa Ingredients:
- 2 large avocados, diced
- 1 tablespoon lime juice, fresh squeezed
- 2 tablespoons coconut oil
- 2 cans diced green chilies with juice
- 2 teaspoons green tabasco sauce
- 6 tablespoons mayo
- 4 teaspoons lime juice, fresh squeezed
- 1 medium Poblano pepper, diced very small
- 1 tablespoon extra-virgin olive oil
- 1 cup cilantro, freshly chopped

Directions:
Remove all excess fat from the meat and cut into strips. Season the meat strips with taco seasoning. Set your instant pot to sauté mode. Add in coconut oil and meat, sauté until meat is no longer pink and browned on all sides. Press the keep warm/cancel button to stop sauté once the meat is browned. Set to meat/stew setting for 1 hour. Release the pressure naturally. Remove the meat from instant pot and shred on chopping board with a fork. Place shredded meat back into your instant pot and replace the lid and keep on the keep warm/cancel setting. Slice the cabbage and the green onions to tiny strips using a slicer. Make the dressing by whisking the green Tabasco, mayo, and lime juice together. Mix the strips of cabbage and onions with the dressing. Slice the avocados and mix with lime juice. Chop cilantro and Poblano pepper very finely, and mix with the avocado. Pour in olive oil and mix. Place slaw in serving bowls. Top with beef and avocado salsa. Serve.

Nutritional Information per serving:
Calories: 296   Fat: 21g   Fiber: 1g   Carbs: 14g   Protein: 33g

31. Cheeseburger Soup
Cook Time: 25 minutes   **Servings:** 4
Ingredients:
- 1 lb lean ground beef
- 4 cups beef broth low sodium
- 1 teaspoon Worcestershire sauce
- 2 teaspoons parsley, fresh chopped
- ½ red bell pepper
- 2 tomatoes, chopped
- 8 ounces tomato paste
- ½ cup onions, chopped
- 1 teaspoon garlic powder
- ½ cup cheese
- Salt and pepper to taste
- 2 tablespoons coconut oil

Directions:

Set your instant pot to sauté mode. Add the coconut oil. Add in the ground beef and sauté until the meat is no longer pink and is browned. Press the keep warm/cancel button to stop sauté mode. Set the instant pot to meat/stew setting for 20 minutes. Add the rest of the ingredients and stir. Close the lid. Once done release pressure naturally. Add to serving dishes. Top with cheese. Serve.

Nutritional Information per serving:
Calories: 187   Fat: 5g   Fiber: 1.4g   Carbs: 32g   Protein: 38g

---

32. *Beef Sirloin Lettuce Wraps*
Cook Time: 40 minutes   **Servings:** 6
Ingredients:
- 2 lbs. sirloin roast, excess fat removed
- 1 teaspoon smoked paprika
- 1 tablespoon chili powder
- 2 cups beef broth
- 1 onion, chopped
- Salt and pepper to taste
- Lettuce leaves to use to wrap meat, as needed

Directions:
Add all your ingredients into your instant pot. Set your instant pot on the meat/stew setting for 40 minutes. Once done release the pressure naturally. Remove the lid and stir. Remove the meat to chopping board and shred the meat with a fork. Return the meat to the instant pot. Place lettuce leaves on serving plates then top them with meat. Serve.

Nutritional Information per serving:
Calories: 296   Fat: 20g   Fiber: 1g   Carbs: 14g   Protein: 37g

---

33. *Ropa Vieja*
Cook Time: 25 minutes   **Servings:** 4
Ingredients:
- 2 lbs. flank steak, cut into strips
- 1 yellow pepper
- 1 green pepper
- 1 onion, thinly sliced
- 4 teaspoons cumin
- 4 teaspoons oregano
- 3 teaspoons garlic, minced
- 3 tablespoons tomato paste
- 1 tablespoon capers
- Sea salt to taste
- 2 tablespoons olive oil

Directions:
Add the olive oil to your instant pot and set it to sauté mode. Add in meat strips and sauté until browned. Press the keep warm/cancel button to turn off the sauté mode. Add remaining ingredients into the pot and set to meat/stew setting for 20 minutes. Release the pressure with quick-release. Remove the lid and stir ingredients. Divide into serving dishes. Serve.

Nutritional Information per serving:
Calories: 282   Fat: 20g   Fiber: 1g   Carbs: 14g   Protein: 39g

34. Italian-style Beef
Cook Time: 45 minutes
Servings: 4
Ingredients:
- 2 lbs. boneless beef brisket
- 6 cloves of garlic, minced
- 1 onion, sliced
- 1 teaspoon red pepper flakes
- ½ cup red wine
- 2 cups fat-free beef broth
- Salt and pepper to taste
- 1 tablespoon Italian seasoning

Directions:
Rub the beef with salt and pepper. Place the beef along with the rest of the ingredients into your instant pot. Set to meat/stew setting for 45 minutes. Once done release the pressure naturally. Remove the lid and stir. Remove the meat and shred with fork then place it back into the instant pot.

Nutritional Information per serving:
Calories: 274   Fat: 22g   Fiber: 1g   Carbs: 16g   Protein: 42g

35. Asian Shredded Beef
Cook Time: 50 minutes
Servings: 4
Ingredients:
- 2 lbs. beef eye of round roast
- ¼ cup rice wine vinegar
- ½ cup soy sauce
- ¼ cup brown sugar
- 2 tablespoons ketchup
- 2 tablespoons sesame seeds
- 1-inch piece of ginger, fresh, grated
- 2 teaspoons Asian chili sauce
- 6 cloves of garlic, minced
- ½ red onion, minced
- 1 jalapeno, minced

Directions:
In a bowl add the soy sauce, brown sugar, vinegar, sesame seeds, ginger, ketchup, Asian chili sauce. Whisk these ingredients, add in the onion, jalapeno, and garlic. Place the roast into the instant pot. Pour the sauce over the roast. Cook on the meat/stew setting for 50 minutes. When done release naturally. Remove the meat and shred the meat with a fork. Replace the meat back into the instant pot. Allow it to sit for 30 minutes on the keep warm setting.

Nutritional Information per serving:
Calories: 287   Fat: 22g   Fiber: 1g   Carbs: 12g   Protein: 36g

36. Instant Pot Beef Ragu with Herbs
Cook Time: 30 minutes
Servings: 4
Ingredients:
- 2 lbs lean chuck beef
- ½ onion, diced
- 1 rib of celery, diced
- 2 tablespoons oregano, fresh, chopped
- 2 tablespoons rosemary, fresh, minced
- 1.5 cups beef broth
- 1-14 ounce can tomatoes, diced

- 1-14 ounce can tomatoes, crushed
- 4 garlic cloves, minced
- 1 carrot, peeled, diced

Directions:
Rub the meat with salt and pepper and place it in the instant pot. Add remaining ingredients to the instant pot. Set to meat/stew setting and cook for 30 minutes. Once done then release the pressure naturally. Remove the lid and stir ingredients. Divide into serving dishes. Serve.

Nutritional Information per serving:
Calories: 292   Fat: 19g   Fiber: 2g   Carbs: 14g   Protein: 36g

---

37. *Hot Roast Machaca*
Cook Time: 45 minutes   **Servings: 4**
Ingredients:

- 2 lbs. rump roast
- 3 serrano chiles, stemmed, seeded, and minced
- 3 garlic cloves, minced
- 1 cup red bell pepper, diced
- 1 ½ cups onion, diced
- 4 tablespoons fresh lime juice
- 2 tablespoons Worcestershire sauce
- 2 tablespoons of Maggi sauce
- Salt and pepper to taste
- ½ cup beef broth
- ½ teaspoon oregano, dried
- ½ 14-ounce can diced tomatoes with juice

Directions:
Rub the meat with salt and pepper and place into your instant pot. In a bowl mix Maggi, beef broth and lime juice. Pour the mixture over the meat. Add all other ingredients into instant pot. Set to meat/stew setting for 45 minutes. Once it is done release pressure naturally. Remove the lid and stir the ingredients, remove meat shred with fork. Return meat to pot. Keep on warm setting for 20 minutes. Divide into serving dishes. Serve.

Nutritional Information per serving:
Calories: 296   Fat: 23g   Fiber: 3g   Carbs: 14g   Protein: 34g

---

38. *Korean-style Beef Tacos*
Cook Time: 55 minutes   **Servings: 6**
Ingredients:

- 2 lbs. beef roast
- ½ tablespoon Truvia
- 1/3 soy sauce
- 4 garlic cloves, minced
- 1-inch ginger root, fresh, peeled, grated
- ½ red onion, diced
- 2 jalapenos, diced
- 2 tablespoons seasoned rice wine vinegar
- 2 tablespoons sesame seeds
- Serve on flour tortillas

Directions:
In a bowl add Truvia, sesame seeds, jalapenos, ginger and mix well. Add in the rice wine vinegar and soy sauce. Add the beef into instant pot, rub garlic into meat. Pour sauce over the meat and place lid on instant pot. Set to meat/stew setting for 55 minutes. When done release the pressure naturally. Remove the meat and shred, then place back into the

instant pot and allow to stay for 20 minutes on keep warm setting. Divide into serving dishes on top of flour tortillas. Serve.
Nutritional Information per serving:
Calories: 302   Fat: 23g   Fiber: 3g   Carbs: 14g   Protein: 34g

---

39. *Instant Pot Beef Stew*
Cook Time: 40 minutes　　　　　　　**Servings: 4**
Ingredients:
- 2 lbs cubed beef
- 1 tablespoon ghee
- 2 cups beef broth
- 1 red onion, sliced
- 1 carrot, peeled, chopped
- 2 celery stalks, diced
- 1 cinnamon stick
- 5 cloves
- ¼ teaspoon nutmeg
- 1-star anise
- Salt and pepper to taste
- Head of lettuce

Directions:
Set your instant pot to sauté mode, add in the ghee. Place your cubed beef into instant pot and brown on all sides. Also add onion. When you are finished with sautéing the meat and onions press the keep warm/cancel button to stop the sauté mode. Place your other ingredients into instant pot along with meat and onions. Set your instant pot to meat/stew setting for 35 minutes. Once done release pressure naturally. Stir the ingredients. Add lettuce leaves to serving dished then top with meat mixture.
Nutritional Information per serving:
Calories: 292   Fat: 21g   Fiber: 3g   Carbs: 14g   Protein: 32g

---

40. *Caribbean Ginger Oxtails*
Cook Time: 45 minutes　　　　　　　**Servings: 4**
Ingredients:
- 2 lbs. beef oxtails
- 2 carrots, diced
- 2 onions, sliced
- 4 sprigs thyme, fresh
- 1 teaspoon fish sauce
- 3 tablespoons tomato paste
- 2 cups beef stock
- 1 jalapeno pepper, minced
- 4 garlic cloves, minced
- 1-inch piece ginger, peeled, minced
- 2 tablespoons of ghee
- Sea salt and pepper to taste

Directions:
Rub the oxtails with seasonings. Set your instant pot to sauté mode and add in the ghee. Add in the oxtails into instant pot and brown them on all sides. Toss in the garlic, onion, jalapeno, carrot, ginger and continue to sauté for a few minutes. Set the instant pot to keep warm/cancel setting to stop sauté mode. Add remaining ingredients into instant pot and set to meat/stew setting for 40 minutes. Once done release pressure naturally. Stir the ingredients. Divide into serving dishes. Serve.
Nutritional Information per serving:
Calories: 303   Fat: 24g   Fiber: 2g   Carbs: 13g   Protein: 33g

Chapter 3. Collection of Pork-Based Instant Pot Recipes

41. Apple Cider Pork

Cook Time: 25 minutes **Servings: 4**

Ingredients:
- 2lbs. pork loin
- 2 tablespoons extra virgin olive oil
- 2 cups apple cider
- 1 yellow onion, peeled, chopped
- 1 tablespoon onion flakes, dried
- 2 apples, cored and chopped
- Salt and pepper to taste

Directions:
Set your instant pot on the sauté mode, add the oil, and heat it up. Add the pork, dried onion, salt, pepper, and stir. Brown the meat on all sides and transfer to a plate. Add the onion to the instant pot, stir and cook for 2 minutes. Add cider, apples, salt and pepper, and return the meat to the instant pot. Stir. Cover and cook on Manual mode for 20 minutes. Release the pressure naturally, and uncover the instant pot. Transfer pork to cutting board, slice and divide amongst serving dishes. Add the sauce and mix from instant pot. Serve.

Nutritional Information per serving:
Calories: 450   Fat: 22g   Fiber: 2.2g   Carbs: 29g   Protein: 37.2g

---

42. Pork Sausages & Sweet Potatoes

Cook Time: 15 minutes **Servings: 6**

Ingredients:

For the sweet potatoes:
- 4 sweet potatoes, peeled and cut into cubes
- 1 teaspoon dry mustard
- Salt and pepper to taste
- 1 tablespoon butter
- 4-ounces milk, warmed
- 6-ounces water

For the sausages:
- 6 pork sausages
- 1 tablespoon of cornstarch mixed with one tablespoon water
- Salt and pepper to taste
- 3-ounces water
- 3-ounces red wine
- ½ cup onion jam
- 2 tablespoons extra virgin olive oil

Directions:
Place the sweet potatoes into the instant pot, add 6-ounces water, salt, pepper, stir and cover, and cook on steam mode for 5 minutes. Release the pressure with quick-release. Drain the sweet potatoes and place them in a bowl. Add the milk and butter, mustard, more salt and pepper and mash them well. Set the dish aside.
Set your instant pot to sauté mode, add the oil and heat it up. Add the sausages and brown them on all sides. Add the onion jam, wine, 3-ounces of water, salt and pepper. Cover the instant pot and cook on the meat/stew setting for 8 minutes. Release the pressure with quick-release and divide the sausages among serving plates. Add cornstarch to mixture in instant pot and stir well. Drizzle the sauce from instant pot over the sausages and serve with mashed sweet potatoes.

Nutritional Information per serving:
Calories: 435 Fat: 33g Fiber: 15g Carbs: 44.2g Protein: 55g

---

43. Sausage & Red Beans
Cooking Time: 30 minutes
Servings: 8
Ingredients:
- 1 lb. smoked sausage, sliced
- 1 bay leaf
- 1 lb. red beans, dried, soaked overnight and drained
- 2 tablespoons Cajun seasoning
- 1 celery stalk, chopped
- Salt and pepper to taste
- ½ green bell pepper, seeded, chopped
- 1 small yellow onion, peeled, chopped
- 1 garlic clove, peeled, chopped
- ¼ teaspoon cumin
- 5 cups water
- 1 teaspoon parsley, dried

Directions:
In your instant pot mix the beans, bay leaf, sausage, Cajun seasoning, celery, salt, bell pepper, parsley, cumin, garlic, onion, pepper, water and stir. Cover and cook on Bean/Chili setting for 30 minutes. Release the pressure using quick-release, uncover the instant pot, divide and mix into serving bowls. Serve.

Nutritional Information per serving:
Calories: 248 Fat: 15g Fiber: 12.3g Carbs: 40g Protein: 29g

---

44. Kulua Pork
Cooking Time: 90 minutes
Servings: 5
Ingredients:
- 4 lbs. pork shoulder, cut into half
- ½ cup water
- 1 tablespoon liquid smoke
- 2 tablespoons coconut oil
- Salt and pepper to taste
- Steamed green beans, for serving

Directions:
Set your instant pot on the sauté mode, add the oil and heat it up. Add in the pork, salt and pepper. Brown the meat for 3 minutes on each side. Transfer meat to a plate. Add the water and liquid smoke to the instant pot and stir. Return the meat to the instant pot and stir ingredients and cover with lid. Cook on Meat/Stew setting for 90 minutes. Release the pressure on quick-release, and transfer meat to cutting board and shred with 2 forks. Divide the pork onto serving plates, add some sauce on top, and serve with steamed green beans on the side.

Nutritional Information per serving:
Calories: 243 Fat: 18g Fiber: 1g Carbs: 15g Protein: 29g

45. Pork with Hominy

Cooking Time: 30 minutes **Servings: 6**

Ingredients:
- 1 ¼ lbs. pork shoulder, boneless, cut into medium pieces
- 2 tablespoons chili powder
- 2 tablespoons almond oil
- Salt and pepper to taste
- 1 white onion, peeled, chopped
- 4 garlic cloves, peeled, minced
- 30 ounces canned hominy, drained
- 4 cups beef stock
- Avocado slices, for serving
- Lime wedges, for serving
- 2 tablespoons cornstarch
- ¼ cup water

Directions:
Set your instant pot on the sauté mode, add one tablespoon of almond oil and heat it. Add the pork, salt, pepper, and brown the meat on all sides. Transfer the meat to a bowl. Add the rest of the almond oil to the instant pot and heat it up. Add the garlic, chili powder, onion, stir and sauté for 4 minutes. Add half of the beef stock, stir and cook for 1 minute. Add the rest of the stock and return the pork to the instant pot. Stir and cover, and cook on Manual setting for 30 minutes.
Release the pressure naturally for 10 minutes. Transfer the pork to a cutting board, shred it using 2 forks. Add the cornstarch into instant pot, mixed with water. Set instant pot on sauté mode. Add the hominy, more salt, and pepper, and the shredded pork, stir and cook for 2 minutes. Divide among serving bowls. Serve with avocado slices and lime wedges.

Nutritional Information per serving:
Calories: 250   Fat: 8.7g   Fiber: 7.7g   Carbs: 29g   Protein: 32g

46. Pork Tostadas

Cook Time: 30 minutes **Servings: 4**

Ingredients:
- 4 lbs. pork shoulder, boneless, cubed
- 2 cups diet cola
- ½ cup picante sauce
- 2 teaspoons chili powder
- 2 tablespoons tomato paste
- ¼ teaspoon cumin
- 1 cup enchilada sauce
- Corn tortillas, for serving
- Mexican cheese, shredded, for serving
- Shredded lettuce, for serving
- Guacamole, for serving

Directions:
In your instant pot mix 1 cup of diet cola with picante sauce, salsa, tomato paste, chili powder, cumin and stir. Add the pork, stir and cover. Cook on Meat/Stew setting for 25 minutes. Release pressure naturally. Uncover the instant pot, drain juice from instant pot, transfer the meat to a cutting board. Shred the meat with 2 forks. Return the meat to instant pot. Add in remaining diet cola and enchilada sauce, stir. Set the instant pot to sauté mode and heat well. Serve with tortillas, lettuce, cheese and guacamole.

Nutritional Information per serving:
Calories: 160   Fat: 13g   Fiber: 3g   Carbs: 16g   Protein: 9g

47. Pork Tamales

Cook Time: 1 hour and 35 minutes **Servings: 24 pieces**
Ingredients:
- 8-ounces dried corn husks, soaked for 1 day and drained
- 4 cups water
- 3lbs. pork shoulder, boneless, cubed
- 1 yellow onion, peeled, chopped
- 3 tablespoons chili powder
- 2 garlic cloves, peeled, crushed
- 1 teaspoon baking soda
- ¼ cup shortening
- ¼ cup almond oil
- 4 cups masa
- 1 teaspoon cumin
- Salt and pepper to taste

Directions:
In your instant pot, mix 2 cups of water with onion, garlic, chili powder, salt, pepper, and cumin. Add in the pork and stir, cover the instant pot. Cook on the Meat/Stew setting for 75 minutes. Release the pressure naturally. Transfer the meat to a cutting board and shred it with 2 forks. Place pork in a bowl. Add one tablespoon of the cooking liquid from instant pot. Add more salt and pepper and set aside. In a bowl mix salt, pepper, masa, baking powder, shortening and almond oil. Combine using hand mixer. Add the cooking liquid from the instant pot and blend well. Add 2 cups water to instant pot.

Place the steamer basket inside of instant pot. Unfold 2 of the corn husks, place them on a work surface, add ¼ cup of the masa mixture near top of husk, press into a square and leave 2-inches at the bottom. Add 1 tablespoon pork in the center of the masa, wrap the husk around the dough and place it standing up in the steamer basket. Repeat with the rest of the husks, cover the instant pot and cook on the Steam setting for 20 minutes Release the pressure naturally. Remove the tamales and place them on serving plates. Serve.

Nutritional Information per serving:
Calories: 150   Fat: 7.2g   Fiber: 2g   Carbs: 11g   Protein: 7g

48. Pork Carnitas

Cook Time: 1 hour and 10 minutes **Servings: 8**
Ingredients:
- 3 lbs. pork shoulder, chopped
- 2 tablespoons ghee
- 1 jalapeno pepper, chopped
- 1 poblano pepper, seeded, chopped
- 1 green bell pepper
- 3 garlic cloves, minced
- 1 lb. tomatillos, cut into quarters
- 1 yellow onion, chopped
- 2 bay leaves
- 2 cups beef stock
- 1 red onion, chopped, for serving
- Cheddar cheese, shredded, for serving
- 1 teaspoon oregano, dried
- Salt and pepper to taste
- 1 teaspoon cumin
- Flour tortillas, for serving

Directions:

Set your instant pot on the sauté mode, add the ghee and heat it up. Add in the pork, salt and pepper. Brown the meat on all sides for about 3 minutes. Add the bell pepper, jalapeno pepper, poblano pepper, tomatillos, onion, oregano, garlic, cumin, bay leaves and stock. Stir and cover, cooking on the Meat/Stew setting for 55 minutes. Release the pressure naturally for 10 minutes. Transfer the meat to cutting board. Puree the mix from instant pot with immersion blender. Shred meat with 2 forks.

Add the meat back into the instant pot with the puree mix. Divide the pork mixture onto flour tortillas on serving plates. Add onion, cheese and serve.

Nutritional Information per serving:
Calories: 355 Fat: 23g Fiber: 1g Carbs: 10g Protein: 23g

49. *Instant Pot Balsamic Pork Tenderloin*

Cook Time: 25 minutes **Servings: 4**

Ingredients:
- 2 lbs. pork tenderloin
- 2 tablespoons coconut oil
- 1 cup chicken stock
- ¼ cup balsamic vinegar
- 2 cloves of garlic, minced
- 1 tablespoon Worcestershire sauce
- ¼ cup water
- Sea salt and black pepper to taste
- 1 teaspoon sage, ground
- 1 tablespoon Dijon mustard

Directions:
Set your instant pot to the sauté mode, add the coconut oil and heat. Add the pork and brown the meat on all sides for five minutes. Add the remaining ingredients, and set to Manual setting for 20 minutes. When cooking is complete, release the pressure naturally in 10-minutes. Cut the pork into medallions and place on serving plates, cover with sauce from instant pot. Serve hot!

Nutritional Information per serving:
Calories: 347 Fat: 26g Fiber: 1g Carbs: 13g Protein: 33g

50. *Asian Pork Short Ribs*

Cooking Time: 60 minutes **Servings: 4**

Ingredients:
- 4 lbs. pork short ribs
- 2 green onions, chopped
- 1 teaspoon coconut oil
- 3 garlic cloves, minced
- 3 ginger slices
- ½ cup water
- 2 teaspoons sesame oil
- 1/4 cup rice wine
- ½ cup soy sauce

Directions:
Set your instant pot onto saute mode, add coconut oil and heat it up. Add the green onions, ginger, garlic, and stir and cook for 1 minute. Add the ribs, water, wine, sesame oil and soy sauce. Stir and cook for 3 minutes. Cover the instant pot and cook on the Meat/Stew setting for 45 minutes. Release the pressure naturally for 15 minutes. Uncover the instant pot and transfer the ribs to a plate. Strain the liquid from the instant pot, divide the ribs among serving plates and drizzle with sauce.

Nutritional Information per serving:
Calories: 300   Fat: 11g   Fiber: 1g   Carbs: 5g   Protein: 10g

---

51. Ribs & Coleslaw
Cooking Time: 35 minutes   **Servings: 4**
Ingredients:
- 2 ½ lbs. pork baby back ribs
- 1 teaspoon onion powder
- ½ teaspoon garlic powder
- ½ teaspoon chili powder
- ½ teaspoon dry mustard
- ½ teaspoon paprika
- Salt and pepper to taste
- 2 tablespoons almond oil

For the sauce:
- ½ teaspoon smoked paprika
- 1/3 cup apple cider vinegar
- ¼ cup coconut Aminos
- 2 garlic cloves, minced
- ¾ cup tomato paste
- 6-ounces tomato paste
- 2 bacon slices, chopped
- 1 small yellow onion, chopped
- ½ cup water
- Salt and pepper to taste

For the coleslaw:
- 2 green onions, chopped
- 2 carrots, grated
- Salt and pepper to taste
- 2 ½ teaspoons caraway seeds
- 3 cups green cabbage, shredded
- 1 cup red cabbage, shredded
- ¾ cup mayonnaise
- ¼ cup apple cider vinegar

Directions:
In a salad bowl, mix the green onions, carrots, with the cabbage. In a small bowl mix the caraway seeds with the mayonnaise, salt, pepper, ¼ cup vinegar and stir well. Pour over the coleslaw, and toss to coat, keep in fridge until ready to serve. In a bowl mix onion powder, paprika, dry mustard, garlic powder, chili powder, salt and pepper. Rub the ribs with this mixture. Set your instant pot to sauté mode, add in almond oil and heat it. Add the bacon and cook until done. Add in onion and garlic and cook for an additional five minutes. Place the ribs into your instant pot. Add some water, cover and cook on the Meat/Stew setting for 15 minutes. Add the remaining ingredients for ribs into instant pot and cook for another 10 minutes. Release the pressure naturally for 15 minutes. Transfer the ribs to a plate. Remove some of the sauce, leave enough in pot to cover bottom. Then place layer of ribs into instant pot and cover with layer of sauce until all the ribs are in the instant pot. Cover and cook on Manual setting for 10 minutes. Release pressure again, and divide the ribs among serving plates, and serve with coleslaw.

Nutritional Information per serving:
Calories: 360   Fat: 15g   Fiber: 1g   Carbs: 4g   Protein: 17g

52. Country-style Ribs
Cooking Time: 20 minutes
Servings: 8
Ingredients:
- 5 lbs. country-style ribs, boneless

For the brine:
- 1 tablespoon Truvia sweetener
- Salt to taste
- 4 cups water
- 3 garlic cloves, crushed
- 2 tablespoons liquid smoke

For the ribs:
- 2 tablespoons butter
- ½ tablespoon water
- 1 cup onion, chopped
- Cayenne pepper
- 1 teaspoon chili powder
- ½ teaspoon cinnamon, ground
- 2 apples, peeled, cored, sliced

For the sauce:
- 2 tablespoons yellow mustard
- 1 tablespoon liquid smoke
- 1 tablespoon Worcestershire sauce
- 1 teaspoon hot sauce
- 1 tablespoon Truvia
- 2 tablespoons Dijon mustard
- 2 tablespoons cornstarch
- 1 tablespoon soy sauce
- ¼ cup honey
- 2 tablespoons water

Directions:
In a bowl, mix the 4 cups water with some salt, and 1 tablespoon Truvia, garlic, and 2 tablespoons liquid smoke. Stir, and add the pork ribs and keep them in fridge to marinate for 2 hours. Set your instant pot to the sauté mode, add 2 tablespoons butter and melt it. Add the ribs and brown them on all sides. Transfer the ribs to a plate. Add the onions, ½ tablespoon water, stir, and cook for 2 minutes. Add the cinnamon, cayenne, chili powder, and apple slices. Return the ribs to the instant pot, cover and cook on the Meat/Stew setting for 15 minutes. Release pressure naturally. Transfer the ribs to a plate. Puree the onions and apples using a food processor, and set the instant pot on sauté mode again. Add the yellow mustard, 1 tablespoon liquid smoke, Dijon mustard, 1 tablespoon Truvia, Worcestershire sauce, hot sauce, soy sauce, honey and stir well. Add cornstarch mixed with 2 tablespoons of water, and cook for 2 minutes. Divide the ribs onto serving plates and drizzle with sauce. Serve.

Nutritional Information per serving:
Calories: 470   Fat: 34g   Fiber: 3g   Carbs: 10g   Protein: 29g

53. Pork Chops & Spinach Salad

Cook Time: 20 minutes **Servings:** 6

Ingredients:

For the pork chops:
- 6 pork chops, boneless
- 2 cups beef stock
- 3 garlic cloves, chopped
- 1 yellow onion, chopped
- 1 bunch mixed sage, rosemary, oregano, thyme
- 2 tablespoons ghee
- 1 teaspoon smoked paprika
- Salt and pepper to taste

For Spinach Salad:
- 1 large package of spinach leaves
- 1 English cucumber, sliced
- ½ red onion, thinly sliced
- Balsamic Vinegar dressing
- 2 large tomatoes, diced

Directions:

Set your instant pot to the sauté mode, and add in the ghee and heat it up. Add in the pork chops and brown them on all sides. Add the rest of the ingredients for porkchops into the instant pot. Set the instant pot to the Meat/Stew setting for 15 minutes. Meanwhile prepare the spinach salad in a large salad bowl adding all ingredients except for the dressing then keep in the fridge until ready to serve, just before serving add dressing and toss to mix. Release the pressure naturally. Put the pork chops onto a plate and remove and discard the herbs from instant pot. Place the pork chops back into pot and place on Manual mode, for 2 minutes. Stir. Divide the pork chops on serving plates along with spinach salad.

Nutritional Information per serving:

Calories: 410 Fat: 20g Carbs: 29g Protein: 30.2g

---

54. Pork Chops & Brown Rice

Cooking Time: 25 minutes **Servings:** 6

Ingredients:
- 2 lbs. pork chops
- 2 hot peppers, minced
- 1 tablespoon peppercorns, crushed
- 2 cups brown rice
- 3 garlic cloves, crushed
- 1 cup onion, chopped
- 2 ½ cups beef stock
- Salt and ground pepper to taste
- 3 tablespoons butter

Directions:

Set your instant pot to the sauté mode, add the butter and melt it. Add in garlic and onions, hot peppers and pork chops. Brown the meat on all sides. Remove the pork chops from instant pot once they are browned and place on a plate. Add the rice and beef stock to instant pot and stir. Add the porkchops back to the pot and set instant pot to the Meat/Stew setting for 25 minutes. Release the pressure naturally for 10 minutes. Add salt and pepper and divide porkchops and rice among serving plates. Serve.

Nutritional Information per serving:

Calories: 430 Fat: 12.3g Fiber: 4.3g Carbs: 53g Protein: 30g

55. Braised Pork

Cooking Time: 75 minutes   **Servings:** 6

Ingredients:
- 4 lbs. pork butt, chopped
- 16-ounces red wine
- 16-ounces beef stock
- 4-ounces lemon juice
- 2 tablespoons extra virgin olive oil
- 1 tablespoon paprika
- ¼ cup garlic powder
- ¼ cup onion, chopped
- Salt and pepper to taste

Directions:
In your instant pot mix the pork with the stock, wine, lemon juice, garlic powder, onion, oil, paprika, salt and pepper. Stir and cover, setting to the Meat/Stew mode for 45 minutes. Release the pressure naturally for 15 minutes. Stir the pork, divide into serving bowls. Serve.

Nutritional Information per serving:
Calories: 452   Fat: 44g   Fiber: 1g   Carbs: 12g   Protein: 27g

56. Chinese Barbecue Pork

Cooking Time: 50 minutes   **Servings:** 6

Ingredients:
- 2lbs. pork belly
- 2 tablespoons dry sherry
- 4 tablespoons soy sauce
- 1-quart beef stock
- 2 teaspoons sesame oil
- 2 teaspoons Truvia
- 1 teaspoon peanut oil

Directions:
Set your instant pot on the Manual mode, add the sherry, stock, soy sauce and stir and cook for 8 minutes. Add the pork, stir, cover and cook on the Meat/Stew setting for 30 minutes. Release the pressure naturally, transfer the pork to a cutting board, allow to cool and chop into smaller pieces. Add the sauce in instant pot into a bowl and set aside. Set your instant pot to sauté mode, add in the peanut oil and add the pork back into the instant pot. Cook for a few minutes browning all sides of the meat. In a bowl mix the sesame oil with the sauce that was put aside and mix well. Add this mix to the instant pot and stir. Set on Manual mode for 10 minutes. Divide the pork onto serving plates, drizzle with sauce. Serve.

Nutritional Information per serving:
Calories: 398   Fat: 22g   Fiber: 1g   Carbs: 15g   Protein: 43g

57. Pork Roast with Fennel

Cooking Time: 1 hour and 20 minutes   **Servings:** 4

Ingredients:
- 2 lbs. pork meat, boneless
- 5-ounces white wine
- 1 yellow onion, chopped
- 2 garlic cloves, minced

- Salt and pepper to taste
- 2 tablespoons extra virgin olive oil
- 5-ounces beef stock
- 1 lb. fennel bulbs, sliced

Directions:
Set your instant pot to the sauté mode, add the oil and heat it up. Add the pork, salt and pepper, stir and brown meat on all sides. Add the wine, garlic and stock to the instant pot. Cook for another few minutes. Transfer the pork to a plate. Stir the sauce in instant pot well. Return pork to pot, cover and cook on Manual setting for 40 minutes. Release the pressure naturally in 15 minutes. Add the onion, and fennel, to instant pot stir and cover. Cook on the Manual setting for 15 minutes. Release pressure again, stir and transfer the pork to serving plates. Serve with onion and fennel on the side with the cooking sauce from the instant pot drizzled over.

Nutritional Information per serving:
Calories: 426   Fat: 15g   Fiber: 1.2g   Carbs: 27g   Protein: 36g

---

58. Pulled Pork
Cook Time: 1 hour and 20 minutes
Servings: 6
Ingredients:
- 3 lbs. pork shoulder, boneless, cut into chunks
- 8-ounces of water

For the sauce:
- 4-ounces hot water
- 2 teaspoons dry mustard
- Cayenne Pepper
- 1 tablespoon Truvia
- 2 teaspoons dry mustard
- 2 teaspoons smoked paprika
- Salt and pepper to taste
- 2 teaspoons Truvia
- 12-ounces apple cider vinegar

Directions:
Mix the Truvia with smoked paprika, 2 teaspoons dry mustard, and salt in a bowl. Rub the pork with this mixture and place the pork pieces into your instant pot. Add the 8-ounces of water and stir. Cover the instant pot and cook on the Meat/Stew setting for 75 minutes. Release the pressure naturally within 10 minutes. Transfer the pork to a cutting board and shred it using 2 forks. Discard half the cooking liquid from instant pot. In a bowl mix the 2 teaspoons of Truvia for sauce, with vinegar, cayenne, salt, pepper and hot water along with 2 teaspoons of dry mustard and stir well. Add to instant pot along with cooking sauce and cook on Manual for 3 minutes. Release the pressure naturally, and divide the pork among serving plates and drizzle with sauce from instant pot. Serve.

Nutritional Information per serving:
Calories: 428   Fat: 11g   Fiber: 4g   Carbs: 38g   Protein: 31g

59. Creamy Pork Chops
Cooking Time: 20 minutes
Servings: 4
Ingredients:
- 4 pork chops, boneless
- 2 tablespoons extra virgin olive oil
- ½ small bunch of fresh parsley, chopped
- Salt and pepper to taste
- 1 cup sour cream
- 10-ounce can of cream of mushroom soup
- 2 teaspoons of chicken bouillon
- 1 cup water

Directions:
Set your instant pot to the sauté mode, add the oil and heat it up. Add in the pork chops, pepper and salt. Brown the meat on all sides. Transfer pork chops to a plate. Add the water and bouillon to the instant pot and stir well. Return the pork chops to the instant pot, cover and cook on Manual setting for 9 minutes. Release the pressure naturally, transfer the pork chops to a platter and set aside. Set the instant pot on Manual mode and heat up the cooking liquid. Add the mushroom soup, stir and cook for 2 minutes. Add the parsley and sour cream, stir and mix well. Pour over pork chops. Serve.

Nutritional Information per serving:
Calories: 282 Fat: 14g Fiber: 1g Carbs: 9g Protein: 22g

60. Pork Chops and Onion
Cooking Time: 15 minutes
Servings: 4
Ingredients:
- 4 pork chops
- 1 lb. onions, sliced
- ½ cup milk
- 2 tablespoons extra virgin olive oil
- 1 garlic clove, minced
- 2 tablespoons parsley, fresh, chopped
- Salt and pepper to taste
- ½ cup white wine
- 1 tablespoon flour
- 2 tablespoons cornstarch mixed with 3 tablespoons water
- 2 tablespoons butter
- 2 tablespoons lime juice

Directions:
Set your instant pot on the sauté mode, add the oil and butter and heat up. Add the pork chops, salt and pepper. Brown the meat on all sides. Transfer meat to a plate. Add the onion, garlic to the instant pot and stir, cook for 2 minutes. Add the lime juice, wine, milk, parsley, and return the pork chops to the instant pot. Stir, cover and cook on Manual setting for 15 minutes. Release the pressure, add the cornstarch and flour, stir well. Cook on Manual mode for 3 minutes. Divide pork chops on serving plates drizzle with sauce. Serve.

Nutritional Information per serving:
Calories: 212 Fat: 6g Fiber: 3g Carbs: 8g Protein: 19g

61. Apple Cider Pork
Cooking Time: 25 minutes
Servings: 4
Ingredients:
- 2 lbs. pork loin
- 2 tablespoons coconut oil
- 2 cups apple cider
- 1 yellow onion, chopped
- 2 apples, cored, chopped
- 1 tablespoon onion flakes, dried
- Salt and pepper to taste

Directions:
Set your instant pot to the sauté mode, add the coconut oil and heat it up. Add the pork loin, salt and pepper, along with the dried onion. Brown the meat on all sides. Transfer to a plate. Add the onion to instant pot and stir for 2 minutes. Add the cider and return the meat to the instant pot, adding chopped apples, more salt and pepper. Cover and cook on Manual mode for 20 minutes. Release the pressure, naturally, and transfer the pork to cutting board, slice it. Divide the pork among serving plates. Add the sauce from instant pot and serve.

Nutritional Information per serving:
Calories: 432   Fat: 21g   Fiber: 2.2g   Carbs: 26g   Protein: 36g

62. Bacon and Egg Omelette
Cook Time: 8 minutes
Servings: 4
Ingredients:
- 5 slices of bacon, chopped into small pieces
- 5 free range eggs
- 1 tablespoon parsley, fresh, chopped
- 2 tablespoons of coconut oil
- Salt and pepper to taste

Directions:
Lightly beat your eggs in a mixing bowl with a fork. Add a dash of salt and pepper. Set your instant pot to the sauté mode, add the coconut oil and heat it up. Add the pieces of bacon and sauté them until they are cooked and slightly crispy for about 5 minutes. Add the mixed eggs and stir into the bacon. Leave the eggs for about 3 minutes or until they are done to your liking. Remove eggs from pot and add to serving plates, and sprinkle tops with chopped parsley. Serve.

Nutritional Information per serving:
Calories: 227   Fat: 14g   Fiber: 1g   Carbs: 21g   Protein: 20g

63. Ham Hock Soup
Cook Time: 1 hour and 10 minutes **Servings:** 8
Ingredients:
- 1 ham hock
- 2 celery stalks, chopped
- 1 onion, chopped
- 2 carrots, chopped
- 2 litres of water

Directions:
Place your ham hock into your instant pot, and sprinkle with salt and pepper, can cover with water. Press the Meat/Stew button and set for 40 minutes. Once it is done, release the pressure naturally, then remove the lid. Remove the ham hock to a cutting board. Remove the meat from the ham hock and replace it back into the instant pot. Add the onion, carrot, and celery to the pot and secure the lid. Press the "Soup" button and set for 30 minutes. Release the pressure once again when it is done, naturally. Stir the soup and serve hot!

Nutritional Information per serving:
Calories: 223 Fat: 11g Fiber: 2g Carbs: 21g Protein: 30g

64. Bacon, Spinach & Mozzarella Bundles
Cook Time: 6 minutes **Servings:** 12 bundles (3 per person)
Ingredients:
- 12 slices of bacon
- 250 g mozzarella cheese, cut into 12 even pieces
- 2 tablespoons extra-virgin olive oil
- Large handful of baby spinach leaves

Directions:
Wrap each piece of mozzarella cheese in spinach leaves, about 4 pieces per piece. Wrap each spinach-coated piece with a piece of bacon. Your bundles should look like round bacon-covered balls. Select the sauté mode on your instant pot. Add the oil to the pot and heat. Add the bundles in groups of 6. Cook on either side for 3 minutes each or until golden and sizzling. Serve hot!

Nutritional Information per serving:
Calories: 232 Fat: 19g Fiber: 2g Carbs: 23g Protein: 33g

65. Keto Carbonara with Bacon & Cream
Cooking Time: 10 minutes **Serving:** 4
Ingredients:
- 5 zucchinis, spiralized as a fettucine-style pasta alternative
- 4 strips of bacon, chopped into small pieces
- ¼ cup grated parmesan cheese
- 1 cup heavy cream
- 1 garlic clove, finely chopped
- 2 tablespoons extra virgin olive oil

Directions:

Select your sauté mode on your instant pot, add the oil and heat it up. Add in the bacon pieces and garlic into instant pot. Cook until they are sizzling for about 3 minutes. Add the zucchini pasta and coat with oil and bacon. Saute zucchini for about 2 minutes. Add cream and parmesan cheese and cream and stir. Cook for another 5 minutes and continue to stir. Turn off your instant pot. Serve Carbonara hot!

Nutritional Information per serving:
Calories: 263   Fat: 20g   Fiber: 1g   Carbs: 23g   Protein: 31g

66. *Chorizo Sausage with Feta, Spicy Tomatoes & Spinach*
Cook Time: 12 minutes   **Servings: 4**
Ingredients:

- 5 chorizo sausages, cut into small chunks
- 4 large tomatoes
- 2 handfuls of baby spinach
- 150gm feta cheese, cut into small cubes
- 1 teaspoon chilli flakes
- 2 tablespoons coconut oil
- Olive oil to drizzle on top of tomatoes

Directions:
Turn the oven on to broil, hi temperature. Cut tomatoes in half and drizzle tops with olive oil, salt, pepper and chilli. Place the tomatoes on baking tray on upper rack in oven. Select sauté mode on your instant pot, add the coconut oil and heat. Add the Chorizo sausage to instant pot and stir. Cook sausage for 5 minutes, when it begins to brown add in the spinach and feta and stir. When tomatoes are browned and soft remove from oven. Turn off the instant pot and serve Chorizo mixture. Serve with tomato halves.

Nutritional Information per serving:
Calories: 273   Fat: 20g   Fiber: 1g   Carbs: 23g   Protein: 32g

67. *Sautéed Asparagus with Bacon*
Cook Time: 15 minutes   **Servings: 4**
Ingredients:

- 4 strips of bacon
- 16 spears of asparagus (4 per person)
- 2 tablespoons of butter
- 1 garlic clove, minced

Directions:
Select the sauté mode on your instant pot. Add the butter and heat it. Add the minced garlic and the bacon strips and sauté until crispy for about 5 minutes. Add in the asparagus spears and stir and coat them, and cook for an additional 10 minutes. Place on serving plates with some salt and pepper to taste. Serve.

Nutritional Information per serving:
Calories: 223   Fat: 12g   Fiber: 3g   Carbs: 17g   Protein: 26g

68. *Instant Pot Scrambled Egg & Sausage*
Cook Time: 17 minutes   **Servings: 4**
Ingredients:

- 1 lb. ground sausage
- 8 large eggs

- 2 tablespoons extra virgin olive oil
- 1 green bell pepper, seeded, diced
- 1 red bell pepper, seeded, diced
- 1 yellow bell pepper, seeded, diced
- 1 large onion, diced
- ¼ cup heavy cream
- Salt and pepper to taste

Directions:
Set your instant pot to the sauté mode, add the oil, and add the onions and bell peppers and cook for five minutes. Add the sausage, stir and select the Manual function at low pressure and choose 10-minute cook time. Once the cook time is done, do a quick-release of pressure. Discard any excess fat in instant pot. Whisk your eggs, heavy cream, salt and pepper. Pour the egg mixture over the sausage mixture. Close the instant pot and select Manual function at low pressure and choose a 2-minute cook time. Divide into serving dishes. Serve.

Nutritional Information per serving:
Calories: 231   Fat: 14g   Fiber: 2g   Carbs: 21g   Protein: 28g

---

69. *Instant Pot Split Pea & Ham Soup*

Cook Time: 17 minutes   **Servings: 4**

Ingredients:
- ½ cup ham, diced
- 2 cups dried peas
- 5 cups of water
- 1 teaspoon onion, finely chopped
- Salt and pepper to taste
- 1 cup carrots, peeled, sliced

Directions:
Place all your ingredients into your instant pot. Select the Manual mode and set for a cook time of 17 minutes. Divide soup up into serving bowls. Serve hot!

Nutritional Information per serving:
Calories: 216   Fat: 14g   Fiber: 2.2g   Carbs: 17g   Protein: 24g

---

70. *Instant Pot Pork Feet & Soy Bean Soup*

Cook Time: 1 hour   **Servings: 4**

Ingredients:
- 2 lbs. pork feet
- 1 cup soaked soy beans
- 6 cups water
- 3 thin slices of ginger
- Salt and pepper to taste
- 2 green onion leaves, minced

Directions:
Add all your ingredients into your instant pot, except the minced green onion leaves. Select the soup mode and cook time for an hour. When soup is done divide it up into serving bowls and top with minced green leaves. Serve hot!

Nutritional Information per serving:
Calories: 228   Fat: 23g   Fiber: 1g   Carbs: 17g   Protein: 35g

Chapter 4. Collection of Lamb-Based Instant Pot Recipes

71. *Instant Pot Lamb Curry*
Cook Time: 20 minutes
Servings: 6
Ingredients:
- 1 ½ lbs. lamb stew meat, cubed
- 4 cloves of garlic, minced
- Cilantro, chopped
- 1 medium zucchini, diced
- 3 medium carrots, sliced
- 1 medium onion, diced
- ¾ teaspoon turmeric
- 1 ½ tablespoon garam masala
- 1 (14-ounce can) tomatoes, diced
- 1 tablespoon ghee
- Sea salt and pepper to taste
- Juice of ½ a lime
- ½ cup coconut milk
- 1-inch piece ginger, fresh, grated

Directions:
Combine your meat, grated ginger, minced garlic, lime juice, coconut milk, sea salt and pepper in a container with a lid. Mix ingredients and marinated in the fridge for 30 minutes.
After marinating is complete, add the meat, tomatoes with their juice, marinade, ghee, garam masala, carrots and onions to your instant pot. Lock the lid in place, then set the steam release handle to 'Sealing' then select the Manual mode and cook at high pressure for 20 minutes. Once the cooking time is complete, allow your instant pot to release pressure naturally for 15 minutes, then flip the steam release handle to 'Venting' to release remaining steam before you attempt to open the lid. Remove the lid then set your instant pot to the sauté mode in the normal setting. Stir in the diced zucchini and simmer for 5-6 minutes without the lid or until the zucchini is tender and the sauce has thickened. Divide into serving dishes, over cauliflower rice, and garnish with chopped cilantro. Serve hot!

Nutritional Information per serving:
Calories: 230   Fat: 9g   Fiber: 3g   Carbs: 11g   Protein: 25g

72. *Instant Pot Lamb Curry with Yogurt*
Cooking Time: 25 minutes
Servings: 4
Ingredients:
- 2 lbs. lamb, boneless, cubed
- 4 Chile pepper, chopped
- 2 tablespoons clarified butter
- 1 onion, diced
- 4 cups plain yogurt
- 1 teaspoon cumin seed
- 2 teaspoons ground turmeric
- 2 tablespoons coriander seeds

Directions:
Add the ginger, garlic, chiles, spices and yogurt into a food processor and process until well blended. Spoon the mixture over lamb, tossing to coat, place in fridge for 3 hours to marinate. Set your instant pot on sauté mode, add butter and heat it up. Add in the onions and brown them. Once onion is browned add in the lamb and yogurt marinade and mix. Place lid on instant pot and set to Meat/Stew setting for 20 minutes. Release pressure naturally for 15 minutes. Divide between serving dishes. Serve.

Nutritional Information per serving:
Calories: 260   Fat: 23g   Fiber: 12g   Carbs: 7g   Protein: 22g

---

73. Instant Pot Mediterranean Lamb Roast
Cooking Time: 60 minutes   **Servings: 6**
Ingredients:
- 4 lbs. lamb shanks
- 2 tablespoons olive oil
- 2 cups beef broth
- 1 teaspoon thyme
- 3 large sweet potatoes, peeled, cubed
- 1 teaspoon ginger
- 3 cloves garlic, minced
- 1 teaspoon sage
- 1 teaspoon marjoram
- Sea salt and pepper to taste

Directions:
Set your instant pot to sauté mode, add the oil and heat it. Add the lamb and swirl it around to coat with oil. Sear one side of lamb then flip it over to sear the other side. Sprinkle lamb shanks with all the herbs, sea salt, pepper and add broth. Cover the instant pot and set to Meat/Stew setting for a cook time of 45 minutes. Once cooking is completed release the pressure naturally for 10 minutes. Add the diced sweet potatoes. Close instant pot and set an additional cook time of 10 minutes on Meat/Stew setting. Release pressure again naturally for 10 minutes. Divide into serving dishes. Serve hot!

Nutritional Information per serving:
Calories: 254   Fat: 20g   Fiber: 9g   Carbs: 7g   Protein: 23g

---

74. Instant Pot Middle Eastern Lamb Stew
Cooking Time: 1 hour and 9 minutes   **Servings: 4**
Ingredients:
- 1 ½ lbs. lamb stew meat, cubed
- 1 onion, diced
- 2 tablespoons ghee
- 6 garlic cloves, chopped
- ¼ cup raisins
- 1 (15-ounce can) chickpeas, rinsed and drained
- 2 tablespoons honey
- ¼ cup apple cider vinegar
- 2 tablespoons tomato paste
- 1 teaspoon each: coriander, cumin, cinnamon, cumin seeds, sea salt and pepper
- 2 cups chicken stock or broth
- Garnish with fresh cilantro or parsley

Directions:
Set your instant pot to the sauté mode, add the ghee and heat it up. Sauté your onions for about 4 minutes. Add the lamb, spices, garlic, salt and pepper, and sauté for an additional 5 minutes. Brown the meat on all sides. Add the stock, vinegar, tomato paste, honey, chickpeas, and raisins, stir. Cover your instant pot and set to the Meat/Stew setting for 1 hour. Release the pressure naturally for 15 minutes. Remove lid and stir. Serve with cauliflower rice or quinoa and garnish with cilantro or fresh parsley. Divide into serving bowls and serve hot!

Nutritional Information per serving:
Calories: 242   Fat: 18g   Fiber: 2g   Carbs: 6g   Protein: 21g

75. Instant Pot Lamb Rogan Josh

Cooking Time: 15 minutes **Servings: 4**

Ingredients:

For the lamb:
- 1 ½ lbs. leg of lamb, cubed into small pieces

For the sauce:
- 1 tablespoon coriander, fresh, chopped for garnish
- 2 tablespoons tomato puree
- 1 1/2 cups water
- 2 tomatoes, finely diced
- 1 teaspoon each: ground coriander, ground cumin, ground ginger
- ½ teaspoon chilli, ground
- 4 tablespoons Greek yogurt
- ½ teaspoon garam masala
- ½ teaspoon garam masala
- 2 cloves garlic, minced
- 1 ½ teaspoons fennel seeds
- 1 ½ teaspoons cumin seeds
- 1-inch cinnamon bark
- 3 green cardamom pods, cracked open
- 1 tablespoon olive oil

Directions:

Mix the lamb, garam masala and yogurt for the marinade in a container with lid. Chill in fridge for 24 hours. When ready to begin cooking set your instant pot to the sauté mode, add the oil and all the whole spices. Sizzle and cook until the aromas are released, then in garlic and powdered spices. Cook for about 5 minutes, add in water, tomatoes, and tomato puree, stir. Add in the marinated lamb and stir before cancelling the sauté mode. Place the lid on your instant pot and set on Manual mode for 10 minutes. When cooking is complete press the quick-release to release the pressure. Once the pressure has come down then remove the lid and gently stir the lamb. Add sea salt to taste. Divide into serving dishes and garnish with chopped fresh coriander. Serve over cauliflower rice.

Nutritional Information per serving:
Calories: 231   Fat: 12g   Fiber: 4g   Carbs: 21g   Protein: 23g

76. Instant Pot Leg of Lamb Stew with Dates & Cinnamon

Cook Time: 1 hour and 40 minutes **Servings: 4**

Ingredients:
- 2 lbs. leg of lamb, boneless
- 1 teaspoon each: black pepper, sea salt, ground cumin powder, ground coriander powder, turmeric powder
- 1 tablespoon balsamic vinegar
- 3 bay leaves
- 1 chicken stock cube
- 1 cup water
- 1 cinnamon stick
- 8 garlic cloves, peeled, whole
- 7 dates, dried
- 4 slices ginger root, fresh
- 1 red onion, sliced
- 1 tablespoon coconut oil
- Cauliflower rice or couscous to serve with
- 1 tablespoon almond flour to thicken sauce

Directions:

Rub the leg of lamb with cumin, coriander seed powder, turmeric, sea salt and pepper. Set your instant pot to the sauté mode, add coconut oil and heat it. Add the lamb and sauté, browning all sides of the meat. Add the onions, ginger around the lamb. Remove the lamb and add remaining ingredients to pot. Stir and bring to a boil. Press the Keep Warm/Cancel setting and return the lamb to the instant pot. Place the lid on the instant pot and set the Manual setting for a cook time of 80 minutes. Once the cook time is complete, release the pressure naturally for 5 minutes, then use the quick-release to let off the rest of the steam.

Remove the lamb to a cutting board, set the instant pot to the sauté mode and allow broth to bubble for 10 minutes, stir it a few times. Cut the lamb meat into bite-size pieces. Add the lamb meat back to the instant pot. Stir the lamb mixture, and turn off the instant pot. If sauce needs to be thickened add in the almond flour. Divide into serving dishes over a bed of cauliflower rice or couscous. Garnish with chopped coriander and serve hot!

Nutritional Information per serving:
Calories: 229   Fat: 11g   Fiber: 3g   Carbs: 23g   Protein: 25g

---

77. *Lavender Lamb Chops*
Cook Time: 25 minutes   **Servings: 2**
Ingredients:
- 2 lamb chops, boneless
- 1 tablespoon lavender, chopped
- 2 tablespoons ghee, melted
- 2 tablespoons coconut oil
- 2 tablespoons rosemary, fresh, chopped
- 1 teaspoon garlic, powder
- Zest and juice from 1 lime
- Zest and juice from 1 orange
- 2 cups water
- Sea salt and black pepper to taste

Directions:
Cover the trivet with aluminum foil. Set your instant pot to sauté mode and heat the coconut oil. Sear lamb chops for 2 minutes per side. Remove and set aside. Press the Keep Warm/Cancel button to end sauté mode. In a bowl, add the lavender, ghee, rosemary, orange zest and juice, lime zest and juice and seasonings. Pour 2 cups of water into the instant pot. Place the trivet inside the instant pot. Set the lamb chops on top of it. Close and seal the lid. Select the Manual setting and cook at high-pressure for 15 minutes. When cooking is completed, release the pressure naturally for 15 minutes. Divide onto serving plates. Serve hot!

Nutritional Information per serving:
Calories: 250   Fat: 5g   Dietary Fiber: 1g   Carbohydrates: 5g   Protein: 8g

---

78. *Leg of Lamb & Spinach Salad*
Cook Time: 40 minutes   **Servings: 4**
Ingredients:
- 1 tablespoons of ghee
- 3 lbs. leg of lamb, boneless and butterflied
- 2 garlic cloves, minced
- 1 teaspoon cumin, ground
- ¼ teaspoon thyme, dried
- Salt and pepper to taste
- 2 cups vegetable stock

For the salad:
- 4-ounces of feta cheese, crumbled
- ½ cup pecans, toasted
- 1 cup mint, chopped
- 1 ½ tablespoons lemon juice
- 2 cups baby spinach
- ¼ cup olive oil

Directions:
Rub the lamb with salt, pepper, 1 tablespoon melted ghee, thyme, cumin and garlic. Add the stock to your instant pot, add leg of lamb, cover and cook on high for 40 minutes. Leave the leg of lamb on a plate, and slice and divide between serving plates.
In a salad bowl mix the spinach, mint, feta cheese, olive oil, lemon juice, pecans, salt, pepper, and toss then divide amongst serving plates next to the lamb slices. Serve right away.

Nutritional Information per serving:
Calories: 234   Fat: 20g   Fiber: 3g   Carbs: 5g   Protein: 12g

---

79. Lamb Shanks & Carrots
Cook Time: 35 minutes   **Servings: 4**

Ingredients:
- 4 lamb shanks
- 2 tablespoons ghee
- 1 yellow onion, chopped
- 3 carrots, sliced
- 1 teaspoon oregano, dried
- 2 tablespoons tomato paste
- 2 garlic cloves, minced
- 2 tablespoons coconut flour
- 4-ounces of beef stock
- 2 tablespoons water
- 1 tomato, chopped
- Sea salt and black pepper to taste

Directions:
In a bowl, mix flour, lamb shanks, salt, pepper, and toss to coat. Set your instant pot to the sauté mode, add the ghee and heat it up. Add the lamb and brown all sides of the meat, then transfer meat to a bowl. Add oregano, carrots, garlic, onion, into instant pot and stir and sauté for 5 minutes. Add the stock, water, tomato paste, tomato and return the lamb to the instant pot. Stir, cover, cook on high for 25 minutes. Divide evenly between serving plates. Serve.

Nutritional Information per serving:
Calories: 400   Fat: 14g   Fiber: 3g   Carbs: 7g   Protein: 30g

---

80. Lamb & Coconut Curry with Cauliflower Rice
Cook Time: 28 minutes   **Servings: 6**

Ingredients:
- 3 lbs. lamb, cubed into small pieces
- 2 tablespoons ghee
- 2 cloves garlic, finely chopped
- 1 onion, finely chopped
- 1 teaspoon chilli powder
- ½ teaspoon coriander, ground
- 1 teaspoon cumin, ground
- ½ teaspoon turmeric, ground
- 1 cup full-fat coconut milk
- 1 cup beef stock
- 1 (14-ounce can) tomatoes, chopped

- 1 head of cauliflower, cut into rough chunks
- 1 tablespoon butter

Directions:
On your instant pot select the sauté mode, add the ghee to instant pot and heat. Add the lamb to pot and brown on all sides for about 5 minutes. Add the onion and garlic along with spices to pot and coat the lamb with them by stirring it all together. Add the stock, tomatoes, coconut milk to instant pot.

Change the setting to the Meat/Stew setting and set the cook time for 20 minutes. When the cooking is done, release the pressure naturally for 10 minutes. Meanwhile, add the cauliflower to a food processor and blend until it has the consistency of rice. Tip the cauliflower into a microwave-proof bowl, top with butter, cover and place in the microwave. Cook the cauliflower in the microwave for 3 minutes on high. Stir through the melted butter, adding some sea salt and pepper to taste. Serve the lamb curry on a bed of cauliflower rice.

Nutritional Information per serving:
Calories: 327   Fat: 11g   Fiber: 2g   Carbs: 9g   Protein: 26g

---

81. *Instant Pot Lamb Chops with Creamed Cauliflower*

Cook Time: 31 minutes   **Servings: 6**

Ingredients:
- 3 lbs. lamb chops
- 3 teaspoons sea salt
- 1 shallot, peeled, halved
- 1 cup beef stock
- 1 tablespoon tomato paste
- 2 tablespoons ghee
- 1 tablespoon extra-virgin olive oil
- 1 rosemary sprig
- Picked red onions for topping

For the Creamed Cauliflower:
- 1 head of cauliflower, cut into florets
- 3 garlic cloves, crushed
- 1 celery stalk, quartered
- 2 cups chicken stock
- Water
- 1 tablespoon unsalted butter
- ¼ cup celery leaves, chopped
- ¾ tablespoon cream
- ½ cup milk
- ½ teaspoon sea salt

Directions:
On a platter evenly distribute the rosemary leaves and salt on both sides of the lamb chops. Set your instant pot to the sauté mode, add the olive oil and butter and heat. Add the lamb chops and brown the meat on all sides for 12 minutes do chops in batches of 3. Once all the lamb chops are browned, and remove chops. Add the shallot, and tomato paste into pot stirring often. Add the beef stock. Return the lamb chops back to the pot. Cover and cook on high-pressure for 2 minutes. Once cooked use quick-release on the pressure. Meanwhile place the cauliflower, chicken stock, garlic, and celery into a pan. Add enough water to cover. Bring to a boil over medium-high heat, cook for about 15 minutes. Drain the liquid. Add cauliflower to food processor along with butter, salt, milk and cream. Puree cauliflower until it is creamy and smooth, then stir in the celery leaves.

Place the lamb chops on top of the creamed cauliflower, top with pan sauce and pickled red onions. Serve hot!

Nutritional Information per serving:
Calories: 312 Fat: 8g Fiber: 3g Carbs: 8g Protein: 26g

---

82. Instant Pot Cooked Lamb Tagine
Cook Time: 25 minutes   **Servings: 6**
Ingredients:

- 3 lbs. leg of lamb, diced
- 2 tablespoons ghee
- 3 teaspoons cumin, ground
- ½ teaspoon cinnamon, ground
- 2 medium onions, sliced
- 2 garlic cloves, peeled and chopped
- 1 (14-ounce can) tomatoes, chopped
- 3 tablespoons honey, organic
- 1 beef stock cube
- 1 medium sweet potato, diced
- 6 no-soak dried apricots
- 1 ½ cups water
- Garnish with parsley, fresh leaf
- Lemon zest for garnish
- 1 (15-ounce can) chickpeas, drained, rinsed

Directions:
Set your instant pot to the sauté mode, add the ghee and heat. Add the lamb, garlic, onions, and sauté, browning meat on all sides, add the spices and stir well for about 5 minutes. Add the chopped tomatoes, honey, chickpeas, sweet potato, apricots, and crumble stock cube on top. Give it a good stir and mix well. Add water. Lock the lid on the instant pot and select the Meat/Stew setting with a cook time of 15 minutes.
Release the pressure naturally, for 15 minutes. Divide into serving dishes and garnish with lemon zest and fresh parsley leaves. Serve warm.

Nutritional Information per serving:
Calories: 323 Fat: 8g Fiber: 2g Carbs: 9g Protein: 27g

---

83. Lamb, Butternut Squash & Chickpea Tagine
Cook Time: 30 minutes   **Servings: 4**
Ingredients:

- 2 lbs. lamb shoulder, cut into small chunks
- 1 (14-ounce can) chickpeas, drained, rinsed
- 1 small butternut squash, peeled, diced into small chunks
- 1 (14-ounce can) tomatoes, chopped
- 1 tablespoon coconut oil
- ½ teaspoon cinnamon, ground
- ½ teaspoon ginger, ground
- 1 teaspoon coriander, ground
- 2 teaspoons cumin, ground
- ½ teaspoon sea salt
- 1 tablespoon runny honey, organic
- 3 cloves garlic, crushed
- 1 onion, diced
- 1 cup water

Directions:
Set your instant pot to the sauté mode, add the coconut oil and heat. Add the onions and garlic, and allow to soften for 3 minutes. Now add the lamb and brown meat on all sides for another 5 minutes. Add spices and allow them to coat the meat, stir to blend.
Add tomatoes with 1 cup water and stir. Add in the honey and stir. Cancel the sauté setting. Put the lid on your instant pot and press the Manual setting with a cook time of

30 minutes. Serve with cauliflower rice or couscous with plain Greek yogurt on top and some fresh coriander, chopped. Divide into serving dishes. Serve warm.

Nutritional Information per serving:
Calories: 283   Fat: 10g   Fiber: 2g   Carbs: 10g   Protein: 24g

---

84. *Lamb Tagine with Orange & Prunes*
Cook Time: 30 minutes   **Servings:** 4
Ingredients:
For Lamb Tagine:
- 2 lbs. lamb shoulder, cut into small pieces
- 2 teaspoons cinnamon
- 2 teaspoons turmeric
- 1 teaspoon ginger
- 2 medium onions, finely sliced
- 1 teaspoon sea salt
- ½ cup prunes
- 1 orange, peeled, and juiced
- 2 cups beef broth
- 2 garlic cloves, crushed
- 2 tablespoons ghee

For Cilantro Buttered Couscous:
- 1 large cauliflower
- ½ bunch cilantro, finely chopped
- 2 tablespoons butter
- 1 ½ teaspoons sea salt

Directions:
Add the spices to a large bowl and add the lamb meat. Mix and blend with hands to coat meat with spices then set aside. Set your instant pot to the sauté mode, add the ghee and heat. Add the garlic, and onions and sauté for 3 minutes. Add in the lamb mix to the instant pot and stir to blend ingredients. Brown the meat on all sides. Add the broth and stir. Cover the instant pot with the lid and set on Meat/Stew setting with a cook time of 30 minutes. When cooking is complete, release the pressure naturally for 15 minutes. Meanwhile cut the cauliflower into florets and place them into your food processor and pulse until the cauliflower has the consistency of large grain rice. In a pan heat the butter and add the cauliflower rice and cook for 5 minutes. Stir in the salt and add the cilantro just before serving. Serve the lamb over a bed of cilantro buttered rice. Serve warm.

Nutritional Information per serving:
Calories: 334   Fat: 15g   Fiber: 1g   Carbs: 11g   Protein: 29g

---

85. *Lamb, Vegetable & Lentil Soup*
Cook Time: 35 minutes   **Servings:** 8
Ingredients:
- 2 lbs. lamb shanks, cut into small pieces
- 2 tablespoons coconut oil
- 2 cloves garlic, minced
- 2 carrots, chopped
- 2 celery ribs, chopped
- ½ cup peas, frozen
- 2/3 cup green lentil, rinsed, drained
- ½ cup dry white wine
- 5 cups water
- 5-ounces pancetta, chopped

Directions:

Set your instant pot to the sauté mode, add coconut oil, and heat. Add the lamb and brown the meat on all sides for about 5 minutes, then remove the meat from pot. Add the garlic, carrot, celery, pancetta, and onion into pot and sauté for about 3 minutes. Return the lamb to the pot along with wine and water, stir. Secure the lid on the pot and set on Manual setting with a cook time of 20 minutes on high pressure. When cooking is done use the quick-release to release the pressure. Add the lentils and set on Manual for a 10-minute cook time. Release pressure again using quick-release method and remove the lamb to cutting board, shred meat using 2 forks. Return the meat back to the pot along with peas. Cook for an additional 5 minutes on simmer setting. Season to taste. Pour into serving bowls. Serve hot!

Nutritional Information per serving:
Calories: 330   Fat: 25g   Fiber: 24g   Carbs: 5g   Protein: 51g

86. *Tuscan Lamb with White Beans*
Cook Time: 25 minutes   **Servings: 4**
Ingredients:

- 2 lbs. lamb shanks
- 2 tablespoons ghee
- 1 medium onion, chopped
- 3 ½ cups water
- 1 cup navy beans, dried, picked over
- 2 rosemary sprigs
- 1 (14-ounce can) tomatoes, diced in juice
- 3 garlic cloves, thinly sliced
- 2 celery ribs, chopped
- 2 carrots, chopped
- Garnish with flat-leaf parsley, extra virgin olive oil for drizzling

Directions:
Set your instant pot to the sauté mode, add the ghee and heat it. Season the lamb shanks with salt and pepper and pat dry. Add the lamb to instant pot and brown the meat on all sides. Remove the meat to a plate. Add the carrots, celery, onion, and garlic to the instant pot and sauté for about five minutes, stirring often. Add the beans, water and salt and pepper to instant pot and stir. Return the lamb shanks to the instant pot and secure the lid of pot and set on Manual setting for 30 minutes. Release the pressure naturally for 10 minutes. Place the meat on a cutting board and shred the meat using 2 forks. Spoon the beans and vegetable mixture into serving bowls and top with lamb and sauce.

Nutritional Information per serving:
Calories: 317   Fat: 12g   Fiber: 20g   Carbs: 8g   Protein: 38g

87. *Moroccan Lamb Stew*
Cook Time: 45 minutes   **Servings: 4**
Ingredients:

- 1 lb. grass-fed lamb, cubed stew meat
- 1 tablespoon coconut oil
- ½ lemon peel zested
- 1 bulb fennel cut into cubes
- ¼ cup raw almonds, toasted
- 3 tablespoons lemon juice, fresh squeezed
- ½ cup flat leaf parsley, fresh, chopped
- 20 green olives, pitted

- 2 turnips peeled, cubed
- ½ cup raisins
- 1 yellow onion, diced
- 4 carrots, peeled, sliced
- 14-ounces of pureed tomatoes
- 1 cinnamon stick
- ¼ teaspoon cloves, ground
- ¼ teaspoon cayenne
- 1 teaspoon black pepper
- Sea salt to taste
- 2 teaspoons cardamom, ground
- 1 teaspoon cumin, ground
- 2 teaspoons coriander ground
- 2 teaspoons smoked paprika
- 2 teaspoons ginger ground

Directions:
In a large container with lid, add lemon zest, coconut oil, ginger, paprika, coriander, cumin, pepper, cayenne, saffron, cinnamon stick, cardamom, and sea salt. Add the cubed lamb and mix well place lid on container and store in the fridge for 24 hours. When ready to begin cooking place the lamb mixture into your instant pot and layer the top of meat with raisins, turnips, carrots, fennel and onions. Mix the tomato puree with enough water to make 3 cups and slowly pour over meat mixture. Stir mixture. Set the lid on the instant pot and set it to the Meat/Stew setting on a cook time of 35 minutes. When the cooking is done release the pressure naturally for 15 minutes. Add the stew to serving bowls and top with chopped parsley, cilantro and toasted almonds. Serve warm.

Nutritional Information per serving:
Calories: 308   Fat: 9g   Fiber: 3g   Carbs: 9g   Protein: 29g

---

88. *Instant Pot Rack of Lamb*
Cook Time: 30 minutes   **Servings: 6**
Ingredients:
- 2 racks of lamb, about 1 lb, with about 8 ribs each
- ¼ teaspoon parsley flakes
- ¼ teaspoon black pepper
- ½ teaspoon seasoned salt
- ¼ teaspoon rosemary, ground
- ¼ teaspoon, marjoram
- ¼ teaspoon, savory
- ¼ teaspoon thyme
- ¼ cup water
- 1 tablespoon extra virgin olive oil

Directions:
Add the water to your instant pot, set racks into pot. Brush the lamb with olive oil. Mix the remaining ingredients in a small bowl. Coat the lamb with this mixture. Secure instant pot lid and set to Manual setting with a cook time of 30 minutes. When cook time is complete, release the pressure naturally for 10 minutes. Place racks on serving dishes. Serve.

Nutritional Information per serving:
Calories: 297   Fat: 15g   Fiber: 4g   Carbs: 9g   Protein: 33g

89. Garlic Rosemary Lamb
Cook Time: 25 minutes **Servings:** 6
Ingredients:
- 1 rack of lamb
- ½ cup vegetable stock
- 4 carrots, chopped
- 4 garlic cloves, minced
- Salt and pepper to taste
- 2 tablespoons coconut oil
- 3 tablespoons coconut flour
- 4 pieces of fresh rosemary

Directions:
Season the lamb with salt and pepper. Set your instant pot to the sauté mode. Cook the lamb in instant pot along with garlic until brown on all sides for about 5 minutes. Add flour and stir. Add stock, rosemary, and carrots. Stir well. Close the lid and cook on Manual setting for 20 minutes. Once cooking is done, release the pressure naturally for 10 minutes. Remove the rosemary. Divide onto serving plates. Serve.

Nutritional Information per serving:
Calories: 287   Fat: 16g   Fiber: 9g   Carbs: 8g   Protein: 34g

90. Lamb Shanks with Garlic & Port Wine
Cook Time: 45 minutes **Servings:** 2
Ingredients:
- 2 lbs. lamb shanks
- 1 tablespoon ghee
- 8 garlic cloves, peeled and left whole
- ½ cup chicken stock
- ½ cup port wine
- 1 teaspoon balsamic vinegar
- 1 tablespoon rosemary, dried
- 1 tablespoon tomato paste
- Salt and pepper to taste
- 1 tablespoon unsalted butter

Directions:
Season the lamb shanks with salt and pepper. Set the instant pot to the sauté mode, add the ghee and heat. Add the lamb shanks and brown them on all sides. Add the garlic cloves. Add the port wine, tomato paste, stock, rosemary, and stir. Close the instant pot and set on Manual setting for 30 minutes. When cooking is done release the pressure naturally for 10 minutes. Remove the lamb shanks. Set the instant pot on cook for an additional 5 minutes to thicken the sauce, add in the butter and vinegar, stir. Serve the sauce over the lamb. Serve hot!

Nutritional Information per serving:
Calories: 282   Fat: 13g   Fiber: 10g   Carbs: 9g   Protein: 36g

91. Instant Pot Irish Lamb Stew
Cook Time: 40 minutes **Servings:** 6
Ingredients:
- 3 lbs. lamb shoulder, boneless, cut into small chunks
- 2 medium onions, sliced thin
- 2 medium russet potatoes, peeled, sliced 1/4 -inch thick
- 2 sprigs of thyme, fresh

- 2 cups beef broth
- ¼ cup parsley, minced
- 2 large carrots, peeled cut into 1 1/2-inch lengths
- Sea salt and black pepper to taste

Directions:
In a vegetable basket that will fit into your instant pot, place the potatoes, carrots, parsley, with a pinch of salt and pepper and set aside. Layer the rest of the ingredients in the instant pot with salt and pepper. Add in the beef stock pouring over everything. Then place the basket on top of them. Set the instant pot to Manual setting for 20 minutes. Now set the pot at high pressure for 20 minutes. Release the pressure naturally for 15 minutes. Remove the basket of vegetables from pot and set on a plate. Remove the thyme sprigs from stew. Add the vegetables in the basket back into instant pot and stir the stew. Add more sea salt and black pepper as needed. Divide into serving bowls. Serve hot!

Nutritional Information per serving:
Calories: 256   Fat: 11g   Fiber: 14g   Carbs: 7g   Protein: 35g

---

92. *Instant Pot Lamb Stew Provencal*

Cook Time: 45 minutes
Servings: 4
Ingredients:

- ¾ cup coconut flour
- 1 lb. lamb stew meat, cubed
- 2 tablespoons coconut oil
- 1 shallot, finely chopped
- 1 cup red wine
- 1 teaspoon garlic, minced
- 4 cups beef stock
- 1-inch rosemary
- 2 bay leaves
- 1 cup pearl onions
- 1 tablespoon Herbes de Provence
- 2 cups mushrooms quartered
- 4 cups vegetable roots, cubed
- Sea salt and black pepper to taste
- Flat leaf parsley for garnish

Directions:
Add the salt, pepper and coconut flour to a zip bag. Add the cubed lamb to bag and zip the top. Shake until the pieces of meat are coated. Set your instant pot to the sauté mode, add the coconut oil and heat it up. Shake excess coating off meat and place the meat into the instant pot along with shallot and garlic.

Stir until the meat is browned on all sides, for about 5 minutes. Add the beef stock and red wine to the instant pot along with bay leaves, rosemary, and Herbes de Provence, and stir to combine. Set to Meat/Stew setting for 30 minutes. When cooking is complete, release the pressure naturally in 15 minutes. While your lamb is cooking, prep your vegetables. Blanch the pearl onions quickly, snip the root end, and pop the onion out of its skin. Add the vegetables to the instant pot, and cook on Manual setting for 10 minutes. Release the pressure again with quick-release. Divide into serving bowls, and garnish with parsley. Serve hot!

Nutritional Information per serving:
Calories: 572   Fat: 46g   Fiber: 10g   Carbs: 42g   Protein: 31g

93. Guinness Lamb Stew with Vegetables
Cook Time: 40 minutes **Servings: 6**
Ingredients:
- 3 lbs. lamb shoulder, cut into small pieces
- 3 tablespoons coconut oil
- 2 medium yellow onions, sliced thin
- 6 cloves garlic, peeled, smashed
- 1 cup frozen peas
- 6 small white potato, cut in half
- 2 teaspoons honey, organic
- 1 sprig rosemary, fresh
- 1 bay leaf
- 1/2 cup water
- 1 cups beef broth
- 1/2 cup Guinness
- 3 tablespoons tomato paste
- ¼ cup coconut flour

Directions:
Pat the lamb dry and season it with salt and pepper. Set your instant pot to sauté mode, add the coconut oil and heat. Add the onions, and garlic and stir for about 3 minutes. Add in the lamb and brown the meat on all sides for about 5 minutes, then remove the lamb from pot. Stir in the tomato paste and cook for another 3 minutes.

Add the lamb and flour back into pot, and stir. Add the water, beef broth, bay leaf, honey, rosemary sprig, and Guinness, stir. Set to Manual setting for 20 minutes and cook. When cooking is completed, release pressure naturally for 10-minutes. Add the carrots and potatoes to the stew and place the lid back on the instant pot and set on Meat/Stew setting for 20 minutes. Release pressure again when cooking is complete, and remove rosemary sprig, and bay leaf. Add the frozen peas and keep the pot on simmer for about 5 minutes. Divide into serving bowls. Serve hot!

Nutritional Information per serving:
Calories: 789   Fat: 52g   Fiber: 6g   Carbs: 36g   Protein: 42g

---

94. Mushroom, Potato Lamb Stew
Total Cook Time: 40 minutes **Servings: 4**
Ingredients:
- 2 lbs. lamb stew meat, cubed
- 1 large onion, chopped
- 2 tablespoons ghee
- 4 potatoes, quartered
- 2 cloves garlic, crushed
- ¼ of 14-ounce can of tomatoes, crushed
- ¼ can of button mushrooms, sliced
- Flat-leaf parsley, chopped for garnish
- Sea salt and black pepper to taste
- 2 cups beef broth

Directions:
Set your instant pot to the sauté mode, add the ghee and heat. Add the lamb with sea salt and pepper, brown meat on all sides for about 5-minutes, remove meat from pot. Add garlic and onions into the instant pot and cook for about 5-minutes stir occasionally. Add the tomato, broth, potatoes, mushrooms and the lamb back into your instant pot. Place the lid on the pot and set on Meat/Stew setting for 30 minutes. Release the pressure naturally for 15 minutes. Divide into serving bowls, and garnish with parsley. Serve hot!

Nutritional Information per serving:
Calories: 682   Fat: 51g   Fiber: 10g   Carbs: 39g   Protein: 42g

95. Greek Lamb Stew with Green Beans
Cook Time: 40 minutes **Servings:** 6
Ingredients:
- 3 lbs. leg of lamb, boneless
- 1 medium onion, finely chopped
- 1 ½ cups water
- 2 tablespoons coconut oil
- 1 lb. of string green beans, fresh, trimmed
- 3 large tomatoes, pulped in blender
- 4 tablespoons tomato sauce
- 5 potatoes, peeled and cut into small chunks
- 1 tablespoon dill, fresh, chopped
- ½ tablespoon mint, fresh chopped
- A pinch of cinnamon, ground

Directions:
Set your instant pot to the sauté mode, add the coconut oil and heat. Add the lamb and brown on sides of the meat, for about five minutes, then remove the meat from the pot. Add the onions to pot and cook for about 5-minutes stirring often. Add in the tomatoes, tomato sauce and some sea salt and stir. Add the meat back into the pot, along with the rest of the ingredients except for parsley, and stir. Cover with lid and set the pot on Meat/Stew setting for 30-minutes. Release the pressure naturally for 10-minutes. Divide into serving bowls, garnish with chopped parsley. Serve hot!

Nutritional Information per serving:
Calories: 589 Fat: 41g Fiber: 10g Carbs: 29g Protein: 46g

96. Ground Lamb with Zucchini Pasta
Cook Time: 45 minutes **Servings:** 6
Ingredients:
- 1 lb. lamb, ground
- 2 tablespoons ghee
- 1 medium white onion, finely chopped
- 2 cups chicken broth
- 1 bay leaf
- 2 stalks celery, chopped
- ½ cup water
- 1 (14-ounce can) tomatoes, crushed
- Sea salt and black pepper to taste
- 1 ½ cups of zucchini pasta
- 1 bunch of parsley, fresh, chopped for garnish

Directions:
Set your instant pot on the sauté mode, add the ghee and heat. Add the white onion and cook for 5-minutes while stirring. Add the ground lamb and cook for an additional 5-minutes. Once meat is browned transfer to a colander and drain. Add the tomatoes, water, broth, celery, bay leaf, sea salt and pepper. Set the instant pot to the Meat/Stew setting for 35-minutes. When cooking is completed, release the pressure naturally for 10-minutes. Divide into serving bowls, serve on top of bed of zucchini pasta, and garnish with parsley. Serve hot!

Nutritional Information per serving:
Calories: 623 Fat: 46g Fiber: 13g Carbs: 12g Protein: 42g

97. Greek Lamb Shanks with Tomatoes
Cooking time: 50 minutes **Servings: 4**
Ingredients:
- 4 lamb shanks
- 2 tablespoons extra-virgin olive oil
- 1 (14-ounce can) tomatoes, crushed
- 1 cup chicken stock
- ½ cup red wine
- ¼ teaspoon cinnamon, ground
- 1 teaspoon, thyme, dried
- 1 teaspoon, oregano, dried
- 1 tablespoon, tomato paste
- 4 cloves garlic, crushed
- 1 carrot, peeled, minced
- 1 stalk of celery, minced
- 1 large onion, minced
- Sea salt and black pepper to taste

Directions:
Set your instant pot to the sauté mode, add the oil and heat it up. Add the shanks and brown the meat on all sides, 3-minutes on each side, then remove the shanks from pot. Add the onion, celery, and carrot to food processor and process until minced. Add the minced vegetables to your instant pot, along with stock, wine, spices, and lamb shanks, stir well. Secure the lid and set the instant pot onto the Meat/Stew setting for 30 minutes. When cooking is completed, release the pressure for 15 minutes naturally. Divide the into serving dishes, drizzle sauce over from instant pot. Serve hot!

Nutritional Information per serving:
Calories: 641   Fat: 48g   Fiber: 16g   Carbs: 13g   Protein: 44g

98. Lamb & White Bean Stew
Cook Time: 50 minutes **Servings: 4**
Ingredients:
- 2 ½ lbs. lamb shoulder, boneless, cubed
- 1 ½ cups white beans, dried
- 2 tablespoons ghee
- 2 bay leaves
- 2 onions, cut into rings
- ½ bunch parsley, fresh, chopped
- 1 large tomato, diced
- 2 tablespoons curry powder
- 2 bunches spring onion, chopped, set aside 2 tablespoons for garnish
- 2 garlic cloves, chopped
- Pinch of cayenne pepper
- 1 teaspoon cumin, ground
- 2 cups chicken stock

Directions:
Soak the white beans overnight in 2 cups cold water. When ready to cook, set your instant pot to the sauté mode, add the ghee and heat. Add the lamb and brown the meat on all sides. Add the onion, garlic, cayenne pepper, cumin, curry powder, salt and pepper, cook for 5 minutes, stirring. Drain the beans and remaining ingredients, except for 2 tablespoons of chopped green onion, then add them to your instant pot along with stock and stir. Put on the lid to instant pot and set it on the Meat/Stew setting 35 minutes. When the cooking is complete, release the pressure for 10-minutes. Divide into serving bowls, and top with chopped spring onion. Serve hot!

Nutritional Information per serving:
Calories: 633   Fat: 49g   Fiber: 10g   Carbs: 32g   Protein: 49g

99. Lamb Trotters with Tomato & Thyme
Cooking Time: 50 minutes
Servings: 4
Ingredients:
- 2 lbs lamb trotters
- 4 cloves of garlic, chopped
- 2 medium white onions, chopped
- 1 chive, chopped
- 3 bay leaves
- 2 carrots, peeled, sliced
- 12 peppercorns
- 1 cup white wine
- 3 chilli peppers
- 1 cup tomato puree
- 1 tablespoon thyme, fresh, chopped
- Sea salt and black pepper to taste
- ½ cup water
- 1 tablespoon olive oil

Directions:
Wash the lamb trotters under cold running water. Set your instant pot to the sauté mode, add the oil and heat. Add the onions, and garlic and sauté for 5 minutes. Place the trotters into your instant pot, along with wine, water, bay leaves, peppercorns, tomato puree and remaining spices, except the thyme. Set the instant pot to the Manual setting for 45 minutes. When cooking is complete, release the pressure for 15 minutes naturally. Divide into servings dishes, and garnish with fresh, chopped thyme. Serve hot!

Nutritional Information per serving:
Calories: 1290   Fat: 53g   Fiber: 28g   Carbs: 14g   Protein: 64g

100. Mensaf (Jordanian Lamb Stew)
Cook Time: 45 minutes
Servings: 8
Ingredients:
- 2 lbs. lamb shoulder, boneless, cubed
- ¼ cup pinenuts
- 1 cups chicken stock
- ½ cup white wine
- 2 cup goat's milk
- 2 tablespoons coconut oil
- Serve with cauliflower rice
- Pita bread for serving

Directions:
Set your instant pot to the sauté mode, add the coconut oil and heat. Add the lamb and brown the meat on all sides for about 5-minutes, then remove meat from pot. Add the pinenuts and toast them for 3-minutes, then remove them. Add in the wine, stock, goats milk and stir. Cook on Manual setting with a cook time of 40-minutes. When cooking is completed, release the pressure naturally in 10-minutes. Stir the stew pour over bed of cauliflower rice that is on top of piece of pita bread. Garnish with toasted pinenuts. Serve hot!

Nutritional Information per serving:
Calories: 642   Fat: 49g   Fiber: 10g   Carbs: 23g   Protein: 47g

Chapter 5. Collection of Poultry-Based Instant Pot Recipes

101. Garlic Chicken
Cook Time: 35 minutes **Servings: 8**
Ingredients:
- 2 lbs. chicken thighs, skinless, boneless
- 1 cup Parmesan cheese, grated
- 8-ounces cream cheese
- 1 cup chicken broth
- 1 teaspoon black pepper, freshly ground
- 2 teaspoons sea salt
- 2 teaspoons paprika
- 8 garlic cloves, minced
- 1 onion, diced
- 12-ounces cremini mushrooms or button mushrooms, halved
- ½ cup unsalted butter, melted
- Parsley, fresh for garnish

Directions:
Place your chicken thighs into your instant pot, and pour the melted butter over the chicken. Add the onion, garlic, mushrooms, salt and pepper, toss to coat the chicken thighs with butter. Cover and set on the Meat/Stew setting for 35 minutes.

Once the cooking is completed, release the pressure naturally for 15 minutes. Remove the chicken and vegetables to a serving platter. Set your instant pot to the sauté mode for 5 minutes. Combine the chicken broth, with Parmesan cheese and cream cheese. Cook, stirring, mixture until the cream cheese is fully melted. Pour the sauce over your chicken thighs and garnish with fresh parsley. Serve hot!

Nutritional Information per serving:
Calories: 495   Fat: 41g   Carbs: 6g   Protein: 26g

102. Ground Turkey & Basil Meatballs
Cook Time: 40 minutes **Servings: 8**
Ingredients:
For the Sauce:
- 1 teaspoon parsley, dried
- 2 teaspoons basil, dried
- 2 garlic cloves, minced
- 1 tablespoon extra-virgin olive oil
- 1 (14-ounce can) tomatoes, crushed
- ½ stick of unsalted butter
- 1 cup heavy whipping cream
- Sea salt and black pepper to taste

For the Meatballs:
- 2 large eggs
- 2 cups cauliflower rice
- ½ teaspoon garlic powder
- ½ teaspoon black pepper, freshly ground
- 1 teaspoon sea salt
- 1 tablespoon Italian seasoning
- 2 cups Parmesan cheese, grated, divided
- ½ cup almond meal
- 12-ounces ground turkey
- 1 lb. Italian sausage, casings removed
- 8-ounces fontina cheese, cut into 24 cubes
- 2 tablespoons coconut oil

Directions:

In a mixing bowl, beat the eggs, then whisk in the almond meal, cauliflower rice, Italian seasoning, 1 cup Parmesan cheese, salt, pepper, and garlic powder. Add the sausage and turkey and mix to combine. Form 24 (1-inch) balls. In the center of each meatball stuff a fontina cheese cube, making sure the cheese is fully encased. Place the stuffed meatballs into your instant pot. Set your instant pot to the sauté mode, and add the coconut oil and heat it. Add the meatballs to the melted coconut oil, and brown them on all sides for 5 minutes. Add in the remaining ingredients to instant pot, except the heavy whipping cream, stir and place the lid securely onto instant pot. Set the instant pot to the Meat/Stew setting for a cook time of 30 minutes. When cooking is completed, release the pressure naturally for 15 minutes. Remove the meatballs from instant pot, and add the cream into the sauce in the instant pot and stir to blend. Add the meatballs back into the pot and set to the Keep Warm/Cancel setting until ready to serve. Serve hot!

Nutritional Information per serving:
Calories: 633   Fat: 50g   Carbs: 9g   Protein: 39g

---

103. Creamy Mushroom, Rosemary Chicken
Cook Time: 45 minutes   **Servings: 6**
Ingredients:
- 2 lbs. chicken breasts, skinless, boneless
- 8-ounces bacon, diced
- 8-ounces button mushrooms, halved
- 1 cup sour cream
- Sea salt and black pepper to taste
- 3 fresh rosemary sprigs
- 6 garlic cloves, minced
- ½ cup dry white wine
- ½ stick butter, cubed
- 2 tablespoons coconut oil
- Fresh parsley, chopped for garnish

Directions:
Set your instant pot to the sauté mode, add the coconut oil and heat. Add the diced bacon to instant pot and cook until semi-crispy. Add the chicken and brown the meat for about five minutes. Add in the wine to instant pot and stir mixture. Add in the remaining ingredients, except for parsley, stir and secure the lid of instant pot. Set to the Meat/Stew setting for 35 minutes. When the cooking is complete, release pressure naturally for 10-minutes. Remove the rosemary sprigs and discard. Divide among serving dishes. Garnish with fresh chopped parsley. Serve hot!

Nutritional Information per serving:
Calories: 570   Fat: 49g   Carbs: 5g   Protein: 27g

---

104. Heavy Cream Chicken Stew
Cook Time: 40 minutes   **Servings: 4**
Ingredients:
- 12-ounces whole chicken thighs and legs
- ¼ cup extra-virgin olive oil
- 1 teaspoon fennel seeds, crushed
- 1 tablespoon tomato paste
- 2 tablespoons dry white wine
- 2 garlic cloves, minced
- ½ onion, diced
- 1 stalk celery, chopped
- 1 cup black olives, pitted
- 1 cup chicken broth

- 1 cup heavy whipping cream
- 2 tablespoons fresh chopped parsley for garnish
- Sea salt and black pepper to taste

Directions:
Place the chicken broth, olives, celery, garlic, onion, white wine, tomato paste, fennel seeds, sea salt, black pepper, stir, then add in chicken pieces, and stir. Cover instant pot and set to Meat/Stew setting for 45 minutes. When the cooking is completed, release the pressure naturally for 15-minutes. Add in the heavy cream and stir. Divide into serving bowls, and garnish with fresh chopped parsley. Serve hot.

Nutritional Information per serving:
Calories: 447   Fat: 34g   Carbs: 7g   Protein: 26g

---

105. *Ginger Spinach Chicken*
Cook Time: 50 minutes   **Servings: 8**

Ingredients:
- 1 tablespoon ginger, minced
- 8 chicken thighs
- 2 cups baby spinach
- 1 teaspoon blackstrap molasses
- 1 tablespoon garlic powder
- 2 cups chicken stock
- Sea salt and black pepper to taste
- Chopped coriander, fresh, for garnish

Directions:
Add the chicken stock, salt, pepper, ginger, garlic powder, and mix, then add in the chicken thighs. Set the instant pot to Meat/Stew setting for a cook time of 45 minutes. When cook time is completed, release pressure within 10-minutes naturally. Add the spinach to the instant pot and stir, set on Manual for 5-minute cook time. Divide into serving dishes, and garnish with fresh, chopped coriander. Serve hot!

Nutritional Information per serving:
Calories: 472   Fat: 35g   Carbs: 3.8g   Protein: 32.7g

---

106. *Ginger Coconut Chicken Wings*
Cook Time: 50 minutes   **Servings: 6**

Ingredients:
- 3 lbs. chicken wings
- 8-ounces curry paste
- 2-ounces Thai basil, minced
- 1 tablespoon coconut milk
- 1 tablespoon ginger, fresh, minced
- 1 tablespoon cilantro, fresh, minced

Directions:
Add your chicken wings into your instant pot. In a mixing bowl, whisk together cilantro, coconut milk, ginger, curry paste and basil. Pour the milk mixture over your chicken wings and toss to coat. Cover and cook on Meat/Stew setting for 50 minutes. When the cook time is complete, release the pressure naturally within 15-minutes. Remove lid and stir. Divide into serving dishes, and serve hot!

Nutritional Information per serving:
Calories: 332   Fat: 14.3g   Carbs: 6.3g   Protein: 39.6g

107. *Spicy, Creamy, Coconut Chicken*
Cook Time: 40 minutes   **Servings:** 5
Ingredients:
- 1 lb. chicken thighs, boneless, skinless
- 2 tablespoons olive oil
- 2 teaspoons onion powder
- 3 garlic cloves, minced
- 1 tablespoon ginger, grated
- 3 tablespoons tomato paste
- 5 teaspoons garam masala
- 2 teaspoons paprika
- 10-ounces tomatoes, diced
- 1 cup heavy cream
- 1 cup coconut milk

Directions:
Cut the chicken up into pieces, and add to your instant pot. Add the grated ginger on top of the chicken pieces, then add the rest of the spices. Add the tomato paste, and tomatoes, along with olive oil, and mix well. Add half a cup of coconut milk and stir well. Secure the lid and set the instant pot on the Meat/Stew setting for 35 minutes. When the cook time is complete, release the pressure naturally for 10-minutes. Add to instant pot the heavy cream, and remaining coconut milk, stir. Replace the lid and set on Manual for 5-minutes of cook time. Divide into serving dishes. Serve hot!

Nutritional Information per serving:
Calories: 444 Fat: 33g Carbs: 10g Protein: 29.2g

---

108. *Jalapeno, Curry, Garlic Chicken Meatballs*
Cook Time: 45 minutes   **Servings:** 3
Ingredients:
- 1 lb. lean ground chicken
- 2 cloves garlic, minced, divided
- 1 tablespoon ginger, fresh, minced, divided
- 2 green onions, chopped
- 1 tablespoon cilantro, fresh, chopped
- ½ cup chicken broth
- 1 tablespoon basil, fresh, chopped
- 2 tablespoons almond meal
- 1 jalapeno, sliced
- 1 cup light coconut milk
- 2 tablespoons Thai green curry paste, divided
- Sea salt and black pepper to taste
- 2 tablespoons coconut oil

Directions:
Add to a mixing bowl, the ground chicken, green onion, cilantro, basil, almond meal, half the ginger, garlic, Thai curry paste, salt and pepper, and mix well. Divide the mixture into 12 equal portions and shape into balls. Add the rest of the ingredients into your instant pot, and mix well. Set your instant pot onto the sauté mode, add the coconut oil and heat. Add the balls into the instant pot.
Brown the meatballs for about 5-minutes, then remove the meatballs from instant pot. Add the rest of the ingredients into the instant pot and stir to combine. Add the meatballs, carefully back into the instant pot. Secure the lid and place on Meat/Stew setting on a cook time of 40 minutes. When the cook time is complete, release the pressure naturally for 15-minutes. Divide into serving dishes, and serve hot!

Nutritional Information per serving:
Calories: 284 Fat: 15g Carbs: 3g Protein: 33g

109. Chicken Breasts & Spicy Sauce
Cook Time: 25 minutes   **Servings: 4**

Ingredients:
- 2 chicken breasts, skinless, boneless, chopped
- ¼ teaspoon ginger, grated
- 1 tablespoon garam masala
- 1 cup Greek yogurt, plain
- 1 tablespoon lemon juice
- Sea salt and black pepper to taste

For the Sauce:
- ¼ teaspoon cayenne
- ½ teaspoon turmeric
- ½ teaspoon paprika
- 15-ounce can of tomato sauce
- 4 garlic cloves, minced
- 4 teaspoons garam masala

Directions:
In a mixing bowl, add lemon juice, chicken, yogurt, 1 tablespoon garam masala, ginger, salt, pepper, and toss well, then leave in the fridge for an hour. Set your instant pot to the sauté mode, add the chicken, and stir and cook for 5-minutes. Add 4 teaspoons garam masala, paprika, turmeric, cayenne, tomato sauce, stir and cover. Set the instant pot to the Meat/Stew setting on a high cook time of 20 minutes. Once the cook time is complete, release the pressure naturally for 20 minutes. Divide between serving plates. Serve hot!

Nutritional Information per serving:
Calories: 452   Fat: 4g   Fiber: 7g   Carbs: 9g   Protein: 12g

110. Chicken & Spaghetti Squash
Cook Time: 20 minutes   **Servings: 4**

Ingredients:
- 1 spaghetti squash, halved, seedless
- 1 lb. chicken, cooked, cubed
- 16-ounces Mozzarella cheese, shredded
- 1 cup water
- 1 cup keto marinara sauce

Directions:
Place a cup of water into your instant pot, add the trivet, add the squash, cover and cook on Manual setting on high for a 20-minute cook time. Shred squash and transfer it into a heatproof bowl. Add the marinara sauce, chicken, and mozzarella, toss. Add the squash back into the instant pot, along with marinara sauce, chicken, and mozzarella, stir and close the lid. Set to Manual setting for 5-minutes. Divide into serving bowls. Serve warm!

Nutritional Information per serving:
Calories: 329   Fat: 6g   Fiber: 6   Carbs: 9g   Protein: 10g

111. Chicken & Cauliflower Rice
Cook Time: 38 minutes   **Servings: 6**

Ingredients:
- 3 lbs. chicken thighs, boneless, skinless
- 3 carrots, chopped
- 3 bacon slices, chopped
- 1 rhubarb stalk, chopped

- 4 garlic cloves, minced
- ¼ cup red wine vinegar
- 2 bay leaves
- 1 cup beef stock
- 1 teaspoon turmeric powder
- 24-ounces cauliflower rice
- 1 tablespoon Italian seasoning
- 1 tablespoon garlic powder
- ¼ cup olive oil
- Sea salt and black pepper to taste

Directions:
Set your instant pot on the sauté mode, add the oil and heat. Add bacon, onion, rhubarb, carrots, and garlic, cook for 8 minutes. Add the chicken and stir for 5 minutes. Add the vinegar, turmeric, Italian seasoning, bay leaves, and garlic powder, stir. Cover with lid and set to Meat/Stew setting and cook on high for 20-minutes. When cooking is complete, release the pressure naturally in 15-minutes. Add the cauliflower rice to instant pot with beef stock, stir, cover, and set on Manual setting and cook on low for 5-minutes. Divide into serving bowls. Serve warm!

Nutritional Information per serving:
Calories: 310   Fat: 6g   Fiber: 3g   Carbs: 6g   Protein: 10g

---

112. Chicken Curry
Cook Time: 30 minutes   **Servings: 4**
Ingredients:

- 2lbs. chicken thighs, skinless, boneless, and cubed
- 3 tomatoes, chopped
- 1 tablespoon water
- 3 red chilies, chopped
- 1 cup white onion, chopped
- 2 garlic cloves, minced
- 14-ounces canned, coconut milk
- 1 cup chicken stock
- 2 tablespoons coconut oil
- 1 tablespoon lime juice
- 1 teaspoon fennel seeds, ground
- 1 teaspoon cumin, ground
- 1 teaspoon turmeric, ground
- 1 teaspoon cinnamon, ground
- 2 teaspoons coriander, ground
- 1 tablespoon ginger, grated
- Sea salt and black pepper to taste

Directions:
In your food processor, mix the garlic, white onion, water, ginger, chilies, coriander, cinnamon, cumin, fennel, turmeric, black pepper, and blend until you have a paste and transfer it to a bowl.
Set your instant pot to the sauté mode, add the coconut oil, and heat. Add the mixed paste and stir and cook for 30 seconds. Add tomatoes, chicken, stock, stir and blend well. Cover and cook on Manual setting on high for 15-minutes. Add the coconut milk and stir mixture in pot. Cover the instant pot again and set on high for an additional 10-minutes more. Add in the lime juice, sea salt and black pepper and divide into serving bowls. Serve warm!

Nutritional Information per serving:
Calories: 430   Fat: 16g   Fiber: 4   Carbs: 7g   Protein: 38g

113. Chicken and Mushrooms

Cooking Time: 15 minutes
Servings: 4
Ingredients:

- 4 chicken thighs
- 2 cups button mushrooms, sliced
- 1 teaspoon Dijon mustard
- ½ cup water
- ½ teaspoon garlic powder
- Sea salt and black pepper to taste
- ¼ cup of ghee
- 1 tablespoon tarragon, chopped
- ½ teaspoon onion, powder

Directions:
Set your instant pot to the saute mode, add the ghee and heat it. Add the chicken thighs, onion powder, garlic powder, salt, pepper, and stir. Cook chicken on each side for 2 minutes, then transfer to a bowl. Add the mushrooms into your instant pot, stir and sauté them for 2 minutes. Return the chicken to your instant pot, add the mustard, water, and stir well, cover and cook on high for 10 minutes on Manual setting. When cooking is completed, release the pressure naturally, for 10-minutes. Add the tarragon and stir, divide between serving plates. Serve warm!

Nutritional Information per serving:
Calories: 263   Fat: 16g   Fiber: 4g   Carbs: 6g   Protein: 18g

114. Chicken and Salsa

Cook Time: 17 minutes
Servings: 6
Ingredients:

- 6 chicken breasts, skinless, boneless
- 2 tablespoons of olive oil
- 1 cup cheddar cheese, shredded
- Sea salt and black pepper to taste
- 2 cups jarred keto salsa

Directions:
Set your instant pot on sauté mode, add the oil and heat. Add the chicken, stir and cook for 2 minutes on each side. Add the salsa, stir, cover and cook on high on Manual setting. When cooking is completed, release the pressure naturally for 10 minutes. Spread the cheese over top of mix in the instant pot. Cook again for an additional 3 minutes more on high setting. Divide between serving plates. Serve warm!

Nutritional Information per serving:
Calories: 220   Fat: 7g   Fiber: 2g   Carbs: 6g   Protein: 12g

115. Chicken, Walnuts, and Pomegranate
Cook Time: 17 minutes   **Servings:** 6
Ingredients:
- 12 chicken thighs
- 3 tablespoons coconut oil
- 2 cups walnuts, toasted, chopped
- 1 yellow onion, chopped
- Juice of ½ a lemon
- ¼ teaspoon cardamom, ground
- ½ teaspoon cinnamon, ground
- 1 cup pomegranate molasses
- 2 tablespoons Truvia

Directions:
Place the walnuts in your food processor, blend and transfer to a bowl. Set your instant pot to the sauté mode, add the oil and heat it up. Add the chicken, salt and pepper and brown for 3-minutes on each side, transfer chicken to a bowl. Add the onion, walnuts, and sauté for 2-minutes. Add the pomegranate molasses, cardamom, lemon juice, chicken, Truvia and stir. Cover and set to Manual cooking on high for 12 minutes. When cooking is completed, release the pressure naturally for 15-minutes. Divide amongst serving plates. Serve hot!

Nutritional Information per serving:
Calories: 265   Fat: 6g   Fiber: 6g   Carbs: 6g   Protein: 16g

116. Turkey Instant Pot Stew
Cook Time: 33 minutes   **Servings:** 4
Ingredients:
- 2 tablespoons avocado oil
- 3 cups turkey meat, cooked, shredded
- Sea salt and black pepper to taste
- 2 carrots, chopped
- 3 celery stalks, chopped
- 1 teaspoon garlic, minced
- 1 yellow onion, chopped
- 1 tablespoon cranberry sauce
- 5 cups turkey stock
- 15-ounce can of tomatoes, chopped

Directions:
Set your instant pot to the sauté mode, add the oil and heat it up. Add the celery, carrots, and onions, stir and cook for 3-minutes. Add the cranberry sauce, stock, garlic, turkey meat, salt and pepper, stir, cover. Cook on Manual setting on low for 30-minutes. When cooking is completed, release the pressure for 15-minutes. Divide into serving bowls. Serve hot!

Nutritional Information per serving:
Calories: 200   Fat: 4g   Fiber: 1g   Carbs: 6g   Protein: 16g

117. Lemongrass Chicken
Cook Time: 20 minutes   **Servings:** 5
Ingredients:
- 1 bunch lemongrass, bottom removed and trimmed
- 1-inch piece ginger root, peeled and chopped

- 4-garlic cloves, peeled and crushed
- 1 tablespoon lime juice
- 1 yellow onion, chopped
- ¼ cup cilantro, diced
- 2 tablespoons coconut oil
- Sea salt and black pepper to taste
- 10-chicken drumsticks
- 2 tablespoons fish sauce

Directions:
In your food processor mix the lemongrass, with the garlic, ginger, fish sauce, five spice powder and pulse well. Add the coconut milk and pulse again. Set your instant pot to the sauté mode, add the coconut oil and heat it. Add the onion, stir and cook for 5-minutes. Add the chicken, salt and pepper, stir and cook for 3-minutes per side of chicken. Add the coconut milk, lemongrass mix, stir, cover. Set on the Poultry mode, and cook for 15-minutes. Release the pressure for 10-minutes naturally. Add lime juice, more salt and pepper and stir. Divide into serving plates. Serve warm!

Nutritional Information per serving:
Calories: 400   Fat: 18g   Fiber: 2g   Carbs: 6g   Protein: 20g

---

118. Chicken and Cabbage

Cook Time: 30 minutes   **Servings:** 3

Ingredients:
- 1 ½ lbs. chicken thighs, boneless
- 1 green cabbage, roughly chopped
- 1 yellow onion, chopped
- 2 chili peppers, chopped
- Sea salt and black pepper to taste
- 2 tablespoons ghee
- 1 tablespoon fish sauce
- 10-ounces coconut milk
- ½ cup white wine
- Cayenne pepper to taste
- 1 tablespoon curry
- 4 garlic cloves, peeled and chopped

Directions:
Set your instant pot to the sauté mode, add the ghee and heat it. Add the chicken, salt, pepper and brown on the sides of meat for about 5-minutes, then transfer chicken to a bowl. Add the chili peppers, onions, garlic to the instant pot and stir, cook for 3-minutes. Add the curry and cook for an additional 2-minutes, stirring. Add the coconut milk, wine, cabbage, fish sauce, salt, pepper, chicken, stir and cover, set to Poultry setting for 20 minutes. Release the pressure naturally, for 15-minutes. Stir and divide into serving plates. Serve hot!

Nutritional Information per serving:
Calories: 260   Fat: 5.5g   Fiber: 4.9g   Carbs: 15.2g   Protein: 30.2g

---

119. Chicken and Corn

Cook Time: 25 minutes   **Servings:** 4

Ingredients:
- 8-chicken drumsticks
- 2 tablespoons extra virgin olive oil
- ¼ cup cilantro, fresh, chopped
- 1 tomato, cored, chopped
- ½ yellow onion, peeled, chopped
- 3 scallions, chopped
- ½ teaspoon garlic powder
- ½ teaspoon cumin

- 2 corns on the cob, husked and cut into halves
- 1 tablespoon chicken bouillon
- 8-ounces tomato sauce
- 2 cups water
- 1 garlic clove, minced

Directions:
Set your instant pot on the sauté mode, add the oil and heat it up. Add the scallions, tomato, onions, garlic, stir and cook for 3-minutes. Add the cilantro, stir and cook for another 1-minute. Add the tomato sauce, water, bouillon, garlic powder, cumin, chicken, salt, pepper, top with corn. Cover the instant pot and cook on Poultry setting for 20-minutes. Release the pressure naturally for 15-minutes. Divide among serving plates. Serve warm!

Nutritional Information per serving:
Calories: 320   Fat: 10g   Fiber: 3g   Carbs: 18g   Protein: 42g

---

120. Duck Chili
Cook Time: 1 hour   **Servings: 4**
Ingredients:
- 1lb. northern beans, soaked and rinsed
- 5 cups water
- 2 cloves

For the Duck:
- 1 lb. duck, ground
- 1 tablespoon olive oil
- 1 yellow onion, minced
- ½ cup cilantro, fresh, chopped for garnish
- 1 bay leaf
- Sea salt and black pepper to taste
- 1 garlic head, top trimmed off
- 1 yellow onion, cut in half
- 15-ounces can of tomatoes, diced
- 1 teaspoon brown sugar
- 4-ounces canned green chilies
- Sea salt and black pepper to taste
- 2 carrots, chopped

Directions:
Set your instant pot to the sauté mode, add the oil, add carrots, chopped onion, season with salt and pepper and cook for 5-minutes, then transfer to a bowl. Add the duck and stir and cook for 5-minutes, transfer to a bowl. Put the beans into the instant pot, add the garlic head, onion halves, bay leaf, cloves, water, salt and stir, cover and cook on the Bean/Chili setting for 25-minutes. Release the pressure naturally for 10-minutes. Add back into the instant pot the duck, carrots, onions, tomatoes, chilies, stir. Cook on high on Manual setting for 5-minutes. Release the pressure again naturally for 10-minutes. Add into the instant pot the beans and brown sugar, stir. Add to serving bowls and garnish with fresh chopped cilantro. Serve warm!

Nutritional Information per serving:
Calories: 270   Fat: 13g   Fiber: 26g   Carbs: 15g   Protein: 25g

121. Chicken Gumbo

Cook Time: 45 minutes
Servings: 4
Ingredients:
- 1 lb. smoked sausage, sliced
- 1 lb. chicken thighs, cut into halves

For the Roux:
- ½ cup almond flour
- ¼ olive oil

Aromatics:
- 1 bell pepper, seeded, chopped
- Tabasco sauce
- 1 yellow onion, chopped
- 1 celery stalk, chopped
- ½ lb. okra

For Serving:
- ½ cup parsley, fresh, chopped
- 2 tablespoon olive oil, divided
- Sea salt and black pepper to taste
- 1 teaspoon Cajun spice
- 15-ounce can of tomatoes, chopped
- 2 cups chicken stock
- 4 garlic cloves, minced
- 1 carrot, peeled, sliced
- Cauliflower rice, already cooked

Directions:
Set your instant pot on the sauté mode, add 1 tablespoon oil and heat it. Add the sausage, stir and brown meat for 4-minutes, then transfer sausage to a plate. Add the chicken pieces, stir, brown chicken for 6-minutes, then transfer to a bowl. Add the remaining tablespoon of oil to the instant pot and heat it up. Add the Cajun spice to instant pot, stir and cook for 5-minutes. Add the onion, bell pepper, carrot, celery, garlic, salt, pepper and stir and cook for an additional 5-minutes. Return the chicken and sausage to the instant pot and stir, adding in the stock and tomatoes. Cover the instant pot and cook on the Meat/Stew setting for 10-minutes. Release the pressure naturally for 10-minutes. Divide into serving bowls, on top of bed of cauliflower rice, and garnish with fresh chopped parsley. Serve warm!

Nutritional Information per serving:
Calories: 208   Fat: 15g   Fiber: 1g   Carbs: 8g   Protein: 10g

122. Chicken Delight

Cook Time: 37 minutes
Servings: 4
Ingredients:
- 6 chicken thighs
- 2 tablespoons coconut oil
- ½ teaspoon thyme, dried
- 1 cup baby carrots
- 1 celery stalk, chopped
- 1 yellow onion, chopped
- Sea salt and black pepper to taste
- 2 tablespoons tomato paste
- 1 ½ lbs. potatoes, chopped
- 2 cups chicken stock
- 15-ounce can of tomatoes, diced
- ½ cup white wine

Directions:
Set your instant pot to the sauté mode, add the oil and heat it up. Add the chicken pieces, salt and pepper to taste, brown the chicken for 4-minutes on each side, then transfer chicken to a bowl. Add the thyme, onion, celery, carrots, tomato paste to your instant pot and stir. Cook for 5-minutes. Add the wine, and cook for an additional 3-minutes, stir. Add the chicken stock, chopped tomatoes, chicken pieces and stir. Place the steamer basket in the instant pot, add the potatoes to it. Cover the instant pot and cook on the Poultry setting for 30-minutes. Release the pressure naturally for 15-minutes. Take the potatoes out of the instant pot. Shred the chicken, add it to bowl with potatoes. Divide among serving plates. Serve warm!

Nutritional Information per serving:
Calories: 237   Fat: 12g   Fiber: 0g   Carbs: 1g   Protein: 30g

123. *Party Chicken Wings*
Cooking Time: 25 minutes
Servings: 6
Ingredients:
- 12 chicken wings, cut into 24 pieces
- 1lb. celery, cut into thin matchsticks
- 1 tablespoon parsley, fresh, diced
- 1 cup yogurt
- ¼ cup tomato puree
- 1 cup water
- Sea salt and black pepper to taste
- 4 tablespoons hot sauce
- ¼ cup honey

Directions:
Add water to the instant pot. Place the chicken wings in the steamer basket of the instant pot, cover and cook on Poultry setting for 19-minutes. In a mixing bowl add honey, hot sauce, tomato puree, salt and stir well. Release the pressure naturally for 10-minutes on your instant pot. Add the chicken wings to the honey mix and toss to coat them. Add the chicken wings to a lined baking sheet and place under a preheated broiler for 5-minutes. Arrange the celery sticks on a serving platter and add the chicken wings next to it. In a bowl, mix the parsley, with yogurt, stir and place on serving platter. Serve warm!

Nutritional Information per serving:
Calories: 300   Fat: 3.1g   Fiber: 2g   Carbs: 14g   Protein: 33g

124. *Roasted Chicken*
Cook Time: 35 minutes
Servings: 8
Ingredients:
- 1 whole chicken
- 2 teaspoons garlic powder
- 1 tablespoon coriander
- 1 tablespoon cumin
- Sea salt and black pepper to taste
- ½ teaspoon cinnamon, ground
- 1 tablespoon thyme, fresh
- 1 cup chicken stock
- 1 ½ tablespoons lemon zest
- 2 tablespoons extra virgin olive oil, divided

Directions:
In a mixing bowl, add the cinnamon, cumin, garlic, salt, pepper, coriander, and lemon zest, stir well. Rub the chicken with 1 tablespoon of oil, then rub it inside and out with the spice mix. Set your instant pot to the sauté mode, add the rest of the oil to it and heat it up. Add the chicken to the instant pot and brown it on all sides for 5-minutes. Add the thyme and stock, stir, cover and cook on the Poultry setting for 25-minutes. Release the pressure naturally for 10-minutes. Transfer chicken to a platter. Pour cooking liquid over it from instant pot. Serve warm!

Nutritional Information per serving:
Calories: 260   Fat: 3.1g   Fiber: 1g   Carbs: 4g   Protein: 26.7g

---

125. *Braised Turkey Wings*

Cook Time: 20 minutes   **Servings: 4**

Ingredients:
- 4 turkey wings
- 2 tablespoons butter
- 2 tablespoons olive oil
- 1 ½ cups cranberries, fresh
- 1 cup orange juice
- 1 cup walnuts
- 1 yellow onion, sliced
- Sea salt and black pepper to taste
- 1 bunch of thyme, chopped

Directions:
Set your instant pot onto the sauté mode, add the oil and butter and heat up. Add the turkey wings, salt, pepper and brown them on all sides for about 5-minutes. Remove the wings from instant pot, add the walnuts, onions, cranberries, thyme to instant pot and stir and cook for 2-minutes. Add the orange juice and return the wings to the instant pot, stir and cover. Cook on the Poultry setting for 20 minutes. Release the pressure naturally for 10-minutes. Divide the wings among serving plates. Heat the cranberry mixture in instant pot with Manual setting on low for 5-minutes. Drizzle the sauce over wings. Serve warm!

Nutritional Information per serving:
Calories: 320   Fat: 15.3g   Fiber: 2.1g   Carbs: 16.4g   Protein: 29g

---

126. *Braised Quail*

Cook Time: 15 minutes   **Servings: 2**

Ingredients:
- 2 quails, cleaned
- 2 cups water
- 3.5 ounces smoked pancetta, chopped
- ½ fennel bulb, cut into matchsticks
- 1 bunch rosemary
- Sea salt and black pepper to taste
- 1 bay leaf
- 1 bunch thyme
- 2 shallots, peeled and chopped
- ½ cup champagne
- 4 carrots, cut into thin matchsticks
- Juice of 1 lemon
- Olive oil
- ½ cup arugula
- 2 tablespoons olive oil

Directions:

Place the carrot and fennel into the instant pot steamer basket. Add water to the instant pot, cover and cook on the Steam setting for 1-minute, release the pressure using quick-release, rinse vegetables with cold water and transfer to a bowl. Put the cooking liquid in a separate bowl. Chop half the rosemary and thyme, then set aside. Set your instant pot to the sauté mode, add the oil and heat. Add the pancetta, shallots, thyme, rosemary, bay leaf, salt, pepper, and cook for 4-minutes.

Stuff the quail with the remaining whole rosemary and thyme and add to the instant pot. Brown all sides of the quail for 5-minutes. Add the champagne, stir and cook for an additional 2-minutes. Add the cooking liquid from the vegetables, cover and cook on the Poultry setting for 9-minutes. Release the pressure naturally for 15-minutes. Remove the quail from your instant pot. Set the instant pot to sauté mode and cook the sauce for 5-minutes stirring often. Arrange the arugula on a platter, add the steamed fennel, and carrots, a drizzle of oil, lemon juice on top with quail. Drizzle the sauce from instant pot over the quail. Serve warm!

Nutritional Information per serving:
Calories: 300   Fat: 17g   Fiber: 0.2g   Carbs: 0.2g   Protein: 40g

---

127. *Crispy Chicken*
Cook Time: 40 minutes
Servings: 4
Ingredients:
- 6 chicken thighs
- 4 garlic cloves, peeled, chopped
- 1 yellow onion, sliced thin
- 2 tablespoons cornstarch, mixed with 2 ½ tablespoons of water
- Sea salt and black pepper to taste
- 1 tablespoon soy sauce
- 1 cup cold water
- Dried rosemary
- 2 eggs, whisked
- 1 cup coconut flour
- 2 tablespoons butter
- 2 tablespoons coconut oil
- 1 ½ cups panko breadcrumbs

Directions:
In your instant pot mix the onion, garlic, rosemary and water. Place the chicken thighs into the steamer basket and place in the instant pot. Cover and cook on the Poultry setting for 9-minutes. Release the pressure naturally for 10-minutes. In a pan heat the oil and butter over medium-high heat. Add the breadcrumbs, stir and toast them, then remove them from the heat. Remove the chicken from instant pot; pat chicken thighs dry, season with salt and pepper, coat them with the flour, dip them in the whisked egg, then coat them in the toasted breadcrumbs.

Place chicken thighs on a lined baking sheet, bake in oven at 300° Fahrenheit for 10 minutes. Set your instant pot to the sauté mode, and heat up the cooking liquid. Add the salt, pepper, soy sauce, cornstarch and stir, then transfer to a bowl. Take the chicken thighs out of the oven, divide between serving plates. Serve with sauce from your instant pot. Serve warm!

Nutritional Information per serving:
Calories: 360   Fat: 7g   Fiber: 4g   Carbs: 18g   Protein: 15g

128. Chicken Salad

Cook Time: 25 minutes　　　　　**Servings: 2**

Ingredients:
- 1 chicken breast, skinless and boneless
- 3 cups water
- 3 tablespoons extra virgin olive oil
- 1 tablespoon honey
- 1 tablespoon balsamic vinegar
- 3 garlic cloves, minced
- Sea salt and black pepper to taste
- 1 tablespoon mustard
- Mixed salad greens
- Half a cup of cherry tomatoes, cut into halves

Directions:
In a bowl, mix 2 cups water with a pinch of salt. Add the chicken to the mixture, stir and place in the fridge for an hour. Add the remaining water to your instant pot, place the chicken breast in the steamer basket of your instant pot, cover and cook on the Poultry setting for 5-m inutes. Release the pressure naturally for 10-minutes. Remove the chicken breast from instant pot. Cut the chicken breast into thin strips. In a bowl mix salt, pepper, mustard, honey, vinegar, olive oil, garlic and whisk well. In a salad bowl, mix chicken strips with salad greens and tomatoes. Drizzle the vinaigrette on top. Serve room temperature.

Nutritional Information per serving:
Calories: 140   Fat: 2.5g   Fiber: 4g   Carbs: 11g   Protein: 19g

129. Stuffed Chicken Breasts

Cook Time: 30 minutes　　　　　**Servings: 2**

Ingredients:
- 2 chicken breasts, skinless, boneless, and butterflied
- 2 cups water
- 1-piece ham, cut in half, cooked
- Sea salt and black pepper to taste
- 16 bacon strips
- 4 mozzarella cheese slices
- 6 pieces of asparagus, cooked

Directions:
In a mixing bowl, mix the chicken with 1 cup water, salt, stir, cover and keep in the fridge for an hour. Pat the chicken breasts dry and place them on a working surface. Add 2 slices of mozzarella, 3 asparagus pieces onto each, 1 piece of ham, add salt and pepper then roll up each chicken breast. Place the bacon strips on a working surface, add the chicken and wrap them in bacon strips. Put the rolls in the steamer basket of your instant pot, add 1 cup of water to your instant pot, cover and cook on the Poultry setting for 10-minutes. Release the pressure naturally for 10-minutes. Pat rolls with paper towel and lay them on a plate. Set your instant pot to the sauté mode, add the chicken rolls to the instant pot and brown them for 5-minutes. Divide among serving plates. Serve warm!

Nutritional Information per serving:
Calories: 270   Fat: 11g   Fiber: 1g   Carbs: 6g   Protein: 37g

130. Turkey Mix and Mashed Potatoes

Cooking Time: 50 minutes **Servings: 3**

Ingredients:
- 2 turkey quarters
- 1 cup chicken stock
- 1 celery stalk, chopped
- 3-garlic cloves, minced
- 1 carrot, chopped
- 1 yellow onion, chopped
- ½ cup white wine
- 2 tablespoons butter
- 3.5-ounces heavy cream
- 2 tablespoons Parmesan cheese, grated
- 5 Yukon gold potatoes, cut in halves
- 2 tablespoons cornstarch, mixed with 2 tablespoons water
- 1 teaspoon thyme, dried
- 1 teaspoon sage, dried
- 2 bay leaves
- 1 teaspoon rosemary, dried
- 2 tablespoons extra virgin olive oil
- Sea salt and black pepper to taste

Directions:
Season your turkey with salt and pepper. Add a tablespoon of oil to your instant pot. Set your instant pot to the sauté mode, and heat it up. Add the turkey and brown for 4-minutes, transfer turkey to a plate and set aside.

Add ½ a cup of chicken stock to your instant pot and stir. Add 1 tablespoon of oil, garlic, and cook for 2-minutes. Add the carrots, celery, pepper, salt and stir for 7-minutes. Add the sage, thyme, bay leaves and rosemary, stir. Add the wine and turkey back into the instant pot and the rest of the stock. Place the potatoes in the steamer basket for instant pot and place in the instant pot. Cook for 20 minutes on the Steam mode. Release the pressure naturally for 10-minutes. Transfer the potatoes to a bowl and mash them. Add some salt, butter, Parmesan cheese and cream, stir well. Divide the turkey quarters onto serving plates. Set your instant pot onto the sauté mode. Add the cornstarch mixture to pot, stir well, and cook for 3-minutes. Drizzle the sauce over the turkey and serve with mashed potatoes. Serve warm!

Nutritional Information per serving:
Calories: 200   Fat: 5g   Fiber: 4g   Carbs: 19g   Protein: 18g

131. Duck & Vegetables

Cooking Time: 40 minutes **Serving: 8**

Ingredients:
- 1 duck, chopped into eight pieces
- 1-inch ginger piece, peeled chopped
- Salt and black pepper to taste
- 2 cups water
- 2 carrots, chopped
- 1 cucumber, chopped
- 1 tablespoon white wine

Directions:
In your instant pot place the pieces of duck. Add the carrots, wine, cucumber, ginger, water, salt, pepper, stir and cover, cook on Poultry mode for 40-minutes. Release the pressure naturally for 15-minutes. Divide the mix onto serving plates. Serve warm!

Nutritional Information per serving:
Calories: 189   Fat: 2g   Fiber: 1g   Carbs: 4g   Protein: 22g

132. Braised Duck and Potatoes

Cook Time: 20 minutes **Servings:** 4

Ingredients:
- 2 duck breasts, boneless, skinless, cut into small chunks
- 1 tablespoon Truvia
- 4 garlic cloves, minced
- 1-inch ginger root, sliced
- 1 potato, cut into cubes
- Sea salt and black pepper to taste
- 4 tablespoons soy sauce
- ¼ cup water
- 4 tablespoons sherry wine
- 2 green onions, roughly chopped
- 1 tablespoon olive oil

Directions:
Set your instant pot to the sauté mode, add the oil and heat it up. Add the duck, stir and brown it for 5-minutes. Add the garlic, green onions, ginger, Truvia, water, wine, soy sauce, salt and pepper. Cover instant pot and set to the Poultry mode, and cook for 18-minutes. Release the pressure naturally for 10-minutes. Add the potatoes, stir, cover, and cook on the Steam setting for 5-minutes. Release the pressure using quick-release. Divide the duck amongst serving plates. Serve warm!

Nutritional Information per serving:
Calories: 238   Fat: 18g   Fiber: 0g   Carbs: 1g   Protein: 19g

133. Chicken in Tomatillo Sauce

Cook Time: 15 minutes **Servings:** 6

Ingredients:
- 1lb. chicken thighs, skinless, boneless
- ½ cup cilantro, diced
- 4-ounces canned green chilies, chopped
- 1 garlic clove, peeled, crushed
- 1 yellow onion, sliced thinly
- 2 tablespoons coconut oil
- 4-ounces black olives, pitted, chopped
- 15-ounces cheddar cheese, grated
- 5-ounces tomatoes, cored, chopped
- 15-ounces cauliflower rice, already cooked
- 5-ounces canned garbanzo beans, drained
- 15-ounces canned tomatillos, chopped
- Sea salt and black pepper to taste

Directions:
Set your instant pot to the sauté mode, add the oil and heat it up. Add the onions, stir and cook for 5-minutes. Add the garlic and stir and cook for 1-minute. Add the chicken, chilies, cilantro, tomatillos, salt, pepper, and stir. Cover your instant pot and cook on the Poultry mode for 8-minutes. Release the pressure naturally for 10-minutes. Remove the chicken from your instant pot. On a cutting board shred the chicken. Return chicken to your instant pot then place the rice and beans on top. Set your instant pot to the sauté mode for 1-minute. Add the tomatoes, cheese, and olives to your instant pot, stir and cook for an additional 2-minutes. Divide among the serving plates. Serve warm!

Nutritional Information per serving:
Calories: 245   Fat: 11.4g   Fiber: 1.3g   Carbs: 14.2g   Protein: 20g

134. Filipino Chicken
Cooking Time: 15 minutes
Servings: 4
Ingredients:
- 5 lbs. chicken thighs
- ½ cup soy sauce
- 3 bay leaves
- 4 garlic cloves, minced
- 1 teaspoon black peppercorns, crushed
- ½ cup white vinegar
- Sea salt and black pepper to taste

Directions:
Set your instant pot on the Poultry mode, add the chicken, soy sauce, vinegar, garlic, peppercorns, salt, pepper, bay leaves, and stir. Cover the pot with lid an cook for 15-minutes. Release the pressure naturally for 10-minutes. Discard the bay leaves, stir, divide the chicken between serving plates. Serve hot!

Nutritional Information per serving:
Calories: 430   Fat: 19.2g   Fiber: 1g   Carbs: 2.4g   Protein: 76g

135. Instant Pot Keto Chicken Stew
Cook Time: 40 minutes
Servings: 6
Ingredients:
- 6 chicken thighs
- 2 ½ cups chicken stock
- 15-ounce can of tomatoes, chopped
- ½ teaspoon thyme, dried
- 1 celery stalk, chopped
- 2 tablespoons tomato paste
- 1 yellow onion, chopped
- Sea salt and black pepper to taste
- ¼ cup baby carrots
- 2 tablespoons coconut oil

Directions:
Set your instant pot to the sauté mode, add the coconut oil, and heat it. Add the chicken and brown on all sides for 4-minutes each, along with salt and pepper, then transfer the chicken to a plate. Add the tomato paste, onion, celery, thyme, carrots, salt, pepper, and sauté for 4-minutes and stir. Add the stock, chicken, tomatoes into instant pot, cover, and set to Manual setting on high for 25 minutes. Once the cooked time is complete, release the pressure for 15-minutes naturally. Transfer the chicken to a cutting board and allow it to cool down, then shred it using 2 forks, remove skin, bones and discard. Return the chicken to the instant pot and heat for an additional 3-minutes on high. Divide into serving bowls. Serve hot!

Nutritional Information per serving:
Calories: 212   Fat: 16g   Fiber: 2g   Carbs: 9g   Protein: 23g

136. Chicken Romano
Cook Time: 15 minutes
Servings: 4
Ingredients:
- 6 chicken thighs, skinless, boneless, cut into chunks
- ½ cup coconut flour
- 2 tablespoons vegetable oil
- 4-ounces mushrooms, sliced
- 1 cup Romano cheese, grated
- 1 yellow onion, chopped
- 1 teaspoon chicken bouillon granules
- 1 teaspoon basil, dried
- 1 teaspoon garlic, minced
- 1 tablespoon oregano, dried
- 1 teaspoon Truvia
- 1 teaspoon white wine vinegar
- 10-ounces tomato sauce

Directions:
Set your instant pot to the sauté mode, add the oil and heat. Add the chicken pieces, stir and brown on all sides for 5-minutes. Add the onion, garlic and stir, cooking for an additional 3-minutes. Add flour, pepper, salt and stir. Add the tomato sauce, vinegar, Truvia, basil, oregano, bouillon granules, mushrooms, and cover. Cook on the Poultry setting for 10-minutes. Release the pressure naturally, for 10-minutes. Add the cheese, stir, then divide among serving plates. Serve warm!

Nutritional Information per serving:
Calories: 450   Fat: 11g   Fiber: 1g   Carbs: 24.2g   Protein: 61.2g

137. Turkey Chili
Cook Time: 10 minutes
Servings: 4
Ingredients:
- 1lb. turkey meat, ground
- 2 ½ tablespoons chili powder
- 12-ounces vegetable stock
- Cayenne pepper
- 1 ½ teaspoons cumin
- 3 garlic cloves, chopped
- 1 yellow onion, chopped
- 15-ounces chickpeas, already cooked
- ½ cup of water
- Salt and black pepper to taste

Directions:
Place the turkey meat into your instant pot, add the water, stir and cover. Cook on the Poultry setting for 5-minutes. Release the pressure naturally for 10-minutes. Add the garlic, chickpeas, bell pepper, onion, chili powder, cayenne pepper, salt, pepper, and stock. Stir, and cover the instant pot, and cook in the Bean/Chili setting for 5-minutes. Release the pressure naturally for 10-minutes. Divide among serving bowls. Serve hot!

Nutritional Information per serving:
Calories: 22.4   Fat: 7g   Fiber: 6.1g   Carbs: 18g   Protein: 19.7g

138. Sweet & Tangy Chicken
Cook Time: 10 minutes
Servings: 4
Ingredients:
- 2 lbs. chicken thighs, boneless, skinless
- 2 teaspoons cilantro, diced
- 1 teaspoon mint, fresh, chopped
- 1 teaspoon ginger, grated
- ¼ cup extra virgin olive oil
- 2 tablespoons coconut nectar
- 1 cup lime juice
- ½ cup fish sauce

Directions:
Place the chicken thighs into your instant pot. In a mixing bowl mix the olive oil, lime juice, fish sauce, coconut nectar, mint, ginger, cilantro, and whisk well. Pour mixture over chicken, cover your instant pot, and cook on the Poultry setting for 10-minutes. Release the pressure naturally for 10-minutes. Divide among serving plates. Serve warm!

Nutritional Information per serving:
Calories: 300   Fat: 5g   Fiber: 4g   Carbs: 23g   Protein: 32g

139. Honey Barbecue Chicken Wings
Cooking Time: 25 minutes
Servings: 4
Ingredients:
- 2 lbs. chicken wings
- ½ cup water
- 2 teaspoons paprika
- 1 teaspoon red pepper flakes
- ½ cup apple juice
- Cayenne pepper
- ¾ cup honey barbecue sauce
- Sea salt and black pepper to taste
- 1 teaspoon Truvia
- ½ teaspoon basil, dried

Directions:
Place the chicken wings into your instant pot. Add the barbecue sauce, salt, pepper, paprika, red pepper, Truvia, water, and apple juice. Stir, cover and cook on the Poultry setting for 10-minutes. Release the pressure naturally for 10-minutes. Transfer the chicken wings to a baking sheet, add the sauce, place under preheated broiler for 7-minutes. Turn chicken wings over and broil for an additional 7-minutes. Divide among serving plates. Serve hot!

Nutritional Information per serving:
Calories: 147   Fat: 2.2g   Fiber: 1g   Carbs: 8g   Protein: 21.8g

140. Sticky Chicken Drumsticks
Cook Time: 20 minutes
Servings: 4
Ingredients:
- 8 chicken drumsticks
- 1 teaspoon ginger, fresh, grated
- 3 garlic cloves, finely chopped
- 3 tablespoons olive oil
- Juice of 1 lemon
- 2 tablespoons soy sauce

Directions:
Mix the lemon juice, olive oil, ginger, garlic, and soy sauce in your instant pot. Add the chicken drumsticks and stir to coat them. Secure the instant pot lid and set it to the Poultry setting for a cook time of 20-minutes. Release the pressure naturally for 15-minutes. Divide drumsticks on to serving plates, and drizzle sauce over them. Serve hot!

Nutritional Information per serving:
Calories: 132   Fat: 3g   Fiber: 1g   Carbs: 10g   Protein: 19g

141. Chicken, Broccoli, & Cheese
Cook Time: 45 minutes
Servings: 6
Ingredients:
- 20-ounces chicken breast, cooked, shredded
- 1 teaspoon oregano, dried
- ½ teaspoon paprika
- 1-ounce pork rinds
- 1 cup cheddar cheese, shredded
- ½ cup heavy cream
- ½ cup sour cream
- 2 cups broccoli, florets
- 2 tablespoons olive oil

Directions:
Place the cooked, shredded chicken into your instant pot. In a bowl mix broccoli, olive oil, and sour cream. Pour over chicken and stir. Pour heavy cream over top and season. On Manual setting cook on low for 40-minutes. Release the pressure naturally for 15-minutes. Crush the pork rinds. Add the pork rinds and cheese on top of mixture, cover with lid and cook for an additional 5-minutes. Divide among serving dishes. Serve warm!

Nutritional Information per serving:
Calories: 210   Fat: 3g   Fiber: 1g   Carbs: 17.3g   Protein: 32g

142. Instant Pot Cream Chicken & Sausage
Cook Time: 48 minutes
Servings: 4
Ingredients:
- 1 ½ lbs. chicken breasts, boneless, skinless, cut into strips
- 1 large Italian sausage, sliced
- 1-8 ounce package of cream cheese
- 2 tablespoons grainy mustard
- 1 small yellow onion, diced
- ½ cup white wine
- 1 cup chicken stock
- Scallions, chopped for garnish
- Salt and black pepper to taste
- 2 tablespoons coconut oil

Directions:
Set your instant pot to the sauté mode, add the oil and heat. Add the sausage, and chicken breast strips, and brown for about 5-minutes. Add the yellow onion, and cook for an additional 3-minutes and stir. In a mixing bowl combine the cheese, mustard, stock, wine, garlic, salt and pepper. Pour the cheese mix over the chicken and sausage mix, and stir to combine. Place the lid onto your instant pot and set it on Poultry setting for 40-minutes. Release the pressure naturally for 10-minutes. Stir mix and serve over a bed of cauliflower rice or zucchini pasta. Serve warm!

Nutritional Information per serving:
Calories: 232   Fat: 14g   Fiber: 4g   Carbs: 9g   Protein: 12g

143. Instant Pot Chicken Hash
Cook Time: 43 minutes
Servings: 4
Ingredients:
- 1 lb. chicken, boneless, skinless, diced
- 2 cups chicken stock
- 1 cup sweet potatoes, peeled, diced
- 4 tablespoons of butter
- 1 cup yellow onion, chopped
- 1 cup red bell pepper, chopped
- Fresh parsley, chopped for garnish

Directions:
Set your instant pot to the sauté mode, add the butter and heat it. Add the chicken and stir, cooking for 5-minutes browning all sides of the chicken. Add the bell pepper, and onion, continue to cook for an additional 3-minutes, stir. Add the chicken stock and sweet potatoes, set the instant pot to the Meat/Stew setting for 35-minutes. Release the pressure naturally for 10-minutes, once the cooking is completed. Divide into serving dishes, and garnish with parsley. Serve warm!

Nutritional Information per serving:
Calories: 212   Fat: 7g   Fiber: 8g   Carbs: 12g   Protein: 12g

144. Instant Pot Chicken Bean Chili
Cook Time: 35 minutes
Servings: 6
Ingredients:
- 1 lb. chicken, boneless, skinless, cubed
- 1 medium, yellow onion, diced
- 2 cups vegetable stock
- 1 15-ounce can of black beans, rinsed, drained
- 2 cups salsa
- 2 tablespoons olive oil

Directions:
Set your instant pot to the sauté mode, add the oil and heat it. Add the cubed chicken to instant pot, and brown on all sides for 5-minutes, stir often. Add the remaining ingredients to instant pot and stir. Close the lid place instant pot on the Bean/Chili setting for 30-minutes. Release the pressure naturally for 15-minutes. Divide among serving bowls. Serve hot!

Nutritional Information per serving:
Calories: 246   Fat: 16g   Fiber: 8g   Carbs: 12g   Protein: 28g

145. Instant Pot Herbal Chicken
Cook Time: 40 minutes
Servings: 4
Ingredients:
- 1 lb. chicken, cubed
- 2 cups chicken stock
- 3 tablespoons rosemary leaves, fresh, chopped
- 3 tablespoons thyme leaves, fresh, chopped
- 3 garlic cloves, minced
- Salt and black pepper to taste
- 1 red bell pepper, chopped
- 1 green bell pepper, chopped
- 1 cup broccoli, florets

Directions:
Blend the garlic and herbs, and rub the mixture over your chicken chunks. In your instant pot heat olive oil with the sauté mode setting. Add the chicken into instant pot, stir and cook for 5-minutes, browning chicken on all sides. Add the chicken stock and veggies, and close the lid on your instant pot. Set to Poultry setting for 35-minutes. Release the pressure naturally for 10-minutes. Divide into serving dishes. Serve warm!

Nutritional Information per serving:
Calories: 217   Fat: 8g   Fiber: 2g   Carbs: 6g   Protein: 9g

146. Instant Pot Chicken Fillets
Cook Time: 45 minutes
Servings: 4
Ingredients:
- 1 lb. chicken fillets, cut into four equal portions
- ¼ cup sour cream, reduced fat
- 2 teaspoons lemon juice
- 2 tablespoons stone-ground mustard
- Salt and pepper to taste
- Lime wedges for garnish

Directions:
Place the chicken fillets into your instant pot. Make a paste with the remaining ingredients except the lime wedges. Spread the mixture over the chicken fillets. Set the instant pot to the Poultry setting for 45-minutes. Release the pressure naturally for 10-minutes. Divide among serving plates, and garnish with lemon wedges.

Nutritional Information per serving:
Calories: 253 Fat: 17g Fiber: 6g Carbs: 11g Protein: 22g

147. Buttery Chicken with Macadamia
Cook Time: 22 minutes
Servings: 4
Ingredients:
- 1lb. chicken breast, sliced into four equal portions
- 2 tablespoons macadamia nuts, toasted
- ¼ teaspoon chili powder
- 2 tablespoons lime juice + ½ teaspoon lime zest
- 2 tablespoons butter

Directions:
Set your instant pot to the sauté setting, add the butter and heat it. Season the chicken with salt and black pepper. Add the chicken to instant pot and cook for 5-minutes or until the chicken is slightly brown in color on all sides. Set on the Poultry setting on low for 17-minutes. Release the pressure naturally for 10-minutes. Make a mixture using the melted butter from instant pot, lime juice, chili powder, lime zest and pour over the chicken on serving plates. Add the toasted macadamia nuts as garnish. Serve warm!

Nutritional Information per serving:
Calories: 254 Fat: 13g Fiber: 2g Carbs: 10g Protein: 19g

148. Mushroom & Chicken Hash
Cook Time: 40 minutes
Servings: 4
Ingredients:
- 2 cups cooked chicken, cubed
- 4 tablespoons butter
- 4 celery ribs, finely chopped
- 1 medium yellow onion, diced
- 1 lb. button mushrooms, sliced

Directions:
Set your instant pot to the sauté mode, add the butter and heat. Add the mushrooms and sauté for 2-minutes. Add the onion, chicken, and celery, stir and cook for an additional 3-minutes. Close the lid and set instant pot on the Poultry setting for 35-minutes. Release the pressure for 10-minutes. Divide into serving plates. Serve warm!

Nutritional Information per serving:
Calories: 232   Fat: 9g   Fiber: 1g   Carbs: 12g   Protein: 21g

---

149. Cheesy Spinach Stuffed Chicken Breasts
Cook Time: 20 minutes
Servings: 2
Ingredients:
- 2 chicken breasts
- 1 teaspoon onion powder
- 1 teaspoon garlic powder
- 2 cups baby spinach
- 3 tablespoons coconut oil
- 1 cup parmesan cheese, shredded
- 1 cup mozzarella cheese, shredded
- 1 red bell pepper, chopped
- 2 cups water
- Sea salt and black pepper to taste

Directions:
Cover your instant pot trivet with foil. Set your instant pot to the sauté mode, add 2 tablespoons of the coconut oil and heat it. Add the chicken and brown on all sides for 5-minutes. Remove the chicken, and allow to cool. Press the Keep Warm/Cancel button to end the sauté mode. In a mixing bowl, combine parmesan cheese, red pepper, mozzarella cheese, remaining 1 tablespoon of coconut oil, baby spinach and seasoning. When the chicken is cool, cut down the middle, but do not cut all the way through. Stuff with spinach mixture. Pour 2 cups of water in the instant pot. Place the trivet inside. Place the chicken on trivet. Close and seal lid. Press the Manual setting, and cook on high pressure for 7-minutes. Release the pressure naturally for 10-minutes. Allow the chicken to rest for 5-minutes. Divide among serving plates. Serve warm!

Nutritional Information per serving:
Calories: 500   Fat: 33g   Fiber: 1.7g   Carbs: 3.8g   Protein: 45g

Chapter 6. Collection of Seafood-Based Instant Pot Recipes

150. Spicy Lemon Salmon
Cook Time: 10 minutes
Servings: 4
Ingredients:
- 4 salmon fillets
- 1 teaspoon cayenne pepper
- 1 tablespoon paprika
- 1 cup water
- Juice from 2 lemons
- Sea salt and black pepper to taste

Directions:
Rinse your salmon, and pat dry. In a mixing bowl, combine cayenne pepper, paprika, salt and pepper. Drizzle the lemon juice over the salmon fillets. Turn over fillets, repeat on the other side. Add 1 cup of water to your instant pot. Place the trivet inside your instant pot. Place your salmon fillets on top of the trivet. Close and seal instant pot, press the Manual button. Cook at high-pressure for 10-minutes. Once cooking time is complete use the quick-release for pressure. Divide up among serving plates. Serve warm!

Nutritional Information per serving:
Calories: 280   Fat: 20g   Fiber: 0.5g   Carbs: 8g   Protein: 20.5g

151. Coconut Shrimp Curry
Cook Time: 34 minutes
Servings: 4
Ingredients:
- 1 lb. of shrimp, peeled, deveined
- 10-ounces coconut milk
- 1 red bell pepper, sliced
- 4 tomatoes, chopped
- 1 teaspoon, fresh ground black pepper
- Juice from 1 lime
- 4 garlic cloves, minced
- 1 tablespoon coconut oil
- ½ cup cilantro, fresh, chopped for garnish

Directions:
Set your instant pot to the sauté mode, add the oil and heat it. Season your shrimp with lime juice, salt and pepper. Sauté the garlic for 1-minute. Add the shrimp and cook for 4-minutes per side. Add the bell peppers and tomatoes. Stir well. Press the Keep Warm/Cancel button to cancel the sauté mode. Add the coconut milk and stir. Close and seal the lid of instant pot. Press the Manual setting, and cook on high pressure for 25-minutes. Once cooking is completed, use the quick-release for pressure. Divide into serving plates, and garnish with fresh, chopped cilantro.

Nutritional Information per serving:
Calories: 150   Fat: 3g   Fiber: 3g   Carbs: 1g   Protein: 7g

152. Mediterranean Fish
Cook Time:
Servings: 4
Ingredients:
- 4 fish fillets (any kind)
- 1 teaspoon parsley, fresh, chopped
- 1 tablespoon thyme, fresh, chopped
- 1 tablespoon coconut oil
- 1 cup water
- 2 garlic cloves, minced
- 1 cup green olives, pitted
- 1 lb. cherry tomatoes, halved
- Sea salt and black pepper to taste

Directions:
Pour 1 cup of water in your instant pot. Cover the instant pot trivet with foil. On a flat surface, rub fish fillets with garlic. Season with thyme, pepper and salt. Place the olives and cherry tomatoes along the bottom of Instant pot. Place the fillets on the trivet. Close the lid and seal. Set on Manual, and cook at high-pressure for 15-minutes. When done, release pressure naturally for 10-minutes. Place the fish with ingredients, stir to coat them. Place on serving plates, and top with fresh, chopped parsley for garnish. Serve warm!

Nutritional Information per serving:
Calories: 225   Fat: 4g   Fiber: 2g   Carbs: 9g   Protein: 30g

153. Ginger, Sesame Glaze Salmon
Cook Time: 25 minutes
Servings: 4
Ingredients:
- 4 salmon fillets
- 2 tablespoons soy sauce
- 1 tablespoon rice vinegar
- 2 tablespoons white wine
- 1 tablespoon sugar-free ketchup
- 1 tablespoon fish sauce
- 4 garlic cloves, minced
- 2 teaspoons sesame oil
- 2 cups water

Directions:
In a mixing bowl, combine fish sauce, garlic, ginger, ketchup, white wine, rice vinegar, soy sauce, and sesame oil. In a large Ziploc bag, add the sauce and salmon fillets. Marinate for 10-hours. Pour 2 cups water in to your instant pot. Cover the trivet with foil. Place the trivet into your instant pot. Place the marinated salmon on the trivet. Close the lid and seal. Press the Manual button, cook on high-pressure for 15-minutes. Once done release the pressure naturally for 10-minutes. Divide onto serving plates. Serve warm!

Nutritional Information per serving:
Calories: 370   Fat: 23.5g   Fiber: 0g   Carbs: 2.6g   Protein: 33g

154. Cauliflower Risotto and Salmon
Cook Time: 30 minutes **Servings:** 4
Ingredients:
- 4 salmon fillets, shredded
- 1 lb. asparagus, stemmed, chopped
- ½ cup parmesan cheese, shredded
- 1 cup chicken broth
- 1 tablespoon coconut oil
- Sea salt and black pepper to taste
- 2 teaspoons thyme, fresh, chopped
- 1 tablespoon rosemary, fresh, chopped
- 8-ounces coconut cream, unsweetened
- 1 head of cauliflower, chopped into florets

Directions:
In a food processor add the cauliflower florets, and pulse until you have rice-like consistency. Set your instant pot to the sauté mode, add the oil and heat it. Add the cauliflower rice, asparagus, and shredded salmon fillet. Cook until light brown and tender. Press the Keep Warm/Cancel setting to stop the sauté mode. Add the remaining ingredients and stir well. Close and seal lid. Press the manual button, cook on high-pressure for 20-minutes. Once done, release the pressure naturally for 10-minutes. Stir, and divide into serving bowls. Serve warm!

Nutritional Information per serving:
Calories: 225 Fat: 6g Fiber: 4g Carbs: 9g Protein: 6g

155. Chili, Lime Cod
Cook Time: 22 minutes **Servings:** 4
Ingredients:
- 4 cod fillets, shredded
- ¼ cup parsley, fresh, chopped
- ½ cup low-carb mayonnaise
- 1 tablespoon rice wine vinegar
- 1 yellow onion, chopped
- 1 celery stalk, chopped
- 4 garlic cloves, minced
- 1 can (14-ounce) tomatoes, diced
- 1 teaspoon paprika
- 1 tablespoon coconut oil
- 1 cup vegetable stock
- Zest from 1 lime
- Sea salt and black pepper to taste

Directions:
Press the sauté mode on your instant pot, and heat the coconut oil. Add the onion, and garlic. Sauté for 2-minutes, and add the celery and shredded cod. Press the Keep Warm/Cancel button to stop the sauté mode. Add the diced tomatoes, rice wine, mayonnaise, parsley, lime juice and zest, along with seasoning. Stir well. Close the lid and seal. Press the Manual button and cook at high-pressure for 20-minutes. Release the pressure naturally for 10-minutes. Divide onto serving plates. Serve warm!

Nutritional Information per serving:
Calories: 215 Fat: 5g Fiber: 2g Carbs: 3g Protein: 35g

156. Instant Pot Halibut Fillets
Cook Time: 30 minutes
Servings: 4
Ingredients:
- 4 halibut fillets
- 1 lemon sliced for garnish
- 2 cups of water
- Zest and juice of 1 lime
- ¼ cup mozzarella cheese, grated
- ¼ cup parmesan cheese, fresh, grated
- ¼ cup ghee, melted
- ¼ cup low-carb mayonnaise
- 4 green onions, chopped
- 6 garlic cloves, minced
- Sea salt and black pepper to taste

Directions:
Pour 2-cups of water in the instant pot. Cover the trivet with foil. In mixing bowl, combine green onions, garlic, ghee, mayonnaise, cheeses, lime juice, lime zest, salt and pepper. Stir well. Coat the halibut fillets with the mixture. Place halibut on trivet. Close and seal the lid. Press the Manual button, cook on high-pressure for 20-minutes. Use the quick-release for pressure. Divide up into serving plates, and garnish with fresh, chopped parsley. Serve warm!

Nutritional Information per serving:
Calories: 250   Fat: 12g   Fiber: 1g   Carbs: 5g   Protein: 25g

157. Fish Fillets & Orange Sauce
Cook Time: 10 minutes
Servings: 4
Ingredients:
- 4 spring onions, finely chopped
- Zest from 1 orange
- Juice from 1 orange
- 4 white fish fillets
- 1 tablespoon olive oil
- 1-inch ginger piece, grated
- Sea salt and black pepper to taste
- 1 cup fish stock

Directions:
Season the fish fillets with salt and pepper, then rub them with oil and place on a plate. Place the onions, orange zest, orange juice, fish stock into your instant pot. Add the steamer basket and place the fish fillets inside it. Cover the instant pot with lid and cook on high-pressure on Manual setting for 10-minutes. Release the pressure using the quick-release. Divide the fish fillets among serving plates, then drizzle the orange sauce from instant pot over fillets. Serve warm!

Nutritional Information per serving:
Calories: 343   Fat: 21g   Fiber: 1g   Carbs: 8g   Protein: 26g

158. Calamari & Tomatoes
Cook Time: 30 minutes
Servings: 4
Ingredients:

- 1 ½ lbs. of calamari, cleaned, heads detached, tentacles separated and cut into thin strips
- 1 tablespoon olive oil
- Juice of 1 lemon
- 2 anchovies, chopped
- A pinch of red pepper flakes
- 1 bunch parsley, chopped
- ½ cup white wine
- 1 garlic clove, minced
- Sea salt and black pepper to taste
- 1 (15-ounce can) tomatoes, chopped

Directions:
Set your instant pot to the sauté mode, add the oil and heat it up. Add the anchovies, garlic, and pepper flakes, stir and cook for 3-minutes. Add the calamari, stir and sauté for 5-minutes more. Add the wine, stir and cook for 3 minutes more. Add the tomatoes, half of the parsley, some salt and pepper, stir and cover pot. Set to manual on high-pressure for 20-minutes. Release the pressure naturally for 15-minutes. Add the lemon juice and zest, remaining parsley and stir. Divide up among serving plates. Serve warm!

Nutritional Information per serving:
Calories: 342   Fat: 18g   Fiber: 1g   Carbs: 3g   Protein: 28g

159. Red Snapper & Chili Sauce
Cook Time: 12 minutes
Servings: 2
Ingredients:

- 1 red snapper, cleaned
- 1 teaspoon Truvia
- 2 cups water
- 1 green onion, chopped
- 1 teaspoon sesame oil
- 2 teaspoons sesame seeds, toasted
- 2 teaspoons Korean plum extract
- ½ teaspoon ginger, grated
- 1 garlic clove, minced
- 1 tablespoon soy sauce
- 3 tablespoons Korean chili paste
- Dash of sea salt

Directions:
Make some slits into your red snapper, season with salt and leave aside for 30-minutes. Put the water into your instant pot, add the steamer basket inside and place the fish in it. Rub the fish with the chili paste, cover your instant pot with lid and secure and cook on Manual on low for 12-minutes. In a mixing bowl, combine Truvia, soy sauce, garlic, plum extract, sesame seeds, sesame oil, green onions, and stir well. Release pressure naturally for 10-minutes. Divide fish among serving plates, and drizzle with sauce you made. Serve warm!

Nutritional Information per serving:
Calories: 284   Fat: 17g   Fiber: 1g   Carbs: 9g   Protein: 27g

160. Baked Red Snapper

Cook Time: 12 minutes
Servings: 4
Ingredients:

- 4 red snappers, cleaned
- 5 garlic cloves, minced
- ½ cup parsley, chopped
- ½ cup olive oil
- 1 lemon, sliced
- 4 tablespoons lemon juice
- Sea salt and black pepper to taste
- 5-ounces of grape leaves, blanched

Directions:
Pat the fish dry and place it in a bowl. Season the fish with salt, pepper, and brush half the oil onto it and rub well, then keep in the fridge for 30-minutes. In a mixing bowl, combine parsley, salt and pepper, stir. Divide this mix into the fish cavities, wrap each in a grape leaf, drizzle with lemon juice over them and place the fish in a heat-proof dish within your instant pot steamer basket. Drizzle the rest of the oil over the fish, cover the dish with some tin foil, place the basket inside your instant pot. Add 2 cups of water to your instant pot, cover with lid, and cook on High-pressure for 12-minutes. Release the pressure using the quick-release. Divide the wrapped fish among serving plates, top with lemon slices. Serve warm!

Nutritional Information per serving:
Calories: 276   Fat: 20g   Fiber: 1g   Carbs: 8g   Protein: 29g

161. Red Snapper & Tomato Sauce

Cook Time: 11 minutes
Servings: 4
Ingredients:

- 4 medium red snapper fillets
- 4 ciabatta rolls, cut in halves, and toasted
- 2 tablespoons parsley, fresh, chopped
- 16-ounces canned tomatoes, crushed
- ¼ cup olive oil
- 1 yellow onion, chopped
- 3 tablespoons hot water
- A pinch of saffron threads
- Sea salt and black pepper to taste

Directions:
In a mixing bowl, combine, hot water, and saffron, then leave aside. Set your instant pot to the sauté mode, and add the oil and heat it up. Add the onion, and stir and cook for 2-minutes. Add the fish, cook for an additional 2-minutes and flip on the other side and cook that side for 2-minutes. Add the tomatoes, drained saffron, some salt and pepper, cover the instant pot with lid. Set the instant pot to low for 5-minutes. Release the pressure with the quick-release. Divide the fish and sauce among serving plates, and garnish with fresh, chopped parsley, serve with ciabatta rolls. Serve warm!

Nutritional Information per serving:
Calories: 243   Fat: 14g   Fiber: 2g   Carbs: 7g   Protein: 26g

162. Thai Red Snapper
Cook Time: 20 minutes **Servings: 2**
Ingredients:
For the Marinade:
- 1 tablespoon Thai curry paste
- 1 cup coconut milk
- 1 tablespoon fish sauce paste
- 1 tablespoon cilantro, chopped
- 2 cups water
- 1 lime, sliced
- 2 red snapper fillets
- 1 teaspoon garlic, minced
- 1 tablespoon ginger, grated
- 1 teaspoon Truvia
- Juice of ½ a lime
- Zest of a lime

For the Salsa:
- 2 jalapenos, chopped
- 2 mangoes, peeled, and chopped
- 1 scallion, chopped
- A handful of cilantro, fresh, chopped for garnish
- Juice from 1 lime

Directions:
In a mixing bowl, combine fish sauce with coconut milk, zest from 1 lime, curry paste, juice from ½ a lime, Truvia, garlic, ginger, and whisk well. Add the fish fillets, toss to coat and set aside for 30-minutes. In another bowl, mix jalapenos, mangoes, scallion, juice from 1 lime, mix well and leave aside. Place the water in your instant pot and put the steamer basket inside. Place the fish in 2-pieces of parchment paper, cover them with lime slices and wrap them. Place them into the steamer basket, cover the instant pot with lid, and cook on high for 10-minutes. Release the pressure using the quick-release. Put the marinade from fish into a pan and heat it up over medium-high heat. Boil for a couple of minutes and take off heat. Drizzle some of the sauce over dish, top with mango salsa and garnish with fresh, chopped cilantro. Serve warm!

Nutritional Information per serving:
Calories: 257 Fat: 17g Fiber: 1g Carbs: 10g Protein: 28g

163. Lobster & Sweet Potatoes
Cook Time: 16 minutes **Servings: 4**
Ingredients:
- 4 lobsters
- 1 onion, cut into wedges
- Water
- 2 garlic heads, not peeled
- 1 ½ lbs of sweet potatoes, peeled, and cubed
- 4 ears of corn, shucked, and halved
- 4 tablespoons butter

Directions:
Place the cubed-sweet potatoes in your instant pot. Add onion, garlic, and some salt with enough water to cover them. Cover your pot and cook on high for 12-minutes. Release the pressure using quick-release. Add the lobsters, and corn to the instant pot and cover once again. Cook on high for 5-minutes. Release the pressure again using quick-release. Divide the corn and sweet potatoes among serving plates, season with some salt and drizzle some melted butter over them. Discard the onion, and garlic. Transfer the lobsters

to cutting board and remove the meat. Divide lobster meat among serving plates next to corn and sweet potatoes. Drizzle the rest of butter over lobster meat. Serve warm!
Nutritional Information per serving:
Calories: 297   Fat: 18g   Fiber: 2g   Carbs: 11g   Protein: 32g

---

164. Steamed Lobster
Cooking Time: 3 minutes
Servings: 1
Ingredients:
- 1 cup non-alcoholic beer
- 2 cups water
- 1 lobster
- Sea salt and white pepper to taste

Directions:
Add the beer and water to your instant pot and place the steamer basket inside it as well. Place the lobster in the basket, cover and cook on high for 3-minutes. Release the pressure with quick-release. Transfer lobster to serving plate and season with some salt and pepper. Serve warm!
Nutritional Information per serving:
Calories: 286   Fat: 19g   Fiber: 1g   Carbs: 16g   Protein: 37g

---

165. Simple Instant Pot Lobster
Cook Time: 3 minutes
Servings: 3
Ingredients:
- 2 lbs. lobster tails
- ½ cup ghee, melted
- 1 cup water
- A dash of sea salt and some black pepper

Directions:
Put the water into your instant pot, add the lobster tails into steamer basket and place in your instant pot. Cook on high for 3-minutes. Release the pressure using the quick-release. Transfer the lobster tails to a bowl, drizzle melted ghee over lobster, and sprinkle with some salt and pepper. Serve warm!
Nutritional Information per serving:
Calories: 289   Fat: 14g   Fiber: 2g   Carbs: 8g   Protein: 30g

166. Spicy Sardines
Cook Time: 15 minutes
Servings: 4
Ingredients:
- 1 lb. of sardines
- 8 garlic cloves, minced
- 2 yellow onions, cut in halves, then thinly sliced
- 2 tablespoons white vinegar
- 3 tablespoons coconut oil
- ½ teaspoon turmeric
- 1 large tomato, chopped
- 1 ½ teaspoons chili powder
- 4 curry leaves
- 1 green chili pepper, chopped
- 1-inch ginger pieces, grated

Directions:
Place the oil into your instant pot, and heat it up on the sauté mode. Add the garlic, ginger, onion, curry leaves, chili, and stir for 2-minutes. Add the chili powder, tomato, turmeric, vinegar, salt, pepper, and stir and cook for an additional 3-minutes. Add the sardines, cover your instant pot and cook on high for 10-minutes. Release the pressure with quick-release. Divide among serving plates. Serve warm!

Nutritional Information per serving:
Calories: 206   Fat: 11g   Fiber: 2g   Carbs: 13g   Protein: 27g

167. Tasty Sardines
Cook Time: 20 minutes
Servings: 5
Ingredients:
- 2 lbs. sardines
- 2 peppercorns
- 10 garlic cloves, minced
- 1 tablespoon, smoked paprika
- 1 teaspoon Truvia
- 1 red chili pepper, chopped
- 2 bay leaves
- 1 pickle, sliced
- 1 carrot, chopped
- 2 cups tomato sauce
- 2 tablespoons olive oil
- 2 cups water

Directions:
Put sardines into a mixing bowl, cover them with water and salt to taste, leave them to sit for 15-minutes. Drain the sardines and put them into your instant pot. Add the peppercorns, cloves, oil, tomato sauce, carrots, bay leaves, chili pepper, pickle, Truvia, paprika, garlic, and stir gently. Cover with pot lid and cook on low for 20-minutes. Release the pressure naturally for 10-minutes. Divide among serving plates. Serve warm!

Nutritional Information per serving:
Calories: 284   Fat: 12g   Fiber: 1g   Carbs: 14g   Protein: 29g

168. Teriyaki Salmon
Cook Time: 10 minutes
Servings: 2
Ingredients:
- ¼ cup water
- 2 teaspoons sesame seeds
- 1 tablespoon sesame oil
- 1 garlic clove, minced
- ½ cup soy sauce
- 2 salmon fillets
- 1 tablespoon cornstarch mixed with 1 tablespoon of water
- 3 green onions, chopped
- 1 cup water for instant pot
- 1 teaspoon Truvia
- 1 tablespoon ginger, grated
- ¼ cup mirin

Directions:
In a mixing bowl, combine mirin, soy sauce, sesame oil, sesame seeds, ginger, garlic, Truvia, and ¼ cup water, stir well. Add the salmon and toss to coat, cover and keep the salmon in the fridge for 30-minutes. Add 1 cup water to your instant pot and place the steamer basket inside. Add a pan in the basket, put the salmon in the pan and reserve the marinade. Cover your instant pot with lid and cook on high for 8-minutes. Put the marinade in a pot and heat it over medium-high heat. Add the cornstarch to it, mix and stir. Release the pressure using quick-release. Divide the salmon among serving plates, and drizzle with the sauce on top. Serve warm!

Nutritional Information per serving:
Calories: 304 Fat: 21g Fiber: 2g Carbs: 16g Protein: 46g

---

169. Simple Salmon & Onion
Cook Time: 6 minutes
Servings: 4
Ingredients:
- 4 salmon steaks
- ½ cup white wine
- 1 yellow onion, sliced thinly
- ½ cup water
- 1 lemon, sliced
- Sea salt and black pepper to taste

Directions:
Add the wine, water, and some salt and pepper into your instant pot. Stir, and place the steamer basket inside your instant pot. Put the salmon steaks in the basket, season with salt and pepper, cover them with onions, and lemon slices. Cover and cook on high for 6-minutes. Release the pressure using quick-release. Divide the salmon steaks among serving plates and top them with onions and lemon slices. Serve warm!

Nutritional Information per serving:
Calories: 321 Fat: 19g Fiber: 1g Carbs: 12g Protein: 43g

170. Simple Instant Pot Salmon
Cook Time: 5 minutes
Servings: 2
Ingredients:
- 2 salmon fillets
- 1 tablespoon thyme, fresh, chopped
- 1 bay leaf
- 2 tablespoons mustard
- Sea salt and black pepper to taste
- 1 cup fish stock
- Slices of lemon for garnish

Directions:
In a mixing bowl, combine mustard, thyme, salt, pepper, and stir. Rub the salmon fillets with this mix. Put the stock and bay leaf into your instant pot. Place the steamer basket inside instant pot and place salmon in it. Cover and cook on high for 5 minutes. Release the pressure using quick-release. Divide the salmon among serving plates and garnish with sliced lemons. Serve warm!

Nutritional Information per serving:
Calories: 326   Fat: 20g   Fiber: 2g   Carbs: 14g   Protein: 47g

171. Salmon Fillets with Sauce
Cook Time: 6 minutes
Servings: 4
Ingredients:
- 4 salmon fillets
- 1 cup water
- 3 tablespoons mayonnaise
- 2 tablespoons butter
- 1 teaspoon Truvia
- 1 tablespoon dill, fresh, chopped
- 1 teaspoon soy sauce
- 1 tablespoon lemon juice

Directions:
Add the water to your instant pot, add the steamer basket inside and add the fish to basket. Cover and cook on high for 5-minutes. Add the lemon juice, butter, Truvia, dill, soy sauce, mayo to a pot, stir well and heat over medium-high heat. Release the pressure of the instant pot naturally for 10-minutes. Divide the salmon among the serving plates and drizzle over the top of fish the sauce. Serve warm!

Nutritional Information per serving:
Calories: 327   Fat: 16g   Fiber: 1g   Carbs: 16g   Protein: 43g

172. Tuna Steaks
Cook Time: 5 minutes
Servings: 4
Ingredients:
- 4 medium tuna steaks
- 1 bunch oregano, fresh
- 3 tablespoons lemon juice
- 2 tablespoons soy sauce
- 1/3 cup white wine
- Sea salt and black pepper to taste
- Some lettuce and tomatoes for serving

Directions:
Place your tuna steaks into your instant pot, add the soy sauce, wine, lemon juice, salt, pepper, and add the steamer basket as well, place the fresh oregano in the steamer basket. Cook on high for 5-minutes. Release the pressure using the quick-release. Divide the tuna steaks among the serving plates, serve with lettuce and tomatoes on the side. Serve warm!

Nutritional Information per serving:
Calories: 298   Fat: 12g   Fiber: 2g   Carbs: 10g   Protein: 26g

173. Tuna Casserole
Cook Time: 4 minutes
Servings: 4
Ingredients:
- 2 ½ cups macaroni pasta
- 10-ounces cream of mushroom soup
- 14-ounces of canned tuna, drained
- 1 cup cheddar cheese, shredded
- 1 cup peas
- 3 cups water
- Salt and black pepper to taste

Directions:
In your instant pot mix the water, mushroom soup, tuna, macaroni, peas, salt, pepper, and stir. Cover and cook on high for 4-minutes. Release the pressure using the quick-release. Add the shredded cheese then cover your pot and allow it to sit for 5-minutes. Divide among serving bowls. Serve warm or cold!

Nutritional Information per serving:
Calories: 287   Fat: 12g   Fiber: 2g   Carbs: 17g   Protein: 28g

174. Zucchini Pasta with Capers

Cooking Time: 8 minutes
Servings: 4
Ingredients:

- 2 tablespoons capers
- Water
- 16-ounces of zucchini pasta
- 11-ounces of canned tuna in oil
- 3 anchovies
- 1 tablespoon olive oil
- 1 garlic clove, minced
- 2 cups tomato puree
- Sea salt to taste

Directions:
Set your instant pot to the saute mode, add the oil and heat it up. Add the anchovies and garlic, stir and sauté them for 2-minutes. Add tomato puree, tuna, salt and stir. Add the water cover and cook for 3-minutes on low. Release the pressure on quick-release. Divide then place the tuna mix on top of bed of zucchini pasta and top with capers. Serve warm!

Nutritional Information per serving:
Calories: 267   Fat: 7g   Fiber: 1g   Carbs: 14g   Protein: 23g

175. Beans & Clams

Cook Time: 10 minutes
Servings: 6
Ingredients:

- 10-ounces canned white beans, drained
- 1 bay leaf
- 2 garlic cloves, minced
- 1 tablespoon olive oil
- 4-ounces white wine
- 14-ounces clams
- A dash of salt

Directions:
Place the beans in your instant pot, add water to cover, a pinch of salt and bay leaf, stir. Cover and cook on high for 10-minutes. Release the pressure using quick-release. Drain the beans and clean your pot. Add the oil and set to sauté mode, and heat oil up. Add the garlic, stir and cook for 2-minutes. Add wine, beans, clams, cover and cook on high for 6-minutes. Release the pressure again using quick-release. Divide the clams and beans in serving bowls. Serve warm!

Nutritional Information per serving:
Calories: 254   Fat: 6g   Fiber: 2g   Carbs: 8g   Protein: 21g

176. Instant Pot Squid
Cook Time: 25 minutes
Servings: 4
Ingredients:
- 1 small ginger piece, grated
- 2 yellow onions, chopped
- 1 lb. squid, cut into medium pieces
- 10-garlic cloves, minced
- 2 green chilies, chopped
- 3 tablespoons olive oil
- ¾ cup water
- 1 teaspoon mustard seeds
- 1 teaspoon garam masala
- Black pepper to taste
- A pinch of sea salt
- Pinch of turmeric powder
- ¾ tablespoon chili powder
- ½ tablespoon lemon juice
- ¼ cup coconut, shredded
- 1 tablespoon coriander, ground

Directions:
Place your instant pot on the sauté mode, add the oil and heat it up. Add the mustard seeds, stir and toast them for 1-minute. Add the coconut, stir, toast for 2-minutes more. Add the ginger, chilies, onions, garlic and stir and cook for 1-minute. Add the curry leaf, pepper, salt, lemon juice, coriander, chili powder, turmeric, garam masala, water, squid and stir. Cover and cook on low for 25-minutes. Release the pressure naturally for 10-minutes. Divide into serving bowls. Serve warm!

Nutritional Information per serving:
Calories: 241   Fat: 12g   Fiber: 1g   Carbs: 11g   Protein: 30g

177. Italian Braised Squid
Cook Time: 20 minutes
Servings: 4
Ingredients:
- 1 lb. peas
- 1 lb. squid, cut into medium pieces
- 1 tablespoon olive oil
- 1 tablespoon white wine
- ½ lb. tomatoes, crushed
- Sea salt and pepper to taste
- 1 yellow onion, chopped

Directions:
Add the oil to your instant pot, set it on sauté mode, and heat the oil up. Add the onion, stir and cook for 3-minutes. Add the squid and cook for an additional 3-minutes. Add the wine, tomatoes, peas, pepper and salt, stir, cover and cook on high for 15-minutes. Release the pressure naturally for 15-minutes. Divide among serving plates. Serve warm!

Nutritional Information per serving:
Calories: 212   Fat: 16g   Fiber: 1g   Carbs: 13g   Protein: 34g

178. Stuffed Squid
Cooking Time: 20 minutes4
Servings:
Ingredients:
- 14-ounces dashi stock
- 4 squid, tentacles separated and chopped
- 1 cup cauliflower rice, cooked
- 2 tablespoons sake
- 1 tablespoon mirin
- 1 teaspoon Truvia
- 4 tablespoons soy sauce

Directions:
In a bowl, mix cauliflower rice, tentacles, stuff the squid with mix. Place the stuffed squid into your instant pot, add the soy sauce, Truvia, mirin, sake, stir and cover. Cook on high for 15-minutes. Release pressure fast, divide squid on plates. Serve warm!

Nutritional Information per serving:
Calories: 223 Fat: 7g Fiber: 1g Carbs: 9g Protein: 29g

179. Seafood Masala
Cooking Time: 15 minutes
Servings: 4
Ingredients:
- 1 ½ tablespoons red chili powder
- 17-ounces squid
- ¼ teaspoon mustard seeds
- 1 small ginger pieces, grated
- 3 tablespoons olive oil
- 4 garlic cloves, minced
- 5 small coconut pieces, shredded
- ¼ teaspoon turmeric
- 2 cups water
- Salt and black pepper to taste

Directions:
In your instant pot, mix the chili powder, squid, turmeric, water, salt, pepper and cook on high for 15-minutes. In your food processor, mix ginger with garlic, ginger, coconut, cumin and pulse. Heat up a pan with the oil over medium-high heat. Add the mustard seeds, and toast them for 2-minutes and remove from heat. Release the pressure on instant pot naturally for 10-minutes. Transfer the squid and its liquid to the pan with mustard seeds. Add the coconut paste as well. Cook for a few minutes, divide among serving plates. Serve warm!

Nutritional Information per serving:
Calories: 216 Fat: 6g Fiber: 1g Carbs: 15g Protein: 23g

180. Mediterranean Octopus Dish
Cook Time: 15 minutes **Servings:** 5
Ingredients:
- 2 rosemary sprigs
- 2 teaspoons oregano, dried
- 1 octopus, prepared
- 4 thyme sprigs
- 1 small yellow onion, chopped
- 3 tablespoons olive oil

- 1 teaspoon black peppercorns

For the Marinade:
- 4 cloves garlic, minced
- 2 thyme sprigs
- 1 sprig of rosemary
- Juice from ½ a lemon
- Juice from ½ a lemon
- Pinch of sea salt and black pepper

Directions:
In your instant pot, mix the octopus with 2 rosemary sprigs, 4 thyme sprigs, juice from ½ a lemon, peppercorns, oregano, onion, olive oil, pinch of salt. Stir, cover and cook on low for 10-minutes. Release the pressure naturally for 10-minutes. Transfer the octopus to a cutting board, cool down and chop, then put in a bowl. Mix the octopus pieces with juice from ½ lemon, ¼ cup oil, 1 rosemary sprig, 2 thyme sprigs, salt and pepper, set aside for 1 hour. Place the marinated pieces on a preheated grill over medium-high heat, cook for 3-minutes on each side. Serve with the marinade drizzled on top. Serve warm or cold!

Nutritional Information per serving:
Calories: 206 Fat: 4g Fiber: 1g Carbs: 11g Protein: 28g

181. *Portuguese Seafood Stew*

Cook Time: 15 minutes
Servings: 4
Ingredients:
- 1 big octopus, prepared
- 1 cup red wine
- 1 cup white wine
- ½ cup olive oil
- 2 garlic cloves, minced
- 1 yellow onion, finely chopped
- 4 potatoes, peeled, cut into quarters
- 1 tablespoon tomato paste
- ½ bunch parsley, chopped
- 1 tablespoon paprika
- 2 teaspoons pepper sauce
- 1 teaspoon hot sauce
- 2 tablespoons olive oil
- ½ cup sunflower oil
- Sea salt and black pepper to taste

Directions:
In a bowl, mix the red and white wine with water, sunflower oil, pepper sauce, tomato paste, hot sauce, paprika, parsley, salt and pepper, stir. Add the octopus, toss and coat, keep in the fridge for a day. Add the olive oil to your instant pot, and heat it using the sauté mode. Add the potatoes and onions, stir and cook for 3-minutes. Add the octopus and its marinade to instant pot, stir and cook on high for 8-minutes. Release pressure using quick-release. Divide among serving bowls. Serve hot!

Nutritional Information per serving:
Calories: 267 Fat: 10g Fiber: 3g Carbs: 16g Protein: 22g

182. *Instant Pot Gumbo*

Cook Time: 25 minutes
Servings: 10
Ingredients:
- 1 cup green bell pepper, chopped
- 1 cup yellow onion, chopped
- ¾ cup coconut oil
- 1 and ¼ cup almond flour

- 3 bay leaves
- 2 tablespoons peanut oil
- A pinch of cayenne pepper
- 24 shrimps, peeled and deveined
- 24 crawfish tails
- 24 oysters
- 2 cups chicken stock
- 1 teaspoon thyme, dried
- 1 lb. sausage, chopped
- 1 teaspoon celery seeds
- ½ teaspoon onion powder
- ½ teaspoon garlic powder
- 6 plum tomatoes, chopped
- ½ cup celery, chopped
- ½ lb. of crabmeat
- Sea salt and black pepper to taste

Directions:
In a pan heat the coconut oil over medium-high heat, add flour, stir very well, cook for 4-minutes and take off heat. Set your instant pot to the sauté mode, add the peanut oil and heat it. Add onion, peppers, celery, and garlic, stir and sauté for 10-minutes. Add stock, sausage, tomatoes, cayenne, onion powder, garlic powder, bay leaves, thyme, celery seeds, paprika, stir and cook for 3-minutes. Add the flour mix, crawfish, crabmeat, salt, pepper, shrimp, oysters, stir, cover and cook on high for 15-minutes. Release pressure naturally for 10-minutes. Divide among serving bowls. Serve warm!

Nutritional Information per serving:
Calories: 253   Fat: 14g   Fiber: 2g   Carbs: 16g   Protein: 31g

---

183. Easy to Prepare Octopus
Cook Time: 35 minutes
Servings: 6
Ingredients:
- 2 lbs. octopus, head discarded, tentacles separated
- 2 lbs. sweet potatoes
- 1 bay leaf
- 2 tablespoons olive oil
- 5 tablespoons vinegar
- 2 tablespoons parsley, chopped
- 3 garlic cloves, minced
- ½ teaspoon of peppercorns
- Sea salt and black pepper to taste

Directions:
Add some water to your instant pot, add the sweet potatoes, cover and cook them on high for 15-minutes. Release the pressure naturally for 10-minutes. Transfer the sweet potatoes to a bowl, cool down and peel and chop them. Clean your instant pot, add some more water, octopus, bay leaf, 1 garlic clove, peppercorns, salt, cover and cook on high for 20-minutes. Release the pressure again naturally for 10-minutes. Drain the octopus, chop and add this to the bowl of potatoes. In a different bowl, mix the rest of the garlic with vinegar, oil, pepper, salt, and whisk well. Add this to your salad, sprinkle parsley, toss to coat. Divide among serving bowls. Serve warm.

Nutritional Information per serving:
Calories: 247   Fat: 16g   Fiber: 2g   Carbs: 14g   Protein: 32g

184. Shrimp Risotto
Cook Time: 20 minutes
Servings: 4
Ingredients:
- 1 lb. shrimp, peeled and deveined
- 2 tablespoons white wine
- ¾ cup parmesan, grated
- ½ cup parsley, chopped
- 2 garlic cloves, minced
- 3 cups chicken stock
- 1 yellow onion, chopped
- 1 cup cauliflower rice, cooked
- 4 tablespoons butter
- Sea salt and black pepper to taste

Directions:
Set your instant pot on the sauté mode, add half of the butter, and heat it up. Add the garlic, onion, and cook and stir for 4-minutes. Add the cooked cauliflower rice, stir and cook for 1-minute more. Add 2 cups of stock, wine a pinch of salt and pepper. Set on high for 10-minutes cook time. Release the pressure naturally for 10-minutes. Add the shrimp, the remaining stock, and switch the pot to Simmer mode. Cook everything for 5-minutes, add cheese, the rest of the butter, parsley and stir. Divide among serving plates. Serve warm!

Nutritional Information per serving:
Calories: 292   Fat: 19g   Fiber: 1g   Carbs: 12g   Protein: 37g

185. Flounder & Shrimp
Cook Time: 5 minutes
Servings: 4
Ingredients:
- 1/2 lb. shrimp, peeled and deveined and cooked
- 2 lbs. flounder
- 4 lemon wedges
- 2 tablespoons butter
- ½ cup water
- Sea salt and black pepper to taste

Directions:
Put the water in your instant pot and place the steamer basket inside. Add the fish into the basket, season with a dash of salt and black pepper. Cover and cook on high for 10-minutes. Release the pressure using the quick-release. Divide the fish among serving plates, and leave to cool down. Clean your instant pot, add butter and set it on the sauté mode. Add the shrimp, salt and black pepper, stir and cook for a few seconds. Divide onto serving plates next to fish. Drizzle with butter all over, and serve with lemon wedges. Serve room temperature!

Nutritional Information per serving:
Calories: 282   Fat: 16g   Fiber: 1g   Carbs: 14g   Protein: 34g

186. Italian Shrimp Scampi
Cook Time: 5 minutes **Servings: 4**
Ingredients:
- 1 lb. shrimp, peeled, deveined, and cooked
- 1 garlic clove, minced
- 10-ounces canned tomatoes, chopped
- 1 tablespoon parsley, chopped
- 1/3 cup water
- 1 cup parmesan, grated
- 1/3 cup tomato paste
- ¼ teaspoon oregano, dried
- 2 tablespoons olive oil
- Zucchini pasta for serving

Directions:
Set your instant pot to the sauté mode, add the oil and heat it up. Add the garlic and cook it for 2-minutes. Add the tomato paste, water, tomatoes, shrimp, oregano, parsley, stir cover and cook on high for 3 minutes. Release the pressure using the quick-release. Divide among serving plates on top of a bed of zucchini pasta. Garnish the tops with parmesan. Serve warm!

Nutritional Information per serving:
Calories: 272   Fat: 12g   Fiber: 2g   Carbs: 17g   Protein: 36g

187. Spicy Shrimp
Cook Time: 10 minutes **Servings: 4**
Ingredients:
- 18-ounces shrimp, peeled and deveined
- 2 green chilies, halved lengthwise
- 2 onions, chopped
- 1 small ginger piece, grated
- Cauliflower rice already cooked for serving
- 1 teaspoon turmeric
- ½ tablespoon mustard seeds
- 3-ounces mustard oil
- Dash of sea salt

Directions:
Place the mustard seeds in a bowl, add water, leave aside for 10-minutes. Drain them and blend in your blender. In another bowl, mix shrimp, mustard oil, turmeric, mustard paste, onions, salt, chilies, and ginger, stir. Transfer this to your instant pot, cover and cook on low for 10-minutes. Release the pressure using quick-release. Divide among serving plates. Serve warm with rice!

Nutritional Information per serving:
Calories: 264   Fat: 14g   Fiber: 3g   Carbs: 17g   Protein: 35g

188. Special Shrimp Dish
Cook Time: 4 minutes **Servings: 4**
Ingredients:
- 1 lb. shrimp, peeled and deveined
- 1 cup chicken stock
- 2 tablespoons soy sauce
- 1 teaspoon Truvia
- ¾ cup unsweetened pineapple juice
- ½ lb. pea pods

- 3 tablespoons vinegar

Directions:
In your instant pot combine, shrimp, pea pods, stock, vinegar, soy sauce, Truvia, pineapple juice, and stir well. Cover the pot and cook on high for 4-minutes. Release the pressure using quick-release. Divide among serving bowls. Serve warm!

Nutritional Information per serving:
Calories: 252   Fat: 15g   Fiber: 1g   Carbs: 16g   Protein: 23g

---

189. Creole Shrimp
Cook Time: 25 minutes   **Servings: 4**
Ingredients:
- 1 cup shrimp, cooked, peeled and deveined
- 2 teaspoons vinegar
- 1 cup tomato juice
- 1 yellow onion, chopped
- 2 tablespoons olive oil
- 1 cup celery, chopped
- ½ teaspoon Truvia
- 1 teaspoon chili powder
- 1 cup of cauliflower rice, cooked
- Dash of sea salt

Directions:
Set your instant pot to the sauté mode, add the oil and heat it up. Add the onion, celery, stir and sauté them for 2-minutes. Add the salt, vinegar, chili powder, rice, Truvia, shrimp, stir and cook on high for 3-minutes. Release the pressure using quick-release. Divide among serving plates. Serving warm!

Nutritional Information per serving:
Calories: 258   Fat: 17g   Fiber: 2g   Carbs: 18g   Protein: 37g

---

190. Shrimp Stew
Cook Time: 15 minutes   **Servings: 3**
Ingredients:
- 2 lbs. shrimp, peeled and deveined
- 1 lb. tomatoes, peeled, chopped
- 4 tablespoons olive oil
- A dash of sea salt
- 4 sweet potatoes, peeled, cubed
- 4 yellow onions, chopped
- 1 teaspoon coriander, dried
- 1 tablespoon watercress, chopped
- Juice from 1 lemon
- 1 teaspoon curry powder

Directions:
Put some water into your instant pot, place the steamer basket inside, add the sweet potatoes, cover and cook on high for 10-minutes. Release the pressure using quick-release. Transfer sweet potatoes to a bowl to cool down. Clean pot, add oil and set on the sauté mode. Add the onion, stir and cook for 4-minutes. Add the coriander, curry powder, and sea salt, cook for an additional 5-minutes. Add shrimp, lemon juice, sweet potatoes, tomatoes, stir. Set to high and cook for 3-minutes. Release pressure once again using quick-release. Divide among serving bowls. Serve hot!

Nutritional Information per serving:
Calories: 247   Fat: 4g   Fiber: 1g   Carbs: 12g   Protein: 32g

Chapter 7. Collection of Soup Instant Pot Recipes

191. Sweet Potato & Broccoli Soup

Cook Time: 40 minutes
Servings: 4
Ingredients:

- 2 lbs. sweet potatoes, peeled, cubed
- 1 cup cheddar cheese, grated, divided
- 4 cups veggie broth
- 2 tablespoons butter
- 1 broccoli head, chopped into florets
- 2 garlic cloves, minced
- 1 cup half and half

Directions:
Set the instant pot to the sauté mode, add the butter and heat it. Add the garlic and cook it for 2-minutes. Stir in the broth and broccoli, add the sweet potatoes. Close the lid and select Manual, cook on high for 5-minutes. To release the pressure, use the quick-release. Stir the half and half cream in a bowl with half of the cheese, and blend with blender. Add to the instant pot and stir. Divide among serving bowls, and garnish with remaining cheddar cheese. Serve warm!

Nutritional Information per serving:
Calories: 522   Fat: 35g   Carbs: 23g   Protein: 28g

192. Squash & Potato Soup

Cook Time: 40 minutes
Servings: 4
Ingredients:

- 2 cups of sweet potatoes
- 2 cups butternut squash
- 2 garlic cloves, minced
- 2 tablespoons coconut oil
- 3 cups bone broth
- ½ teaspoon turmeric
- ½ teaspoon nutmeg
- 1 teaspoon tarragon
- 1 ½ teaspoon curry powder
- 1 onion, chopped
- 1 teaspoon grated ginger
- Sea salt and black pepper to taste

Directions:
Set your instant pot to the sauté mode, add the coconut oil, and cook for 3-minutes. Add ginger and garlic, and cook for an additional 1-minute. Stir the remaining ingredients, close the lid, and select Manual, and cook for 10-minutes. Allow the pressure to release using the quick-release. Blend the soup with a hand blender. Divide into serving bowls. Serve warm!

Nutritional Information per serving:
Calories: 236   Fat: 9g   Carbs: 35g   Protein: 8g

193. Parsnip Soup

Cooking Time: 15 minutes
Servings: 4
Ingredients:

- 4 parsnips, chopped
- 4 cups vegetable stock
- Juice from 1 lemon
- ½ teaspoon chili powder

- 2 garlic cloves, crushed
- 2 tablespoons coconut oil
- 1 red onion, finely chopped
- Sea salt and black pepper to taste

Directions:
Set your instant pot to the sauté mode, add the coconut oil and heat it up. Add the parsnips, onions, garlic, and cook for 5-minutes, or until softened. Add the chili powder, and stir constantly for a few seconds. Stir in the stock, lemon juice, and lock the lid securely in place. Select the Manual setting, and cook on high for 5-minutes. To release the pressure, use the quick-release. Transfer to a food processor, and blend until smooth. Return the soup to the instant pot and set on warm for 2-minutes. Season with salt and black pepper. Divide among serving bowls. Serve warm!

Nutritional Information per serving:
Calories: 110   Fat: 7.3g   Carbs: 11g   Protein: 1.7g

194. *Turkey & Carrot Soup*
Cook Time: 15 minutes   **Servings:** 3
Ingredients:
- 5-ounces of turkey breast, chopped into pieces
- 2 carrots, sliced
- 3 cups chicken broth
- 2 tablespoons cilantro, chopped
- Sea salt and white pepper to taste

Directions:
Add all the ingredients into your instant pot and secure the lid. Press the Manual mode and set for a cook time of 35-minutes. Release the pressure naturally for 15-minutes. Divide among serving bowls. Serve hot!

Nutritional Information per serving:
Calories: 116   Fat: 2.5g   Carbs: 9g   Protein: 15g

195. *Fish Soup*
Cook Time: 45 minutes   **Servings:** 4
Ingredients:
- 6-ounces of mackerel fillets
- 4 cups fish stock
- 1 teaspoon rosemary, fresh, chopped
- ½ lb. tomatoes, peeled, diced
- ¼ cup sweet corn
- ½ cup wheat groats, soaked
- ½ cup kidney beans, soaked
- 2 tablespoons olive oil
- Sea salt and pepper to taste

Directions:
Grease the stainless-steel insert for your instant pot with olive oil. Press the sauté mode and add the tomatoes. Cook for 4-minutes, stir occasionally. Add the rosemary, fish stock, corn, wheat groats, beans, a pinch of salt. Close the lid and set the steam release handle. Press Manual and set for a cook time of 30-minutes. To release pressure, use the quick-release. Open the lid and add the mackerel fillets. Close lid again and press the Fish button, and cook for 10-minutes.

Nutritional Information per serving:
Calories: 464   Fat: 21g   Carbs: 39g   Protein: 29g

196. Asparagus & Sour Cream Soup
Cook Time: 25 minutes **Servings:** 4
Ingredients:
- 2 lbs. asparagus, chopped
- 8-ounces sour cream
- 1 onion, chopped
- 5 cups bone broth
- 2 garlic cloves, minced
- 3 tablespoons butter
- ½ teaspoon thyme
- Salt and black pepper to taste

Directions:
Set your instant pot to the sauté mode, add the butter and heat it. Add the onions and cook for 3-minutes. Add the thyme and garlic, cook for an additional minute. Stir in the asparagus, broth, salt, pepper, and stir. Close the lid and select Manual, cook on high for 5-minutes. Allow the pressure to release naturally for 10-minutes. Stir in the sour cream. Divide among serving bowls. Serve warm!

Nutritional Information per serving:
Calories: 317 Fat: 5.6g Carbs: 16g Protein: 13g

197. Turkey & Black Bean Soup
Cook Time: 55 minutes **Servings:** 4
Ingredients:
- 6-ounces turkey, chopped
- 1 cup black beans, dried
- 1 onion, chopped
- 1 garlic clove, minced
- 3 cups water
- 1 carrot, chopped
- ½ tablespoon olive oil
- Sea salt and black pepper to taste

Directions:
Set your instant pot to the sauté mode, and add the oil and heat. Add the onions, and carrots for 5-minutes. Add the garlic and cook for one minute more. Stir in the remaining ingredients, except the salt and pepper. Close the lid, select Manual, setting and cook on high for 45-minutes. Allow the pressure to release naturally for 10-minutes. Season with salt and pepper. Divide into serving bowls. Serve hot!

Nutritional Information per serving:
Calories: 90 Fat: 8g Carbs: 13g Protein: 10g

198. Brussels Sprouts Soup
Cook Time: 35 minutes **Servings:** 4
Ingredients:
- 1lb. Brussels sprouts, halved, chopped
- 8-ounce baby spinach, torn chopped
- 4 tablespoons sour cream
- 1 cup milk
- 2 cups water
- 1 tablespoon celery, chopped
- 1 tablespoon butter
- ½ teaspoon Truvia
- Sea salt and black pepper to taste

Directions:

Combine all the ingredients in the instant pot. Secure the lid, and select the Soup setting and cook for 35-minutes on high pressure. Release the pressure using quick-release. Transfer the soup to a food processor and blend.
Nutritional Information per serving:
Calories: 191   Fat: 10g   Carbs: 22g   Protein: 10g

199. Chicken & Spinach Soup
Cook Time: *5 minutes*   **Servings:** *6*
Ingredients:
- 1 lb. chicken, cut into chunks
- 4 scallions, chopped
- ½ onion, chopped
- 1 bulb fennel, chopped
- 2 cups chicken broth
- 1 cup spinach
- 3 garlic cloves, minced
- Sea salt and black pepper

Directions:
Place all the ingredients into your instant pot. Select Soup, and cook for 30-minutes. Allow pressure to release naturally for 10-minutes. Divide into serving bowls. Serve warm!
Nutritional Information per serving:
Calories: 181   Fat: 3g   Carbs: 6g   Protein: 25g

200. Tomato Soup
Cook Time: *30 minutes*   **Servings:** *4*
Ingredients:
- 1 ½ lbs. tomatoes, diced
- 1 cup white beans, cooked
- 2 tablespoons sour cream
- 2 tablespoons extra virgin olive oil
- 1 garlic clove, minced
- 1 onion, diced
- 1 tablespoon parsley, fresh, chopped
- ½ cup vegetable broth
- ½ teaspoon Truvia
- Sea salt and black pepper to taste

Directions:
Set your instant pot to the sauté mode, add the oil, and heat it. Add the garlic and chopped onion, cook for 2-minutes. Add the white beans, tomatoes, vegetable broth, 2 cups water, parsley, Truvia, salt and pepper. Press the Soup setting and cook for 25-minutes on high pressure. Release the pressure naturally for 10-minutes. Top with 2 tablespoons of sour cream and parsley prior to serving. Serve warm!
Nutritional Information per serving:
Calories: 319   Fat: 16g   Carbs: 35g   Protein: 13g

201. Chicken Soup with Noodles
Cook Time: *40 minutes*   **Servings:** *4*
Ingredients:
- 1 lb. chicken meat, cut in pieces
- 4 cups chicken broth
- ½ cup soup noodles
- Parsley for garnish
- Sea salt and black pepper to taste
- 1 cup of baby spinach, chopped
- 1 large carrot, peeled, sliced

Directions:
Sprinkle the chicken bites with salt, and place them into the instant pot. Pour the chicken broth, over the chicken, carrot, spinach, and close the lid. Set the steam release handle. Press Soup and cook for 20-minutes. Press the Cancel and release the pressure naturally for 10-minutes. Add the soup noodles and cook for 5 more minutes on the Soup setting. Release the pressure again naturally for 10-minutes. Divide into serving bowls. Add black pepper and parsley for garnish. Serve hot!

Nutritional Information per serving:
Calories: 285   Fat: 11g   Carbs: 7g   Protein: 38g

---

202. Creamy Sausage & Kale Soup
Cook Time: 25 minutes   **Servings:** 6
Ingredients:
- 1 lb. Italian sausage, sliced
- 3 potatoes, cubed
- 1 onion, chopped
- 1 cup heavy cream
- 2 cups kale, chopped
- ¼ cup water
- 4 garlic cloves, minced
- 1 ½ cups chicken broth
- 4 bacon slices, chopped
- 1 tablespoon olive oil

Directions:
Set your instant pot to the sauté mode, add the oil and heat it. Add the bacon and cook until crispy. Transfer to a plate. Add the onions to your instant pot and cook for 3-minutes. Add the garlic and cook for 1 more minute. Add the sausage and cook for 3 more minutes. Stir in potatoes, water and kale. Close the lid and select the Manual setting and cook for 3-minutes on high pressure. Release the pressure naturally for 10-minutes. Stir in the heavy cream, and season with salt and pepper. Divide into serving bowls. Serve warm!

Nutritional Information per serving:
Calories: 500   Fat: 35g   Carbs: 35g   Protein: 28g

---

203. Lentils & Tomato Soup
Cook Time: 15 minutes   **Servings:** 4
Ingredients:
- 4 cups vegetable broth
- 1 medium-sized onion, chopped
- ½ teaspoon thyme, dried, ground
- 1 tablespoon parsley, chopped
- 1 carrot, thinly sliced
- 2 tomatoes, wedged
- 2 cups lentils, soaked overnight, drained
- 3 garlic cloves, peeled, crushed
- 3 tablespoons tomato paste
- ½ teaspoon cumin, ground
- Pinch of salt and black pepper

Directions:
Combine all the ingredients in your instant pot. Set the instant pot on the Manual setting, and cook on high for 8-minutes. Release the pressure naturally for 10-minutes. Divide into serving bowls. Serve warm.

Nutritional Information per serving:
Calories: 326   Fat: 3g   Carbs: 26g   Protein: 35g

---

204. Mixed Veggie Soup
Cook Time: 25 minutes   **Servings: 6**
Ingredients:
- 12-ounces green beans
- ¼ cup parsley, chopped
- 1 can of tomatoes, diced
- 12-ounces frozen veggies
- 2 cups veggie broth
- 2 teaspoons olive oil
- 1 teaspoon thyme
- 1 teaspoon oregano
- 2 garlic cloves, minced
- Salt and pepper to taste

Directions:
Set your instant pot to the sauté mode, add the oil and heat it. Add the onion and cook for 3-minutes. Add the thyme, garlic, oregano, and cook for another minute. Stir in the remaining ingredients. Close the lid and set to Manual setting, cook on high for 5-minutes. Allow the pressure to release naturally for 10-minutes. Divide among serving bowls. Serve hot!

Nutritional Information per serving:
Calories: 94   Fat: 3g   Carbs: 14g   Protein: 7g

---

205. Pork Soup
Cook Time: 55 minutes   **Servings: 4**
Ingredients:
- 4 pork chops with bones
- 2 tablespoons soy sauce
- 1 tablespoon cayenne pepper
- 1 teaspoon chili and garlic powder
- 2 tablespoons olive oil
- 2 celery stalks, diced
- 2 onions, diced
- 2 bay leaves
- 3 medium carrots, sliced

Directions:
Set your instant pot to the sauté mode, add the oil and heat it. Add the onions, cook for 3-minutes. Add the carrots, celery, chili pepper, and cook for another 8-minutes and give it a good stir. Press the Keep Warm/Cancel button then add the pork chops, garlic powder, bay leaves, and soy sauce. Pour in the broth, and seal the lid. Set to Manual mode for 35-minutes. Release the pressure using the quick-release. Divide among serving bowls. Serve warm!

Nutritional Information per serving:
Calories: 259   Fat: 52g   Carbs: 29g   Protein: 47g

---

206. Sweet Potato, Carrot & Turmeric Soup
Cook Time: 35 minutes   **Servings: 4**
Ingredients:
- 3 cups veggie broth
- 2 sweet potatoes, chopped

- 3 carrots, sliced
- 2 garlic cloves, minced
- ½ teaspoon paprika
- 1 tablespoon olive oil
- 1 onion, diced
- Salt and pepper to taste

Directions:
Set your instant pot to the sauté mode, add the oil and heat it. Heat the oil and cook your onions, garlic, carrots for 3-minutes. Stir in the remaining ingredients. Close the lid and set to the Manual mode, and cook on high for 20-minutes. Release the pressure using the quick-release. Blend the soup with a hand blender. Divide among serving bowls. Serve warm!

Nutritional Information per serving:
Calories: 100   Fat: 3g   Carbs: 17g   Protein: 4g

---

207. Creamy Bean Soup
Cook Time: 20 minutes   **Servings: 4**
Ingredients:

- 4 cups beef broth
- 1 cup white beans, cooked
- 1 potato, chopped
- 1 teaspoon garlic powder
- 1/3 cup heavy cream
- Sea salt and black pepper

Directions:
Add all the ingredients and cook on Manual setting for 10-minutes on high. Release the pressure naturally for 10-minutes. Transfer to food processor and blend until smooth. Return the soup to the clean stainless-steel insert and add half cup of water. Cook on sauté mode for 5-minutes. Divide among serving bowls. Serve warm!

Nutritional Information per serving:
Calories: 175   Fat: 8g   Carbs: 16g   Protein: 7.9g

---

208. Cauliflower Soup
Cook Time: 45 minutes   **Servings: 4**
Ingredients:

- 1 lb. cauliflower, chopped into florets
- 4 cups chicken broth
- 1 potato, cubed
- 1 cup milk
- ¼ cup sour cream
- ½ teaspoon salt and pepper
- Parsley, fresh, chopped for garnish
- ¼ cup cooking cream

Directions:
Add the vegetables to your instant pot, add the chicken broth. Close the lid and press the Manual setting and cook on high for 20-minutes. To release the pressure, use the quick-release. Transfer to food processor and pulse until smooth. Pour back into the instant pot, add remaining ingredients. Cook on Manual for 5-minutes. Release pressure again using quick-release. Add to serving bowls, top with fresh, chopped parsley for garnish. Serve warm!

Nutritional Information per serving:
Calories: 167   Fat: 7g   Carbs: 20g   Protein: 12g

209. Garlicky Leek & Potato Soup

Cook Time: 45 minutes
Servings: 4
Ingredients:
- 4 potatoes, diced
- 1 ½ teaspoons oregano
- 3 leeks, sliced
- 1 ½ cups of half and half
- 2 bay leaves
- 4 garlic cloves, minced
- 4 thyme sprigs
- 5 cups veggie broth
- 2 tablespoons butter
- Sea salt and black pepper to taste
- ¾ cup dry white wine

Directions:
Set your instant pot to the sauté mode, add the butter and heat it. Add the garlic and cook for 1-minute. Stir in the wine, broth, bay leaves, oregano, thyme, and potatoes. Close the lid and select the Manual setting and cook on high for 10-minutes. Release the pressure naturally for 10-minutes. Stir in the half and half and blend with hand blender until smooth. Divide into serving bowls. Serve warm!

Nutritional Information per serving:
Calories: 198   Fat: 9g   Carbs: 21g   Protein: 7g

210. Bean Soup with Chili

Cook Time: 35 minutes
Servings: 4
Ingredients:
- 15-ounces of red kidney beans, rinsed
- 14-ounce can of tomatoes
- 1 green bell pepper, diced
- ½ teaspoon Truvia
- 1 clove garlic, minced
- 1/3 cup tomato pasta sauce
- 2 ½ tablespoons olive oil
- 2 fresh red chilies, finely chopped

Directions:
Set your instant pot to the sauté mode, add the oil and heat it. Add the chili, garlic, and onion, stir and cook for 3-minutes. Add the remaining ingredients, then secure the lid to instant pot. Press the Manual setting, and cook on high-pressure for 25-minutes. Release the pressure naturally for 10-minutes. Divide into serving bowls. Serve hot!

Nutritional Information per serving:
Calories: 195   Fat: 8g   Carbs: 25g   Protein: 7g

211. *Instant Pot Vegan Soup*
Cook Time: 25 minutes
Servings: 4
Ingredients:
- 6-ounces broccoli, chopped
- 2 cups vegetable broth
- 1 cup water
- ¼ cup tofu, seasoned and crumbled
- ½ cup almond flour
- 1 cup soy milk
- 1 onion, chopped
- 1 carrot, sliced
- 1 garlic clove, minced

Directions:
Set your instant pot on the sauté mode, add the oil and heat it up. Add the garlic, onion, and cook for 2-minutes. Add the vegetable broth, 1 cup of water, carrot, and broccoli. Seal the lid and press the Manual setting for 5-minutes. Perform a quick-release for pressure. Transfer to a food processor and blend until creamy. Add back into the instant pot, add remaining ingredients. Press the Manual setting and cook on high for 13-minutes. Release the pressure again naturally for 10-minutes. Divide into serving bowls. Serve hot!

Nutritional Information per serving:
Calories: 210   Fat: 9g   Carbs: 23g   Protein: 8g

212. *Chicken Soup with Eggs*
Cook Time: 35 minutes
Servings: 6
Ingredients:
- 1 lb. chicken breast, boneless, skinless, chopped
- 2 carrots, peeled and sliced
- 2 onions, chopped
- 4 cups water
- 2 tablespoons almond flour
- 3 tablespoons olive oil
- 3 egg yolks
- 2 teaspoons cayenne pepper
- 3 small potatoes, peeled, chopped

Directions:
Set your instant pot to the sauté mode, add the oil and heat it. Add the onions, and cook them for 2-minutes. Add the remaining ingredients and seal the lid. Press the Soup button and release the pressure naturally.

Nutritional Information per serving:
Calories: 340   Fat: 15g   Carbs: 23g   Protein: 26g

213. Smoky Ham Hock & Pinto Bean Soup
Cook Time: 50 minutes
Servings: 3
Ingredients:
- 2 lbs. of Smoked Ham Hock
- 4 cups chicken stock
- Pinch of oregano, dried
- 2 cups Pinto beans
- 2 bay leaves
- 1 teaspoon cumin powder
- 6 cloves garlic, crushed
- 1 small onion, sliced
- Minced tomatoes for garnish
- Cilantro, fresh, chopped for garnish
- Sea salt and black pepper to taste

Directions:
Clean your pinto beans with cold running tap water. Place all your ingredients into your instant pot, and secure the lid and set on Manual, for a cook time of 50-minutes. Release the pressure naturally for 10-minutes. Divide among serving bowls, and garnish with minced tomatoes and cilantro. Serve warm!

Nutritional Information per serving:
Calories: 178   Fat: 23g   Carbs: 16g   Protein: 29g

214. Potato Soup
Cook Time: 10 minutes
Servings: 4
Ingredients:
- 4 cups Yukon Gold Potatoes, diced
- ¼ cup bacon, chopped, cooked
- 16-ounces cream cheese
- 1 tablespoon of seasoned salt
- 1 ¼ cups onion, diced
- 4 cups chicken stock
- 5 teaspoons of garlic, minced
- ¼ cup cheddar cheese, shredded

Directions:
Add the chicken stock, garlic, seasoning, onion, and potatoes to your instant pot. Secure the lid, and choose the Soup setting for 10-minutes cook time. Release the pressure using quick-release. Stir in your cream cheese, until well blended. Divide into serving bowls, and garnish with shredded cheese and bacon. Serve hot!

Nutritional Information per serving:
Calories: 192   Fat: 11g   Carbs: 18g   Protein: 6g

215. Chicken, Ranch & Rice Soup
Cook Time: 13 minutes **Servings:** 8
Ingredients:
- 2 ½ cups celery, diced
- 2 tablespoons olive oil
- 1 ½ cups carrots, diced
- 1 ¼ cups onions, diced
- 1 tablespoon of Ranch dressing
- 2 tablespoons Dijon mustard
- 1 cup of cooked rice
- 2 ½ cups of chicken breasts, boneless, cooked diced
- 8 cups chicken broth/stock
- 3 teaspoons garlic cloves, minced
- Sea salt and black pepper to taste

Directions:
Set your instant pot to the sauté function, add the oil and heat it. Add the carrots, onions, celery, and cook for 2-minutes. Add the garlic and cook for another minute or so. Add the chicken, rice, mustard, ranch dressing, chicken stock, pepper and salt. Secure the lid and set to the Soup setting for a 10-minute cook time. Release the pressure naturally for 10-minutes. Divide among serving bowls. Serve hot!

Nutritional Information per serving:
Calories: 167   Fat: 23g   Carbs: 19g   Protein: 21g

216. Bean Soup with Pork
Cook Time: 23 minutes **Servings:** 12
Ingredients:
- 20-ounces of 15 Bean Soup mix
- 1 ¼ lbs. of pork chops, boneless
- 2 ½ cups carrots, diced
- 2 tablespoons Worcestershire sauce
- 1 cup onion, diced
- 1/3 cup bacon, diced, cooked
- 2 tablespoons of bacon fat
- ¼ cup parsley, fresh, chopped
- 4 cups chicken broth/stock
- 3 tablespoons lemon juice
- 1 tablespoon of chili powder
- 3 whole bay leaves
- 14-ounces of canned tomatoes, diced
- 4 teaspoons garlic cloves, minced
- 2 tablespoons Dijon mustard
- Sea salt and black pepper to taste

Directions:
Drain and rinse your soaked beans. Set to the side. Set your instant pot to the sauté mode, add half of the bacon drippings into your instant pot. Sear the pork chops on both sides in instant pot, then put them on a plate.
In the remaining bacon drippings, sauté the celery, onions, carrots and garlic for 3-minutes. Add the tomatoes and cook for another 2-minutes and stir. In your instant pot combine your beans, onion/tomato mixture, pork chops, bacon, bay leaves, mustard, chili powder, lemon juice, Worcestershire sauce, salt and pepper. Pour your chicken stock over the ingredients, and gently stir to combine. Seal the lid in place, set to Manual setting, and cook for 18-minutes. Release the pressure naturally for 15-minutes. Divide among serving bowls. Serve hot!

Nutritional Information per serving:
Calories: 183   Fat: 26g   Carbs: 20g   Protein: 24g

217. Hamburger Barley Vegetable Soup
Cook Time: 34 minutes
Servings: 4
Ingredients:
- 1 lb. ground hamburger
- 28-ounce can of Petite tomatoes, undrained
- ¼ cup celery, chopped
- 1 teaspoon garlic, minced
- ½ cup onion, chopped
- 5 cups beef broth
- 1 cup quick barley
- 2 medium potatoes, peeled, diced
- 12-ounce bag of frozen mixed vegetables
- ½ teaspoon basil, dried
- 4 cups cabbage, chopped
- 2 carrots, peeled, sliced
- Sea salt and black pepper to taste
- 2 tablespoons olive oil

Directions:
Set your instant pot to sauté mode, add the oil and heat it up. Add the hamburger and sauté it until it is no longer pink. Drain off the fat, on meat. Add the onion to instant pot and cook for 3-minutes. Add the garlic and cook for another 1-minute. Add the tomatoes, barley and beef broth. Set to the Soup setting with a cook time on high for 10-minutes. Release the pressure using quick-release. Add the vegetables and spices and stir. Place the lid onto the instant pot and set on Soup setting for another 15-minutes. Then use the quick-release again. Divide among serving bowls. Serve hot!

Nutritional Information per serving:
Calories: 204   Fat: 31g   Carbs: 19g   Protein: 37g

218. Black-Eyed Pea Soup
Cook Time: 19 minutes
Servings: 4
Ingredients:
- 1 smoked ham hock
- 3 large carrots, peeled, sliced
- 1 large onion, chopped
- 2 cups black-eyed peas, dried, picked over and rinsed
- 1 clove garlic, minced
- 5 cups chicken broth
- 10-ounces of frozen Okra, sliced, defrosted
- 2 tablespoons olive oil
- Sea salt and black pepper to taste

Directions:
Set your instant pot to the sauté mode, add the oil, and heat it up. Add the onion, cook for about 3-minutes, then add the garlic, and cook for 2-minutes more, stir. Add your peas, ham hock, broth. Secure the lid in place and on Manual setting cook on high for 10-minutes. Release the pressure using the quick-release. Remove the ham hock and add the carrots, and okra. Cut off the meat from ham hock. Add back to the instant pot and stir. Set on Simmer for 4-minutes. Divide among the serving bowls. Serve hot!

Nutritional Information per serving:
Calories: 163   Fat: 37g   Carbs: 28g   Protein: 41g

219. Curried Coconut Chicken Soup
Cook Time: 10 minutes
Servings: 8
Ingredients:
- 3 cups chicken breasts, cooked, diced
- 4 cups chicken stock
- 4 teaspoons garlic cloves, minced
- 1 tablespoon ginger, peeled, fresh, minced
- 3 cups red bell pepper, sliced
- 2 cups carrots, sliced
- 2 tablespoons olive oil
- 2 cups onions, diced
- 8 individual limes
- 2 cups of Basmati Rice, cooked
- 1 tablespoon curry powder
- 2 tablespoons soy sauce
- 1 ½ tablespoons lemongrass, chopped
- 2 tablespoons creamy peanut butter
- 1 cup of canned coconut milk
- 2 tablespoons Sriracha sauce
- ¼ cup cilantro, fresh, chopped
- Sea salt and black pepper to taste

Directions:
Set your instant pot to the sauté mode, add the oil and heat it up. Add onions, carrots, pepper, and cook for about 4-minutes. Add the curry powder, garlic and ginger and cook for another minute or so. Pour your broth, lemongrass, and salt into the instant pot. Add the chicken. Mix your coconut milk, peanut butter, soy sauce, Sriracha sauce in a bowl and at this mix to your instant pot. Secure the lid in place and set to Manual on high for 3-minutes. Release the pressure using quick-release. Stir in the cooked rice and cilantro. Divide into serving bowls, and garnish with lime wedges. Serve warm!

Nutritional Information per serving:
Calories: 152   Fat: 21g   Carbs: 18g   Protein: 23g

220. Split-Pea & Ham Soup
Cook Time: 17 minutes
Servings: 4
Ingredients:
- ½ cup ham, diced
- 5 cups vegetable stock
- 1 small onion, diced
- 2 cups dried peas
- Sea salt and pepper to taste

Directions:
Add all the ingredients into your instant pot and set it to the Manual mode for 17-minutes on high. Release the pressure using the quick-release. Divide among your serving bowls. Serve hot!

Nutritional Information per serving:
Calories: 122   Fat: 32g   Carbs: 25g   Protein: 31g

Chapter 8. Collection of Keto- Friendly Grain-Based Recipes

221. Chicken & Wild Rice Soup
Cook Time: 56 minutes   **Servings: 4**
Ingredients:
- 1 lb. chicken breasts, skinless, boneless, cut in half
- 4 carrots, peeled, chopped
- 2 egg yolks
- 4 cups chicken broth, divided
- 1 bay leaf
- 1 cup water
- 1 large zucchini, chopped
- ¾ cup wild rice-brown rice blend
- ½ teaspoon thyme, dried
- 1 tablespoon butter
- 2 tablespoons garlic-infused olive oil
- 1 small leek, green parts, sliced
- 3 tablespoons lemon juice
- Sea salt and black pepper to taste
- Parmesan cheese, grated for garnish
- Italian parsley, fresh, chopped for garnish

Directions:
Set your instant pot to the sauté mode, add the oil and heat it. Sauté the leek, in oil, seasoned with salt and pepper for 6-minutes. Place the chicken breasts on a cutting board to rest for a few minutes

Shred the chicken and add to the instant pot and brown meat on all sides for 5-minutes. Transfer chicken and leek to a bowl. Whisk the egg yolks, and pour in ½ a cup of chicken broth, whisking to temper the yolks. Add the yolk mixture to the instant pot along with the rest of the ingredients and stir. Return the shredded chicken and leeks to the instant pot and secure the lid. Set on Manual setting on high with a cook time of 45-minutes. Divide among serving bowls, and garnish with grated parmesan and fresh, chopped Italian parsley. Serve hot!

Nutritional Information per serving:
Calories: 227   Fat: 1g   Fiber: 2g   Carbs: 24g   Protein: 16g

222. Quinoa Beef Pot
Cook Time: 20 minutes   **Servings: 1**
Ingredients:
- 2 tablespoons of any quinoa, rinsed
- 2 tablespoons cheddar cheese, diced
- 2 tablespoons baby spinach, fresh, chopped
- 2 tablespoons beef, shredded. cooked
- 1 tablespoon ghee, melted
- Grated peel of ½ a lime and a dash of its juice
- 1 fluid ounce of water
- Sea salt and black pepper to taste

Directions:
Before cooking, rinse the quinoa under running water, until it is clear. Pour the quinoa, salt, water, and lime zest into the instant pot. Close the instant pot lid, and press the Manual button, and set it for 1-minute of pressure cooking. When the cooking is done, release the pressure naturally for 10-minutes. Add some lime juice, ghee, shredded beef,

pepper, cheese, spinach and mix. You can serve it at room temperature or you may decide to serve it at room temperature or place it in the fridge to cool before serving.
Nutritional Information per serving:
Calories: 636   Fat: 61g   Carbs: 9g   Protein: 14g

---

223. Keto Clam Chowder
Cook Time: 20 minutes   **Servings: 2**
Ingredients:

- 4 tablespoons of clams
- The juice contained from the clam jar
  in addition to water
- 2 tablespoons bacon, diced
- 4 tablespoons heavy cream
- 2 tablespoons of flour
- 2 tablespoons ghee
- 2 tablespoons butter
- 4 tablespoons sour cream
- 1 pinch of cayenne pepper, crushed
- 1 pinch of thyme, dried
- 1 bay leaf
- 4 tablespoons white wine
- 4 tablespoons onion, finely chopped

Directions:
Set your instant pot to the sauté mode, add the ghee and heat it. Add the bacon, without the lid. When the bacon begins to release fat and starts to sizzle, add the salt, pepper, onion, and cook for 5-minutes and stir. Add the wine into the instant pot once the onion has dried and stir. Allow the wine to evaporate almost completely, add the thyme, bay leaf, and cayenne pepper.
Close the lid on the instant pot and set to Manual on high for a 5-minute cook time. Release the pressure naturally for 10-minutes. Prepare the roux that will thicken the clam chowder in a pan over a low flame. Mix in the flour with butter, stirring constantly with a wooden spoon until it thickens. Add the roux, heavy cream, sour cream, add drain the clams and set them in a bowl. Set the instant pot on sauté mode and cook the ingredients for 5-minutes, stirring constantly. Then add the clams back in and stir well. Divide into serving bowls. Serve warm!
Nutritional Information per serving:
Calories: 580   Fat: 47g   Carbs: 12g   Protein: 25g

---

224. Stuffed Cuttlefish
Cook Time: 20 minutes   **Servings: 3**
Ingredients:

- 3 small cuttlefish, cleaned
- 2 tablespoons of shallot, chopped
- 1 tablespoon of tomato sauce
- 2 tablespoons of olive oil

For the Dip:

- 1 tablespoon anise seeds
- 1 pinch of chili powder

- 1 pinch of parsley, dried
- 2 tablespoons of flour
- 2 bay leaves
- 2 tablespoons water

- 2 tablespoons of mayonnaise

Directions:

Add all the ingredients in a mixer, except the sauce, bay leaves, water, and cuttlefish. Make the mixture homogenous. Take the cuttlefish and fill with the mixture. Put the sauce on the bottom of the instant pot, add some salt, bay leaves. Add the cuttlefish and water. Close the lid to instant pot, set to the Manual setting for 10-minutes cook time. In the meantime, prepare the dip by combining the ingredients in a small bowl. Release the pressure use the quick-release. Divide among serving plates, drizzle the sauce over fish and serve with dip. Serve warm!

Nutritional Information per serving:
Calories: 590   Fat: 47.92 g   Carbs: 10g   Protein: 27g

225. *Saffron Chicken*
Cook Time: *14 minutes*   **Servings: *2***
Ingredients:

- 1 lb. chicken, skinless, boneless, cut into small strips
- 3 tablespoons olive oil
- 2 tablespoons flour
- 1 teaspoon saffron
- 1 pinch of sea salt
- 1 teaspoon rosemary needles
- 2 tablespoons of cocoa butter
- 2 tablespoons of white onion, diced
- 4 tablespoons water
- 2 teaspoons of triple tomato concentrate

Directions:
Cover the chicken strips with the flour. Set your instant pot to the sauté mode, add the oil to pot and heat it. Brown the chicken strips on all sides for 5-minutes. Add water, salt and saffron and stir. Close the lid and set to Manual setting on high with a cook time of 14-minutes. Release the pressure naturally for 10-minutes. Remove the chicken from pot, set to sauté mode to reduce the sauce. Smear the cocoa butter over the chicken. Divide among serving plates, and drizzle with sauce. Serve warm!

Nutritional Information per serving:
Calories: 713   Fat: 63g   Carbs: 9g   Protein: 36g

226. *Sesame Meatball Stew*
Cook Time: *30 minutes*   **Servings: *2***
Ingredients:

For the Meatballs:
- 1 tablespoon cheddar cheese, grated
- 2 tablespoons of zucchini, grated
- 1 small egg
- 1 pinch of fresh basil, chopped
- 2 tablespoons olive oil

For the Stew:
- 1 clove of garlic, minced
- 4 tablespoons tomato sauce

- 1 tablespoon of sesame seeds
- 4 tablespoons flour
- 4 tablespoons mozzarella cheese
- Dash of salt
- 1 tablespoon parsley, dried

- ½ small onion, finely chopped

Directions:

Grate the zucchini, and add a little salt in a bowl, and flour, mix. Add the egg and grated cheddar cheese and mix well. Cut the mozzarella into cubes. Take a little of the zucchini dough and form a meatball, add three cubes of mozzarella into the middle. Add the sesame seeds, parsley in a small bowl. Roll the zucchini meatball in the sesame seeds. Prepare a baking sheet with baking paper and place the meatballs on top of it. Sprinkle the meatballs with olive oil and bake at 400° Fahrenheit for 20-minutes. Pour the tomato sauce, garlic, and onion into your instant pot. Add the meatballs and stir. Set to the Meat/Stew setting for 10-minutes. Release the pressure naturally for 10-minutes. Divide among serving plates, drizzle with sauce. Serve warm!

Nutritional Information per serving:
Calories: 696   Fat: 140g   Carbs: 15g   Protein: 18g

---

227. Burrito with Chili Colorado
Cook Time: 40 minutes
Servings: 2
Ingredients:

- 4 tablespoons of scaled cheese
- 1 cup of water
- 4 teaspoons meat broth

For the Tortillas:

- 2 tablespoons of ghee
- 1 pinch of baking powder
- 4 tablespoons of water

- 4 tablespoons of enchilada sauce
- 1 cup roasted beef chops, boneless, cubed

- 4 tablespoons of coconut flour
- 1 egg white

Directions:
First to prepare your tortillas: Add the egg whites, coconut flour, baking powder, ghee, and water in a mixing bowl. Mix well. Heat a skillet (the size that you want your tortillas to be) on low heat. Wait until the skillet is hot, spray it with cooking spray, and drop some of the mix into the center. Tilt the skillet to spread the batter as thin as possible. Allow it to cook for a few minutes, until it starts to rise/bubble then flip it over to the other side. Flip and cook for an additional minute. Repeat the process until you have used up all the batter.

Prepare the stuffing: In your instant pot add the beef, half of the enchilada sauce, broth, and water, stir. Press the Manual setting and set for a cook time of 30-minutes. Release the pressure naturally for 10-minutes. Place the tortillas on an aluminum coated baking pan adding some beef to center of tortilla, fold the ends upwards and roll into a burrito. Repeat with other tortillas, sprinkle tops with the remaining enchilada sauce, and cheese shavings. Grill until cheese bubbles for about 4-minutes.

Nutritional Information per serving:
Calories: 502   Fat: 67g   Carbs: 8.96g   Protein: 33.82g

228. Sour Dumplings
Cook Time: 45 minutes **Servings:** 4
Ingredients:
- ½ cup sour cream
- 1 cup broth
- 4 tablespoons coconut oil
- 4 tablespoons tomato paste
- Salt and black pepper to taste
- 4 tablespoons of coconut flour
- 2 cloves of garlic, minced
- 1 small onion, minced
- 2 eggs
- 2 strips of bacon, minced
- 1 lb. ground pork

Directions:
In a mixing bowl mix the bacon, egg, onion, flour, seasonings, and garlic. Shape into small balls and place on a flat surface. Set your instant pot to the sauté mode, add the coconut oil and heat it. Place the meatballs into the pot, evenly spaced. Cook for 5-minutes, browning all sides of meatballs. Once they are browned remove them and set them on a plate. Add broth to pot, add meatballs back into pot. Close the lid and set pot on Manual setting for 7-minutes. After cook time is complete, release the pressure using the quick-release. Remove the meatballs from pot. Set instant pot back on to sauté mode. Add the sour cream, salt and pepper and stir the pots contents. Allow the to heat for 2-minutes. Add the meatballs back into the sauce and stir. Remove meatballs and sauce and place in bowls. Serve warm.

Nutritional Information per serving:
Calories: 608   Fat: 45g   Carbs: 12g   Protein: 41g

229. Sausage Radish Cakes
Cook Time: 42 minutes **Servings:** 2
Ingredients:
- ½ cup Chinese radish, peeled and chopped, cooked
- 1 teaspoon ginger, chopped
- 2 tablespoons of olive oil
- ½ cup of sausage, drained, minced
- 4 tablespoons coconut flour
- 1 cup water
- 1 cup chicken broth
- 2 tablespoons spring onions, chopped
- Pinch of salt

Directions:
Set your instant pot to the sauté mode, add the oil and heat it. Add the ginger, spring onions, and chopped sausage and cook for 5-minutes stirring often. Add the chopped Chinese radishes, and brown for 2-minutes. In a bowl mix the flour and water. Add mixture from instant pot into mixing bowl with flour and water. Add mix into a small oven-dish. Add trivet to instant pot, add the water. Place the oven-dish onto the trivet, set instant pot to Steam for 35-minutes. Release the pressure naturally for 10-minutes. Remove the steamed radish cake from instant pot. Allow for it to cool and refrigerate for a few hours. Serve room temperature.

Nutritional Information per serving:
Calories: 692   Fat: 60g   Carbs: 10g   Protein: 26g

230. Seafood Jambalaya

Cook Time: 45 minutes
Servings: 4
Ingredients:

- 4-ounces cod, chopped
- 4-ounces shrimp, peeled, deveined
- 1 cup brown rice, cooked
- 1 cup chicken broth
- ½ teaspoon cumin, ground
- 1 tablespoon parsley, chopped
- Sea salt and black pepper to taste
- 1 lb. Roma tomatoes, peeled, crushed
- 1 cup Russet potatoes, chopped
- ¼ cup yellow onion, diced
- ½ teaspoon cayenne pepper
- 2 teaspoons paprika, ground
- ¼ cup carrots, chopped
- 6 ½-ounces of crab meat

Directions:
Combine all ingredients in your instant pot, and cook on Meat/Stew setting for 45-minutes. Divide into serving bowls, garnish with fresh chopped parsley. Serve hot!

Nutritional Information per serving:
Calories: 137   Fat: 2g   Carbs: 13g   Protein: 20g

231. Shredded Pork Fajitas
Cook Time: 40 minutes
Servings: 4
Ingredients:
- 1lb. stewing pork, chopped
- 8 whole-wheat fajitas
- ½ small onion, sliced
- 1 green pepper, diced
- 1 jalapeno, minced
- 1 tablespoon olive oil
- ½ teaspoon cumin, ground
- Sea salt and black pepper to taste
- 2 cloves garlic, minced

Directions:
Combine all the ingredients in your instant pot, except the fajitas. Cook on Manual setting for 40-minutes on high. Release the pressure naturally for 10-minutes. Remove the pork to a cutting board and shred it with two forks, then add back to the instant pot and stir. Place fajitas on serving plates and top with pork mix from instant pot and roll up. Serve warm!

Nutritional Information per serving:
Calories: 238   Fat: 17g   Carbs: 18g   Protein: 21g

232. Sausage Gumbo

Cook Time: 35 minutes **Servings:** 6

Ingredients:
- 8-ounces, Andouille sausage, whole
- 4 cups pork stock
- 1 cup of brown rice, cooked
- 1 tablespoon thyme, fresh, chopped
- ½ teaspoon ginger, ground
- ½ teaspoon cumin, ground
- ½ teaspoon cayenne pepper, ground
- 1 teaspoon paprika, ground
- Sea salt and black pepper to taste
- 2 cups Roma tomatoes, peeled and diced
- ¼ cup yellow onion, sliced

Directions:
Combine all the ingredients in your instant pot, except the brown rice. Cook on Manual setting on high for a cook time of 35-minutes. Release the pressure naturally for 10-minutes. Add in the cooked brown rice and mix well. Spoon into serving bowls, topped with fresh chopped thyme for garnish. Serve warm!

Nutritional Information per serving:
Calories: 118   Fat: 4g   Carbs: 13g   Protein: 10g

233. Pork Fried Whole Grain Rice

Cooking Time: 45 minutes **Servings:** 4

Ingredients:
- 1lb. stewing pork, diced
- 1 tablespoon green onion, chopped
- 2 eggs, scrambled
- ½ teaspoon ginger, ground
- ½ teaspoon cumin, ground
- 1 clove garlic, minced
- 1 teaspoon rice vinegar
- 2 cups whole grain rice, cooked
- ¼ cup green beans, diced
- ¼ cup carrots, diced
- ¼ cup yellow onion, diced

Directions:
Add all the ingredients to your instant pot, except for eggs and green onion. Cook on Manual setting for 45-minutes. Release the pressure naturally for 10-minutes. Stir in the scrambled eggs and green onions. Divide among serving dishes. Serve warm!

Nutritional Information per serving:
Calories: 218   Fat: 16g   Carbs: 24g   Protein: 21g

234. Bacon Wrapped Jalapenos

Cook Time: 32 minutes **Servings:** 4

Ingredients:
- 12 large jalapenos
- 6 slices of bacon
- ½ teaspoon salt
- ½ tablespoon olive oil
- ½ red bell pepper, diced
- ½ cup brown rice, cooked

Directions:

Slice the tops off the jalapenos, then take a spoon to remove and scoop out the seeds. Set the hollowed jalapenos aside. In a mixing bowl, combine the cooked brown rice, olive oil, bell pepper, and salt. Stuff the mixture into each jalapeno. Slice each piece of bacon in half longways, and wrap one slice around each jalapeno, use toothpick to hold in place. Place the wrapped jalapenos gently inside your instant pot. Cook on Manual setting for 32-minutes. Release the pressure naturally for 15-minutes. Divide among serving plates. Serve warm!

Nutritional Information per serving:
Calories: 187   Fat: 18g   Carbs: 12g   Protein: 14g

---

235. *Shredded Beef Tacos*
Cook Time: 35 minutes   **Servings: 2**
Ingredients:
- 6-ounces beef tenderloin, chopped
- 4 taco shells
- 1 jalapeno, diced
- ½ red bell pepper, sliced
- 1 tsp. red wine vinegar
- ½ tsp. cumin, ground
- 2 cloves garlic, minced
- Salt and black pepper to taste

Directions:
Combine all your ingredients in your instant pot, except for the taco shells. Set your instant pot to the Manual setting on a high cook time of 35-minutes. Once the cook time is completed, release the pressure naturally for 10-minutes. Shred the beef with a pair of forks. Scoop the mixture into the taco shells and serve warm.

Nutritional Information per serving:
Calories: 299   Fat: 21g   Carbs: 13g   Protein: 22g

---

236. *Beef Stuffed Eggplant*
Cooking Time: 35 minutes   **Servings: 4**
Ingredients:
- 1 tablespoon olive oil
- ¼ cup yellow onion, diced
- ½ cup brown rice
- ½ tablespoon mint, fresh, chopped
- 1 tablespoon basil, fresh, chopped
- Sea salt and black pepper to taste
- 8-ounces lean ground beef, browned
- 1 eggplant, cut in half vertically and horizontally (4-pieces)

Directions:
Scoop out the insides of the eggplant using a spoon. Leave each piece with a ½-inch thick wall. Dice the removed fruit. Combine the diced eggplant with the remaining ingredients (except the olive oil) in a mixing bowl. Fill each eggplant slice with the mixture. Place the stuffed eggplants into your instant pot, and drizzle with olive oil over each piece. Set to Manual setting for a cook time of 35-minutes. When cooking is completed, release the pressure naturally for 10-minutes. Divide among serving plates. Serve warm!

Nutritional Information per serving:
Calories: 284   Fat: 12g   Carbs: 26g   Protein: 22g

237. Spicy Fire Chicken with Rice
Cook Time: 45 minutes **Servings:** 2
Ingredients:
- 8-ounces chicken breasts, skinless, boneless, chopped
- 1 red chili, diced
- 1 teaspoon crushed red pepper
- ½ teaspoon paprika, ground
- Salt and black pepper to taste
- ½ tablespoon olive oil
- 2 cups brown rice, cooked

Directions:
Combine all your ingredients in your instant pot except for the rice. Stir and set to Meat/Stew setting for 45-minutes. When the cooking is completed, release the pressure naturally for 15-minutes. Serve on top of a bed of rice the spicy fire chicken. Serve warm.

Nutritional Information per serving:
Calories: 288 Fat: 7.5g Carbs: 13g Protein: 40g

238. Spiced Apple & Walnut Chicken
Cook Time: 40 minutes **Servings:** 2
Ingredients:
- 8-ounces chicken breast, skinless, boneless, chopped
- ¼ cup walnuts, chopped
- ½ teaspoon nutmeg, ground
- ½ teaspoon ginger, ground
- 1 small apple, peeled and diced
- 1 tablespoon ghee
- Salt and black pepper to taste
- 2 cups brown rice, cooked

Directions:
Set your instant pot to the sauté mode, and add the ghee and heat it. Add the chicken to instant pot and cook for 5-minutes, browning all sides of meat. Add the remaining ingredients to pot, except cooked brown rice. Set the setting to Manual for a cook time of 35-minutes. When the cook time has completed, release the pressure naturally for 10-minutes. Serve on a bed of brown rice. Serve warm!

Nutritional Information per serving:
Calories: 296 Fat: 8g Carbs: 18g bProtein: 49g

239. Pulled Chicken in Soft Whole Wheat Tacos
Cook Time: 38 minutes **Servings:** 6
Ingredients:
- 1 lb. chicken breast, skinless, boneless, cubed
- ½ cup chicken broth
- 2 tablespoons cilantro, chopped, fresh
- ½ teaspoon cayenne pepper, ground
- Salt and black pepper to taste
- ½ teaspoon cumin
- 2 Roma tomatoes, peeled, diced
- ¼ red onion, diced
- ½ green bell pepper, sliced
- ½ red bell pepper, sliced
- ¼ yellow onion, diced
- ½ teaspoon mustard powder, ground

- 1 tablespoon coconut oil

Directions:
Set your instant pot to the sauté mode, add the coconut oil and heat it up. Add the chicken and cook for 5-minutes, stir. Add bell peppers, onion and cook for an additional 3-minutes. Add the remaining ingredients to instant pot, except the soft tacos. Secure the lid of instant pot in place, and set to Manual setting for 30-minutes on high cook time. When the cook time is complete, release the pressure naturally for 10-minutes. Spoon the chicken mix on top of soft tacos. Serve warm!

Nutritional Information per serving:
Calories: 158   Fat: 3.5g   Carbs: 17g   Protein: 25g

240. *Pesto Chicken & Whole Wheat Pasta*

Cook Time: 35 minutes   **Servings: 2**

Ingredients:
- 2 cups whole wheat pasta, cooked
- 2 chicken breasts, skinless, boneless
- 2 tablespoons pesto sauce
- 2 cloves garlic, minced
- Sal and black pepper to taste
- ½ cup of parsley, fresh, chopped for garnish

Directions:
Mix the seasonings together, then run them into each chicken breast. Place the chicken breasts inside instant pot, add a tablespoon of pesto on top of each piece of chicken. Set to Manual setting on high cook time of 35-minutes. When the cooking is completed, release the pressure naturally for 10-minutes. Serve on top of a bed of whole wheat pasta. Garnish with fresh chopped pasta. Serve warm!

Nutritional Information per serving:
Calories: 258   Fat: 6g   Carbs: 10g   Protein: 44g

241. *Pasta & Brown Turkey Sauce*

Cook Time: 35 minutes   **Servings: 4**

Ingredients:
- 1 cup cooked turkey, shredded
- ¼ cup cashew cream
- ½ cup baby portabella mushrooms, chopped
- ¼ cup carrots, chopped
- ¼ cup yellow onion, diced
- 1 clove garlic, minced
- 2 cups whole wheat pasta, cooked
- 1 teaspoon rosemary, fresh, chopped

Directions:
Combine all the ingredients, except for the pasta in your instant pot. Set to manual setting on a low cook time of 35-minutes. Once the cook time is completed, release the pressure naturally for 10-minutes. Serve over a bed of whole wheat pasta, and garnish with fresh, chopped rosemary. Serve warm!

Nutritional Information per serving:
Calories: 218   Fat: 7g   Carbs: 12g   Protein: 34g

242. Orange Chicken Drumsticks & Rice
Cook Time: 40 minutes **Servings:** 4
Ingredients:
- 1 lb. of chicken drumsticks
- 1 tablespoon olive oil
- ½ tablespoon basil, fresh, chopped
- ½ tablespoon parsley, fresh, chopped
- 1 orange, thin round slices
- 1 teaspoon rosemary, fresh, chopped for garnish
- 1 clove garlic, minced
- Salt and black pepper to taste
- 2 cups brown rice

Directions:
Toss the drumsticks, seasonings (except rosemary), and oil and coat drumsticks in mix. Place the drumsticks into your instant pot, and evenly distribute the orange slices evenly around them. Cook on Manual setting on high for a cook time of 40-minutes. Serve on a bed of rice, and garnish with fresh, chopped rosemary. Serve warm!

Nutritional Information per serving:
Calories: 256   Fat: 1g   Carbs: 9g   Protein: 38g

243. Mediterranean Mint & Basil Chicken & Rice
Cook Time: 40 minutes **Servings:** 2
Ingredients:
- 2 chicken breasts, skinless, boneless, cubed
- 2 teaspoons mint, fresh, chopped for garnish
- 1 cup arugula, fresh, chopped
- ½ red bell pepper, sliced
- 1 tablespoon basil, chopped
- ½ yellow onion, diced
- Salt and black pepper to taste
- 2 cups brown rice, cooked

Directions:
Add all your ingredients into your instant pot, except for the arugula and rice. Cook on Manual setting on a high cook time of 40-minutes. When the cook time is completed, release the pressure naturally for 10-minutes. Add the arugula to pot and stir in with chicken mixture. Serve on top of a bed of rice, add fresh, chopped mint as garnish. Serve warm!

Nutritional Information per serving:
Calories: 211   Fat: 5g   Carbs: 12g   Protein: 43g

244. Mango Citrus Chicken & Rice
Cook Time: 40 minutes **Servings:** 2
Ingredients:
- 2 chicken breasts, skinless, boneless, chopped
- 1 cup long-grain rice
- 1 cup mango, fresh, chopped
- 1 tablespoon orange juice, fresh squeezed
- 1 clove garlic, minced
- ½ teaspoon crushed red pepper
- Salt and black pepper to taste
- 1 tablespoon olive oil
- 1 cup arugula, fresh
- ¼ cup yellow onion, diced

- 2 teaspoons mint, fresh, chopped for garnish

Directions:
Combine all the ingredients, except for mango and rice in your instant pot. Set to Manual setting for a high cook time of 40-minutes. When the cook time is completed, release the pressure naturally for 15-minutes. Gently stir in the mango to the instant pot. Serve over a bed of rice, garnish with fresh, chopped mint. Serve warm!

Nutritional Information per serving:
Calories: 295   Fat: 12g   Carbs: 26g   Protein: 40g

---

245. *Lemon, Capers, Chicken & Chinese Black Rice*
Cook Time: 35 minutes   **Servings:** 2

Ingredients:
- 2 chicken breasts, boneless, skinless
- 4 thin slices lemon
- 1 sprig of rosemary
- 1 tablespoon capers
- 2 garlic cloves, minced
- ½ tablespoon olive oil
- 2 cups Chinese black rice, cooked
- Salt and black pepper to taste

Directions:
Coat the chicken breasts evenly with salt, pepper, and olive oil. Place the chicken breasts into your instant pot, sprinkle with minced garlic, and capers. Lay a sprig of rosemary in the middle of instant pot, and place two lemon slices on each chicken breast. Cook on Manual setting for a high cook time of 35-minutes. When the cook time is completed, release the pressure naturally for 10-minutes. Serve over a bed of Chinese black rice. Serve warm!

Nutritional Information per serving:
Calories: 278   Fat: 8g   Carbs: 12g   Protein: 39g

---

246. *Jerk Chicken Strips & Wild Rice*
Cook Time: 40 minutes   **Servings:** 2

Ingredients:
- 2 chicken breasts, boneless, skinless cut into slices or strips
- 2 cups wild rice, cooked
- ½ tablespoon olive oil
- ½ tablespoon red wine vinegar
- 1 small habanero chili, ground into a paste
- ¼ teaspoon nutmeg, ground
- ¼ teaspoon ginger, ground
- ½ teaspoon cumin, ground
- ½ teaspoon cayenne pepper, ground
- Salt and black pepper to taste
- 2 tablespoons cilantro, fresh, chopped for garnish

Directions:
Combine all the ingredients in your instant pot, except the wild rice. Set to Manual setting and cook on high for a cook time of 40-minutes. When the cook time is completed, release the pressure naturally for 15-minutes. Serve over a bed of wild rice, and garnish with fresh, chopped cilantro.

Nutritional Information per serving:
Calories: 235   Fat: 7.5g   Carbs: 9g   Protein: 40g

247. *Greek Chicken & Sprouted Rice*
Cook Time: 35 minutes   **Servings:** 2
Ingredients:
- 2 chicken breasts, boneless, skinless
- 2 cups sprouted rice, cooked
- ½ red bell pepper, chopped
- 2 tablespoons Kalamata olives, chopped
- ¼ cup artichoke hearts, chopped
- 1 teaspoon basil, fresh, chopped
- 1 teaspoon oregano, fresh, chopped
- Salt and black pepper to taste
- ½ tablespoon olive oil
- 2 teaspoons of parsley, fresh, chopped for garnish

Directions:
Coat the chicken breasts evenly with the olive oil and seasonings. Place them into your instant pot, and pour the remaining ingredients over them, except the sprouted rice. Set the instant pot to the Manual setting on high with a cook time of 35-minutes. When the cook time is completed, release the pressure using the quick-release. Serve alongside the sprouted rice, and garnish with fresh, chopped parsley. Serve warm!

Nutritional Information per serving:
Calories: 275   Fat: 8g   Carbs: 18g   Protein: 41g

248. *Chicken Fried Wild Rice*
Cook Time: 25 minutes   **Servings:** 4
Ingredients:
- 2 cups wild rice, cooked
- 1 cup cooked chicken breast, chopped
- 1 clove garlic, minced
- 1 teaspoon rice vinegar
- 1 tablespoon green onion, chopped
- ¼ cup scrambled eggs
- ¼ cup green beans, chopped
- ½ red bell pepper, diced
- ¼ cup carrots, diced
- Salt and black pepper to taste
- 2 teaspoons cilantro, fresh chopped for garnish

Directions:
Combine all the ingredients in your instant pot, except for the wild rice. Set the instant pot to Manual on a high cook time of 25-minutes. When the cook time is completed, release the pressure using the quick-release. Add the wild rice into the instant pot and stir to blend. Divide among serving plates, and top with fresh, chopped parsley for garnish. Serve warm!

Nutritional Information per serving:
Calories: 112   Fat: 6g   Carbs: 22g   Protein: 21g

249. *Stuffed Bell Peppers*
Cook Time: 40 minutes   **Servings:** 4
Ingredients:
- 4 green bell peppers
- 1 cup of brown rice
- ¼ cup eggplant, diced
- 1 tablespoon olive oil

- ½ tablespoon basil, fresh, chopped
- 1 teaspoon paprika, ground
- 1 clove garlic, minced
- Salt and black pepper to taste
- ¼ cup butternut squash, diced

Directions:
Slice the tops off the bell peppers and scoop out the seeds, and discard. Dice the tops that were sliced off. In a bowl combine chopped bell pepper tops with other ingredients. Stuff each bell pepper as much as you can with the filling mixture. Place each bell pepper inside of your instant pot. Pour about ½ an inch of water in bottom of pot. Set to Manual setting for a cook time of 40-minutes. When the cook time is completed, release the pressure naturally for 15-minutes. Divide among serving bowls. Serve warm!

Nutritional Information per serving:
Calories: 71   Fat: 1g   Carbs: 13g   Protein: 4g

250. Chipotle Tacos
Cook Time: 22 minutes
Servings: 2
Ingredients:
- ½ cup black beans, cooked
- 2 tablespoons chili sauce
- ½ cup water
- ½ teaspoon salt
- ½ teaspoon cinnamon powder
- ¼ cup sweet corn kernels
- 4 tacos
- 4 leaves of spinach, finely, chopped

Directions:
Combine all your ingredients into your instant pot, except the tacos. Close the lid and set to Manual setting for 22-minutes. When the cook time is completed, release the pressure naturally for 10-minutes. Fill the tacos with the mixture in instant pot mixture and garnish with some finely chopped spinach. Serve warm!

Nutritional Information per serving:
Calories: 202   Fat: 5g   Carbs: 8g   Protein: 11g

251. Breakfast Burritos
Cook Time: 24 minutes
Servings: 4
Ingredients:
- ½ cup lentils
- 1 teaspoon coconut oil
- 2 avocados, chopped
- Salt and black pepper to taste
- ¼ cup mushrooms, diced
- 1 green bell pepper, chopped
- ¼ cup sundried tomatoes, chopped
- 2 garlic cloves, minced
- ½ cup tomato puree
- 4 whole wheat tortillas
- ½ cup yellow onions, diced

Directions:
Set your instant pot to the sauté mode, add the onions to instant pot and sauté for 4-minutes. Add the rest of the ingredients, except the tortillas, and set to Manual setting on a cook time of 20-minutes. When the cook time is complete, release the pressure naturally for 10-minutes. Serve the mixture in tortillas. Serve warm!

Nutritional Information per serving:
Calories: 232 Fat: 11g Carbs: 14g Protein: 29g

---

252. *Wild Mushroom Rice*
Cook Time: 13 minutes
Servings: 2
Ingredients:
- 1 cup long grain rice
- ½ cup vegetable stock
- ½ cup water
- 1 teaspoon salt
- ½ cup Portobello mushrooms, diced
- 2 onions, finely chopped
- 1 teaspoon olive oil

Directions:
Set your instant pot to sauté mode, add the oil and heat it. Sauté the mushrooms, and onions for 3-minutes. Add the rice and stir for about 30-seconds. Add remaining ingredients, set instant pot to the rice setting for a cook-time of 10-minutes. Release the pressure naturally for 10-minutes. Serve the rice in a large bowl. Serve warm!

Nutritional Information per serving:
Calories: 163 Fat: 6g Carbs: 9g Protein: 11g

---

253. *Spiach Casserole*
Cook Time: 23 minutes
Servings: 4
Ingredients:
- 1/8 cup whole wheat pastry flour
- 1 cube vegetable bouillon
- 4 tablespoons olive oil
- 1 tablespoon vegetarian gravy (chicken flavor)
- 1 tablespoon nutritional yeast
- 4 tablespoons barbecue sauce (hickory
- 1 tablespoon light miso paste
- 1 lb. firm tofu (crumbled)
- ½ lb. mushrooms, sliced
- 1 teaspoon paprika
- 1 cup corn kernels
- 8 whole black peppercorns
- 1 bay leaf
- 1 garlic clove, crushed
- 1 tablespoon tamari
- ¾ cup red onion, diced
- 1 yellow onion, chopped
- 1 bunch parsley, fresh, chopped
- 1 celery stalk, chopped
- 1 cup spinach, chopped
- 2 cups Wehani rice, cooked

Directions:
Set your instant pot to sauté mode, add the oil and heat it up. Add the mushrooms, garlic, and onions, cook for 3-minutes. Set the instant pot to Manual setting on high with a cook time of 20-minutes. Add the gravy mix, tofu, paprika, yeast, tamari and barbeque sauce and mix well. Release the pressure naturally for 10-minutes. Add in the spinach and cooked rice, and corn, stir well. Divide up into serving bowls. Serve warm!

Nutritional Information per serving:
Calories: 232 Fat: 8g Carbs: 14g Protein: 10g

254. Mexican Rice
Cook Time: 30 minutes
Servings: 6
Ingredients:
- 2 cups brown basmati rice
- 1 small jalapeno
- 3 cloves garlic, minced
- Salt and black pepper to taste
- 2 cups water
- ½ white onion, chopped
- ½ cup tomato paste
- 2 tablespoons olive oil

Directions:
Set the instant pot to the sauté mode, add the oil and heat it. Add the onion, rice, garlic and some salt. Sauté for 4-minutes or until fragrant. Mix the water and tomato paste in a bowl until they are well combined, pour mix into instant pot, throw in whole jalapeno. Set to Manual setting on high cook time of 22-minutes. When the cook time is completed, release the pressure naturally for 15-minutes. Using a fork, fluff the rice then serve hot!

Nutritional Information per serving:
Calories: 253   Fat: 1.8g   Carbs: 53.7g   Protein: 5.9g

255. Rice Pilaf
Cook Time: 15 minutes
Servings: 4
Ingredients:
- 2 ½ cups wild rice
- 2 ½ cups chicken stock
- 1 cup leftover cooked, meat, chopped
- 1 tablespoon oyster sauce
- Green onions, chopped for garnish
- 1 tablespoon rice wine
- 1 tablespoon olive oil
- 1 lb. white mushrooms, halved
- 2 carrots, chopped
- 2 tablespoon soy sauce
- 3 cups kale, chopped
- 1 lb. green beans, chopped

Directions:
Rinse the rice with tap water about three times. Drain excess water. Combine the rice with stock in your instant pot, along with rest of ingredients except kale and green onions. Set your pot to manual setting for 15-minutes. When cooking is completed, release the pressure using the quick-release. Gently stir in the chopped kale. Divide among serving bowls, and garnish with chopped green onions. Serve warm

Nutritional Information per serving:
Calories: 417   Fat: 5.6g   Carbs: 32g   Protein: 24g

256. Red Beans Over Sprouted Brown Rice
Cook Time: 53 minutes **Servings:** 8
Ingredients:
- 1 lb. dry red kidney beans
- 1 red bell pepper, diced
- 1 yellow onion, diced
- 1 ½ lb. smoked ham, cubed
- Salt and black pepper to taste
- 6 cups water, divided
- 3 garlic cloves, minced
- 3 stalks celery, chopped
- 2 tablespoons olive oil
- 2 bay leaves
- ¼ teaspoon cayenne pepper
- ½ teaspoon thyme, dried
- 2 cups sprouted brown rice

Directions:
Add two cups of water, and two cups of sprouted brown rice to your instant pot. Set it to the rice setting for 10-minutes. When rice is cooked remove from instant pot and place in large bowl. Clean instant pot. Set the instant pot to the sauté mode, add the oil and heat it. Add the onion, celery, pepper, and cook for 5-minutes. Add the garlic and meat and cook for an additional 3-minutes, stir well.

Rinse the kidney beans and drain. Add all the ingredients into pot, except the cooked rice in bowl. Set the instant pot to Manual setting on high with a cook time of 45-minutes. Release the pressure naturally for 15-minutes. Mash the beans into a creamy gravy and serve over a bed of sprouted rice. Serve warm!

Nutritional Information per serving:
Calories: 369 Fat: 11g Carbs: 32g Protein: 27g

257. Israeli Couscous
Cook Time: 5 minutes **Servings:** 10
Ingredients:
- 1 (16-ounce) package of Israeli couscous
- 2 tablespoons butter
- 2 ½ cups chicken broth
- Salt and black pepper to taste

Directions:
Set your instant pot to the sauté mode, add the butter and heat it. Add the broth and couscous, stir to combine. Close the lid and set to Manual setting on high with a cook time of 5-minutes. When the cook time is completed, release the pressure using quick-release. Fluff the couscous with a fork, season with salt and pepper. Serve as a side dish. Serve warm!

Nutritional Information per serving:
Calories: 201 Fat: 2g Carbs: 30g Protein: 9g

258. Wild Rice & Black Beans
Cook Time: 28 minutes **Servings:** 4
Ingredients:
- 2 cups wild rice
- 5 cups water
- 1 cup onion, diced
- 4 cloves garlic, minced

- 2 limes
- 1 teaspoon salt
- 1 avocado
- 2 cups dry black beans

Directions:
In your instant pot add the wild rice, onions, garlic, black beans, pour in water and sprinkle with salt. Set to the Manual setting on high for a cook time of 28-minutes. When the cook time is completed, release the pressure using quick-release. Divide into serving bowls, squeeze a lime wedge over bowl, and serve with a couple of avocado slices for garnish. Serve warm!

Nutritional Information per serving:
Calories: 691   Fat: 4g   Carbs: 36.5g   Protein: 28.6g

---

259. *Perfect Brown Rice*
Cook Time: 22 minutes   *Servings: 12*
Ingredients:
- 2 cups brown rice
- ½ teaspoon salt
- 2 ½ cups of fish broth
- Coriander, fresh, chopped for garnish

Directions:
Add the rice to your instant pot and pour the fish broth over it and add salt. Seal the lid of instant pot, and set it to Manual setting on high with a cook time of 22-minutes. When the cook time is completed, release the pressure naturally for 10-minutes. Add rice to a large serving bowl, and garnish with fresh, chopped coriander. Serve warm!

Nutritional Information per serving:
Calories: 245   Fat: 2.3g   Carbs: 48.5g   Protein: 6.8g

---

260. *Lentil & Wild Rice Pilaf*
Cook Time: 14 minutes   *Servings: 4*
Ingredients:
- ¼ cup black/wild rice
- ¼ cup brown rice
- ½ cup black or green lentils
- 1 stalk celery, finely chopped
- 1 cup mushrooms, sliced
- ½ onion, finely chopped
- 3 cloves garlic, minced
- 1 bay leaf
- 2 cups vegetable broth
- ¼ teaspoon red pepper flakes
- ½ teaspoon ground black pepper
- 1 teaspoon fennel seeds
- 1 teaspoon coriander, dried
- 1 teaspoon Italian seasoning blend

Directions:
Combine the rice and lentils in a mixing bowl and allow to soak for 30-minutes. Drain and then rinse thoroughly. Set the instant pot to the sauté mode, add veggies with a bit of water and cook for 5-minutes. Add the rice and lentils, vegetable broth, spices into the instant pot. Close the lid and set to Manual on high for 9-minutes. When the cook time is completed, release the pressure using the quick-release. Stir the pilaf and serve with steamed or fresh veggies. Serve warm!

Nutritional Information per serving:
Calories: 211   Fat: 2.6g   Carbs: 35.5g   Protein: 12g

Chapter 9. Collection of Keto-Friendly Egg-Based Instant Pot Recipes

261. *Eggs En Cocotte*

Cook Time: 4 minutes
Servings: 3

Ingredients:

- 3 eggs, fresh
- Sea salt and black pepper to taste
- 1 cup water, for the pot
- Butter, at room temperature
- 1 tablespoon of chives
- 3 tablespoons cream

Directions:
Take 3 four-ounce ramekins, and wipe the insides of them with butter applied using a paper towel. Pour 1 tablespoon of cream into each ramekin. Carefully crack an egg into each ramekin, making sure not to break the yolks. Then sprinkle with chives. Pour the water into the bottom of the instant pot and place trivet into instant pot. Place the ramekins on top of trivet. Close the instant pot and set to the Manual setting on low for a cook time of 4-minutes. When the cook time is completed, release the pressure using quick-release. Remove the ramekins from pot using a kitchen towel. Season eggs en cocotte with salt and pepper. Serve with toast. Serve warm!

Nutritional Information per serving:
Calories: 173 Fat: 9g Carbs: 6.5g Protein: 8.6g

262. *Spinach & Tomato Crustless Quiche*

Cook Time: 20 minutes
Servings: 6

Ingredients:

- 12 large eggs
- ¼ teaspoon fresh ground black pepper
- 1 ½ cups water for the instant pot
- 1 cup tomato, seeded, diced
- ½ cup milk
- 4 tomato slices, for topping for quiche
- Salt as needed
- 3 large green onions, sliced
- ¼ cup Parmesan cheese, shredded
- 3 cups baby spinach, roughly chopped

Directions:
Pour the water into the instant pot. In a mixing bowl, add eggs, milk, pepper, salt and whisk. Add the tomato, spinach, and green onions into a 1 ½ quart-sized baking dish; mix well to combine. Pour the egg mixture over the vegetables, stir until well combined. Place the tomato slices gently on top. Sprinkle with shredded Parmesan cheese. Place the trivet inside instant pot, then place baking dish onto trivet. Secure the lid to instant pot, and set on the Manual setting to high with a cook time of 20-minutes. When the cook time is completed, release the pressure naturally for 10-minutes. Remove the baking dish from instant pot, can broil in oven for a few minutes to brown top if you wish. Divide among serving dishes, and serve warm!

Nutritional Information per serving:
Calories: 179 Fat: 3.8g Carbs: 5g Protein: 48.6g

263. Bacon & Cheese Egg Muffins

Cook Time: 8 minutes
Servings: 4
Ingredients:
- 4 eggs
- 4 slices bacon, cooked, crumbled
- 4 tablespoons pepper jack cheese, or cheddar
- ¼ teaspoon lemon pepper seasoning
- 1 green onion, diced
- 1 ½ cups of water for instant pot

Directions:
Add the water to your instant pot, then place a steamer basket into the pot. In a large mixing bowl, add the eggs, lemon pepper, and beat well. Divide the bacon, cheese, and green onions between 4 silicone muffin cups. Pour the egg mix into each muffin cup, stir with a fork. Put the muffins into steamer basket, cover and secure lid to instant pot. Set to Manual setting at high with a cook time of 8-minutes. Remove the steamer basket from instant pot, and serve the egg muffins right away. Serve warm!

Nutritional Information per serving:
Calories: 127   Fat: 9.4g   Carbs: 0.9g   Protein: 9.7g

264. Meaty Crustless Quiche

Cook Time: 30 minutes
Servings: 4
Ingredients:
- 6 large eggs, well beaten
- ½ cup milk
- 1 cup ground sausage, cooked
- 4 slices bacon, cooked and crumbled
- Salt and black pepper to taste
- 1 ½ cups water for the instant pot
- 1 cup cheese, shredded
- 2 large green onions, chopped
- ½ cup ham, diced

Directions:
Add the water to your instant pot, place a trivet into the pot. In a large mixing bowl, whisk the milk, eggs, salt and pepper. Add the sausage, cheese, ham, bacon, and green onions. Add this mix to a 1-quart soufflé dish; mix well. Pour egg mix over meat, stir to combine. Loosely cover the dish with aluminum foil. Put on to the trivet, and secure the instant pot lid into place. Set to Manual setting on high with a cook time of 30-minutes. When the cook time is completed, release the pressure naturally for 10-minutes. Remove dish from instant pot and sprinkle the top of quiche with additional cheese and broil until melted and slightly browned. Divide into serving dishes. Serve warm!

Nutritional Information per serving:
Calories: 419   Fat: 14g   Carbs: 6.5g   Protein: 29g

265. Breakfast in a Jar
Cook Time: 5 minutes
Servings: 3
Ingredients:
- 6 eggs
- Tater tots
- 6 pieces bacon, cooked
- 6 tablespoons peach-mango salsa, divided
- 9 slices sharp cheese, shredded, divided

Directions:
You will need three mason jars, that can hold about 2-cups worth of ingredients. Add 1 ¼ cups of water to your instant pot. Add enough tater tots to cover the bottom of mason jars. Crack 2 eggs into each mason jar. Poke the eggs using a fork. Add two bacon slices into each mason jar. Add 2 slices of cheese into each mason jar, covering the ingredients. Add 2 tablespoons of salsa into each jar, on top of cheese. Add a few more tater tots on top of salsa. Then top with a slice of cheese in each jar. Cover each jar with foil, making sure to cover them tightly to prevent moisture getting into the jars. Place the jars right into the water inside your instant pot. Cover and secure the lid, setting to Manual setting on high for a cook time of 5-minutes. When cook time is completed, release the pressure using quick-release. Remove jars carefully, transfer contents onto serving plates. Serve warm!

Nutritional Information per serving:
Calories: 632   Fat: 18g   Carbs: 15g   Protein: 38g

266. Bread Pudding
Cook Time: 25 minutes
Servings: 8
Ingredients:
- 6 slices of raisin bread, dried out
- 3 large eggs
- 3 cups milk
- 1 teaspoon vanilla
- 2 cups water
- 1 tablespoon butter
- Truvia to taste
- Cinnamon to taste

Directions:
In a mixing bowl add 3 cups milk, 3 eggs, 1 teaspoon vanilla, ½ teaspoon salt, Truvia to taste, cinnamon to taste. Butter a 5-cup stainless steel bowl that will fit into your instant pot. Put the cut bread pieces into the bowl. Pour the custard mix over bread and allow to stand for 15-minutes. Dot the top with 1 tablespoon of butter. Butter a piece of aluminum foil with buttered piece facing down, and tightly cover the bowl. Pour water into instant pot and then place the trivet into pot. Place the bowl on top of trivet. Secure the lid in place and set to Manual on high with a cook time of 25-minutes. When the cook time is completed, release pressure naturally for 15-minutes. Lift bowl out of instant pot, puncture the foil with a fork to allow the pudding to cool. Serve pudding warm or cold!

Nutritional Information per serving:
Calories: 152   Fat: 5.4g   Carbs: 20g   Protein: 5.9g

267. Boiled Eggs
Cook Time: *3 minutes*
Servings: *6*
Ingredients:
- 12 large eggs
- 1 cup water

Directions:
Add the water to your instant pot, and then place the steamer basket into pot. Place the eggs into the basket. Secure the lid on instant pot, and set to the Manual setting on low with a cook time of 3-minutes. When the cook time is completed, release the pressure using the quick-release. Serve the boiled eggs warm or cold!

Nutritional Information per serving:
Calories: 63   Fat: 4.4g   Carbs: 0.3g   Protein: 5.5g

268. Turkey Meatballs with Mushroom Gravy
Cook Time: *40 minutes*
Servings: *4*
Ingredients:
- 1 lb. ground turkey
- 1 large egg, beaten
- 1 onion, small-sized, minced
- 1 teaspoon oregano, dried
- ½ cup panko bread crumbs
- 1 teaspoon light soy sauce
- 1 teaspoon fish sauce
- 4 cloves garlic, minced
- 20 grams Parmesan cheese, freshly grated
- ¼ teaspoon Italian parsley, finely chopped
- Sea salt and black pepper to taste

For the Mushroom Gravy:
- 12 cremini mushrooms, roughly chopped
- 3 shiitake mushrooms, dried, about 14 grams, roughly chopped
- Salt and black pepper to taste
- 2 tablespoons cornstarch with 2 tablespoons cold tap water
- 1 tablespoon olive oil
- 1 cup chicken stock
- Dash of sherry wine
- 1 teaspoon light soy sauce
- 2 tablespoons butter, unsalted

Directions:
Add all the dry ingredients to a large-sized mixing bowl. Add the wet ingredients into the dry ingredients. With clean hands mix thoroughly until well combined. Roll and form about 16 meatballs from mixture. Set your instant pot to sauté mode, add the olive oil and heat. Add the meatballs into pot and stir, brown meat on all sides for about 5-minutes.
Remove the meatballs and set on a plate. Add chicken stock to pot, and scrape off brown bits from pot. Add the butter to pot, add the mushrooms, and season with pepper and salt. Stir to coat the mushrooms with cooking fat. Cook for 12-minutes, until mushrooms are brown and crisp. Add the shiitake mushrooms into pot and stir immediately. Pour a dash

of sherry into pot and stir. Add soy sauce, and meatballs back into pot. Cover the pot with lid, and press the Manual setting on high for a cook time of 6-minutes.

When the cook time is completed, release the pressure using quick-release. In a bowl mix the cornstarch with the water until dissolved. Remove meatballs from pot onto large serving plate. Add cornstarch mix into pot and mix, until the sauce reaches your desired thickness. Drizzle the mushroom gravy over meatballs, serve with mashed potatoes, pasta, cooked rice etc. Serve warm!

Nutritional Information per serving:
Calories: 112   Fat: 2g   Carbs: 12g   Protein: 6g

---

269. Cheese-Stuffed Mini Turkey Meatloaves & Mushroom Gravy
Cook Time: 25 minutes
Servings: 4 servings
Ingredients:

- 1 lb. ground turkey
- 4 tablespoons gournay cheese spread, such as Boursin Garlic and Fine Herbs
- 3 cups mushrooms, sliced, divided
- 2 tablespoons butter
- ½ teaspoon onion powder
- ½ teaspoon garlic powder
- ½ cup breadcrumbs, plain
- 1 teaspoon Italian seasoning
- 1 tablespoon water
- 1 tablespoon cornstarch
- 1 cup chicken broth
- 1 egg
- Salt and black pepper to taste

Directions:
Grease four mini meatloaf, disposable pans, with non-stick cooking spray. Set your instant pot to the sauté mode, add 2 tablespoons butter and heat. Add the mushrooms to pot and sauté for 5-minutes, then remove mushrooms and set on a plate. Pour broth into instant pot.

Set aside 2/3 of mushrooms for the gravy, and dice the remaining 1/3 into fine pieces. In a large mixing bowl, combine the ground turkey with diced mushroom, egg, breadcrumbs, garlic powder, onion powder, Italian seasoning, salt and pepper. Mix the ingredients with clean hands, until well combined. Divide the mixture into 4 portions and place portions into pans. Create a row in the center of each meatloaf. Fill the row with 1 tablespoon of gournay cheese. Close row by pinching it. Set a trivet into the bottom of instant pot. Add 2 meatloaf pans on top of trivet.

Place a second trivet on the first, place the remaining meatloaf pans on top of second trivet. Cover and lock the lid of instant pot, setting to Manual on high for a cook time of 12-minutes. When the cook time is completed, release pressure naturally for 15-minutes. Remove the meatloaf pans and trivets. Cover the meatloaves with foil to keep them warm. Add the reserved 2/3 mushrooms into the instant pot. In a bowl mix the cornstarch with water until dissolved. Pour into instant pot and stir until sauce thickens. Season to taste with salt and pepper. Serve the mushroom gravy over the mini cheese-stuffed meatloaves. Serve with pan roasted sweet potatoes and green beans. Serve warm!

Nutritional Information per serving:
Calories: 404   Fat: 23g   Carbs: 14g   Protein: 39g

270. Mushroom Stroganoff

Cook Time: 10 minutes **Servings: 4**

Ingredients:
- 1 egg, large-sized, beaten
- 1 lb. ground turkey, lean
- ½ teaspoon Worcestershire sauce
- ½ teaspoon paprika
- ½ cup onion, chopped
- ½ cup sour cream, light
- 1 teaspoon olive oil, divided
- 1 sprig thyme, fresh
- 8-ounces cremini mushrooms, sliced
- Sea salt and black pepper to taste
- ¾ cup water
- 3 tablespoons milk, fat-free
- 2 teaspoons tomato paste
- 2 teaspoons beef bouillon
- 2 tablespoons all-purpose flour
- ¼ parsley, chopped, divided
- 1/3 cup seasoned breadcrumbs, whole-wheat

Directions:
Set your instant pot to the sauté mode, add ½ teaspoon olive oil and heat. Add onion and sauté for 3-minutes. Remove and divide into two portions. Turn off the instant pot. In a large mixing bowl, combine turkey, half of sautéed onions, bread crumbs, egg, milk, 2 tablespoons parsley, ¾ teaspoon black pepper, ¾ teaspoon salt, shape into meatballs.
Pour the sour cream, water, flour, Worcestershire sauce, tomato paste, bouillon and paprika into blender, blend until smooth. Set your instant pot to sauté mode, add remaining olive oil. Add half of the meatballs into pot, and brown them on all sides for about 5-minutes. Transfer the browned meatballs onto a plate and set aside. Repeat the process with remaining meatballs. After second batch is cooked add the first batch back into pot along with remaining onions. Pour the sauce over meatballs, add mushrooms and thyme. Cover and secure the lid on pot and press the Manual setting on high for 10-minutes. When the cook time is completed, release the pressure using the quick-release. Remove and discard the thyme. Add the parsley and serve over your favorite noodles. Serve warm!

Nutritional Information per serving:
Calories: 391   Fat: 21g   Carbs: 16.3g   Protein: 37.2g

271. Korean Style Steamed Eggs

Cook Time: 5 minutes **Servings: 1**

Ingredients:
- 1 large egg
- 1/3 cup cold water
- Pinch of garlic powder
- 1 teaspoon scallions, chopped
- Salt and pepper to taste

Directions:
Mix the egg and water in a small bowl. Strain the egg mixture over a fine mesh strainer into a heat proof bowl. Add the rest of the ingredients and mix well. Add 1 cup of water to instant pot, place the trivet into pot. Place the bowl with egg mixture on top of trivet. Close and secure the lid to pot, set to the Manual setting on high for a cook time of 5-

minutes. When the cook time is completed, release the pressure using quick-release. Serve with some hot rice of your choice. Serve warm!
Nutritional Information per serving:
Calories: 114   Fat: 2g   Carbs: 9g   Protein: 6g

---

272. Eggs De Provence
Cook Time: 30 minutes   **Servings: 6**
Ingredients:

- 6 eggs
- 1/8 teaspoon sea salt and black pepper
- 1 onion, small, chopped
- 1 cup cooked ham
- ½ cup heavy cream
- 1 teaspoon Herbes de Provence
- 1 cup cheddar cheese

Directions:
Whisk the eggs with the heavy cream in a mixing bowl. Add the rest of the ingredients and combine well. Pour the mixture into a heat proof dish and cover. Add one cup of water in the instant pot. Place the trivet into the instant pot. Place the heat proof dish with egg mixture, on top of trivet. Close and secure the lid on pot, and set to Manual setting on high for a cook time of 20-minutes. Serve warm!

Nutritional Information per serving:
Calories: 109   Fat: 2.3g   Carbs: 14g   Protein: 21g

---

273. Instant Pot Poached Eggs Over Spicy Potato Hash
Cook Time: 15 minutes   **Servings: 2**
Ingredients:

- 1 cup sweet potatoes, peeled, cubed into 1-inch cubes
- 2 eggs
- 1 teaspoon taco seasoning, for garnish
- 1 tablespoon cilantro, fresh, chopped, for garnish
- 1 jalapeno pepper, sliced
- 2 tablespoons bacon fat
- 1 tablespoon bacon, cooked, chopped

Directions:
Add a cup of water to the inside of your instant pot, and place trivet inside. Place the heat proof bowl with potatoes on top of trivet. Close the lid and secure, set to Manual setting on high for 2-minutes. Meanwhile chop onions, bacon, jalapeno pepper, and cilantro. When the cook time is completed, release the pressure using the quick-release. Remove the potatoes and set aside. Remove the trivet and drain the water from instant pot. Set your instant pot to the sauté mode, add the bacon fat. Add the onions and sauté for 3-minutes. Add the potatoes, bacon, pepper and mix well. Pat down the potatoes to create a crater in the middle. Crack both eggs into the crater of the potato hash. Close the lid and set on Manual setting on high for 1-minute. Use the quick-release to release the pressure. Place carefully on serving plates and try not to break eggs yolks. Garnish with taco seasoning and cilantro. Serve warm!

Nutritional Information per serving:
Calories: 123   Fat: 2.4g   Carbs: 19   Protein: 18g

274. Instant Pot Ham & Egg Casserole

Cook Time: 25 minutes
Servings: 5
Ingredients:
- 4 medium red potatoes
- 1 cup milk
- 10 large eggs
- 2 cups cheddar cheese, shredded
- 1 cup ham, chopped
- ½ onion, diced
- Sea salt and black pepper to taste

Directions:
Spray the insert of your instant pot with non-stick cooking spray. Add eggs and milk into a heat proof bowl, and whisk to blend. Add the potatoes, onions, cheese, ham, salt and pepper into the bowl with eggs, and whisk until well combined. Cover the bowl with foil. Place your trivet into your instant pot, and add 2 cups of water into pot. Place the bowl with egg mixture on top of the trivet. Close and secure the lid to pot, and set to Manual on high with a cook time of 25-minutes. When the cook time is completed, release the pressure using the quick-release. Serve with favorite toppings some of mine are: more cheese and tomatoes, sour cream, avocado, and salsa. Serve warm!

Nutritional Information per serving:
Calories: 172   Fat: 2g   Carbs: 27   Protein: 32g

275. Instant Pot Aromatic Egg

Cook Time: 20 minutes
Servings: 6
Ingredients:
- 8 eggs
- 1 tablespoon mustard
- ¼ cup cream
- 1 cup water
- 1 teaspoon minced garlic
- 1 teaspoon ground white pepper
- ¼ cup dill
- 1 teaspoon mayo sauce

Directions:
Add a cup of water to your instant pot. Add the stainless steamer basket inside the pot. Place the eggs in the steamer basket. Cook the eggs on Manual setting on high for a cook time of 5-minutes. Remove the eggs from the instant pot and allow to chill in some cold water. Peel the eggs, and cut them in half. Remove the egg yolks and mash them in a bowl. Add the mustard, cream, salt, mayo sauce, ground white pepper, and minced garlic in with mashed yolks. Sprinkle dill into the yolk mix and combine well. Put egg yolk mixture into a pastry bag. Fill the egg whites with yolk mixture. Serve cold!

Nutritional Information per serving:
Calories: 62   Fat: 1g   Carbs: 11g   Protein: 15g

276. Instant Pot Western Omelette Quiche
Cook Time: 30 minutes
Servings: 4
Ingredients:
- 6 large eggs, beaten
- ¼ cup cheddar cheese, shredded, for garnish
- ¾ cup cheddar cheese, shredded
- 3 spring onions, thinly sliced, reserve the tops for garnish
- ¾ cup red and green bell peppers, diced
- 8-ounces Canadian bacon, diced, cooked
- Sea salt and black pepper to taste
- ½ cup half and half
- 1 ½ cups water for instant pot

Directions:
Add the water to bottom of your instant pot, place the trivet inside pot. Spray a soufflé dish with non-stick cooking spray. In a large mixing bowl whisk together the eggs, milk, salt and pepper. Add the bacon, diced peppers, spring onion slices, cheese into 1-quart soufflé dish and combine well. Pour the egg mixture over the meat and stir to combine ingredients. Cover your soufflé dish loosely with a piece of foil. Place the lid onto instant pot and secure it in place, set to Manual setting on high with a cook time of 30-minutes. When the cooking is completed, release the pressure naturally for 10-minutes. Remove the dish from pot and remove foil, sprinkle top with cheese. Broil until lightly browned. Divide among serving plates, and garnish with chopped spring onion. Serve warm!

Nutritional Information per serving:
Calories: 365   Fat: 24g   Fiber: 1g   Carbs: 6g   Protein: 29g

277. Instant Pot French Baked Eggs
Cook Time: 8 minutes
Servings: 4
Ingredients:
- 4 eggs
- 4 slices of ham or favorite meat slices or veggies
- 4 slices of favorite cheese
- 4 fresh herbs, garnish
- 1 cup water for instant pot

Directions:
Add cup of water to your instant pot, and place the trivet inside. Prepare four ramekins by adding a drop of olive oil into each ramekin, rubbing sides and bottom of dish. Lay a slice of preferred meat into dish. Break an egg into ramekin, then add a slice of cheese of choice. For a soft yolk, cover tightly with tin foil, for a fully-cooked hard yolk leave uncovered. Place the ramekins into steamer basket and place on top of trivet. Close the lid and secure, set to Manual setting on low with an 8-minute cook time. When the cook time is completed, release the pressure using the quick-release. Remove ramekins and garnish with fresh herbs of choice. Serve warm!

Nutritional Information per serving:
Calories: 312   Fat: 4g   Fiber: 1g   Carbs: 9g   Protein: 21g

278. Instant Pot Mexican Egg Casserole
Cook Time: 25 minutes **Servings: 8**
Ingredients:
- 8 large eggs, well-beaten
- 1 cup mozzarella cheese, divided
- ½ cup almond flour
- ½ cup green onions
- 1 can black beans, rinsed
- 1 red bell pepper, chopped
- ½ large red onion, chopped
- 1 lb. ground sausage
- Sour cream, and cilantro for garnish
- 1 tablespoon olive oil
- 1 cup Cotija cheese

Directions:
Set your instant pot to the sauté mode, add oil and heat it. Add the sausage and onions, cook for about 6-minutes. In a mixing bowl mix the eggs and flour until well combined. Add the egg mixture into the instant pot with the sausage and onions. Add in the chopped vegetables, cheeses, beans to the instant pot. Set aside some mozzarella cheese to use for garnish. Secure the lid into place on instant pot, set to Manual setting on high with a cook time of 20-minutes. Remove the casserole from instant pot, add mozzarella for garnish. Serve warm!

Nutritional Information per serving:
Calories: 294   Fat: 16g   Fiber: 2g   Carbs: 21g   Protein: 23g

279. Eggs Papin Poached Eggs in Bell Pepper Cup
Cook Time: 10 minutes **Servings: 2**
Ingredients:
- 2 fresh eggs
- 2 red bell peppers, ends cut off
- 1 small bunch of Rucola

For the Mock Hollandaise sauce:
- 1 teaspoon turmeric
- 1 tablespoon white wine vinegar
- 1 teaspoon fresh lemon juice
- 2 slices of Smoked Scamorza, Mozzarella or Gouda
- 2 slices whole wheat bread, toasted
- 1 cup of water for instant pot
- 3 tablespoons orange juice
- 2/3 cup mayonnaise
- ½ teaspoon salt

Directions:
Make the Mock Hollandaise sauce by whisking all the ingredients until smooth, you can refrigerate over night to be used the next day. Add the cup of water to your instant pot, add trivet and steamer basket on top of trivet. Cut the bell pepper ends to form cups, then break an egg inside of the cups. Cover with foil and place inside of steamer basket. Close and lock the instant pot lid, set it to Manual setting on low with a cook time of 4-minutes. When the cook time is completed, release the pressure using quick-release. Stack toast, smoked cheese, Rucola, pepper cups, and cover with a generous dollop of mock-hollandaise sauce, and serve warm!

Nutritional Information per serving:
Calories: 163   Fat: 18g   Fiber: 2g   Carbs: 17g   Protein: 16g

280. Egg Bake

Cook Time: 10 minutes **Servings:** 4

Ingredients:
- 6 eggs
- ½ green bell pepper, diced
- 1 tablespoon milk
- 1/3 cup cheddar cheese shredded
- ½ red bell pepper, diced
- 2/3 cups hash browns, frozen
- Green onion, chopped, fresh, for garnish
- 1 tablespoon coconut oil

Directions:
Set your instant pot to the sauté mode, add oil and heat. Add diced peppers, hash browns and cook for 5-minutes, stir. Whisk the eggs, milk along with a pinch of salt. Pour the eggs over the pepper mixture, add the cheese and stir to combine. Secure the lid and set to high pressure and a cook time of 10-minutes. Once the cook time is completed, release the pressure naturally for 10-minutes. Divide among serving dishes, garnish with green onions. Serve warm!

Nutritional Information per serving:
Calories: 165 Fat: 20g Fiber: 1g Carbs: 15g Protein: 19g

281. Bacon and Egg Risotto

Cook Time: 10 minutes **Servings:** 2

Ingredients:
- 3 slices center cut bacon, chopped
- 2 tablespoons Parmesan cheese, grated
- 2 eggs
- 1 ½ cups chicken broth
- 3 tablespoons dry white wine
- ¾ cup wild rice
- Salt and pepper to taste
- Chives for garnish
- 1 tablespoon olive oil

Directions:
Set your instant pot to the sauté mode, add the oil and heat it. Add the bacon and cook for 5-minutes. Stir in the onion and cook for an additional 3-minutes. Stir in the rice and sauté for 1-minute. Pour in the wine and stir, once the wine is absorbed add in the chicken broth. Place and secure the lid of instant pot, set to Manual setting on high for 5-minutes. When cook time is completed, release the pressure using quick-release. Remove the lid and add in the parmesan cheese, salt and pepper. Cook the eggs to your liking such as poached or sunny side up. Divide between 2 serving plates, garnish with chives. Serve warm!

Nutritional Information per serving:
Calories: 292 Fat: 11g Fiber: 1g Carbs: 16g Protein: 12g

282. Instant Pot Sausage & Egg Breakfast Burritos

Cook Time: 15 minutes **Servings:** 6

Ingredients:

- 8-ounces ground pork
- ¼ cup milk
- 8 eggs
- 6 burrito size tortilla shells
- Olive oil for brushing aluminum
- 1 tablespoon water
- 1/8 teaspoon nutmeg
- 1 teaspoon light brown sugar
- ½ teaspoon crushed red pepper flakes
- 1 teaspoon crushed fennel seed
- 1 teaspoon thyme
- 1 teaspoon sage
- Salt and black pepper to taste
- 1 ½ cups water for instant pot
- Cheddar cheese, shredded for garnish
- Chunky salsa for garnish

Directions:
In a mixing bowl combine the ground pork, thyme, fennel seed, red pepper, brown sugar, nutmeg, salt and pepper along with 1 tablespoon of water. Cover with plastic wrap and place in the fridge while you work on the rest of the recipe. Use 2 pieces of foil to wrap the tortilla shells in. Lightly brush the sides that will be touching the tortillas with olive oil. Place tortillas in the center of one sheet of foil and top them with the other sheet of foil. Tightly fold and seal all four corners. In an oven-safe bowl whisk the eggs. Add milk, salt and pepper. Add the ground pork mixture in with eggs, and break into small pieces. Cover the bowl with a sheet of foil, tightly. Add 1 ½ cups water to instant pot, and place the trivet inside. Place bowl with egg mixture on trivet inside instant pot. Secure the lid in place on instant pot, set to Manual setting with a cook time of 15-minutes. Once the cook time is completed, release the pressure naturally for 10-minutes. Remove the eggs and tortillas from instant pot. Assemble the burritos with eggs, and garnish with cheddar and salsa. Serve warm!

Nutritional Information per serving:
Calories: 265 Fat: 20g Fiber: 2g Carbs: 19g Protein: 26g

---

283. Poached Tomato Eggs
Cook Time: 15 minutes **Servings:** 4
Ingredients:

- 4 eggs
- 1 cup of water for instant pot
- 3 medium tomatoes, chopped
- 1 tablespoon dill, fresh
- ½ teaspoon paprika
- ½ teaspoon white pepper
- 1 tablespoon olive oil
- Salt to taste
- 1 red onion, diced

Directions:
Add the 1 cup of water to your instant pot, along with the trivet. Spray 4 ramekins with olive oil inside. Beat an egg in each ramekin. In a small mixing bowl combine the white pepper, fresh dill, paprika, and salt together. Chop the onions, and tomatoes, and combine them. Sprinkle onion and tomato mixture on top of eggs. Add the spice mixture and transfer the eggs to the instant pot on top of the trivet. Close the lid to pot and set Manual setting on high for a cook time of 5-minutes. When the cook time is completed, release the pressure using the quick-release. Serve immediately and serve warm!

Nutritional Information per serving:
Calories: 152 Fat: 14g Fiber: 2g Carbs: 12g Protein: 19g

284. Instant Pot Scrambled Eggs
Cook Time: 15 minutes **Servings:** 4
Ingredients:
- 7 eggs
- 1 tablespoon cilantro
- 4-ounces of bacon, chopped
- 1 teaspoon paprika
- Salt and black pepper to taste
- ¼ cup parsley, fresh
- 1 teaspoon basil
- 1 tablespoon butter
- ½ cup milk
- 1 tablespoon olive oil

Directions:
Beat the eggs in a small mixing bowl. Add the milk, salt, paprika, black pepper, basil and cilantro. Mix to combine ingredients. Chop the bacon and parsley. Set your instant pot on the sauté mode, add the oil and heat it. Add the bacon and cook for 3-minutes. Add the whisked eggs and cook for an additional 5-minutes more. Using a wooden spoon mix up the eggs. Sprinkle with chopped parsley and cook for another 4-minutes. Once eggs are cooked—remove them from instant pot and serve warm!

Nutritional Information per serving:
Calories: 152   Fat: 16g   Fiber: 1g   Carbs: 11g   Protein: 20g

285. Instant Pot Soft Eggs
Cook Time: 10 minutes **Servings:** 4
Ingredients:
- 3 eggs
- 2 tablespoons chives, fresh, chopped
- ¼ teaspoon ginger, ground
- 1 teaspoon paprika
- ½ teaspoon white pepper, ground
- 1 teaspoon salt
- 6-ounces ham, chopped, cooked

Directions:
Beat an egg inside of each ramekin, sprinkle eggs with paprika, white pepper, salt and set inside instant pot. Set the pot onto Steam mode for 4-minutes. Meanwhile chop the chives and ham, and combine both. Add the ground ginger to mixture and stir. Transfer the mixture to serving plates. When eggs are done cooking place the eggs over the ham mixture on serving plates and serve warm!

Nutritional Information per serving:
Calories: 157   Fat: 10g   Fiber: 2g   Carbs: 9g   Protein: 21g

286. Instant Pot Soft-Boiled Eggs
Cook Time: 6 minutes **Servings:** 2
Ingredients:
- 4 eggs
- 1 cup of water for instant pot
- 2 toasted English Muffins
- Salt and pepper to taste

Directions:

Pour the cup of water into your instant pot and insert the steamer basket. Place four canning lids into the basket before placing the eggs on top of them, so they will stay separated. Secure the instant pot lid. Select the Steam mode for 4-minutes. To release pressure, use the quick-release. Use a pair of tongs to remove the eggs from instant pot and dunk them into a bowl of cold water. Wait 2-minutes, peel and serve with one egg per half of English muffin. Serve warm!

Nutritional Information per serving:
Calories: 141   Fat: 10g   Fiber: 1g   Carbs: 8g   Protein: 15g

---

287. Mushroom & Spinach Crustless Quiche

Cook Time: 40 minutes   **Servings:** 6

Ingredients:
- 12 large eggs
- ¼ teaspoon fresh ground black pepper
- 1 cup of mushrooms, diced
- ½ cup milk
- 3 cups baby spinach, chopped
- ¼ cup Parmesan cheese, shredded
- 2 tablespoons of red onion, diced
- Sea salt and black pepper to taste
- 1 ½ cups of water for the instant pot

Directions:
Pour the water into the instant pot. In a large mixing bowl whisk the eggs, milk, pepper and salt. Add the mushrooms, spinach and onion, into a 1 ½ quart-sized baking dish; and mix well to combine. Pour the egg mix over the vegetables; stir until combined. Sprinkle the top with shredded parmesan cheese. Place the baking dish onto a trivet with handle and place it inside the baking dish. Secure the lid of instant pot in place, and set to Manual on high for a cook time of 20-minutes. When the cooking is completed, then release the pressure naturally for 10-minutes. Using the handles of rack lift dish out from the pot. Serve warm!

Nutritional Information per serving:
Calories: 167   Fat: 1g   Fiber: 3g   Carbs: 10g   Protein: 14g

---

288. Instant Pot Scotch Eggs

Cook Time: 17 minutes   **Servings:** 4

Ingredients:
- 4 large eggs
- 1 tablespoon olive oil
- 1 lb. country style ground sausage
- 1 cup of water for the instant pot

Directions:
Add the water to your instant pot, then place steamer basket into your instant pot, and add the eggs to basket. Lock the lid of instant pot in place, and set on Manual on high with a cook time of 6-minutes. When the cooking is completed, release the pressure naturally for 6-minutes. Remove the steamer basket from the pot and place the eggs in a bowl of cold water to cool down.

Once the eggs have cooled, remove the shells. Divide the ground sausage into four-equal pieces. Flatten each piece into a flat round. Place a hard-boiled egg in the middle of each piece, gently wrapping the sausage around the egg.

Set your instant pot onto the sauté mode, add in oil and heat it. Add in the Scotch eggs and brown them on all sides. Remove them from the instant pot once they have been browned. Add a cup of water to the instant pot and place trivet inside pot. Place the Scotch eggs on top of trivet.

Lock and secure the instant pot lid setting on Manual on high for a cook time of 6-minutes. When the cook time is completed, to release the pressure do a quick-release. Serve warm!

Nutritional Information per serving:
Calories: 134   Fat: 12g   Fiber: 0g   Carbs: 16g   Protein: 27g

289. Instant Pot Banana French Toast

Cook Time: 25 minutes   **Servings:** 6

Ingredients:
- 3 eggs
- 4 bananas, sliced
- ¼ cup cream cheese
- 1 teaspoon Truvia
- 1 tablespoon brown sugar
- 1 teaspoon vanilla extract
- ¼ cup pecans, chopped
- 2 tablespoons butter, chilled, sliced
- ½ teaspoon cinnamon, ground
- 6-slices of French bread, cubed
- ¾ cup water for the instant pot

Directions:
Slice the bread into cubes, then spray a 1 ½ QT round baking dish with non-stick cooking spray. Add a layer of bread to the bowl. Layer one sliced banana over the bread, then sprinkle with some brown sugar over banana slices. In a microwave melt the cream cheese for about 30-seconds, or until it is creamy enough to spread. Cover bread and bananas with cream cheese. Add remaining bread and another layer of bananas, sprinkle top with brown sugar and half of pecans.

Place slices of butter on top layer. In a bowl whisk the eggs with milk, Truvia, cinnamon, and pour it over the bread. Pour water into instant pot, place the trivet into pot, and place baking dish on the trivet. Secure pot lid in place and select porridge button, and add 5-minutes of cook time.

When the cook time is completed, release the pressure naturally for 6-minutes. Then remove the baking dish and top it with sliced bananas, remaining pecans and perhaps some maple syrup if you desire. Serve warm!

Nutritional Information per serving:
Calories: 167   Fat: 2g   Fiber: 5g   Carbs: 11g   Protein: 7g

290. Potato Egg Frittata, Quiche

Cook Time: 19 minutes   **Servings:** 4

Ingredients:
- 6 large eggs
- 4-ounces French fries (defrosted)
- 1 tablespoon butter, melted
- 4-ounces cheddar cheese, grated
- 1 teaspoon tomato paste
- ¼ cup milk
- 2 tablespoons Bisquick or other baking mix

- 1 clove garlic, minced
- 1 teaspoon seasoning
- Sea salt and black pepper to taste
- ¼ cup Spanish onions, diced
- 1 ½ cups of water for the instant pot

Topping:
- 1-ounce of cheese, grated

Add in Options:
- Sausage
- Ham
- Bacon
- Green bell pepper
- Spinach

Directions:
Peel and slice the potatoes into thin strips and soak in water for 20-minutes. In a mixing bowl, whisk eggs and seasonings until frothy. In a mixing cup, whisk baking mix, tomato paste and milk, add to egg mixture and whisk. Add onions and garlic to egg mix. Grease a casserole dish. Remove the potatoes from water and dry them with paper towel. Add raw potatoes and pour in melted butter. If using defrosted French fries skip using melted butter. Pour in the egg mixture and any add ins and top with cheese. Add 1 ½ cups of water to instant pot and add in the trivet. Place uncovered casserole dish on top of trivet. Close the pot lid and set to Manual mode, on high, with a cook time of 20-minutes. When cook time is completed, release the pressure naturally for 10-minutes. Top with grated cheese and allow it to melt on top before serving.

Nutritional Information per serving:
Calories: 182   Fat: 3g   Fiber: 4g   Carbs: 14g   Protein: 17g

291. Instant Pot Cheesy, Bacon & Potato Egg Bake
Cook Time: *7 minutes*   **Servings:** *4*
Ingredients:
- 8 eggs
- 1 cup cheddar cheese, shredded
- 2 cups hash brown potatoes, thawed
- ½ cup milk
- 6-pieces of bacon, diced
- Salt and pepper to taste
- Green onions, chopped for garnish
- 1 tablespoon olive oil

Directions:
Set your instant pot to the sauté mode, add oil and heat it. Add the bacon to pot and lightly brown it for 2-minutes. Once the bacon is browned leave it in the pot, you will be layering with other ingredients. Layer the hash brown potatoes over the bacon. Sprinkle half a cup of shredded cheese over the top of potatoes. In a mixing bowl beat the eggs with milk and some salt, then pour it over the bacon and potatoes in pot. Sprinkle remaining cheese on top of mixture. Secure the lid to pot in place, and set at Manual on high for a cook time of 7-minutes. After the time is up there should be no pressure to release. Open the pot and divide among serving bowls, and garnish with chopped green onion. Serve warm!

Nutritional Information per serving:
Calories: 184   Fat: 4g   Fiber: 2g   Carbs: 10g   Protein: 20g

292. Instant Pot Eggs Ketogenic Style
Cook Time: 16 minutes **Servings:** 4
Ingredients:
- 4 beaten eggs
- 1 tablespoon shallot, chopped
- 3 tablespoons ghee
- 1 green bell pepper, coarsely chopped
- ½ cup cilantro, chopped
- 1 teaspoon cinnamon, ground
- Salt and pepper to taste
- ½ teaspoon turmeric
- ½ teaspoon ginger, ground
- 2 tomatoes, chopped
- 3 cloves garlic, sliced
- 1 jalapeno, matchstick sliced
- 1 teaspoon cumin seeds

Directions:
Set your instant pot to the sauté mode, add in the ghee and heat it. Add the cumin seeds and cook until they are aromatic for about 2-minutes. Add the shallots and cook for an additional 3-minutes. Blend in the bell pepper, jalapeno, garlic, and tomatoes, then stir. Add the eggs and cook them for about 30-seconds without stirring to allow eggs to set up. Continue with cooking and stir occasionally until dry. Blend in the salt, pepper and cilantro to taste. Cover and seal with pot lid and set to Manual setting on high for 13-minutes cook time. Release the pressure using the quick-release. Serve hot!

Nutritional Information per serving:
Calories: 141 Fat: 14.4g Fiber: 1g Carbs: 8.3g Protein: 7.3g

293. Breakfast Egg Bread Spread
Cook Time: 7 minutes **Servings:** 6
Ingredients:
- 8 eggs
- ½ cup mayonnaise
- 2 tablespoons extra virgin olive oil
- Salt and pepper to taste
- 3 tablespoons mustard
- 2 cups of water for the instant pot

Directions:
Place the 2 cups of water into the bottom of instant pot, and set the steam basket in the pot, and place the eggs into basket. Cover and seal the pot lid in place, and set on Manual for 7-minutes cook time. Release the pressure using quick-release, and remove the eggs and place in ice water. Peel the eggs after they have cooled. Using a large mixing bowl, mash the eggs with a fork, add in the rest of the ingredients, and blend together. Spread mixture onto bread. Serve cold or at room temperature!

Nutritional Information per serving:
Calories: 161 Fat: 17.4g Fiber: 2g Carbs: 6.5g Protein: 6.7g

294. Cocoa & Bacon Muffins
Cook Time: 25 minutes **Servings:** 12
Ingredients:
- 6 eggs
- 1 cup coconut milk
- 1 tablespoon lemon juice
- 2 avocados, cored, cubed
- Salt and black pepper to taste
- 1 tablespoon baking soda

- 1 teaspoon baking powder
- 1 cup crispy cooked bacon
- ½ cup cheddar cheese, shredded
- 1 tablespoon green onions, chopped
- ¼ teaspoon red pepper flakes
- ¼ cup flaxseed meal
- ½ cup almond flour
- 3 tablespoons butter
- 2 cups of water for the instant pot

Directions:
Spray a dozen silicon muffin holders with food release. Using a large mixing bowl, mix all the ingredients except the avocados, and stir mix until smooth. Ladle batter into each of the muffin holders. Arrange the muffin holders on top of the steaming basket. Garnish each muffin with avocado cubes and cover with foil. Add water into pot and gently place muffins into cooker.

Set the instant pot to Manual setting for 25-minute cook time. When the cook time has completed, release the pressure using the quick-release and allow the muffins to cool on a rack for at least an hour before serving. Serve slightly warm, or room temperature!

Nutritional Information per serving:
Calories: 174   Fat: 29.1g   Fiber: 2g   Carbs: 6.4g   Protein: 14.1g

295. Keto Style Sunny Side Up Eggs
Cook Time: 8 minutes   **Servings: 4**
Ingredients:

- 4 eggs
- 1 cup honey-cured bacon
- 1 ½ cups cherry tomatoes
- 2 teaspoons garlic, minced
- ½ teaspoon rosemary
- 2 teaspoons olive oil

Directions:
Cut the bacon into ½ inch square pieces, and slice the cherry tomatoes in half. Turn the instant pot onto the sauté mode, add oil to pot and heat it. Add the bacon and sauté it for 3-minutes. Remove the bacon and crack the eggs into pot, add the garlic, chopped tomatoes, rosemary and stir to combine. Stir in the bacon pieces, seal and secure the pot lid and place on Manual setting for 5-minutes. When cooking is completed, release the pressure using the quick-release.

Nutritional Information per serving:
Calories: 189   Fat: 21g   Fiber: 1g   Carbs: 4.2g   Protein: 22g

296. Mug Cake with Berries & Cream
Cook Time: 5 minutes   **Servings: 4**
Ingredients:

- 2 large eggs
- ¼ cup heavy whipping cream
- ¼ cup mixed berries
- ¼ cup almond flour
- 2 tablespoons cream cheese
- 2 tablespoons ghee, melted

Directions:
In a blender mix eggs, cream cheese, and melted ghee. Pour the mix into a large, microwave-safe coffee mug. Stir in the berries and almond flour. Place the mug inside of the instant pot, and set to Manual setting with a cook time of 5-minutes. When cook time

is completed, release the pressure using the quick-release. Allow it to cool for a few minutes. Serve warm!
Nutritional Information per serving:
Calories: 178   Fat: 15g   Fiber: 2g   Carbs: 13.3g   Protein: 10g

---

297. Cauliflower & Cheesy Muffins
Cook Time: 20 minutes   **Servings:** 4
Ingredients:
- 2 beaten eggs
- 3 tablespoons butter, melted
- 2 tablespoons jalapeno, minced
- 2 cups cauliflower, florets
- 1 teaspoon garlic powder
- 1 teaspoon baking powder
- 1 tablespoon onion flakes, dried
- 1-ounce parmesan, grated
- 1 cup mozzarella cheese, shredded
- 1 cup cheddar cheese, shredded
- Salt and black pepper to taste
- ½ cup coconut flour
- 2 cups of water for the instant pot

Directions:
In a large mixing bowl combine all ingredients. Spray silicone muffin cups with food release. Fill cups with batter. Pour the two cups of water in pot, and place the steamer basket over water. Set the muffin cups on the steamer basket. Cover and seal the pot, and set on Manual on high for 20-minutes cook time. When cook time is completed, release the pressure using quick-release. Remove muffins from pot and serve warm!
Nutritional Information per serving:
Calories: 182   Fat: 23g   Fiber: 1g   Carbs: 14g   Protein: 16.2g

---

298. Ketogenic Grilled Toast
Cook Time: 6 minutes   **Servings:** 4
Ingredients:
- 2 eggs
- 2 slices of keto bread
- ½ cup unsweetened almond milk
- 1 teaspoon cinnamon, ground
- 1 teaspoon vanilla
- Sugar-free syrup and butter as toppings

Directions:
Set your instant pot to the sauté mode, and heat it up. Whisk the eggs, vanilla, almond milk, and cinnamon. Coat both sides of the keto bread with the egg mixture. Cook each piece of bread until it is brown. Serve warm using butter and sugar-free syrup as toppings!
Nutritional Information per serving:
Calories: 189   Fat: 8g   Fiber: 1g   Carbs: 4g   Protein: 6.7g

---

299. Sausage, Pepper, & Cheese Rings
Cook Time: 13 minutes   **Servings:** 4
Ingredients:
- 4 large eggs
- 2 red bell peppers

- 1 lb. breakfast sausage
- 4 tablespoons parmesan cheese, shredded for garnish
- 2 tablespoons coconut oil
- Salt and black pepper to taste

Directions:
Take out the seeds and cores of the bell peppers, and cut into rings about ½ an inch thick. Set the instant pot to the sauté mode, add the coconut oil and heat it up. Slice the sausages into small rings and sauté for 3-minutes. Set to side when they are finished. Carefully place the pepper rings into your instant pot. Crack an egg on a saucer, then carefully tip the plate over the top of pepper to fill in center of ring. Set the sausage slices on top of the eggs. Set to Manual setting on high for 10-minute cook time. Remove rings from pot and serve warm with a garnish of parmesan shredded cheese.

Nutritional Information per serving:
Calories: 192   Fat: 26g   Fiber: 1g   Carbs: 3.6g   Protein: 28g

---

300. Egg, Beef & Bacon Fest
Cook Time: 35 minutes
Servings: 4
Ingredients:
- 3 hard-boiled eggs
- 3 slices of bacon
- 1 teaspoon cumin
- 1 lb. lean ground beef
- 2 tablespoons ketchup
- 1 green bell pepper, finely chopped
- 1 teaspoon chili powder
- 1 yellow onion, finely diced
- Salt and black pepper to taste
- 1 cup cabbage, shredded

Directions:
Fry bacon in a skillet, then pat of excess grease and crumble it and set aside. Keep the bacon grease to use later in recipe. Quarter the boiled eggs and set aside with bacon. Using a mixing bowl, combine the remaining ingredients then place in fridge to marinate for 1 hour. Set your instant pot to sauté mode and heat up the saved bacon grease in pot. Pour the beef mixture into the instant pot, and cook for 5-minutes without sealing. Cover and seal the pot lid in place, setting on Manual on high with a cook time of 30-minutes. When the cook time is completed, release the pressure naturally for 10-minutes. Add the crumbled bacon and stir. Place on serving plates and garnish with eggs, and black pepper. Serve warm!

Nutritional Information per serving:
Calories: 203   Fat: 7g   Fiber: 1g   Carbs: 3.2g   Protein: 24g

Chapter 10. Collection of Bean & Lentil-Based Instant Pot Recipes

301. Mung Bean Dahl

Cook Time: 25 minutes **Servings:** 6
Ingredients:
- ½ cup mung beans, dry
- 2 teaspoons curry powder
- 2 cups vegetable stock
- ½ teaspoon onion powder
- ¼ teaspoon garlic powder
- Salt and black pepper to taste
- 1 cup spinach, chopped finely

Directions:
Add the stock, curry powder, mung beans, onion and garlic powder into instant pot with some salt. Secure the pot lid in place, and set on Manual setting for a cook time of 25-minutes. When the cook time is completed, release the pressure naturally for 10-minutes. Using a fork, smash about the beans and stir to thicken sauce. Add the spinach and stir allowing it cook within the residual heat. Serve warm!

Nutritional Information per serving:
Calories: 203 Fat: 7g Fiber: 1g Carbs: 6g Protein: 8g

302. Red Bean & Lentil Chili

Cook Time: 38 minutes **Servings:** 6
Ingredients:
- ½ cup red beans, dried, soaked in water overnight
- ½ cup brown lentils, soaked in water overnight
- 1 teaspoon cumin powder
- ½ teaspoon coriander powder
- 1 ½ teaspoons chili powder
- 1 teaspoon smoked paprika
- 5 cloves garlic, minced
- 1 green bell pepper, chopped
- 1 cup carrot, chopped
- ½ cup yellow onion, chopped
- 1 cup frozen corn
- ¼ cup tomato paste
- 14.5 ounce can of tomatoes, diced
- 2 tablespoons soy sauce
- ½ teaspoon cayenne pepper
- ½ teaspoon allspice
- ½ teaspoon oregano, dried
- 1 ½ cups water

Directions:
Soak the beans and lentils in water overnight. When you are ready to cook your chili, rinse and drain the beans and lentils in a fine mesh strainer, then set aside for now. Get all your veggies prepped and measure out all your spices for your chili. Set your instant pot on the sauté mode, and allow it to heat up for 2-minutes. Add the onion, bell pepper, carrot, and garlic and sauté for 5-minutes, stir occasionally. Add in the smoked paprika, coriander powder, chili powder, dried oregano, cumin powder, cayenne, allspice, soy sauce, diced tomatoes, salt, tomato paste, lentils and red beans, stir to combine ingredients. Cook and stir for about a minute then add in the water and stir once more. Secure the lid to pot in place, set it to Manual setting on high with a cook time of 30-minutes. When the cooking

is completed, release the pressure using natural release of 15-minutes. Add the corn and stir. Divide among serving bowls, and serve hot!
Nutritional Information per serving:
Calories: 206   Fat: 8g   Fiber: 2g   Carbs: 9g   Protein: 25g

---

303. Falafel
Cook Time: 5 minutes   **Servings: 6**
Ingredients:
- 1 cup chickpeas, cooked
- 1 tablespoon lemon juice
- 2 teaspoons water
- 3 tablespoons tahini
- 4-ounces shallots
- 1 teaspoon garlic powder
- 3 garlic cloves
- 1 teaspoon chili flakes
- 1 teaspoon paprika
- ½ cup parsley, chopped
- 1 tablespoon sesame seeds
- ½ teaspoon coriander
- 1 teaspoon cumin
- ½ teaspoon sea salt
- 1 teaspoon salt

Directions:
Place the chickpeas, coriander, cumin, parsley, salt, chili flakes, paprika, garlic powder, and water into a blender. Blend the mix until it is a smooth mass. Slice garlic cloves and shallot and add to the chickpea mixture. Continue to blend for another minute. Combine the sea salt and sesame seeds in a mixing bowl, and stir.
Make medium-sized balls with chickpea mixture, and coat them with sesame seed mix. Pour olive oil into instant pot and set it to sauté mode. Allow oil to heat up for a few minutes, then toss in the falafel to cook for a 5-minutes. Once they have formed a crust transfer them to a paper towel to remove the excess oil. Combine the tahini, sliced garlic, and lemon juice together and whisk. Drizzle tahini sauce over cooked falafel. Serve warm!
Nutritional Information per serving:
Calories: 296   Fat: 13g   Fiber: 1g   Carbs: 9g   Protein: 26g

---

304. Chickpea Curry
Cook Time: 11 minutes   **Servings: 6**
Ingredients:
- 2 cans (15-ounce) of chickpeas, rinsed and drained
- 1 packed cup kale, chopped
- 2 tablespoons cilantro leaves, for garnish
- 1 lime juiced
- 1 tablespoon honey
- 1 cup vegetable broth
- 1 cup okra, frozen, sliced
- 1 cup corn, frozen
- 1 (14.5-ounce) can tomatoes, crushed, with juice
- 1 tablespoon curry powder
- 2 cloves garlic, minced
- 1 green bell pepper, diced
- 2 tablespoons olive oil

Directions:

Set your instant pot to the sauté setting, add the oil and heat it. Add onion and stir, cook for 4-minutes. Add the bell pepper and garlic and cook for an additional 2 minutes. Add the curry powder and stir, cooking for another 30 seconds. Add the corn, okra, kale, broth, honey, tomatoes and juice, stir. Select the Manual setting on high with a cook time of 5-minutes. Once the cook time is completed, release the pressure naturally in 10-minutes. Divide into serving dishes, and garnish with cilantro leaves. Serve hot!

Nutritional Information per serving:
Calories: 232   Fat: 10g   Fiber: 1g   Carbs: 23g   Protein: 37g

305. Lentil Sloppy Joe's
Cook Time: 30 minutes   **Servings:** 6
Ingredients:

- 2 cups green lentils
- 3 cups veggie broth
- 1 red bell pepper, stemmed and chopped
- 1 yellow onion, chopped
- 1 (14-ounce) can of tomatoes, crushed
- 1 tablespoon dark brown sugar
- 1 tablespoon Dijon mustard
- 2 tablespoons soy sauce
- 1 tablespoon olive oil
- Salt and black pepper to taste

Directions:
Set your instant pot to the sauté mode, add the oil and heat it. Add the pepper and onion, cook for 3-minutes or until they have softened. Pour in the broth, then add in soy sauce, mustard, lentils, tomatoes, brown sugar, and pepper. Stir until the sugar has dissolved. Close and seal the pot lid. Select Manual setting on high for a cook time of 27-minutes. When the cook time is completed, release the pressure naturally for 15-minutes. Stir before serving on hamburger buns. Serve hot!

Nutritional Information per serving:
Calories: 208   Fat: 17g   Fiber: 1g   Carbs: 8g   Protein: 27g

306. Lentil and Wild Rice Pilaf
Cook Time: 14 minutes   **Servings:** 6
Ingredients:

- ¼ cup black or green lentils, soak for 30 minutes before cooking
- ¼ cup black/wild rice, soak for 30 minutes before cooking
- ¼ cup brown rice, soak for 30 minutes before cooking
- 3 cloves garlic, minced
- ½ onion, finely chopped
- 1 stalk celery, finely chopped
- 1 cup mushrooms, sliced
- 2 cups vegetable broth
- ¼ teaspoon red pepper flakes
- Salt and black pepper to taste
- 1 teaspoon fennel seeds
- 1 teaspoon coriander, dried
- 1 tablespoon Italian seasoning
- 1 bay leaf

Directions:

Combine the lentils and rice in a bowl, and allow them to soak for 30-minutes. Drain then rinse well. Set your instant pot to the sauté mode. Sauté veggies in pot for about 5-minutes, add a bit of water to prevent the veggies from burning. Add the rice and lentils, vegetable broth, and spices into pot. Close the lid and set to Manual on high pressure with a cook time of 9-minutes. When the cook time is completed, release the pressure naturally for 10-minutes. Serve dish with fresh or steamed veggies. Serve warm!

Nutritional Information per serving:
Calories: 187   Fat: 11g   Fiber: 1g   Carbs: 7g   Protein: 23g

---

307. Instant Pot Hummus
Cook Time: 18 minutes   **Servings: 6**
Ingredients:

- 1 cup soaked chickpeas
- 6 cups water
- 1 bay leaf
- 4 garlic cloves, crushed
- ¼ cup parsley, chopped
- 2 tablespoons tahini
- Dash of paprika
- ¼ teaspoon cumin
- ¼ teaspoon salt

Directions:
Soak your chickpeas in water overnight. When you are ready to make the hummus, rinse them and place them into instant pot. Pour in 6 cups of water to pot, add garlic cloves, and bay leaf. Seal the lid of pot shut, and set to Manual on high for a cook time of 18-minutes. When the cook time is completed, release the pressure naturally for 10-minutes. When it is safe to do so, once the pressure has come down, then drain the chickpeas, saving 1 cup of cooking liquid. Remove the bay leaf, before pureeing the chickpeas. Add the tahini, lemon juice, cumin, and ½ cup of cooking liquid to start. Keep pureeing, and if the mixture is not creamy enough, add a bit more liquid. Add salt and puree once more when you reach the right creaminess. Serve with a sprinkle of paprika and fresh, chopped parsley as garnish. Serve at room temperature!

Nutritional Information per serving:
Calories: 153   Fat: 4g   Fiber: 2g   Carbs: 8.2g   Protein: 21g

---

308. Stewed Chickpeas
Cook Time: 27 minutes   **Servings: 4**
Ingredients:

- 2 (14-ounce) cans of chickpeas, rinsed and drained
- 1 ½ tablespoon smoked paprika
- 3 small onions, chopped
- ¼ teaspoon allspice
- ½ teaspoon sea salt
- ½ teaspoon cumin
- 1 jar (24-ounces) tomatoes, strained
- 2/3 cup dates, pitted, chopped
- 3 tablespoons water, or as needed

Directions:
Set your instant pot to the sauté mode, add water as needed to prevent sticking. Cook for about 7-minutes, occasionally stirring. Add the tomatoes, dates, chickpeas, and stir until combined. Cover and lock the pot lid in place and set to Manual on high for a cook time of

20-minutes. When cook time is over, release the pressure using quick-release. Serve over cooked whole-grain, such as millet, quinoa, and brown rice.
Nutritional Information per serving:
Calories: 192   Fat: 16g   Fiber: 1g   Carbs: 6.2g   Protein: 24g

---

309. Rainbow Beans
Cook Time: 20 minutes   **Servings:** 6
Ingredients:

- 1 cup chicken stock
- 1 cup black beans, cooked
- ½ cup red beans, cooked
- ½ cup green beans, chopped
- ½ cup white beans, cooked
- 1 red sweet pepper, chopped, seeded
- 1 yellow sweet pepper, chopped, seeded
- 1 red onion, chopped
- 3 tablespoons sour cream
- 1 teaspoon turmeric
- 3 tablespoons tomato paste
- Salt as needed

Directions:
Add the water and chicken stock into your instant pot. Add the red, white, and black beans. Add the chopped veggies to instant pot. Sprinkle mixture with turmeric, tomato paste, sour cream, and salt. Mix gently and close the lid. Set to the Stew mode and cook for a 20-minute cook time. When the cooking is completed, transfer to serving bowls. Serve hot!
Nutritional Information per serving:
Calories: 205   Fat: 17g   Fiber: 1g   Carbs: 8.2g   Protein: 27g

---

310. Northern White Bean Dip
Cook Time: 13 minutes   **Servings:** 2
Ingredients:

- ¾ cup Great Northern white beans, soaked overnight
- Pinch of red pepper flakes
- 1 ½ teaspoons chili powder
- 2 teaspoons cumin, ground
- 3 tablespoons cilantro, minced
- 3 tablespoons lemon juice
- 2 garlic cloves
- 1/3 cup extra virgin olive oil
- Salt and black pepper to taste
- Water as needed

Directions:
Drain the beans before putting them in the instant pot. Cover beans with 1-inch of fresh water, close the pot lid and seal. Select Manual setting on high with a cook time of 13-minutes. When the cook time is completed, release the pressure naturally for 10-minutes. Once the pressure is gone, drain the beans and run under cold water. In a food processor, chop up the garlic. Add the rest of the ingredients (except cilantro) and puree till smooth. Serve with cilantro on top as a garnish. Serve at room temperature!
Nutritional Information per serving:
Calories: 203   Fat: 11g   Fiber: 2g   Carbs: 19g   Protein: 36g

311. *Greek-Style Gigantes Beans with Feta*
Cook Time: 25 minutes **Servings:** 8

Ingredients:
- 3 cups Gigantes white beans, dried
- 8 cups water
- 1 teaspoon oregano, dried
- 1 can (about 28-ounces) crushed tomatoes
- 1 large yellow onion, finely diced
- 1 garlic, clove, peeled
- ¼ cup extra virgin olive oil
- 1 teaspoon salt
- ¼ teaspoon black pepper
- ¼ cup flat-leaf parsley, fresh, chopped, for garnish
- ½ cup feta cheese, crumbled, for garnish or topping

Directions:
Combine the beans, salt, and water in the instant pot. Allow the beans to soak in the water for 12 hours before cooking. Secure the lid in place when you are ready to cook. Select the Bean/Chili setting and set the cook time for 15-minutes at high pressure. When the cook time is completed, release the pressure naturally for 15-minutes. Remove lid and ladle out 1 cup of cooking liquid and set aside. Wearing oven-mitts, lift the inner pot out of instant pot and drain the beans in a colander. Return the now empty pot to the instant pot housing for it. Now, select sauté mode, and heat the ¼ cup olive oil in the pot. Add the garlic, onion, celery and sauté for 15-minutes. Add the drained beans, and reserved cup of cooking liquid, tomatoes, oregano, pepper, and stir well.

Close and lock the lid, and reset the instant pot to Bean/Chili setting and set the cook time for 5-minutes on high. Let the pressure release using quick-release. Ladle the beans into a serving dish and garnish or top with feta cheese, parsley, and remaining olive oil, and serve warm!

Nutritional Information per serving:
Calories: 215 Fat: 18g Fiber: 2g Carbs: 7.4g Protein: 28g

312. *Chili Con Carne*
Cook Time: 10 minutes **Servings:** 6

Ingredients:
- 1 can (28-ounces) ground and peeled tomatoes
- 1 teaspoon oregano, dry
- 1 tablespoon Worcestershire sauce
- 1 tablespoon chili powder
- 1 ½ cups onion, large, diced
- 1 ½ teaspoons cumin, ground
- 1 ½ lbs. ground beef
- 1 can (14-ounce) black beans, rinsed and drained
- 1 can (14-ounce) kidney beans, rinsed and drained
- 3 tablespoons extra virgin olive oil
- 2 tablespoons garlic, minced
- 1-2 jalapenos, stems and seeds removed, finely diced
- Salt and black pepper to taste
- 1 cup sweet red bell pepper, large, diced
- ½ cup water

Directions:

Press the sauté button, allow pot to heat, add in oil. Add the ground beef, and break it up using a wooden spoon, cook for 5-minutes or until beef is browned. Remove excess fat, add the onions, bell pepper, jalapenos, and sauté for 3-minutes. Add the garlic, chili powder, oregano, cumin, salt and pepper, and sauté for 1-minute. Add the beans, water, tomatoes, and Worcestershire sauce and stir to combine. Close and secure the lid. Select Manual setting on high with a cook time of 10-minutes. When the cook time is completed, release the pressure using the quick-release. Serve hot!

Nutritional Information per serving:
Calories: 204   Fat: 22g   Fiber: 2g   Carbs: 17g   Protein: 26g

---

313. Smokey Sweet Black-Eyed Peas & Greens
Cook Time: 13 minutes   **Servings: 6**
Ingredients:
- 1 ½ teaspoon chili powder
- 2 teaspoons smoked paprika
- 1 ½ cups black-eyed peas, dried and soaked overnight
- 1 cup red pepper, diced
- 1 onion, thinly sliced
- 1 teaspoon oil
- 4 dates, chopped fine
- 1 cup water or vegetable stock
- 1 (15-ounce) can of fire roasted tomatoes with green chilies
- 2 cups greens, chopped, kale or Swiss chard
- Salt to taste

Directions:
Set your instant pot to the sauté mode, add the oil and heat it. Add the onions, and cook for 3-minutes. Add the garlic and peppers and sauté for another 2-minutes. Add the smoked paprika and chili powder along with the peas and dates. Stir to coat them with spices. Add water, stirring to combine. Close and lock lid of pot, select Manual setting on high with a cook time of 3-minutes. When the cook time is completed, release the pressure naturally for 5-minutes. Add the tomatoes and greens and lock the lid, setting for an additional 5-minutes of cook time. Serve warm!

Nutritional Information per serving:
Calories: 207   Fat: 5g   Fiber: 8g   Carbs: 22g   Protein: 29g

---

314. Tex Mex Pinto Beans
Cook Time: 42 minutes   **Servings: 6**
Ingredients:
- ¼ cup cilantro, chopped
- 1 jalapeno, diced
- 1 onion, chopped
- 1 packet taco seasoning
- ½ cup Salsa Verde
- 1 clove garlic, diced
- 5 cups chicken broth
- 20 ounces package pinto beans with ham

Directions:
Rinse and sort out the dried beans, then place them into your instant pot. Add the broth to the pot. Add onion, garlic, jalapeno, and stir. Add taco seasoning and stir to combine, then close the lid and secure it. Select the Manual setting on high for a cook time of 42-minutes. When the cook time is completed, release the pressure naturally for about 15-

minutes. Drain the excess liquid from the pot. Stir in the Salsa Verde, ham seasoning, and cilantro. Add salt to taste. Serve tacos, over rice, or a side dish. Serve hot!

Nutritional Information per serving:
Calories: 232   Fat: 21g   Fiber: 3g   Carbs: 22g   Protein: 27g

---

315. *Instant Pot Charros*
Cook Time: 56 minutes   *Servings: 8*
Ingredients:

- 1 lb. pinto beans dried, rinsed and picked over
- ½ lb. double smoked bacon
- ½ lb. Mexican Chorizo raw, Mexican chorizo sausage, not the dried Spanish chorizo
- 1 large onion, chopped
- 1 large jalapeno, seeded and finely chopped
- 4 cloves garlic
- 1 can of tomatoes and chilies
- 3 cups chicken stock
- 2 cups Mexican beer
- 2 chipotle chilies canned in adobo, minced
- 1 teaspoon salt
- 2 bay leaves
- 1 tablespoon Epazote, crushed
- 1 tablespoon Mexican oregano
- 2 tablespoons cumin
- 1 tablespoon olive oil
- 1 cup cilantro, fresh, chopped, for garnish

Directions:
Set your instant pot to the sauté mode, add the oil and heat it up. Add the bacon and fry until it starts to brown for about 5-minutes. Remove the chorizo meat from the casing and add it to pot to brown. Cook for another 4-minutes or until meat is cooked.
Add the onion, add cook for another 5-minutes. Add the jalapenos, cumin, garlic, oregano, Epazote and cook for one more minute. Now add in the pinto beans, bay leaves, chipotle chilies, beer, salt, chicken stock, and give it a nice stir. Close the lid and set to cook for 45-minutes on Manual high with a cook time of 45-minutes. When the cook time is completed, release the pressure naturally for 15-minutes. Remove the lid and stir the beans, and set to sauté mode, cooking for an additional 5-minutes. Serve hot! Top with cilantro for garnish.

Nutritional Information per serving:
Calories: 243   Fat: 20g   Fiber: 2g   Carbs: 21g   Protein: 31g

---

316. *Three Bean Salad*
Cook Time: 15 minutes   *Servings: 4*
Ingredients:

- 1 cup chickpeas/garbanzo beans, soaked or quick-soaked
- 1 cup Borlotti or cranberry beans, soaked or quick-soaked

For the dressing:
- 2 celery stalks, chopped finely
- 1 ½ cups of green beans, fresh or frozen
- 1 bay leaf
- 1 clove of garlic, lightly crushed
- ½ red onion, chopped finely

- 4 tablespoon olive oil
- 1 teaspoon Truvia
- 5 tablespoon apple cider vinegar
- 1 bunch parsley, finely chopped
- Salt and pepper to taste

Directions:
Wrap the green beans inside some aluminum foil. Add 4 cups of fresh water to your instant pot, then add the soaked or rinsed chickpeas, garlic clove, and bay leaf. Add the steamer basket with the soaked Borlotti beans. Finally, add the packet of tin foil wrapped green beans. Use a second trivet to keep your packet suspended above the Borlotti. Close and lock the pot lid, and set to Manual on high for a cook time of 15-minutes.

When the cook time is completed, release the pressure naturally for 10-minutes. While the beans are cooking prepare dressing. Slice the onion nice and fine, add to a bowl with vinegar and Truvia, mix and set aside. Remove and open the packet of green beans. Pour the beans from the steamer basket and into a strainer. Rinse beans under cold water. Slice the green beans and place in with other beans and mix well. In a serving bowl add the beans along with dressing and mix well. Add salt and pepper to taste. Serve chilled!

Nutritional Information per serving:
Calories: 198   Fat: 18g   Fiber: 3g   Carbs: 19g   Protein: 29g

317. Beans Stew

Cook Time: 67 minutes   **Servings: 8**

Ingredients:

- 1 lb. red beans, dry—water as needed
- 2 carrots, chopped
- 2 tablespoons vegetable oils
- ¼ cup cilantro leaves, chopped
- 1 small onion, diced
- 2 green onions, chopped
- 1 tomato, chopped
- Salt and black pepper to taste
- 2 carrots, chopped
- Water as needed

Directions:
Add the beans to your instant pot and set to Manual on high for a cook time of 35-minutes. When the cook time is completed, release the pressure naturally for 10-minutes. Add carrots, and salt and pepper to taste, cover instant pot again, setting for a cook time of 30-additional minutes. Meanwhile heat a pan with vegetable oil over medium high heat, add onion, stir for 2-minutes. Add tomatoes, green onions, some salt and pepper and stir again, cook for an additional 3-minutes, then remove from heat. Release the pressure naturally for 10-minutes. Divide among serving plates, and garnish with fresh, chopped cilantro. Serve warm!

Nutritional Information per serving:
Calories: 211   Fat: 23g   Fiber: 1g   Carbs: 26g   Protein: 29g

318. Not Re-Fried Beans
Cook Time: 13 minutes **Servings: 8**
Ingredients:
- 2 cups Borlotti beans, dried, soaked
- 2 cups water
- ½ teaspoon cumin
- ¼ teaspoon chipotle powder
- 1 bunch cilantro or parsley, leaves and stems, chopped, divided
- 1 onion, chopped
- 1 tablespoon vegetable oil
- 1 teaspoon salt

Directions:
Set your instant pot to the saute mode, add the oil and heat. Add the onion and cook for 3-minutes. Add beans and water. Close and lock the lid to pot, and set on Manual on high with a cook time of 10-minutes. When the cook time is completed, release the pressure naturally for 10-minutes. Remove a heaping spoonful of beans from pot and set aside (to use as garnish). Sprinkle the rest of the beans inside pot with salt and mash with potato masher for desired consistency. Serve with sprinkled whole beans, parsley, and a dollop of sour cream as garnish. Serve warm!

Nutritional Information per serving:
Calories: 213 Fat: 20g Fiber: 2g Carbs: 14g Protein: 31g

319. Baked Beans
Cook Time: 23 minutes **Servings: 8**
Ingredients:
- 1 lb. dried navy beans, soaked overnight for at least 16 hours
- 1 teaspoon apple cider vinegar
- 2 teaspoons Dijon mustard
- 2 bay leaves
- ¼ teaspoon fine table salt
- 1 tablespoon light soy sauce
- ¼ cup maple syrup
- ¼ cup blackstrap molasses
- 1 ¾ cup cold water
- 2 cloves garlic, roughly chopped
- 1 small onion, roughly diced
- 6 strips thick-cut bacon, roughly diced
- 6 cups cold water

Directions:
Allow the navy beans to soak overnight in a container filled with 6 cups of water with 1 ½ tablespoons of fine table salt. After they have soaked for the night drain the water out of the navy beans using a mesh strainer. Rinse the beans with cold water, drain well. The soaked beans should double in weight. Place the chopped bacon into your instant pot and set it to the sauté mode, stir occasionally, cooking for 3-minutes. Add in the diced onion, pepper, and sauté for another additional minute. Add in the chopped garlic cloves and sauté for 30 seconds.

Combine ¼ cup blackstrap molasses, ¼ cup maple syrup, 1 tablespoon light soy sauce, and 1 ¾ cup cold water in a 1-liter glass measuring cup, and mix well. Pour ½ cup of molasses mixture into your instant pot. Mix well.

Add ¼ teaspoon fine table salt, 2 bay leaves, soaked navy beans, and the remaining molasses mixture into instant pot. Mix well. Close the lid and set to Manual on high with a cook time of 20-minutes. When the cook time is completed, release the pressure naturally for 20-minutes. Add 2 teaspoons of Dijon mustard, and 1 teaspoon apple cider vinegar into the cooked baked beans. Mix well. Set your instant pot to the sauté mode and heat the pot and stir baked beans until they get the desired consistency. Serve this as a side dish at family picnics, or potlucks, or dinner. Serve hot!

Nutritional Information per serving:
Calories: 206   Fat: 23g   Fiber: 3g   Carbs: 19g   Protein: 33g

---

320. Stewed Tomatoes & Green Beans
Cook Time: 10 minutes   **Servings:** 10
Ingredients:
- 1 lb. green beans
- 2 cups tomatoes, fresh, chopped
- 1 crushed garlic clove
- 1 teaspoon olive oil
- ½ cup water
- Salt to taste

Directions:
Set your instant pot to the sauté mode, add the oil and heat it. Add the garlic, and once it becomes fragrant add tomatoes, and ½ cup water. Fill the steamer basket with green beans and sprinkle salt and lower into instant pot. Close and seal the lid to pot and set to Manual on high for a cook time of 5-minutes. When the cook time is completed, release the pressure naturally for 10-minutes. Remove steamer basket from pot and pour the beans into the tomato sauce and stir. Serve warm!

Nutritional Information per serving:
Calories: 198   Fat: 6g   Fiber: 2g   Carbs: 15g   Protein: 23g

---

321. White Beans with Greens & Lemon
Cook Time: 11 minutes   **Servings:** 6
Ingredients:
- 1 onion, chopped
- 2 teaspoons olive oil
- 1 cup white beans, soaked overnight
- 2 bay leaves
- 2 tablespoons lemon juice
- 1 teaspoon lemon zest
- 4 cups greens chard, spinach or kale, stems removed, chopped
- 3 cloves garlic, minced
- ¾ cup vegetable stock or water

Directions:
Set your instant pot to the sauté mode, add the oil and heat it. Add the onion, and cook for 3-minutes. Add beans and vegetable stock and set to Manual mode on high for 7-minutes cook time. Begin preparing the greens while the contents of instant pot are cooking. Zest and juice lemon. Peel and mince the garlic. When the cooking is completed, release the pressure naturally for 7-minutes. Open the pot and add lemon zest, greens, and garlic. Close the instant pot and set on Manual on high for 1-minute cook time. Use quick-release for the pressure, and remove the bay leaves and discard them. Serve alone or with your favorite noodles or grain. Serve warm!

Nutritional Information per serving:
Calories: 203   Fat: 16g   Fiber: 1g   Carbs: 18g   Protein: 24g

322. White Bean Dip with Tomatoes

Cook Time: 19 minutes
Servings: 8
Ingredients:

- 1 can cannellini beans, soaked overnight
- 1 small white onion, diced
- 1 ½ teaspoons garlic, minced, divided
- 6 sun-dried tomatoes
- 2 tablespoons lemon juice
- 3 tablespoons olive oil
- 1 teaspoon paprika
- 1/8 black pepper, ground
- 1 teaspoon salt
- 1 ¼ cups water
- 3 tablespoons parsley, chopped
- 1 tablespoon capers

Directions:
Drain beans and place them into your instant pot. Pour water and add 1 teaspoon garlic salt, and black pepper. Secure the lid on pot and set to Manual on high for a cook time of 14-minutes. When the cook time is completed, release the pressure naturally for 10-minutes. In a frying pan add oil and fry onion and remaining garlic and cook for 5-minutes. When they are done set the pan aside of the heat. Uncover the instant pot and drain beans, reserving ½ cup of cooking liquid. Let the beans cool and transfer them to food processor and add the garlic and onion, lemon juice and paprika. Pulse until smooth, slowly add in the reserved liquid. Tip the mix into a serving bowl. Dice tomatoes and stir together with capers and parsley. Add this mixture into the bean dip and stir. Serve at room temperature.

Nutritional Information per serving:
Calories: 201   Fat: 17g   Fiber: 2g   Carbs: 19g   Protein: 26g

323. Bacon & Black Beans

Cook Time: 43 minutes
Servings: 4
Ingredients:

- 3 strips bacon, cut into halves
- 1 lb. black beans, dried
- 6 garlic cloves, crushed
- 1 small onion, cut in half
- 1 orange, cut in half
- 2 cups chicken stock
- 2 bay leaves
- 2 teaspoons salt
- 1 tablespoon olive oil

Directions:
Set your instant pot to the sauté mode, add oil and heat it. Add the bacon and cook it for 5-minutes turning often. Add the rest of the ingredients into instant pot and close and secure the lid. Set to Manual on high with a cook time of 40-minutes. When the cook time is completed, release the pressure naturally for 15-minutes. Discard the bay leaves, onion, and orange. Season with salt to taste and serve warm.

Nutritional Information per serving:
Calories: 204   Fat: 16g   Fiber: 2g   Carbs: 23g   Protein: 29g

324. Black Bean & Sweet Potato Hash
Cook Time: 6 minutes
Servings: 4
Ingredients:
- 1 cup onion, chopped
- 2 cups sweet potatoes, chopped and peeled
- 2 teaspoons hot chili powder
- 1 garlic clove, minced
- ¼ cup scallions, chopped
- 1 cup black beans, drained
- 1/3 veggie broth
- 1 tablespoon olive oil

Directions:
Prep your vegetables, and turn on your instant pot to the sauté mode, add oil and heat it. Add chopped onions and cook for 3-minutes, stir. Add the garlic and cook for an additional 2-minutes. Add the potatoes, chili powder and stir. Pour in the broth, and stir. Set pot to Manual on high for a cook time of 3-minutes. When the cook time is completed, release the pressure using quick-release. Add the black beans, scallions and stir to combine. Serve warm!

Nutritional Information per serving:
Calories: 189   Fat: 16g   Fiber: 1g   Carbs: 18g   Protein: 24g

325. Refried Bean Nachos
Cook Time: 28 minutes
Servings: 6
Ingredients:
- 2 cups pinto beans, dried, soaked, rinsed
- 1 onion, large, diced
- 1 jalapeno pepper, seeded
- 1 teaspoon chili powder
- 1 teaspoon paprika
- 1 teaspoon salt
- 4 cloves garlic, peeled and roughly chopped
- 3 cups vegetable broth or water
- ½ cup salsa cilantro, to taste
- ½ teaspoon black pepper
- 1 teaspoon cumin

Directions:
Add all the ingredients into the instant pot and stir to combine. Close and lock the lid and set to Manual and cook on high with a cook time of 28-minutes. When the cook time is completed, release the pressure naturally for 10-minutes. Mash the beans using a potato masher to desired consistency. Serve warm.

Nutritional Information per serving:
Calories: 210   Fat: 24g   Fiber: 2g   Carbs: 21g   Protein: 36g

326. Green Bean Casserole

Cook Time: 18 minutes **Servings: 4**

Ingredients:
- 16-ounces green beans
- 12-ounces mushrooms, sliced
- 2 tablespoons butter
- 1 cup chicken broth
- 1 cup heavy cream
- 1 onion, small-size
- ½ cup French's onions, for garnishing
- 2 tablespoons cornstarch

Directions:
Set your instant pot on the sauté mode, add butter and heat it. Add the mushrooms and onion, and cook for about 3-minutes. Add the green beans, heavy cream, and chicken broth. Cover and lock lid in place and set to Manual on high for a cook time of 15-minutes. When the cook time is completed, release the pressure using the quick-release. Add 2 tablespoons of cornstarch to dish to help thicken. Serve hot with French's onions for garnish.

Nutritional Information per serving:
Calories: 218   Fat: 19g   Fiber: 2g   Carbs: 21g   Protein: 33g

327. Green Bean, Sweet Potato & Spinach Risotto

Cook Time: 28 minutes **Servings: 4**

Ingredients:
- 1 ½ cups carnaroli rice
- 1 ½ cups green beans, cut into 1/3-inch pieces
- 1 cup spinach, chopped
- 1 sweet potato, peeled, diced into 1/3-inch cubes
- 1 pinch saffron
- 1 tablespoon sage, finely minced
- 4 shallots, finely diced
- 3 ½ cups vegetable broth
- 2 cloves garlic, minced
- Sea salt and black pepper to taste
- 1 tablespoon olive oil

Directions:
Preheat oven to 410°Fahrenheit. Line a shallow baking tray with parchment paper. In a large-sized bowl, toss the sweet potatoes with 2-tablespoons veggie broth. Place potato pieces onto baking sheet and spread them over it. Roast in the center of oven for 15-minutes or until they begin to brown. Remove the tray and flip potatoes over and bake for another 5-minutes. Once they are baked allow them to rest on baking tray. Set your instant pot to the sauté mode, add olive oil and heat it up. Add the onion and sauté for 3-minutes. Add the garlic and cook for another 30-seconds. Pour in the ¼ cup of stock, add the rice and remaining broth, sage, and saffron. Cover and lock the lid and set to Manual on high for 5-minutes cook time. When the cook time is completed, release the pressure using quick-release.

Stir in the spinach and the beans in the rice mixture in the pot. Cover the lid and allow it to steam for 3-minutes. Add the roasted potatoes and stir, and serve hot.

Nutritional Information per serving:
Calories: 221   Fat: 21g   Fiber: 2g   Carbs: 27g   Protein: 36g

328. Steamed Green Beans
Cook Time: 20 minute **Servings:** 4
Ingredients:
- 1 lb. green beans, washed
- 2 tablespoons parsley, fresh, chopped for garnish
- 1 cup water

For dressing:
- 3 cloves garlic, sliced
- 3 tablespoons olive oil
- 2 tablespoons white wine vinegar
- Pinch of salt
- Pinch of pepper

Directions:
Pour water into your instant pot and set the steamer basket inside pot. Place the green beans in the steamer basket. Set to Manual on high for a cook time of 1-minute. When the cook time is complete, release the pressure using quick-release. Transfer the beans to a serving bowl. Toss in the dressing ingredients and allow it to stand for 10-minutes. Remove the slices of garlic, then garnish with parsley. Serve cold or room temperature.

Nutritional Information per serving:
Calories: 183 Fat: 14g Fiber: 2g Carbs: 16g Protein: 27g

329. Spicy Green Beans
Cook Time: 8 minutes **Servings:** 3
Ingredients:
- 1 tablespoon olive oil
- 2 cups green beans
- 4 cloves garlic, chopped
- ½ teaspoon cumin seeds
- 1 green chili, chopped
- 1 potato, cubed into small pieces

Spices:
- ¼ teaspoon turmeric powder
- 2 teaspoons coriander powder
- ¼ teaspoon red chili powder
- 1 teaspoon mango, dry powder
- 1 ½ teaspoons salt

Directions:
Set your instant pot on the sauté mode, add oil and heat it. Add cumin seeds, green chili and garlic. When the cumin seeds begin to sputter add the potatoes, and green beans, stir and cook for 5-minutes. Add the spices except the dry mango powder and mix. Sprinkle water in pot using your hand. Close and secure the lid to pot and set on Manual on high for a cook time of 2-minutes. When the cook time is completed, release the pressure using quick-release. Mix in the dry mango powder. Serve dish with roti or naan. Serve warm.

Nutritional Information per serving:
Calories: 211 Fat: 22g Fiber: 3g Carbs: 23g Protein: 34g

330. Italian Cannellini Beans & Mint Salad

Cook Time: 8 minutes **Servings: 4**

Ingredients:
- 1 cup cannellini beans, soaked overnight
- 1 clove garlic, smashed
- 4 cups water
- 1 bay leaf
- 1 sprig mint fresh
- 1 dash vinegar
- Olive oil
- Salt and pepper to taste

Directions:
Add soaked beans, garlic clove, water and bay leaf to your instant pot. Close and secure the lid and set to Manual on high for a cook time of 8-minutes. When the cook time is completed, release the pressure using quick-release. Strain the beans and mix with mint, vinegar, olive oil, salt and pepper. Serve chilled.

Nutritional Information per serving:
Calories: 202   Fat: 12g   Fiber: 2g   Carbs: 19g   Protein: 35g

331. Refried Pinto Beans

Cook Time: 45 minutes **Servings: 8**

Ingredients:
- 2 lbs. pinto beans, dried, sorted
- 2 teaspoons oregano, dried
- 3 tablespoons olive oil
- 1 teaspoon sea salt
- 4 cups vegetable broth
- 1 jalapeno, seeds removed, and chopped
- 4 cups water
- 1 ½ teaspoons cumin, ground
- 5 garlic cloves, roughly chopped
- 1 ½ cups onion, chopped

Directions:
Soak the pinto beans in a large bowl of water that covers the beans, allow to soak for 15-minutes. Add garlic cloves, oregano, onion, jalapeno, cumin, olive oil, vegetable broth, black pepper and water into instant pot and stir. Place the soaked beans into a colander to strain. Discard the soaking liquid. Rinse beans with fresh water. Add the beans into the pot and mix. Cover and lock the pot lid, and set to Bean/Chili mode for a cook time of 45-minutes. When the cook time is completed, release the pressure naturally for 40-minutes. Season beans with sea salt to taste. Use an immersion blender to blend beans to desired consistency. Serve cool.

Nutritional Information per serving:
Calories: 204   Fat: 14g   Fiber: 2g   Carbs: 21g   Protein: 37g

332. Spice Black Bean & Brown Rice Salad
Cook Time: 24 minutes　　　　　**Servings: 8**
Ingredients:
- 1 can (14-ounce) black beans, drained and rinsed
- 1 cup brown rice
- 12 grape tomatoes, quartered

For spicy dressing:
- 3 tablespoons extra-virgin olive oil
- 3 tablespoons lime juice, fresh squeezed
- ¼ teaspoon salt
- ¼ cup cilantro, minced
- 1 ½ cups water
- 1 avocado, diced
- 2 garlic cloves, minced
- 2 teaspoons tabasco

Directions:
Combine the rice with water and salt in your instant pot. Close and lock the lid in place, select the Manual setting on high with a cook time of 24-minutes. When the cook time is completed, release the pressure naturally for 10-minutes. Use a fork to fluff the rice and allow it to cool at room temperature. When it is cool, refrigerate until ready to use. In a large bowl, stir the brown rice with black beans, tomato, avocado, and cilantro. In a small bowl, whisk the dressing ingredients together, except olive oil. While whisking slowly add the olive oil. Pour the dressing over the brown rice mix and stir to combine. Serve cold.

Nutritional Information per serving:
Calories: 196　Fat: 10g　Fiber: 2g　Carbs: 17g　Protein: 34g

333. Quick-Soaking Dry Beans
Cook Time: 8 minutes　　　　　**Servings: 3**
Ingredients:
- 1 cup beans
- 4 cups water
- 1 teaspoon salt, optional

Directions:
Place the beans, water and salt into your instant pot. Set your instant pot to Manual on high for a cook time of 8-minutes. Once the cook time is completed, release the pressure naturally for 10-minutes. Strain, rinse and drain the beans. Serve warm.

Nutritional Information per serving:
Calories: 204　Fat: 13g　Fiber: 2g　Carbs: 17g　Protein: 32g

334. Black-Eyed Pea Chili
Cook Time: 45 minutes　　　　　**Servings: 4**
Ingredients:
- 1 ½ cups black-eyed peas, dried
- 3 cups water
- 1 whole chicken breast, boneless, cooked, cut into pieces
- 1 large onion, chopped
- 1 green pepper, chopped
- 3 cloves garlic, minced
- 2 tablespoons chili powder

- Salt and pepper to taste

Directions:
In your instant pot add the water, beans and some salt. Set the pot to the Bean/Chili setting for a cook time of 40-minutes. When the cook time is completed, release the pressure naturally for 15-minutes. Add the chicken and other ingredients to instant pot and stir to combine. Set to sauté mode and cook and stir for about 5-minutes. Serve hot.

Nutritional Information per serving:
Calories: 172   Fat: 7g   Fiber: 2g   Carbs: 18g   Protein: 23g

---

335. *Moroccan Chicken*
Cook Time: 45 minutes   **Servings:** 4

Ingredients:
- 2 boneless, chicken breasts, cut in half
- 2 tablespoons olive oil
- 1 medium onion, chopped
- 2 tablespoons raisins
- 1 cup canned chickpeas, drained and rinsed
- ½ teaspoon cinnamon, ground
- 2 teaspoons cumin, ground
- 1 teaspoon oregano, dried
- 1 (14-ounce) can tomatoes, diced
- 1 medium zucchini, halved lengthwise and sliced thick
- Salt to taste
- 1 ½ cups cooked rice

Directions:
Set your instant pot to sauté mode, add in the oil and heat it. Add the chicken and cook until brown on all sides for about 5-minutes. Once browned remove chicken from pot and set aside. Add in onion to pot and sauté for 3-minutes. Add tomatoes. Return the chicken to the pot and stir and simmer for 25-minutes. Add in zucchini, and spices. Cover pot with lid set on Manual for 5-minutes. Add the chick peas and raisins and set pot on Manual for another 5-minutes cook time. Once the cook time is completed, release the pressure naturally for 10-minutes. Serve over a bed of rice. Serve hot.

Nutritional Information per serving:
Calories: 287   Fat: 9g   Fiber: 2g   Carbs: 29g   Protein: 34g

---

336. *Baked Bean Mix*
Cook Time: 48 minutes   **Servings:** 6

Ingredients:
- ½ cup each of black beans, dried, navy beans, kidney beans, pinto beans
- ¼ lb. bacon, cut into matchstick pieces
- 2 medium onions, chopped
- 1 teaspoon allspice
- 2 tablespoons light molasses
- 2 tablespoons brown sugar
- 1 tablespoon tomato ketchup
- 1 tablespoon soy sauce
- 1 cup water
- 1 (14-ounce) can tomato sauce
- 1 tablespoon olive oil

Directions:
Combine the beans, rinse, and use quick-soak method on soaking and cooking dried beans, drain. In your instant pot add beans and cover with water, and set on Manual for 40-

minutes cook time. When cook time is completed, release the pressure naturally for 15-minutes. Drain and rinse the beans. Set the instant pot to the sauté mode, add in the olive oil and heat it. Add the bacon and cook for 5-minutes or until crispy. Remove bacon and set aside. Add onions, and green pepper to pot and sauté for 3-minutes. Add the bacon back to pot along with remaining ingredients, stir to combine. Close and secure lid for pot and set to Beans/Chili mode for 40-minutes. Serve hot.

Nutritional Information per serving:
Calories: 298   Fat: 10g   Fiber: 26g   Carbs: 27g   Protein: 29g

---

337. Bean Counter's Medley
Cook Time: 45 minutes   **Servings:** 10
Ingredients:

- 1 can (14-ounce) can tomatoes, crushed
- ¼ cup vinegar
- ½ cup tomato ketchup
- 1 cup celery, chopped
- 1 can (14-ounce) baked beans, drained
- 1 can (14-ounce) cut yellow beans
- 1 can (14-ounce) lima beans
- 1 can (19-ounce) kidney beans
- 1 large onion, chopped

Directions:
Add all the ingredients into your instant pot, and set to Bean/Chili mode for 45-minutes. When the cook time is completed, release the pressure naturally for 15-minutes. Stir the mixture well. Serve hot.

Nutritional Information per serving:
Calories: 243   Fat: 11g   Fiber: 3g   Carbs: 29g   Protein: 38g

---

338. Tomato Lima Bean Parmigiana
Cook Time: 25 minutes   **Servings:** 4
Ingredients:

- 4 strips bacon in 1/2-inch slices
- ½ cup parmesan cheese, grated
- 2 medium tomatoes, chopped
- 1 cup water
- 2 cloves garlic, minced
- 1 (14-ounce) can lima beans, rinsed and drained
- 1 onion, chopped finely
- 1 tablespoon olive oil

Directions:
Set your instant pot to sauté mode, add olive oil and heat it. Add the bacon and cook for 5-minutes or until crisp, then remove and set aside. Set your instant pot to Bean/Chili mode for 40-minutes, add all ingredients except cheese. When cook time is completed, release the pressure naturally for 15-minutes. Add mixture to a casserole dish, sprinkle the top with grated parmesan, then broil in oven for 3-minutes or until cheese is melted. Serve hot.

Nutritional Information per serving:
Calories: 256   Fat: 13g   Fiber: 2g   Carbs: 27g   Protein: 39g

339. Curried Cauliflower & Beans
Cook Time: 13 minutes
Servings: 6
Ingredients:
- 1 cup cauliflower, cut into florets
- 2 cups tomatoes, finely chopped
- 2 tablespoons lime juice
- 1 teaspoon curry powder
- 1 cup water
- 1 cup red kidney beans, drained and rinsed
- 1 tablespoon olive oil
- ½ teaspoon ginger, ground

Directions:
Set your instant pot to the sauté mode, add the oil and heat it. Add the ginger and garlic and cook for 2-minutes. Stir in the tomatoes, lime juice, curry powder, water and cook for an additional 3-minutes. Add in the cauliflower, and stir to combine, set to Manual on high for a cook time of 8-minutes. Add the beans and stir to blend. Serve hot.

Nutritional Information per serving:
Calories: 256   Fat: 14g   Fiber: 2g   Carbs: 24g   Protein: 38g

340. Black Beans & Black Chinese Rice
Cook Time: 10 minutes
Servings: 6
Ingredients:
- 1 ½ cups Black Chinese Rice, cooked
- 1 tablespoon olive oil
- 2 cloves garlic, minced
- 3 tablespoons white vinegar
- ½ teaspoon oregano, dried
- ½ green pepper, chopped
- 1 can (14-ounces) black beans, rinsed and drained
- ½ cup water

Directions:
Set your instant pot to the sauté mode, add the oil and heat it. Add the green pepper and garlic and cook for 3-minutes. Add beans, oregano, vinegar, water and rice to pot, stir to combine. Set to manual on a cook time of 8-minutes. When the cook time is completed, release the pressure naturally for 10-minutes. Serve hot.

Nutritional Information per serving:
Calories: 248   Fat: 12g   Fiber: 4g   Carbs: 31g   Protein: 39g

Chapter 11. Collection of Vegetable Instant Pot Recipes

341. Sweet Potato, Red Lentil, Hemp Burgers
Cook Time: 16 minutes **Servings:** 10
Ingredients:

- 1 cup onion, minced
- 1 cup cremini mushrooms, minced
- 2 ¼ cups vegetable stock
- 2 teaspoons ginger, fresh, grated
- 1 ½ sweet potatoes, peeled, cut into large pieces
- 1 cup red lentils, rinsed and picked over
- ¼ cup of hemp seeds
- 4 tablespoons of brown rice flour
- ¼ cup flat leaf parsley, fresh, chopped finely
- 1 cup quick oats
- ¼ cup cilantro, chopped finely
- 1 tablespoon curry powder

Directions:
Set your instant pot on the sauté mode, add in the mushrooms, ginger, and onion, dry sauté for 3-minutes. Add in the sweet potatoes, lentils and vegetable stock. Close and secure the lid, set to Manual on high for a cook time of 6-minutes. When the cook time is completed, release the pressure naturally for 10-minutes. Transfer the lentil mixture to a bowl, and allow to stand for 15-minutes at room temperature. Heat your oven to 375° Fahrenheit. Line a large baking sheet with parchment paper, and lightly coat it with cooking spray. Mash the lentil mixture with a potato masher, when cool. Stir in the cilantro, parsley and hemp seeds, as well as curry powder, then stir in oats.
Add in the brown rice flour, and form the mixture into 10 patties using wet hands and place each patty onto the already prepared baking sheet. Bake for 10-minutes; flip and bake until they are firm and brown, cook for an additional 10-minutes. Allow to cool for a couple of minutes. Serve immediately, or freeze, or refrigerate for later use. Serve warm.

Nutritional Information per serving:
Calories: 263 Fat: 1.3g Carbs: 53.6g Protein: 9.8g

342. Creamy Kidney Beans & Lentils
Cook Time: 45 minutes **Servings:** 6
Ingredients:

- 3 cups kidney beans, cooked
- 6 garlic cloves, minced
- 1 teaspoon cardamom, ground
- 1 cup of whole black lentils, dry
- 2 tablespoons ginger, grated
- 1 ½ teaspoons chili powder
- 3 teaspoons cumin, ground
- ¼ teaspoon nutmeg, ground
- 1 teaspoon turmeric, ground
- 5 cups of water
- ¼ teaspoon mustard, ground

Before serving:

- 2 teaspoons ginger, grated
- ½ cup cashew creamer
- Cilantro, fresh, chopped for garnish
- 1 teaspoon garam masala
- Salt to taste

Directions:
Add all the ingredients to your instant pot, and set on Manual on high for a cook time of 45-minutes. When the cook time has completed, release the pressure naturally for 15-minutes. Once the cooking is completed stir in the serving ingredients and serve hot.
Nutritional Information per serving:
Calories: 250   Fat: 1.4g   Carbs: 45.6g   Protein: 16.5g

---

343. *Sweet Potato, Lentil & Coconut Curry*
Cook Time: 13 minutes   **Servings:** 4
Ingredients:
- 3 ½ cups vegetable broth
- 1 carrot, large, sliced lengthwise and chopped
- 1 cup red or green lentils, dried
- 1 ½ tablespoons coconut oil
- 1 cup onion, diced
- 1 tablespoon curry powder
- ½ teaspoon turmeric, ground
- ½ cup coconut milk
- Fresh ground black pepper to taste
- 1 teaspoon ginger powder
- 1 sweet potato, medium, cubed into 1-inch cubes
- Sea salt to taste

Directions:
Set your instant pot to sauté mode, and heat the oil. Sauté the onion for 3-minutes. Add in the carrot, potato, lentils and seasonings to taste; stir several times to combine. Add the broth and close and secure the lid. Set to Manual on high for a cook time of 10-minutes. When the cook time is completed, release the pressure naturally for 10-minutes. Stir in the coconut milk and season with salt and pepper to taste. Serve warm.
Nutritional Information per serving:
Calories: 234   Fat: 11.8g   Carbs: 27.2g   Protein: 7.2g

---

344. *Millet & Lentils with Vegetables & Mushrooms*
Cook Time: 15 minutes   **Servings:** 4
Ingredients:
- ½ cup French green lentils, rinsed and picked over
- 1 cup sugar snap peas, sliced
- 2 garlic cloves, minced
- 1 cup millet, rinsed
- 2 ¼ cups vegetable stock
- 1 cup leek, sliced
- ½ cup Bok Choy, sliced thinly
- Drizzle of lemon juice, fresh
- ¼ cup herbs, fresh, chopped such as parsley mixed with chives and garlic
- ½ cup oyster mushrooms, sliced thinly
- 1 cup asparagus, cut into 1-inch pieces
- Sesame salt for garnish

Directions:
Set your instant pot to the sauté mode, then add the leek, mushrooms, and garlic, dry sauté for 3-minutes. Add the lentils and millet; toast for a minute and then add in the vegetable stock. Close and secure the lid on the pot, and select the Manual setting on high with a cook time of 10-minutes. Once the cook time is completed, release the pressure naturally for 10-minutes. Add in the asparagus, Bok Choy, and peas. Place the lid back on

pot and set on Manual for an additional 5-minutes cook time. Stir and add the herbs, and then transfer to a large bowl. Add the lemon juice and sprinkle sesame salt over before serving. Serve warm.

Nutritional Information per serving:
Calories: 146   Fat: 1g   Carbs: 28g   Protein: 7.9g

---

345. *Basmati Rice*
Cook Time: 6 minutes   **Servings: 6**
Ingredients:
- 1 red bell pepper, diced
- 2 cups long-grain or basmati rice
- 1 medium onion, chopped
- 1 carrot, grated
- 1 tablespoon olive oil
- ½ cup peas, fresh or frozen
- 1 teaspoon salt
- Water as needed
- 1 teaspoon turmeric, powder

Directions:
Set your instant pot to the sauté mode, add the olive oil and heat it. Add the onion and cook for 3-minutes. Add carrot, bell pepper in a 1 litre liquid measuring cup; lightly pat down into an even layer. Pour water into the veggie container until you reach the 750ml mark then set aside. Add rice, peas, turmeric and salt to your instant pot; add the ingredients from measuring cup and give mix a good stir. Close and secure the lid of pot, and set on Manual on high for a cook time of 3-minutes. When the cook time is completed, release the pressure naturally for 10-minutes. Use a large fork to fluff the rice and serve warm.

Nutritional Information per serving:
Calories: 114   Fat: 2.5g   Carbs: 20.2g   Protein: 2.5g

---

346. *Vegan Butter Chickpeas*
Cook Time: 6 minutes   **Servings: 6**
Ingredients:
- 1 can of garbanzo beans, drained
- 1 cup of coconut milk
- 1 ½ cups vegetable broth
- 1 packet of extra firm tofu
- 1 teaspoon of chili powder
- 1 cup of rice
- 1 tablespoon curry powder
- 1 tablespoon of garam masala
- ½ cup tomatoes, crushed
- Pepper and salt to taste

Directions:
Cube the tofu and add to instant pot along with crushed tomatoes, garbanzo beans, coconut milk, and spices. Close and secure the lid and set to Manual on high with a cook time of 2-minutes. Once the cooking is completed, release the pressure naturally for 10-minutes. Add the veggie broth and rice to instant pot and close lid, set to Manual on high with a cook time of 4-minutes. When the cook time is completed, release the pressure naturally for 10-minutes. Serve hot.

Nutritional Information per serving:
Calories: 200   Fat: 10.6g   Carbs: 22.1g   Protein: 6.8g

347. *Potatoes & Peas*
Cook Time: *12 minutes* **Servings:** *4*

Ingredients:
- 1 large tomato
- ½ teaspoon cumin, ground
- 1 teaspoon coriander, ground
- ½ teaspoon garam masala
- 1-inch of ginger, chopped
- 7 garlic cloves
- 1 teaspoon mustard seeds
- ½ teaspoon of red chili powder
- 1 red onion, small, chopped
- 3 medium potatoes, chopped into ½-inch pieces
- ½ teaspoon turmeric
- ¼ cup peas, fresh
- 2 teaspoons coconut oil
- ¾ teaspoon salt
- 1 cup water
- 1 cup cilantro, fresh, chopped for garnish

Directions:
Set your instant pot to the sauté mode, and heat the coconut oil. Add cumin and mustard seeds, and cook for 2-minutes. Add in onion, mix well and cook for an additional 3-minutes. Blend the ginger, tomato and garlic until you get a coarse puree. Add the tomato puree and spices to your instant pot.
Cook for 5-minutes or until puree thickens. Add the potatoes, water and salt, set to Manual setting with a cook time of 4-minutes. When the cook time completes, release the pressure naturally for 10-minutes. Add in the spinach and peas, mix well. Sauté mix for 2-minutes. Garnish with fresh, chopped cilantro and serve warm.

Nutritional Information per serving:
Calories: 209 Fat: 3.2g Carbs: 40.6g Protein: 6.8g

---

348. *Spicy Veggie Mix*
Cook Time: *17 minutes* **Servings:** *2*

Ingredients:
- 2 cups cauliflower florets
- 1 ½ teaspoons mustard, ground
- ¼ teaspoon turmeric
- ¼ cup water
- 1 cup sweet potato, chopped
- 1 cup green beans, chopped
- ½ cup green peas
- 1/8 teaspoon asafetida
- 1 teaspoon olive oil
- ½ teaspoon sugar
- 1 cup potato, chopped
- Salt to taste
- 1 teaspoon of Panch Phoron

Directions:
Add the ground mustard with water and turmeric, potato, green beans, cauliflower florets and salt into your instant pot. Set to Manual on high with a cook time of 5-minutes. When the cook time is completed, release the pressure naturally for 10-minutes. In a small skill over medium heat add the oil along with Panch pharon, and spices and cook for 2-minutes. Add chilies and asafetida to pan and cook for an additional 2-minutes. Add mixture to instant pot with peas and some salt and sauté for 2-minutes. Serve hot.

Nutritional Information per serving:
Calories: 106   Fat: 3.3g   Carbs: 17.3g   Protein: 4.8g

---

349. Vegetable Masala Mix
Cook Time: 10 minutes   **Servings: 4**
Ingredients:

- 3 cups veggies, chopped such as peppers, carrots and cauliflower, Green beans, potatoes, zucchini, cabbage etc.
- ½ teaspoon cayenne
- 3 garlic cloves, minced
- ½ teaspoon each of mustard, cumin, coriander, turmeric
- 1/3 cup green peas
- Cilantro, fresh, chopped, and lemon for garnish
- Black pepper and salt to taste
- 1 teaspoon oil
- ½ teaspoon cinnamon

Directions:
Mix all the spices in a mixing bowl, and set aside. Set your instant pot to the sauté mode, and heat oil and add in the garlic, cooking it for 2-minutes. Add in the spice mix and cook for an additional minute. Add the veggies, water and salt into instant pot and stir. Close the lid to pot and select the Manual setting with a cook time of 2-minutes. Release the pressure using quick-release. Add in the peas to the pot then close the lid and set to Manual on a cook time for 5-minutes. Garnish with fresh, chopped cilantro and lemon. Serve warm.

Nutritional Information per serving:
Calories: 278   Fat: 3.3g   Carbs: 56.2g   Protein: 12.4g

---

350. Masala Eggplant
Cook Time: 10 minutes   **Servings: 3**
Ingredients:

- 2 tablespoons cashews
- ½ teaspoon mustard seeds
- ½ teaspoon turmeric
- 1 hot green Chile, chopped
- ½ teaspoon cardamom, ground
- 1 ½ ginger, chopped
- 2 tablespoons coconut shreds
- 2 garlic cloves, chopped

For Curry:

- 6 baby eggplants
- 1 cup water
- ½ teaspoon cumin seeds
- 1 tablespoon coriander seeds
- 3 tablespoons chickpea flour
- Water as needed
- ½ teaspoon salt
- 1 teaspoon lime juice
- ½ teaspoon raw sugar
- ½ teaspoon cayenne
- Fresh cilantro, garam masala, and coconut for garnish

Directions:
Set your instant pot to the sauté mode, add the mustard, coriander and cumin seeds and brown for 2-minutes. Add the chickpea flour and mix for a minute. Add in nuts and coconut and mix well. Allow to cool and transfer to a food processor and process to

coarsely grind. Add in the garlic, Chile, lime, ginger and remaining ground spices; pulse until you get a coarse mixture, add a teaspoon of water. Make cross cuts on the eggplants and fill the cross cuts with the stuffing. Place the eggplants into your instant pot. Add a cup of water and some salt, along with a cup of cooked beans. Set to Manual setting for 5-minutes cook time. When the cook time is completed, release the pressure naturally for 10-minutes. Garnish with fresh, chopped cilantro, coconut, garam masala, and serve with rice or flatbread. Serve warm.

Nutritional Information per serving:
Calories: 783   Fat: 21.6g   Carbs: 144.7g   Protein: 20.9g

---

351. Mushroom Matar Masala
Cook Time: 20 minutes   **Servings: 2**
Ingredients:

- ½ teaspoon paprika
- 1 cup spinach, fresh, chopped
- ¾ cup peas
- 1-inch of ginger
- 1/3 cup cashews, raw and soaked for 15-minutes
- 5 garlic cloves
- ½ teaspoon garam masala
- 1 green chile, remove seeds
- 2 large tomatoes
- ½ large onion, chopped
- 8-ounces of white mushrooms, sliced
- 1 teaspoon fenugreek leaves, dried
- ¼ teaspoon sugar
- Cayenne to taste
- ½ teaspoon salt
- 1 teaspoon coconut oil
- Cilantro, fresh, chopped for garnish

Directions:
Puree the garlic with onion, chile, ginger and a few tablespoons of water in a blender on high speed. Set your instant pot to the sauté mode, and heat the oil. Add the pureed mixture to instant pot and heat for 3-minutes, stirring occasionally.
In the meantime, blend the tomatoes and cashews until smooth. Add this puree with the garam masala, fenugreek, and paprika into the instant pot. Saute for 7-minutes, stirring occasionally. Add the peas, mushrooms, other veggies, sugar, salt and ½ cup of water and mix well. Cover and cook on Manual for a cook time of 10-minutes. Garnish with fresh chopped cilantro and serve with rice or flat bread. Serve warm.

Nutritional Information per serving:
Calories: 334   Fat: 14.6g   Carbs: 43.7g   Protein: 15.2g

---

352. Curried Potato Eggplant
Cook Time: 8 minutes   **Servings: 2**
Ingredients:

- 1 eggplant, medium, thinly chopped
- 6 curry leaves, chopped
- 4 garlic cloves, minced
- 1 tomato, large, crushed, chopped finely
- 1 teaspoon coriander powder
- ¾ cup water
- Garam masala or pure red chili powder to taste
- 1 teaspoon coconut oil
- Cilantro, fresh, chopped for garnish
- ¾ teaspoon salt

- 1 potato, large, cubed into small pieces
- ½ teaspoon mustard seeds, cumin and turmeric seeds
- 1 hot green chile, chopped finely
- ½ an inch of ginger, minced

Directions:
Set your instant pot to the sauté mode, add the oil and heat it. Add the mustard and cumin seeds and cook for a minute. Add in the curry leaves, ginger, garlic and chili. Add in turmeric, coriander, tomatoes and mix well, cooking for an additional 2-minutes. Now add everything into your instant pot and close and secure the lid. Select the Manual setting on high for a cook time of 5-minutes. Once the cook time is completed, release the pressure naturally for 10-minutes. Give everything a good stir. Divide into serving bowls, garnish with fresh chopped cilantro, and serve hot.

Nutritional Information per serving:
Calories: 394   Fat: 22.6g   Carbs: 28.8g   Protein: 29.2g

---

353. *Coconut Tofu Curry*
Cook Time: 4 minutes   **Servings:** 4
Ingredients:
- 1 ½ teaspoons salt
- 1 cup onion, chunks
- 2 cups green bell pepper, chunks
- 1 tablespoon curry powder
- 10-ounces coconut milk, light, canned
- 2 tablespoons peanut butter, creamy
- 1 tablespoon garam masala
- 8-ounces tomato paste
- 2 teaspoons garlic cloves, minced
- 1 cup tofu, firm, diced

Directions:
Add everything to a food processor, except the tofu. Put the tofu inside your instant pot and pour sauce from food processor on top of tofu pieces. Close and secure the pot lid, and set to Manual with a cook time of 4-minutes. Once the cook time has completed, release the pressure using the quick-release. Serve over a bed of rice. Serve hot.

Nutritional Information per serving:
Calories: 259   Fat: 13.8g   Carbs: 27.5g   Protein: 15.2g

---

354. *Tomato Stewed Green Bean*
Cook Time: 10 minutes   **Servings:** 4
Ingredients:
- 1 teaspoon extra virgin olive oil
- 2 pinches of salt
- 1 tablespoon olive oil
- 2 cups tomatoes, fresh, chopped
- 1 sprig basil, leaves removed
- 1 clove garlic, crushed
- 1 lb. green beans, fresh or frozen, remove ends

Directions:
Set your instant pot to the sauté mode, add tablespoon olive oil and heat it. Add the crushed garlic clove and cook for 2-minutes. Add in tomatoes and swirl everything to mix. Add steamer basket filled with green beans. Sprinkle some salt on the beans. Close and lock lid to pot, and set to Manual with a cook time of 5-minutes. When the cook time is completed, release the pressure using the quick-release. Remove the steamer basket and

add the beans in with the tomato sauce at bottom of instant pot. Set on sauté mode for 5-minutes, stirring often. Add bean mix to a large serving bowl, and top with fresh basil leaves and 1 teaspoon of extra-virgin olive oil. Serve warm.

Nutritional Information per serving:
Calories: 95   Fat: 5g   Carbs: 12.4g   Protein: 2.9g

---

355. Sesame Tofu
Cooking Time: 8 minutes   **Servings: 4**
Ingredients:
- 1 cup sweet potato, peeled, diced
- 2 teaspoons sesame oil, toasted
- 2 tablespoons sesame seeds
- 1 carrot, peeled, cut diagonally into ½-inch pieces
- 1/3 cup vegetable stock
- 3 garlic cloves, minced
- 2 cups snow peas
- 1 lb. tofu, extra firm, cut into 1-inch cubes
- 2 tablespoons of sweet & spicy red pepper sauce
- 2 tablespoons of tamari
- 2 tablespoons tahini
- 2 cups yellow onion, sliced
- 2 tablespoons scallion, chopped
- 1 tablespoon rice vinegar

Directions:
Set your instant pot to the sauté mode, and add sesame oil and heat it. Add in onion, sweet potato, carrot and sauté for 2-minutes. Add the garlic and tablespoon of sesame seeds, and sauté for an additional 2-minutes. Add in the tofu, tamari, stock, and vinegar. Close and secure the lid of pot, and set to Manual on high with a cook time of 3-minutes. When the cook time is completed, release the pressure using quick-release. Add in the peas and close the lid again, and cook for another 3-minutes, then use the quick-release again. Stir in the tahini and pepper sauce. Use the leftover sesame seeds as a garnish along with green onions chopped. Serve warm.

Nutritional Information per serving:
Calories: 283   Fat: 13.6g   Carbs: 27.3g   Protein: 16.1g

---

356. Lentil & Spinach Dal
Cooking Time: 13 minutes   **Servings: 6**
Ingredients:
- 1 red onion, large, chopped
- 3 garlic cloves, minced
- 1 teaspoon coriander, ground
- 4 cups spinach, fresh, chopped
- 1 teaspoon turmeric, ground
- ¼ cup cilantro, fresh, chopped
- 2 teaspoons vegan butter
- 1 teaspoon cumin, ground
- 1 tomato, large, cut into wedges
- 3 cups water
- 1 ½ cups yellow split peas
- ½ teaspoon salt
- ¼ teaspoon cayenne pepper, dried
- 2 tablespoons of olive oil

To Serve:
- Fresh cilantro, chopped
- Plain yogurt

- Cooked naan or brown rice

Directions:
Set your instant pot to the sauté mode, add oil and heat it. Add onions and cook for 2-minutes. Add garlic and stir well. Turn off the heat then add in the cumin, coriander, cayenned, turmeric, and mix until well combined. Add the lentils, tomato wedges, salt and water into instant pot and stir. Close and secure the lid, and set to Manual on a cook time of 10-minutes. When the cook time is completed, release the pressure using the quick-release. Remove and discard the tomato skins, and whisk the lentils to blend. Add in the spinach, cilantro, and vegan butter, stir to combine. Top it with plain yogurt and fresh cilantro, serve with naan or brown rice. Serve hot.

Nutritional Information per serving:
Calories: 210   Fat: 2.7g   Carbs: 35.2g   Protein: 13.5g

---

357. Spinach Chana Masala

Cook Time: 18 minutes   **Servings: 6**

Ingredients:
- 1 green chili, chopped
- ½ teaspoon turmeric
- 1 tablespoon Chana masala/cholay
- 1 tablespoon garlic, grated
- 2 cups tomato puree, fresh
- ½ tablespoon ginger, grated
- 1 bay leaf
- 3 tablespoons olive oil
- 1 cup onions, chopped
- 1 cup Chana/cholay/chickpeas, raw, soaked for overnight
- 2 teaspoons chili powder
- 1 teaspoon coriander powder
- 2 cups baby spinach, fresh, chopped
- Lemon, fresh
- Handful of cilantro, fresh, chopped
- Salt to taste

Directions:
Clean the chickpeas under cold running water, the next morning drain excess water from the soaked chickpeas. Set your instant pot to the sauté mode, add oil and heat it. Add onions and cook for 2-minutes. Add green chili, bay leaf, ginger, and garlic paste and cook for an additional 2-minutes.
Add in the Chana masala, turmeric, chili powder, coriander powder along with a tablespoon of water. Continue to sauté for a few more seconds. Add in the roasted chickpea flour and sauté for a few more seconds. Now add in the drained chickpeas, tomato puree, and water, mix well. Close and lock the lid to pot, and set to Manual for a cook time of 15-minutes. Once the cook time is completed, release the pressure naturally for 10-minutes. Set pot to sauté mode again and add in the spinach and salt and cook for another 3-minutes, stir. Add in some lemon juice, and chopped coriander. Serve warm, with chapatti, or over quinoa/rice.

Nutritional Information per serving:
Calories: 362   Fat: 14.9g   Carbs: 46.4g   Protein: 14.3g

358. Lentil Bolognese
Cook Time: 15 minutes **Servings:** 4
Ingredients:
- 1 cup of Beluga black lentils, washed
- 3 carrots, medium, diced
- 4 garlic cloves, minced
- 1 can of fire roasted tomatoes, chopped
- Red pepper flakes to taste
- 2 tablespoons Italian seasoning, dry
- 1 can tomato paste
- Pepper and salt to taste
- 4 cups water
- Balsamic vinegar to taste
- 1 yellow onion, diced

Directions:
Add everything into your instant pot, except the vinegar, salt and pepper. Stir well to mix ingredients. Close the lid of pot, and set to Manual on high with a cook time of 15-minutes. When the cook time is completed, release pressure with quick-release. Add drizzle of balsamic and stir. Serve hot over pasta.

Nutritional Information per serving:
Calories: 137   Fat: 1.1g   Carbs: 28g   Protein: 7.8g

359. Coconut Quinoa Curry
Cook Time: 45 minutes **Servings:** 6
Ingredients:
- 1 tablespoon turmeric, ground
- ¼ cup quinoa
- 1 can (15-ounce) of organic chickpeas, drained, rinsed
- 3 cups sweet potato, peeled, chopped
- 1 cup white onion, diced
- 2 cups broccoli crowns, cut into florets
- 1 can (28-ounce) tomatoes, diced
- 2 cans coconut milk (14.5 ounce each)
- 1 tablespoon garlic cloves, minced
- 2 teaspoons tamari sauce, wheat free
- 1 tablespoon ginger, freshly grated
- 1 teaspoon chili flakes
- 1 teaspoon tamari

Directions:
Add 1 cup of water into your instant pot, and add all ingredients into pot. Stir well. Close and lock the pot lid, and set to Manual for a cook time of 45-minutes. When the cook time is completed, release the pressure naturally for 15-minutes. Serve hot.

Nutritional Information per serving:
Calories: 412   Fat: 10.3g   Carbs: 72.1g   Protein: 13.7g

360. Garlic Mashed Potatoes
Cook Time: 4 minutes **Servings:** 4
Ingredients:
- ¼ cup parsley, fresh, chopped
- Salt to taste
- 6 garlic cloves, peeled and cut in half
- ½ cup non-dairy milk
- 4 Russet potatoes, cut into chunks
- 1 cup vegetable broth

Directions:
Add the potato chunks, broth, and garlic into your instant pot. Close and secure the lid, and set to Manual with a cook time of 4-minutes on high. When the cook time is completed, release the pressure using quick-release. Mash the potatoes, add soy milk. Add the parsley and salt to taste. Serve hot.
Nutritional Information per serving:
Calories: 146   Fat: 1g   Carbs: 32.4g   Protein: 5.1g

---

361. Marinara Sauce
Cook Time: 12 minutes   **Servings: 4**
Ingredients:
- 1 ½ cups of water
- 2 sweet potatoes, large, diced
- 2 cans (28-ounce) tomatoes, crushed
- ½ cup red lentils, remove shriveled lentils
- 3 garlic cloves, minced
- Salt to taste

Directions:
Set your instant pot to sauté mode and cook the garlic, sweet potatoes, lentils and salt for 2-minutes. Add crushed tomatoes and stir well. Set to Manual on high with a cook time of 12-minutes. When the cook time is completed, release the pressure naturally for 15-minutes. Stir and puree using an immersion blender. Serve warm.
Nutritional Information per serving:
Calories: 94   Fat: 0.2g   Carbs: 20.1g   Protein: 3.5g

---

362. Cauliflower Rice
Cook Time: 1 minute   **Servings: 4**
Ingredients:
- 1 head of cauliflower, medium, washed and trim leaves, chopped
- ½ teaspoon parsley, dried
- ¼ teaspoon salt
- 2 tablespoons olive oil

Optional Seasonings:
- ¼ teaspoon cumin
- ¼ teaspoon cilantro, fresh, chopped
- ¼ teaspoon turmeric
- Lime juice or lime wedges, fresh
- ¼ teaspoon paprika

Directions:
Place the cauliflower pieces into the steamer and then insert it into your instant pot. Add a cup of water in the steamer basket. Close and secure the pot lid, and set it on Manual on high with a cook time of 1-minute. When the cook time is completed, release the pressure using quick-release. Transfer the cauliflower to a plate. Remove the water from instant pot, and set to sauté mode. Add oil into instant pot, add in the cauliflower and mash with potato masher to break pieces up. Add lime juice and cilantro and stir. Serve warm.

363. Delicious Dumplings
Cook Time: 9 minutes   **Servings: 4**
Ingredients:

- 1 teaspoon ginger, fresh, grated
- ½ cup carrot, shredded
- 1 cup white mushrooms, minced
- 1 ½ cups cabbage, minced
- 1 tablespoon oil
- 2 tablespoons soy sauce
- 1 teaspoon sesame oil
- 12 dumpling wrappers
- 1 tablespoon rice wine vinegar

Directions:
In a large pan over medium heat sauté the minced mushrooms, then add in the carrot, cabbage, vinegar, and soy sauce and cook until mixture becomes dry. Add in sesame oil and ginger in instant pot. Lightly coat vegetable steamer with oil then place it in instant pot. Set a small bowl of water on cutting board. On the cutting board arrange a wrapper using your fingertip; spread water just about the edge. Add a tablespoon of filling to center and fold wrapper in half and match the edges. Press edges together. Add 1 ½ cups of water and the trivet to your instant pot, then place the steamer on top of it. Set to Manual setting for a cook time of 6-minutes. When cook time is completed, release the pressure using quick-release. Serve warm.

Nutritional Information per serving:
Calories: 299   Fat: 10.1g   Carbs: 44.9g   Protein: 8.4g

---

364. Sweet Potato Pie
Cook Time: 13 minutes   **Servings: 4**
Ingredients:

- 1 cup tomatoes, fresh, diced
- ½ cup carrot, diced
- 1 cup onion, diced
- ½ cup sweet potato, peeled, diced
- 1 cup French green lentils, rinsed and picked over
- 1/3 cup celery, diced
- 1 garlic clove, minced
- ¼ teaspoon parsley, dried
- ½ teaspoon rosemary, fresh, chopped
- 1 bay leaf
- 1 ¾ cups vegetable stock
- 1 teaspoon thyme, dried
- 1 cup celery, diced
- 2 tablespoons browned rice flower
- 1 tablespoon tomato paste
- 2 teaspoons of tamari
- 1 tablespoon Worcestershire sauce

Directions:
Set your instant pot to sauté mode, add in onion, celery, carrot and cook for 2-minutes. Add in the lentils, potatoes, bay leaf, thyme, stock and rosemary. Secure the lid closed on pot and set to Manual on high for a cook time of 10-minutes. When the cook time is completed, release the pressure with quick-release.
Add in a tablespoon of browned flour, along with tamari, Worcestershire sauce, tomato paste and tomatoes, and stir. Close the lid again and let it cook on sauté mode for 3-minutes and use the quick-release again. Transfer to a large casserole dish; discard the bay leaf. Top the cooked pie with the mashed potatoes. Run under broiler for a few minutes to brown potatoes. Serve hot.

Nutritional Information per serving:
Calories: 163   Fat: 0.7g   Carbs: 33.4g   Protein: 7.5g

---

365. Tasty Tofu
Cook Time: 45 minutes   **Servings:** 4
Ingredients:
For Instant Pot Ingredients:
- 1 cup carrot coins
- 1 heaping teaspoon of corn starch
- 1 package firm tofu (14-ounces) cubed
- ¼ cup onions, sliced

For Sauce Ingredients:
- ½ cup water
- 1 teaspoon garlic, minced
- ½ tablespoon rice vinegar
- 3 tablespoons maple syrup
- 3 tablespoons nutritional yeast
- 1 tablespoon ginger, minced
- ¼ cup gluten free soy sauce

For Serving:
Cooked quinoa, brown rice or other grain or lettuce leaves to make fresh wraps, and sesame seeds for garnish.

Directions:
Wrap the block of tofu in paper towels and press for 5 minutes. Remove the paper towels and cut the tofu into ½ inch thick pieces. In a mixing bowl add the sauce ingredients and whisk together.
Set your instant pot to the sauté mode, add the oil and heat it. Add the tofu, carrots, and onions, and brown tofu on all sides, cooking for about 5-minutes. Add the sauce mix to the pot and stir. Close the pot lid and set to Manual mode, on high, with a cook time of 5-minutes. When the cook time is completed, release the pressure using quick-release. Serve with choice of quinoa or brown cooked rice.

Nutritional Information per serving:
Calories: 162   Fat: 0.8g   Carbs: 31g   Protein: 7.1g

---

366. Instant Pot Broccoli & Tomato Pasta
Cook Time: 10 minutes   **Servings:** 8
Ingredients:
- 1 bag of organic Broccoli, frozen (10-ounces)
- 1 box of organic pasta (16-ounces)
- 1 jar of organic tomato, basil pasta sauce (25-ounces)
- 4 quarts of water

Directions:
In a large pot bring the water to boil, and add pasta and stir, cook for 5-minutes. Once pasta is cooked, add in the broccoli and stir. Add the tomato, basil pasta sauce to instant pot and set to Manual setting with a cook time of 5-minutes. Drain the pasta and add it along with broccoli into instant pot and mix with sauce. Close the lid, when the cook time is completed, release pressure naturally for 10-minutes. Serve hot.

Nutritional Information per serving:
Calories: 262   Fat: 6.2g   Carbs: 42.1g   Protein: 9g

367. Refried Beans

Cook Time: 28 minutes **Servings: 4**
Ingredients:
- 1 onion, large, cut into fourths
- 3 cups vegetable broth
- 1 teaspoon chili powder
- ½ cup salsa
- 1 teaspoon paprika
- ½ teaspoon black pepper
- 1 Jalapeno, seeded
- 4 garlic cloves, peeled, chopped roughly
- 1 teaspoon cumin
- 2 cups pinto beans, rinsed well, dried
- Salt to taste

Directions:
Add all ingredients into your instant pot and stir. Close and secure the pot lid and set to Manual setting on high with a cook time of 28-minutes. When the cook time is completed, release the pressure naturally for 10-minutes. Using a high-speed blender blend the beans to get the consistency you want. Serve hot.

Nutritional Information per serving:
Calories: 369   Fat: 1.6g   Carbs: 67.9g   Protein: 22.1g

368. Peanut & Sweet Potato Stew

Cook Time: 20 minutes **Servings: 4**
Ingredients:
- 2 cups of kale or another leafy green
- 1 tablespoon ginger, fresh, minced
- 1 teaspoon coriander, dried
- ½ cup peanut butter
- 1 sweet potato, medium, peeled, diced
- ½ teaspoon red chili pepper, crushed
- 1 onion, medium, minced finely
- 3 garlic cloves, finely minced
- 2 cups vegetable broth
- 1 (14.5 ounce) can of tomatoes, diced or crushed
- 1 ½ cups peas frozen or canned
- 1 can black kidney beans, drained and rinsed
- 2 tablespoons olive oil
- Salt and pepper to taste

Directions:
In a food processor or blender, blend the diced tomatoes along with their juice for a few seconds. Set your instant pot to the sauté mode, add oil and heat. Add the onion and cook for 2-minutes. Add the garlic, ginger and chili, and cook for an additional 3-minutes. Add in the tomatoes and stir, then add the peanut butter, coriander while stirring frequently. Add sweet potatoes and broth. Close and lock the pot lid, and set to Manual on high with a cook time of 10-minutes. When the cook time is completed, release the pressure using quick-release. Add the peas, black beans, and greens, and set on sauté mode for 5-minutes, stirring occasionally. Season with salt and pepper. Serve hot.

Nutritional Information per serving:
Calories: 457   Fat: 24.4g   Carbs: 47.8g   Protein: 18.8g

369. White Bean Stew with Kale & Winter Squash

Cook Time: 25 minutes **Servings:** 6

Ingredients:
- 1 ½ teaspoons of cumin, ground, divided
- 5 cups water
- 1 bunch of kale, stems removed, sliced
- ½ cup basil, fresh, chopped
- 1 can (15-ounce) tomatoes, diced, fire-roasted
- 1 Jalapeno pepper, seeded, finely chopped
- 1 red bell pepper, large, chopped
- Salt to taste
- 1 onion, large, chopped
- 2 teaspoons oregano, dried, divided
- 1 cup corn, fresh or frozen
- 4 garlic cloves, minced
- 1 lb. navy beans, dried, quick soaked or soaked overnight
- 4 teaspoons smoked paprika, divided
- 1 lb. winter squash, cubed into ¾ dice
- 1 teaspoon basil, dried

Directions:
Set your instant pot to the sauté mode, add oil and heat. Add in onion with a pinch of baking soda, and cook for 2-minutes. Add the garlic and cook for an additional 3-minutes. Add the beans, 1 teaspoon oregano, 2 teaspoons paprika, dried basil, 1 teaspoon cumin and water into instant pot. Close and lock the pot lid and set to Manual on high with a cook time of 8-minutes.

When the cook time is completed, release the pressure using the quick-release. Add the squash and tomatoes to instant pot, along with leftover peppers, seasonings and salt. Close and lock the lid and set to Manual setting for another 8-minutes of cook time. When the cook time is completed, use the quick-release once again. Add in the peas, and kale and stir. Set the pot on sauté for a 5-minute cook time, stirring often. Serve hot.

Nutritional Information per serving:
Calories: 205 Fat: 1.7g Carbs: 42.3g Protein: 9.8g

370. Lasagna Soup

Cook Time: 35 minutes **Servings:** 6

Ingredients:

For the Pesto Ricotta:
- ¼ lb. extra firm tofu, drained
- 1 tablespoon lemon juice, freshly squeezed
- Pepper and salt to taste
- 4 tablespoons of prepared vegan pesto
- ¼ cup almond milk, unflavored
- 1 cup cashews, raw, soaked in water for 8 hours, drained and rinsed

For the Lasagna Soup:
- 1 can (14-ounce) tomatoes, diced
- 3 cups spinach leaves, fresh, chopped
- 1 teaspoon oregano, dried
- ¾ cup brown lentils, dried
- 1 can (14-ounce) tomatoes, crushed
- 3 cloves garlic, minced
- 1 onion, medium, diced
- 4 ½ cups vegetable broth

- 1 teaspoon basil, dried
- 8 lasagna noodles, broken into pieces

Directions:
In the bottom of your instant pot add onion, broth, basil, garlic, lentils, oregano, and stir to blend. Set to Manual setting with on high with a cook time of 20-minutes. When the cook time is completed, release the pressure naturally for 10-minutes. Add in the crushed tomatoes and stir. Close lid to pot and set on Manual with a cook time of 5-minutes. When the cook time is completed, release the pressure using quick-release. Add in the spinach and noodles and stir. Season with salt and pepper. Set to Manual with a cook time of 10-minutes. Place the soaked cashews and milk into a food processor and blend on high until smooth. Add in the tofu; and pulse a few times, until mix has a ricotta-like texture. Add lemon juice, pesto and season with salt and pepper to taste. Divide the soup into serving bowls, and top each bowl with a dollop of vegan pesto ricotta. Serve warm.

Nutritional Information per serving:
Calories: 300   Fat: 10.3g   Carbs: 40.1g   Protein: 14.7g

---

371. Chickpea & Rice Soup
Cook Time: 40 minutes   **Servings:** 6
Ingredients:

- ½ teaspoon paprika
- 2 cups carrots, sliced
- 1 teaspoon parsley flakes
- ½ cup nutritional yeast
- 2 cups celery, chopped
- 1 cup onion, diced
- 8 cups water
- 1 cup chickpeas, dry
- 2 teaspoons garlic powder
- 1 cup brown rice
- 2 teaspoons onion powder

Directions:
Add the rice and chickpeas and half of water into your instant pot. Close and lock the pot lid, and select the Manual setting with a cook time of 35-minutes. When the cook time has completed, release the pressure naturally for 15-minutes. Add in the remaining ingredients into pot and stir. Close and lock the lid and select the Manual setting with a cook time of 5-minutes. Once cooking is completed, release the pressure using quick-release. Serve hot.

Nutritional Information per serving:
Calories: 249   Fat: 3.4g   Carbs: 44.2g   Protein: 14.3g

---

372. Veggie Stew
Cook Time: 20 minutes   **Servings:** 8
Ingredients:
For Sauté Mode:

- 8-ounces white mushrooms, sliced
- 1 carrot, minced
- 1 teaspoon Italian seasoning
- 8-ounces Portabella mushrooms, chopped
- ¼ cup vegetable broth
- 1 teaspoon rosemary
- ½ onion, minced
- 2 garlic cloves, minced
- ½ teaspoon rubbed sage

For Manual Mode:
- ½ cup red wine
- 8-ounces tomato sauce
- 15-ounces tomatoes, diced
- 1 tablespoon balsamic vinegar
- 2 tablespoons cornstarch
- ¾ cup pearl onions
- 4-ounces frozen peas
- ½ teaspoon salt
- 1 cup green beans, fresh, diced
- ¼ teaspoon pepper, ground
- 3 cups vegetable broth
- ½ teaspoon of kitchen bouquet
- 2 Yukon gold potatoes, diced
- 1 stalk of celery, diced
- 2 carrots, large, diced

Directions:
Set your instant pot to the sauté mode, add the garlic, carrot, onion, and celery and cook for 3-minutes. Add in the Italian seasoning, rosemary, and sage stir well and cook for an additional 2-minutes. Deglaze the pan using the red wine, then add in the tomatoes, sauce followed by the veggie broth (except the peas & pearl onions) and other seasonings. Close and lock the pot lid, and set to Manual with a cook time of 15-minutes. When the cook time is competed, release the pressure naturally for 15-minutes. Add in cornstarch, peas, and pearl onions. Give mixture a good stir and serve warm.

Nutritional Information per serving:
Calories: 159   Fat: 0.8g   Carbs: 32.3g   Protein: 5.5g

---

373. *Mung Bean Stew*
Cook Time: 25 minutes   **Servings: 2**
Ingredients:
- ¼ teaspoon cayenne
- ½ cup whole mung beans, soaked for 15-minutes, dry
- 1 teaspoon coriander, ground
- ½ cup brown basmati rice, soaked for 10-minutes
- 2 tomatoes, medium, chopped finely
- ½ teaspoon cumin seeds
- 5 garlic cloves, minced
- ½ cup red onion, chopped
- ½ teaspoon turmeric
- ¼ teaspoon black pepper
- 4 cups water
- 1 tablespoon olive oil
- 1 teaspoon lemon juice, freshly squeezed
- Salt to taste

Directions:
In a blender blend ginger, garlic, tomato, spices, onions, and a couple of tablespoons of water. Blend until smooth, and set aside. Set your instant pot to the sauté mode, add the oil and heat it. Add in the cumin seeds and toast them for 30 seconds. Add the puree and cook and stir for an additional 15-minutes. Drain the rice and beans and add them to your instant pot. Add lemon juice, water and salt. Add chopped veggies and mix well. Close and lock the lid to the pot, and select the Manual setting with a cook time of 10-minutes. Once the cook time is completed, release the pressure naturally for 10-minutes. Serve hot with some toasted bread or crackers.

Nutritional Information per serving:
Calories: 185   Fat: 2.3g   Carbs: 36.2g   Protein: 7.4g

374. Curried Butternut Squash Soup
Cook Time: 42 minutes **Servings: 6**
Ingredients:
- Hulled pumpkin seeds for topping
- Dried cranberries for topping
- 3 cups water
- 1 tablespoon olive oil
- ½ cup coconut cream or coconut milk
- 1 tablespoon curry powder
- 3 lbs. butternut squash, peeled and cut into 1-inch cubes
- 1 ½ teaspoons sea salt
- 1 onion, large, chopped
- 2 garlic cloves, minced

Directions:
Set your instant pot to the sauté mode, add the oil and heat it. Add onions and cook for 6-minutes. Add garlic, and curry powder and cook for an additional 6-minutes. Add in the butternut squash to instant pot, along with water and salt. Close the lid and set to the Soup setting on a cook time of 30-minutes. When the cook time is completed, release the pressure naturally for 15-minutes. Using an immersion blender puree the soup in the pot. Stir in the coconut cream or milk and adjust seasonings to suit your taste. Top with dried cranberries and hulled pumpkin seeds. Serve warm.

Nutritional Information per serving:
Calories: 140   Fat: 7.1g   Carbs: 18.4g   Protein: 13.2g

375. Split Pea Soup with Navy Beans & Sweet Potatoes
Cook Time: 20 minutes **Servings: 6**
Ingredients:
- 5 cups water
- ½ teaspoon liquid smoke
- 3 bay leaves
- ½ cup nutritional yeast
- 1 cup split peas
- ½ cup navy beans, dried
- 1 sweet potato, medium, diced

Directions:
Add everything to instant pot except the yeast, pepper and salt. Close and secure the pot lid, and set to Manual on high with a cook time of 20-minutes. When the cook time is completed, release the pressure naturally for 10-minutes. Add in the nutritional yeast, pepper and salt and stir well. Serve warm.

Nutritional Information per serving:
Calories: 140   Fat: 7.1g   Carbs: 18.4g   Protein: 3.2g

376. Lentil Red Curry & Coconut Milk Soup
Cook Time: 11 minutes **Servings: 4**
Ingredients:
- 2 cups vegetable broth
- Pinch of red pepper flakes
- 1 can coconut milk (15-ounces)
- 1/8 teaspoon ginger powder
- 2 tablespoons red curry paste
- 1 onion, large, diced
- 3 garlic cloves, minced

- 1 (14-ounce) can tomatoes, diced, don't drain
- 1 cup spinach, fresh, chopped

Directions:
Set your instant pot to the sauté mode, cook onion, and garlic with a splash of vegetable broth for 5-minutes. Add in the ginger powder, red curry paste, red pepper flakes and stir. Add in the coconut milk, vegetable broth, lentils and diced tomatoes, stir well. Close the lid of pot and set to Manual with a cook time of 6-minutes. Once the cooking is completed, release the pressure using quick-release. Stir in chopped spinach and serve warm.

Nutritional Information per serving:
Calories: 584   Fat: 29.3g   Carbs: 59.3g   Protein: 24.9g

---

377. Lentil Risotto
Cook Time: 10 minutes   **Servings: 4**

Ingredients:
- 1 cup Arborio rice
- 1 cup lentils, dry, soaked overnight
- 1 tablespoon olive oil
- 1 stalk celery, chopped
- 2 cloves garlic, mashed lightly
- 1 medium onion, chopped
- 1 tablespoon of parsley, leaves and stems chopped
- 3 ¼ cup vegetable stock

Directions:
Set your instant pot to sauté mode, add the oil, and heat it. Add the onion and cook for 2-minutes. Add in celery and parsley and cook for another minute and stir. Add in the garlic cloves, and rice mix well and continue to cook for another 2-minutes. Add in the stock and strained lentils and mix. Close the lid to pot and set to Manual on high with a cook time of 5-minutes. When the cook time is completed, release the pressure using the quick-release. Serve warm.

Nutritional Information per serving:
Calories: 387   Fat: 4.8g   Carbs: 70.4g   Protein: 16g

---

378. Mushroom Risotto
Cook Time: 10 minutes   **Servings: 4**

Ingredients:
- 1 tablespoon olive oil
- ¼ cup lemon juice, freshly squeezed
- 1 ½ tablespoons nutritional yeast
- 3 cups vegetable broth
- 1 tablespoon vegan butter substitute
- ½ cup white wine, dry at room temperature
- 3 garlic cloves, minced
- 1 cup Arborio rice
- ½ cup white onion, minced
- 2 cups spinach, fresh, chopped
- 1 teaspoon thyme
- 4-ounces mushrooms, chopped
- Salt and pepper to taste

Directions:
Set your instant pot to the sauté mode, add the oil and heat it. Add garlic and onions and cook for 5-minutes. Add in the rice, wine, vegetable broth, water, salt, mushrooms, and thyme. Close the lid to the pot and set to Manual on high and set on a cook time of 5-

minutes. Once the cook time is completed, release the pressure naturally for 15-minutes. Add in the spinach, nutritional yeast, vegan butter, pepper and stir. Serve warm.
Nutritional Information per serving:
Calories: 291   Fat: 5.3g   Carbs: 45.0g   Protein: 10.3g

---

379. Garlic Mushrooms with White Beans
Cook Time: 30 minutes   **Servings: 4**
Ingredients:
- 2 medium tomatoes, diced
- 1 tablespoon Thai Red curry paste
- ½ Jalapeno pepper, finely chopped
- 4 cups water
- 1 tablespoon shallot powder
- 2 tablespoons barley, hulled
- 3 cups mushrooms, finely chopped
- 9 cloves garlic, finely chopped
- 2 tablespoons onion powder
- 1 cup white navy beans, dried
- Cilantro, fresh, chopped for garnish
- Scallions, chopped for garnish

Directions:
Add all your ingredients to your instant pot, except for tomatoes, cilantro, and scallions. Set the pot to the Soup setting with a cook time of 30-minutes. When the cook time is completed, release the pressure naturally for 15-minutes. Add in the tomatoes and stir. Serve with cilantro and scallions as garnish. Serve hot.
Nutritional Information per serving:
Calories: 331   Fat: 2.3g   Carbs: 38.2g   Protein: 8.2g

---

380. Potato Risotto
Cook Time: 10 minutes   **Servings: 6**
Ingredients:
- 1 ½ teaspoons salt
- Couple of sprigs of thyme
- 1 medium red potato, chopped into ½-inch cubes
- 4 cups vegetable stock
- ¼ cup white wine
- 2 cups Arborio rice
- 1 tablespoon olive oil
- 1 tablespoon tomato paste
- 1 yellow onion, medium, chopped

Directions:
Set your instant pot to the sauté mode, add the oil and heat it. Add the onion and cook for 2-minutes. Add in the rice, and stir constantly, cooking for an additional 3-minutes. Add the wine and stir. Add the stock, potatoes, tomato paste and salt. Close the pot lid, and set to Manual on high for a cook time of 5-minutes. When the cook time is completed, release the pressure using the quick-release. Sprinkle with fresh thyme and serve warm.
Nutritional Information per serving:
Calories: 303   Fat: 1.2g   Carbs: 41.2g   Protein: 19.2g

---

381. Pumpkin, Chicken, Corn Chowder
Cook Time: 9 minutes   **Servings: 4**
Ingredients:

- 2 large boneless, skinless chicken breasts, uncooked, diced
- 2 (14.5-ounce) cans of chicken broth
- 2 large Russet potatoes, cubed
- 1 cup onion, diced
- 2 tablespoons butter
- 1/8 teaspoon red pepper flakes, dried
- ½ cup half and half
- 1 clove garlic, minced
- 1/8 teaspoon nutmeg, freshly grated
- 2 cups frozen corn
- ½ teaspoon Italian seasoning
- 1 (15-ounce) can pumpkin puree
- Salt and black pepper to taste
- Parsley, fresh, chopped for garnish
- Crumbled cooked bacon for garnish

Directions:
Add the butter to your instant pot. Set your instant pot on the sauté mode. Add onion once the butter is melted, and cook for 2-minutes. Add the garlic and cook for another 3-minutes. Add the chicken broth, pumpkin puree, pepper, Italian seasoning, red pepper flakes, and nutmeg into pot. Stir well. Add your diced potatoes and diced chicken.
Close the lid and set to Manual on high with a cook time of 4-minutes. When the cook time is completed, release the pressure using quick-release. Stir in the corn and half and half. Divide into serving bowls and top with crumbled bacon and chopped parsley as garnishes. Serve hot.

Nutritional Information per serving:
Calories: 278   Fat: 2.4g   Carbs: 47.1g   Protein: 21.3g

---

382. *Sweet Summer Corn Chowder*
Cook Time: 15 minutes   **Servings: 4**

Ingredients:
- 1 cup shredded cheddar cheese
- 1 cup zucchini, diced
- ¼ cup green onion, sliced
- 4-ounces cream cheese
- 1 cup chicken broth
- 2 cups corn on the cob, peeled and chopped
- 2 teaspoons garlic, minced
- ½ cup green onion, sliced
- 1 cup yellow squash, diced
- ¼ cup white whole wheat flour
- 1 tablespoon thyme, fresh, chopped
- ¼ cup celery, diced
- ¼ cup butter
- 2 cups milk
- Salt and pepper to taste
- 4 pieces of bacon

Directions:
Set your instant pot to the sauté mode, add bacon and cook until crisp. Remove bacon when cooked and place on paper towel and set aside. Leave the bacon drippings in instant pot. Add your green onions, garlic, squash, celery, corn kernels, and zucchini. Cook for 5-minutes. Remove mixture from instant pot. Add butter to instant pot and keep on sauté mode. Whisk in the flour, slowly add the milk and cream cheese.
Cook, whisking frequently until mixture begins to thicken and your cream cheese melts. Add in your veggie mix, bacon, and chicken broth. Season with thyme, salt and pepper. Sprinkle with cheddar cheese and green onions as garnish. Serve hot.

Nutritional Information per serving:
Calories: 282   Fat: 2.3g   Carbs: 43.1g   Protein: 18.2g

383. Winter Minestrone
Cook Time: 10 minutes **Servings: 6**
Ingredients:
- 6 cups vegetable broth
- 1 ½ cups canned cannellini white beans
- 2 teaspoons oregano, dried
- 1 cup celery, diced
- 16-ounces canned tomatoes, diced
- 4 teaspoons garlic cloves, minced
- 1 ¼ cups onion, diced
- 1 ½ cups carrot, diced
- 1 ¼ cups wild rice
- 1 cup leek, diced
- 1 tablespoon olive oil
- Salt and black pepper to taste

Directions:
Add all your ingredients into your instant pot. Secure the lid onto pot and set to Manual on high for a cook time of 10-minutes. When the cook time is completed, release the pressure naturally for 10-minutes. Serve hot.

Nutritional Information per serving:
Calories: 306   Fat: 1.2g   Carbs: 32.4g   Protein: 18.4g

384. Potato Soup
Cook Time: 10 minutes **Servings: 4**
Ingredients:
- 1 ¼ cups onion, diced
- 8 cups chicken broth
- 10 teaspoons garlic cloves, minced
- ¼ cup cheddar cheese, shredded
- 16-ounces cream cheese
- ¼ cup bacon
- 5 cups Yukon gold potato, diced
- Salt and pepper to taste

Directions:
Add in your garlic, onion, potatoes, seasoning, and chicken stock to your instant pot. Cover and secure the pot lid, and set to Manual on high with a cook time of 10-minutes. When the cook time is completed, release the pressure naturally for 10-minutes. Stir in the cream cheese and stir. Divide into serving bowls, and top with shredded cheese and bacon as garnishes. Serve hot.

Nutritional Information per serving:
Calories: 314   Fat: 1.3g   Carbs: 52.1g   Protein: 20.1g

385. Bean Soup with Pork
Cook Time: 23 minutes **Servings: 12**
Ingredients:
- 20-ounces of 15 Bean soup mix
- 1 ¼ lbs. pork chops, boneless
- 2 tablespoons bacon fat
- 1/3 cup cooked bacon, diced
- 3 cups celery, diced
- 1 cup onion, diced
- 2 tablespoons Worcestershire sauce
- 2 ½ cups carrot, diced

- 2 tablespoons Dijon mustard
- 4 teaspoons garlic cloves, minced
- 14 ½ ounces canned tomatoes, diced
- 3 whole bay leaves
- 1 tablespoons chili powder
- 3 tablespoons of lemon juice
- 4 cups chicken broth
- ¼ cup of parsley, fresh
- Salt and pepper to taste

Directions:
Drain and rinse your soaked beans. Set to the side. Heat half of your reserved bacon drippings in your instant pot. Set the instant pot to the sauté mode. Sear the pork chops on both sides until they are browned, for about 5-minutes then set aside.
In the remaining bacon drippings sauté the onion, celery, carrots, and garlic for 5-minutes. Add your tomatoes, and stir well to combine. Combine soaked beans, onion, tomato mixture, pork chops Worcestershire sauce, bay leaves, mustard, chili powder, pepper, salt and lemon juice. Pour the chicken broth over and stir gently to combine. Secure the pot lid in place and set to Manual on high with a cook time of 18-minutes. When the cook time is completed, release the pressure naturally for 15-minutes. Remove the bay leaves and pork chops from your soup. Cut the meat off the bones and return to soup. Stir in fresh parsley and serve hot.

Nutritional Information per serving:
Calories: 342   Fat: 2.6g   Carbs: 45.2g   Protein: 23.4g

386. *Vegetable Barley Soup*

Cook Time: 26 minutes   **Servings:** 4

Ingredients:
- 1 teaspoon garlic, minced
- ¼ cup celery, chopped
- 1 (28-ounce) can of Petite tomatoes, undrained
- ½ cup onion, chopped
- 6 cups vegetable broth
- 1 cup quick barley
- 4 medium potatoes, diced
- 4 carrots, peeled, cut into coins
- 4 cups cabbage, chopped
- ½ teaspoon basil, dried
- 12-ounce bag of frozen mixed vegetables
- Salt and pepper to taste
- 1 tablespoon olive oil

Directions:
Set your instant pot to the sauté mode, add oil and heat it. Add the onions, and cook for 2-minutes. Add in the garlic and cook for an additional 3-minutes. Add the tomatoes, barley and beef broth. Close the lid and set on Soup setting on high with a cook time of 10-minutes. When the cook time is completed, release the pressure using the quick-release. Add the rest of the vegetables into instant pot and stir. Close the lid and set to Soup setting with a cook time of 15-minutes. Serve hot.

Nutritional Information per serving:
Calories: 311   Fat: 1.5g   Carbs: 51.2g   Protein: 20.1g

387. Maple Bacon Acorn Squash

Cook Time: 16 minutes
Servings: 6
Ingredients:
- 4 lbs. Acorn squash
- 2 tablespoons butter
- ½ cup bacon, diced, cooked
- 1 teaspoon sea salt
- 2 tablespoons maple syrup

Directions:
Wash your acorn squash. Pour the 1 cup of water into your instant pot, and place trivet inside. Set your squash on the trivet. Lock your lid in place, and select the Manual option and set for an 8-minute cook time. When the cook time is completed, release pressure with quick-release. Using oven mitts remove the squash from pot. Cut the squash in half and remove the seeds. Place the squash back inside pot on trivet. Close the lid and set on Manual for again for another 8-minute cook time. When cook time is done, use the quick-release again. Remove the squash and scrape the flesh from the shell. Mash the squash and add the butter and maple syrup. Fold in the bacon and sea salt. Serve hot.

Nutritional Information per serving:
Calories: 267   Fat: 1.6g   Carbs: 42.1g   Protein: 20.3g

388. Sweet Potato Soup

Cook Time: 30 minutes
Servings: 8
Ingredients:
- ¼ teaspoon oregano, dried
- ¼ cup lime juice for garnish
- 1 tablespoon chili powder
- 1 cup water
- 1 tablespoon cumin
- 2/3 cup sweet potato, diced
- 1 onion, diced
- 1 cup Pinto beans, cooked, dried
- 2 tablespoons tomato paste
- 1 cup black beans, cooked, dried
- 3 teaspoons garlic cloves, minced
- 20-ounces of diced tomatoes with green chiles
- 3 cups of ground beef, cooked
- Salt and pepper to taste
- Coriander, fresh, chopped for garnish

Directions:
Add all the ingredients into your instant pot, except the lime juice and cilantro. Close and secure the lid, and select the Bean/Chili setting for a cook time of 30-minutes. When the cook time is completed, release the pressure naturally for 15-minutes. Divide among serving bowls, and top with fresh chopped cilantro and lime juice as garnishes. Serve hot.

Nutritional Information per serving:
Calories: 243   Fat: 1.2g   Carbs: 32g   Protein: 21.2g

389. Tomato, Basil & Beef Soup

Cook Time: 20 minutes
Servings: 6

Ingredients:
- ¼ cups of basil, fresh
- 1 cup onion, diced
- 1 cup chicken broth
- 3 teaspoons garlic cloves, minced
- 30-ounces of canned tomatoes, diced
- 1 tablespoon coconut oil
- 1 cup canned coconut milk
- 1 ½ lbs. of ground beef, cooked
- Salt and pepper to taste

Directions:
In a blender, blend the diced tomatoes, and coconut milk until smooth. Set your instant pot to the saute mode, add oil and heat it. Add the onions and garlic and cook for 5-minutes. Add in the tomato/coconut milk mixture to instant pot, along with chicken broth, and salt. Close and secure the lid in place and set on Manual for a cook time of 10-minutes. When cook time is completed, release the pressure naturally for 10-minutes. Mix in the ground beef and basil. Set on saute mode for 5-minutes of cook time, stirring often. Serve hot.

Nutritional Information per serving:
Calories: 310 Fat: 2.5g Carbs: 52.3 Protein: 25.1g

390. African Chickpea, Coconut Soup

Cook Time: 10 minutes
Servings: 4

Ingredients:
- 1 ½ cups red bell pepper, diced
- 15-ounces Garbanzo beans, rinsed and drained
- 2/3 cups sweet potato, peeled, diced
- 4-ounces mild green chiles, diced
- 4 teaspoons garlic cloves, diced
- 3 cups vegetable stock
- 13 ½ fluid ounces of canned coconut milk
- 14-ounces Fire roasted tomatoes, diced
- 1 ½ cups Granny Smith apples, diced and peeled
- 1 tablespoon green curry paste
- ½ teaspoon cumin
- 1 tablespoon lime, juiced
- ½ teaspoon cinnamon
- 2 tablespoons cilantro, dried
- ½ cup quinoa, cooked
- Sea salt and black pepper

Directions:
Add all the ingredients into your instant pot. Close the lid and set to the Soup setting with a cook time of 10-minutes. When the cook time is completed, release the pressure naturally for 10-minutes. Serve hot.

Nutritional Information per serving:
Calories: 314 Fat: 1.4g Carbs: 44.2g Protein: 20.3g

391. Lentil Vegetable Soup

Cook Time: 15 minutes
Servings: 6
Ingredients:

Sauté:
- 1 clove garlic, minced
- 1 small onion, minced
- 1 tablespoon olive oil

Soup:
- 1 medium potato, peeled and cubed
- 5 cups of water
- 1 sweet potato, peeled and cubed
- 1 teaspoon Marjoram
- 2 carrots, medium, cubed
- ½ teaspoon smoked paprika
- 1 teaspoon thyme
- 1 bay leaf
- ¼ teaspoon rosemary powder
- 1 cup lentil blend

Finish:
- Pepper and salt to taste
- ¼ cup nutritional yeast

Directions:
Set your instant pot to the sauté mode, and add oil and heat it. Add onion and garlic and cook for 5-minutes. Add all the rest of the ingredients, except the yeast and salt and pepper. Close the lid of pot and set to the Manual setting for a cook time of 10-minutes. When the cook time is completed, release the pressure naturally for 10-minutes. Add in the yeast, pepper and salt, stir. Serve hot.

Nutritional Information per serving:
Calories: 305 Fat: 1.3g Carbs: 47.3g Protein: 23.2g

392. Creamy Tomato Soup

Cook Time: 5 minutes
Servings: 6
Ingredients:

- 1 (28-ounce) can of whole peeled tomatoes
- 1 (28-ounce) can crushed tomatoes
- 3 tablespoons of oats, rolled, Scottish, or steel-cut
- 2 vegetarian bouillon cubes
- ½ cup of cashew pieces
- 1 tablespoon dried basil
- 3 cups water
- 4 cloves of garlic
- Pepper and salt to taste
- 1 tablespoon of Agave Nectar (optional)

Directions:
Add all your ingredients to your instant pot, except for agave nectar, pepper and salt. Set the pot to Manual on high with a cook time of 5-minutes. When the cook time is completed, release the pressure naturally for 10-minutes. Pour the cooked mixture into a blender and blend until mixture is smooth. Add the agave, salt and pepper. Serve hot.

Nutritional Information per serving:
Calories: 243 Fat: 1.1g Carbs: 21.3g Protein: 6.2g

393. Taco Soup
Cook Time: 10 minutes **Servings: 12**
Ingredients:
- 3 cups of cooked ground beef
- 45-ounces of canned Pinto beans
- 1-ounce of Ranch Dressing mix
- 15 ½ ounces of canned Whole kernel corn
- 1 ¼ cups onion, diced
- 10-ounces of tomatoes, diced with green chilies
- Salt and pepper to taste
- 6 cups vegetable stock

Directions:
Add all the ingredients into your instant pot. Set the instant pot to the Soup setting on high with a cook time of 10-minutes. When the cook time is completed, release the pressure naturally for 10-minutes. Serve hot.

Nutritional Information per serving:
Calories: 253   Fat: 1.5g   Carbs: 32.2g   Protein: 26.2g

394. Mango Dal
Cook Time: 35 minutes **Servings: 6**
Ingredients:
- 1 cup of Chana Dal
- 1 tablespoon coconut oil
- 1 onion, medium, minced
- 2 mangos', peeled and diced
- 1 tablespoon ginger, minced, fresh
- 4 cloves garlic, minced
- 1 teaspoon coriander, ground
- 4 cups chicken broth
- ½ cup cilantro, fresh, chopped
- 1 teaspoon turmeric, ground
- 1 teaspoon cumin, ground
- Juice of ½ a lime
- 1/8 teaspoon cayenne pepper
- Sea salt to taste

Directions:
Add the Chana dal to a colander and rinse until the water runs clear. Set your instant pot to the sauté mode, add coconut oil and heat it. Add the cumin and stir for 30 seconds. Add in the onion and garlic, coriander, ginger, cayenne and sea salt and continue to cook for another 5-minutes. Add in the Chana dal, chicken broth and turmeric, and keep on sauté mode for another 10-minutes. Remove any foam that appears on top. Add in the mangos'. Set the lid on the pot, and set on the Beans/Chili setting for a cook time of 20-minutes. When the cook time is completed, release the pressure naturally for 15-minutes. Add in the cilantro and lime juice and stir to blend them into mixture. You can add chicken or rice to this meal. Serve hot.

Nutritional Information per serving:
Calories: 316   Fat: 2.1g   Carbs: 42.1g   Protein: 6.3g

395. Tuscan Chicken Stew

Cook Time: 15 minutes **Servings:** 6

Ingredients:
- 3 cups of chicken breasts, boneless, cooked, shredded
- 1 cup leek, diced
- 15-ounces of Garbanzo beans, canned, rinsed and drained
- 1 cup kale, chopped
- ¼ teaspoon basil, dried
- ¼ teaspoon oregano, dried
- 1 cup red potato, peeled and diced
- ½ teaspoon paprika
- ½ teaspoon red pepper flakes
- 1 teaspoon thyme, dried
- 15-ounce can of tomatoes, diced
- 1 cup celery, diced
- 4 cups chicken broth
- 1 cup carrot, diced
- 4 teaspoons garlic cloves, minced
- 2 tablespoons olive oil

Directions:
Set your instant pot on the sauté mode, and add oil and heat it. Add the onions, leeks, and garlic, cooking for 3-minutes. Add in the celery and carrots and cook for an additional 2-minutes. Add the chicken stock, chicken, thyme, garbanzo beans, paprika, pepper flakes, potatoes, basil, kale, oregano, and diced tomatoes. Cover and secure the lid to pot and set of the Soup setting with a cook time of 10-minutes.

When the cook time is completed, release the pressure naturally for 10-minutes. Serve hot.

Nutritional Information per serving:
Calories: 261 Fat: 1.4g Carbs: 38.2g Protein: 25.2g

396. Butternut Squash & Spinach Lasagna Rolls

Cook Time: 12 minutes **Servings:** 8

Ingredients:
- 8 tablespoons Italian blend cheese, shredded
- 1 tablespoon parsley, fresh, chopped
- 1 ¼ cups frozen spinach, drained
- ½ cup Parmesan cheese, shredded #2
- 2 teaspoons garlic cloves, minced
- 15-ounces fat-free ricotta cheese
- ¼ cup shallot, diced
- 2 tablespoons Parmesan cheese #1
- ¼ teaspoon kosher salt for #1
- ¼ teaspoon black pepper #1
- ¼ teaspoon kosher salt #2
- ¼ teaspoon black pepper #2
- 1 teaspoon olive oil
- 1 egg
- 3 ¼ cups of Butternut squash, peeled and diced, cooked
- 8 individual cooked lasagna noodles

Directions:
Using a blender, blend the squash until it is smooth, add a bit of water to thin out. Set your instant pot to the sauté mode, add oil and heat it. Add the shallots, and garlic to instant pot and cook for 5-minutes. In pan add your pureed squash, season with salt #1 and pepper #1, and add more water if needed. Stir in the Parmesan cheese #1. Remove the mixture from your instant pot and set to the side.

In the bottom of your instant pot, add about ½ cup of butternut squash mixture. Combine the ricotta, spinach, Parmesan #2, egg, salt #2, pepper #2 in mixing bowl. Lay out the lasagna noodles and spread about 1/3 cup of spinach mixture over each noodle. Roll up noodles and place with seam side down in your instant pot. Pour your butternut squash sauce over the lasagna rolls. Close the lid to pot, and set on Manual for a cook time of 7-minutes. When the cook time is completed, release the pressure using quick-release. Serve hot.

Nutritional Information per serving:
Calories: 308   Fat: 1.2g   Carbs: 28.3g   Protein: 7.6g

---

397. Summer Garden Boiled Peanut Salad

Cook Time: 20 minutes   **Servings: 4**

Ingredients:
- 2 tablespoons olive oil
- 1 bay leaf
- 2 tablespoons lemon juice, fresh
- ¼ cup hot peppers, finely diced
- ½ cup green pepper, diced
- 2 tomatoes, medium, chopped
- ½ cup sweet onion, diced
- 1 lb. raw peanuts, shelled
- Salt and black pepper to taste

Directions:
To skin the peanuts, blanch them in boiling salt water for about 1-minute, then drain. Slip off the skins and discard. Add 2 cups of water to your instant pot, along with bay leaf. Add the peanuts into instant pot, and set to Manual cook time of 20-minutes. When the cook time is completed, release the pressure naturally for 15-minutes. Drain. In a large bowl, combine peanuts with diced vegetables. Whisk together lemon juice, salt, pepper, and oil. Pour over mixture and toss to combine. Serve at room temperature.

Nutritional Information per serving:
Calories: 212   Fat: 1.1g   Carbs: 21.2g   Protein: 6.3g

---

398. Wheat Berry Salad

Cook Time: 20 minutes   **Servings: 2**

Ingredients:
- ½ cup slivered apricots, dried
- 2 tablespoons parsley, fresh, chopped
- ¾ cup green onions, thinly sliced
- ½ cup toasted almonds, chopped
- 1 tablespoon Balsamic vinegar
- ¾ cup blueberries, dried
- 2 teaspoons Dijon mustard
- ¼ cup raspberry vinegar
- 3 tablespoons olive oil
- 2 cups water
- 1 cup Wheat berries
- Salt and black pepper to taste

Directions:
Rinse your wheat berries in cold water, and allow them to soak overnight, then rinse and drain them. Add the wheat berries to your instant pot with 2 cups of water, and set on Manual with a cook time of 20-minutes. When the cook time is completed, release the pressure naturally for 15-minutes. Whisk the raspberry vinegar, mustard, balsamic vinegar, salt, pepper and oil. Stir in apricots, onions, almonds, blueberries, and parsley.

Allow it to stand for about 30-minutes. Stir in the wheat berries, cover and refrigerate for about 4-hours before serving. Serve cold.
Nutritional Information per serving:
Calories: 206   Fat: 1.2g   Carbs: 23.1g   Protein: 5.2g

---

399. Green Bean Casserole
Cook Time: 20 minutes   **Servings: 4**
Ingredients:

- 2 tablespoon butter
- 1 cup chicken broth
- 1 cup heavy cream
- 1 onion, small, diced
- ½ cup French's onions, for garnish
- 12-ounces mushrooms, sliced
- 16-ounces green beans, frozen
- 2 tablespoons cornstarch

Directions:
Set your instant pot to the sauté mode, and add butter and heat it. Add the mushrooms, and onions and cook for 5-minutes. Add the heavy cream, green beans, and chicken broth to your instant pot. Cover and secure the lid, and set to Manual on high with a cook time of 15-minutes. When the cook time is completed, release the pressure naturally for 15-minutes. Add two tablespoons cornstarch and mix. Serve hot topped with French's onions for garnish.
Nutritional Information per serving:
Calories: 219   Fat: 1.4g   Carbs: 17g   Protein: 5.8g

---

400. Red, White & Green Brussels Sprouts
Cook Time: 3 minutes
Servings: 4
Ingredients:

- 1 lb. Brussels sprouts
- ¼ cup pine nuts toasted
- 1 tablespoon pomegranate seeds
- 1 tablespoon extra-virgin olive oil
- Salt and black pepper to taste

Directions:
Remove the outer leaves and trim the stems of your Brussels sprouts and wash them. Cut the large ones in half. Prepare your instant pot by adding 1 cup of water into it, and the steamer basket. Place the sprouts into basket. Close and secure pot lid, and set to Manual on high with a cook time of 3-minutes. When the cook time is completed, release the pressure using the quick-release. Move the sprouts into a serving dish and dress in salt, pepper, olive oil. Serve warm and sprinkle the top with toasted pine nuts and pomegranate seeds for garnish.
Nutritional Information per serving:
Calories: 207   Fat: 1.1g   Carbs: 17.8g   Protein: 6.4g

Chapter 12. Collection of Desserts & Appetizer Instant Pot Recipes

401. Chocolate Almond Fudge Cake
Cook Time: 2 hours   **Servings:** 8
Ingredients:
- 1 cup almond flour
- 2 tablespoons Truvia
- ½ cup chocolate almond milk
- 2 tablespoons canola oil
- 2 tablespoons dark cocoa powder
- 2 teaspoons baking soda
- 1 teaspoon vanilla extract
- Pinch of salt
- ½ cup almonds, slivered

Directions:
Mix the Truvia, flour, baking powder, pinch of salt in a mixing bowl. Add the oil, vanilla extract, almond slivers and almond milk, then whisk until smooth. Pour the batter into a greased instant pot. Place the lid on and secure, then set to Manual on high for a 2-hour cook time using the slow cooking feature. Once the cook time is completed, release the pressure naturally for 15-minutes. Remove the lid and allow the cake to cool completely. Garnish the cake with chocolate sauce and whipped cream.

Nutritional Information per serving:
Calories: 322   Fats: 3g   Carbs: 19g   Proteins: 4g

402. Pumpkin Chocolate Chip Bundt Cake
Cook Time: 35 minutes   **Servings:** 8
Ingredients:
- ¾ cup unbleached all-purpose flour
- ¾ cup whole wheat flour
- ½ a can (15-ounce) of 100% pureed pumpkin
- 1 teaspoon baking soda
- 2 tablespoons canola oil
- ½ cup 2% Greek yogurt
- 2 tablespoons Truvia or ¾ cup sugar
- 1 medium banana, mashed
- ½ teaspoon baking powder
- ¾ teaspoon pumpkin pie spice
- ½ teaspoon salt
- 1 egg
- ½ teaspoon pure vanilla extract
- 2/3 cup semi-sweet chocolate chips
- 1.5 cups of water for instant pot

Directions:
In a mixing bowl combine, salt, baking soda, flour, baking powder, pumpkin pie spice and set aside. Using an electric mixer to combine Truvia, yogurt, oil, banana, pureed pumpkin, egg and vanilla extract (in a separate bowl from dry ingredients). With the mixer on low, gradually add the dry ingredients. Fold in the chocolate chips.
Grease the pan or use cooking spray, and transfer the batter to the bundt pan. Add water into the inner stainless steel pot, and place the trivet inside. Place the bundt pan on top of trivet, and close the lid and lock it. Press the Manual mode and set for a cook time of 35-minutes. When the cook time is completed, release the pressure naturally for 10-minutes. Allow the pan to cool before trying to remove it.

Nutritional Information per serving:
Calories: 356   Fats: 4g   Carbs: 22g   Proteins: 7g

---

403. Tapioca Pudding
Cook Time: 7 minutes
Servings: 6
Ingredients:
- 3 cups milk
- 2 tablespoons Truvia or ½ cup sugar
- 4 tablespoons tapioca
- 1 teaspoon vanilla extract
- 1 egg

Directions:
Spray the inside of your instant pot with non-stick cooking spray. Add all ingredients except the egg, and stir well. Place the lid on your instant pot and set to Manual for a cook time of 7-minutes. When the cook time is completed, release the pressure naturally for 10-minutes. Lightly beat the egg in a bowl. Once the tapioca starts to bubble in the pot stir and temper the egg by adding a spoonful of the tapioca mixture to the egg. Add the tempered egg slowly to the pudding and stir until fully integrated. Eat warm or chill to serve cold.

Nutritional Information per serving:
Calories: 272   Fats: 2g   Carbs: 20g   Proteins: 5g

---

404. Carrot Cake
Cook Time: 32 minutes
Servings: 8
Ingredients:
- 2 eggs
- 1 ½ cups shredded carrots
- 2/3 cup vegetable oil
- ½ teaspoon nutmeg
- ½ teaspoon salt
- ½ teaspoon baking soda
- 1 teaspoon baking powder
- 2 tablespoons Truvia or 1 cup sugar
- 1 cup flour
- ½ cup water for instant pot

Directions:
In a large mixing bowl combine, carrots, oil, sugar (or Truvia), and eggs together. In another bowl mix the dry ingredients. Fold the wet ingredients into dry, mixing until just wet. Spray a 6-inch springform pan with cooking spray and pour in the batter. Pour ½ cup water into instant pot, place in the trivet, and place pan on top of trivet. Set to Manual setting for a cook time of 35-minutes. When cook time is completed, release the pressure naturally for 10-minutes. Serve.

Nutritional Information per serving:
Calories: 274   Fats: 3g   Carbs: 21g   Proteins: 18g

405. Brownies
Cook Time: 18 minutes **Servings: 8**
Ingredients:
- ¼ cup cocoa powder
- ½ cup almond flour
- 1 teaspoon vanilla extract
- 3 eggs
- ¼ cup brown sugar
- 2 tablespoons Truvia, or ½ cup white sugar
- 2 tablespoons chocolate chips
- 4 tablespoons unsalted butter
- 1 cup water for instant pot

Directions:
Melt the chocolate and butter together in the microwave. Beat the butter/chocolate mixture together with sugars until well combined. Add the eggs one at a time, add vanilla while beating. Sift flour, cocoa over the wet ingredients and stir to combine. Add 1 cup of water into instant pot, add the trivet. Add batter to ramekins, and place them on top of trivet. Close the instant pot lid, and set to Manual mode with a cook time of 18-minutes. When the cook time is competed, release the pressure naturally for 15-minutes. Serve.

Nutritional Information per serving:
Calories: 312 Fats: 2g Carbs: 24g Proteins: 21g

406. Apple Crisp
Cook Time: 8 minutes **Servings: 8**
Ingredients:
- 5 medium Granny Smith apples
- 2 teaspoons cinnamon
- ¼ brown sugar
- ¼ cup almond flour
- ¾ cup old fashioned rolled oats
- 4 tablespoons butter
- ½ cup water
- ½ teaspoon nutmeg
- ½ teaspoon salt

Directions:
Peel, core, and dice granny smith apples. Insert the apples on the bottom of your instant pot. Sprinkle with cinnamon and nutmeg. Top with water. In a bowl melt butter, add oats, flour, brown sugar and salt and mix. Drop the crumble mix by the spoonful into your instant pot on top of apples. Close and secure the instant pot lid, set to Manual setting for a cook time on high of 8-minutes. When the cook time is completed, release the pressure naturally for 10-minutes. Serve warm.

Nutritional Information per serving:
Calories: 314 Fats: 4g Carbs: 23g Proteins: 8g

407. Vanilla Fruit Cake
Cook Time: 20 minutes **Servings: 6**
Ingredients:
- 10-ounces fruit
- 2 eggs
- Powdered sugar
- 1 tablespoon olive oil

- 1 teaspoon vanilla extract
- 1 cup milk
- 7 tablespoons almond flour
- 4 tablespoons sugar, or 2 tablespoons Truvia
- 2 cups water for instant pot

Directions:
Add the trivet and 2 cups of water to your instant pot. Wash and prepare the fruit of your choice. In a mixing bowl, add eggs, sugar, vanilla and mix them well with a whisk or a fork. Next add the milk and flour. Oil the form and line with wax paper. Pour the mixture, and then sprinkle the fruit into mixture. Cover tightly with tin foil. Place on trivet, and set on Manual mode, with a cook time of 20-minutes. When the cook time is completed, release the pressure naturally for 10-minutes. Allow to cool, then transfer to serving dishes, sprinkle with powdered sugar right before serving.

Nutritional Information per serving:
Calories: 343   Fats: 3g   Carbs: 25g   Proteins: 19g

---

408. Creamy Chocolate Cheesecake

Cook Time: 45 minutes   **Servings: 8**

Ingredients:
- 8-ounces cream cheese
- 4-ounces milk chocolate
- 1 cup sugar or 3 tablespoons Truvia
- 4-ounces white chocolate
- 4-ounces dark chocolate
- 1 ½ teaspoons vanilla extract
- ½ cup plain Greek yogurt
- 3 large eggs
- 1 tablespoon cornstarch
- 1 cup sugar or 3 tablespoons Truvia

Directions:
Take a 7-inch springform pan and spray with non-stick cooking spray. Use parchment paper to line the bottom of the pan. In mixing bowl, mix cookie crumbs and melted butter and press straight to the bottom of the pan. Store in the freezer to set for a day. Blend the cream cheese with a handheld mixer until smooth. Add the sugar and cornstarch, while mixing on low speed, do this until well combined. Add the eggs to mixture, one at a time, continuing to beat and scrape the bowl. Add yogurt and vanilla, mixing until well combined. Divide your batter into three separate bowls (about 2 cups each).

In the microwave, melt your milk chocolate for 30 seconds, stir. Return chocolate to the microwave for an additional 30 seconds, stir until completely melted and smooth. Whisk it into one of the bowls of cheesecake batter. Repeat this process with the white and dark chocolate (each being mixed in a different bowl of dough). Store the bowls in the fridge for about 20-minutes so they will be firmer for layering. Remove the bowls from the fridge and remove the pan, with the crust out of freezer.

Add the dark chocolate batter into center of the crust, making sure to smooth, to form an even layer. Carefully spoon dollops of your white chocolate mixture on top of the dark chocolate, carefully smoothing over the top. Repeat process with the milk chocolate mixture. Add 1 cup of water to your instant pot, placing the trivet inside it. Place the cake pan on top of trivet, and set to Manual setting on high for a cook time of 45-minutes. When the cook time is completed, release the pressure naturally for 15-minutes. Carefully remove the cake pan from your instant pot. Allow the cake to cool completely and then cover with plastic wrap, and place it in the fridge overnight.

Before serving allow the cake to stand at room temperature for an hour or so. To make the cake look even more pleasing to the eye, decorate the cake with sugared cranberries, if desired.

Nutritional Information per serving:
Calories: 358   Fats: 4g   Carbs: 28g   Proteins: 24g

---

409. Apple Crumb Cake
Cook Time: 20 minutes   **Servings: 8**
Ingredients:
- ¼ cup raw sugar
- 6-ounces butter
- 2 tablespoons all-purpose flour

Crumb filling:
- 5 teaspoons cinnamon
- 5 tablespoons sugar or 2 tablespoons Truvia
- 6 small apples
- 2 tablespoons all-purpose flour
- 5-ounces dry breadcrumbs
- ½ a lemon's juice and rind
- 1 tablespoon ginger powder

Directions:
Prepare the crumb filling by combining the breadcrumbs, lemon juice, ginger, cinnamon, sugar, lemon zest and melted butter. Mix the ingredients well and set aside. Take your unpeeled washed apple, make sure to remove their cores. Then, slice them very thinly, using a mandolin, if you can. Butter the interior of your container all the way around the edge of it. Add the flour to the container and swoosh the flour around so it will evenly coat container. Start layering your apple slices. The bottom of your cake will become the top when you flip the cake out of the container. So, arrange apple slices carefully for the first layer of your cake. Add a layer of breadcrumb mixture to it.

Alternate apple and breadcrumb layers until you have filled your container. Once you have finished filling your bowl, cover tightly with tin foil. Add 1 cup of water to your instant pot, also and the trivet inside your instant pot. Place the container on top of the trivet, set to Manual on high for a cook time of 20-minutes. When the cook time is completed, release the pressure naturally for 10-minutes. Sprinkle the top of cake with a layer of raw sugar and grill until the sugar has melted and the top of the cake has a nice golden brown color to it.

Nutritional Information per serving:
Calories: 258   Fats: 1g   Carbs: 8g   Proteins: 5g

---

410. Raspberry Cream Cheesecake
Cook Time: 25 minutes   **Servings: 8**
Ingredients:
- 28g butter, melted

Filling:
- 2 eggs
- 12 crushed Oreo cookie crumbs
- 1 tablespoon all-purpose flour

- ¼ cup sour cream
- ¼ cup sugar

Topping:
- Fresh raspberries
- 3 ½ ounces milk chocolate

- 16-ounces cream cheese
- ½ cup seedless raspberry jam
- 1/3 cup heavy cream

Directions:
Begin by preparing a 7-inch springform pan, and coating it with a non-stick spray. You can also line it with parchment paper if desired. Combine Oreo cookie crumbs and butter in a mixing bowl. Spread mixture, evenly on the bottom and 1-inch up the side of pan. Store in the freezer for at least 10-minutes. In a mixing bowl, mix cream cheese, and sugar at medium speed with blender until smooth. Blend in the jam, sour cream, and flour. Mix in the eggs, one at a time, until mixture is well combined. Add the batter into the springform pan on top of the crust.

Add 1 cup of water into instant pot and place trivet inside. Place the cake pan on top of trivet, and close lid of pot. Set to Manual setting on high for a cook time of 25-minutes.

When the cook time is completed, release the pressure naturally for 15-minutes. Carefully remove the cheesecake from your instant pot. Place the springform pan on a wire rack to cool. Once the cheesecake has cooled, cover it with plastic wrap and place in the fridge for at least 4 hours or overnight. When the cheesecake is cooled, prepare topping, place half of the chocolate into a mixing bowl. Heat your heavy cream over medium-high heat until it reaches a boil. Remove the cream from heat, and pour the cream over chocolate and stir until chocolate is fully melted. Add the remaining chocolate and stir until it has all melted and well combined. Allow it to cool until it has thickened enough to drip down the sides of the cheesecake. Drizzle the chocolate over top of the cheesecake. Decorate the top of cake with fresh raspberries, to add to the taste and look of this yummy treat. Keep cake refrigerated until ready to serve.

Nutritional Information per serving:
Calories: 318   Fats: 4g   Carbs: 21g   Proteins: 19g

---

411. *Crema Catalana*

Cook Time: 13 minutes
Ingredients:
- 1 stick of cinnamon
- 1 orange zested
- 3 tablespoons white sugar

Garnish:
- 1 teaspoon nutmeg

Servings: 4

- 6 egg yolks
- 18-ounces fresh cream

- 2 tablespoons raw sugar for caramelizing

Directions:
Begin with heating up the citrus zest, cream, cinnamon in a small saucepan over low heat, and stirring occasionally. Once the cream begins to boil, turn off the heat, allow it to infuse for 30-minutes. In the meantime, add 2 cups of water to your instant pot, and place the steamer basket inside of instant pot. Set aside. In a small mixing bowl, add egg yolks, sugar, and whisk until the sugar is dissolved. Once the cream has cooled to room

temperature, add the yolks and whisk, just enough to mix ingredients well. Pour the mixture slowly through a strainer into a spouted container. Put the mixture into ramekins, cover tightly with foil and place them into steamer basket. Close and secure the lid of your instant pot. Set it to Manual mode with a cook time of 8-minutes. When the cook time has completed, release the pressure naturally for 10-minutes.

Remove the custards from your instant pot, and allow them to cool on a wire rack. Cover custards with some plastic wrap and keep them in the fridge for 4-hours to chill. Before serving custards, grate some nutmeg over top of them, and sprinkle a layer of sugar over them as well. Serve warm or cold.

Nutritional Information per serving:
Calories: 302   Fats: 3g   Carbs: 23g   Proteins: 22g

---

412. Cranberry Cake

Cook Time: 50 minutes   **Servings: 10**

Ingredients:
- 3 ½ ounces apricots, dry
- 3 ½ ounces of cranberries, dry
- 1 teaspoon olive oil
- 8 tablespoons sugar or 3 tablespoons Truvia
- 2 teaspoons baking powder
- 1 teaspoon ginger
- 3 ½ ounces carrot, grated
- 2-ounces maple syrup (can use sugar-free syrup)
- 4 large eggs
- 7-ounces butter
- Pinch of salt
- 1 teaspoon cinnamon

Directions:
Add dried apricots and cranberries into a deep bowl, cover them with boiling water. Prepare a pudding mold, by adding a drop of olive oil, then spreading it around with a paper towel until the inside of the bowl is well covered, then set mold aside. Add 2 cups of water to your instant pot, also place the trivet inside of your instant pot.

Add the sugar, flour, baking powder, ginger, cinnamon, and salt into a food processor. Pulse a few times to mix the mixture. Add chopped butter, and pulse a few more times. Add the eggs and maple syrup, and pulse a few times until well blended. Strain dried food and rinse it under cold water. Now, lightly sprinkle the dried fruit and grated carrot on top of the mixture. Add to the prepared bowl, your pudding batter. Place the uncovered bowl onto top of trivet. Close and secure the lid to the instant pot. Set to the Brown/Sauté setting, when the steam starts to come out of the instant pot (in about 10-minutes), start counting down 15-minutes of steam without the pre-cooking time. Set your instant pot to Manual on high with a cook time of 35-minutes. When the cook time is completed, release the pressure naturally for 15-minutes. Remove the pudding from your instant pot and cover it tightly, until ready to invert and serve. Just before serving, give it a dousing of fresh cream.

Nutritional Information per serving:
Calories: 353   Fats: 3g   Carbs: 27g   Proteins: 34g

413. Chocoflan

Cook Time: 20 minutes **Servings: 8**

Ingredients:

For Caramel:
- 1 cup sugar
- 2 tablespoons butter
- 1 teaspoon vanilla extract
- 2 tablespoons heavy cream
- ¼ cup corn syrup

For Flan:
- 1 cup whole milk
- 2 eggs
- 1 cup condensed milk
- 1 teaspoon vanilla extract

For Cake:
- 7 tablespoons almond flour
- 6 tablespoons sugar or 2 tablespoons Truvia
- 1 ½ tablespoons cocoa powder
- 8 tablespoons yogurt
- 2 tablespoons olive oil
- 1 egg
- 1/3 teaspoon salt
- ½ teaspoon baking powder
- ½ teaspoon baking soda

Directions:

Add 2 cups of water to your instant pot, and place the trivet inside of it. Prepare the caramel by heating all ingredients in a small saucepan over low heat. Stir often, and when it begins to boil remove from heat, and pour into tube pan. In a mixing bowl, make the flan by breaking up the eggs well using a fork, mix in the milk, sweetened condensed milk, and vanilla. In another mixing bowl, mix all the dry ingredients for the cake. Add the cocoa, flour, sugar, baking soda, baking powder and salt, mix well. Using a small bowl, break up the egg mix in the oil and yogurt. Scrape out all the yogurt and egg from small bowl using a spatula. Combine this mix with flour/cocoa mixture using a fork to mix until well combined.

Spatula out the chocolate cake mixture into the caramel-coated tube pan, and flatten into a flat layer. Pour the flan mixture on top of that. Set the tube pan in the middle of a foil sling and lower it on top of trivet. Close and secure lid to instant pot, and set to Manual on high with a cook time of 20-minutes. When the cook time is completed, release the pressure naturally for 15-minutes. Lift the dessert out of instant pot and allow it to cool. Cover it with plastic wrap and place in the fridge overnight. Top with upside down serving plate and quickly flip. Remove the tube pan from the cake and serve with an optional sprinkling of pecans or ground pistachios.

Nutritional Information per serving:
Calories: 326   Fats: 2g   Carbs: 26g   Proteins: 32g

414. Cheese Flan Cake
Cook Time: 15 minutes **Servings:** 10
Ingredients:
- 1 teaspoon nutmeg
- Caramel: 4 tablespoons sugar
- 1 teaspoon cinnamon
- 1 teaspoon vanilla extract
- 5 eggs
- 8-ounces cream cheese
- 1 ½ cups evaporated milk
- 2 cups sweetened condensed milk

Directions:
Make caramel; use your flan pan to melt sugar. Stir until melted and is medium brown in color. Remove from heat and swirl the liquid sugar to coat the sides of the pan. Allow it cool, meanwhile make custard. Put the cream cheese in a mixing bowl. Add one egg at a time until well blended. Add the remaining ingredients and then add to your caramelized pan. Add a cup of water into instant pot, and place trivet inside of it. Place the pan on top of trivet, and set on Manual mode with a cook time of 15-minutes. When the cook time is completed, naturally release the pressure for 15-minutes. Remove the flan and allow it to cool to room temperature, then place it in fridge overnight. Run a knife around the edge of the pan, flip onto a plate that has a rim to catch caramel. Slice and serve!

Nutritional Information per serving:
Calories: 357   Fats: 5g   Carbs: 25g   Proteins: 37g

415. Raspberry Curd
Cook Time: 5 minutes **Servings:** 4
Ingredients:
- 4 egg yolks
- 24-ounces raspberries
- 4 tablespoons butter
- 4 tablespoons lemon juice
- 2 cups sugar or 2 tablespoons Truvia

Directions:
Add the raspberries, sugar, lemon juice into your instant pot and stir. Cover and cook on the Manual setting with a cook time of 1-minute. When the cook time is completed, release the pressure using the quick-release. Strain the contents through a fine wire mesh strainer and discard the seeds. Whisk the yolks. Add the strained raspberry pulp into the yolks and whisk. Pour into instant pot and sauté for 5-minutes, stirring constantly. Add butter and turn off pot. Pour into serving bowls and chill for a couple of hours before serving.

Nutritional Information per serving:
Calories: 224   Fat: 1.2g   Carbs: 32g   Protein: 6.4g

416. Fruit Clafoutis Cake
Cook Time: 20 minutes
Servings: 8
Ingredients:
- 5 cups fruits, of your choice, chopped
- 1 ½ cups sugar or 2 tablespoons Truvia
- 4 medium eggs
- 1 ½ cups all-purpose flour
- 2 tablespoons vanilla extract
- 2 cups milk

Directions:
Whisk the eggs, sugar, and vanilla together in a mixing bowl. Add the flour and milk and whisk well until smooth. Grease a heatproof dish and line it with parchment paper. Pour the batter into the dish. Sprinkle the assorted chopped fruit over the top of mixture. Cover with foil. Place a trivet into your instant pot, and pour 2 cups of water into pot. Place the dish with mixture on top of trivet. Close the pot lid, and select Manual setting on high with a cook time of 20-minutes. When the cook time is completed, release the pressure naturally for 10-minutes. Remove the dish from instant pot and allow it to sit for awhile. Sprinkle powdered sugar over it just before serving. Serve warm or chilled.

Nutritional Information per serving:
Calories: 272   Fat: 1.5g   Carbs: 38g   Protein: 5.2g

417. Yams Citrus
Cook Time: 7 minutes
Servings: 2
Ingredients:
- 2 yams, halved
- ¼ teaspoon salt
- 1 tablespoon butter
- ¾ cup brown sugar or to taste
- 1 ½ tablespoons orange zest, grated
- 1 cup orange juice

Directions:
Set the yams facing up on the bottom of your instant pot. Pour in the orange juice. Sprinkle yams with salt and half the orange zest. Sprinkle yams with brown sugar. Close the lid, and select Manual setting on high with a cook time of 7-minutes. When the cook time is completed, release the pressure using the quick-release. Mash the yams with a potato masher. Add butter, more brown sugar is desired, and remaining orange zest. Serve warm.

Nutritional Information per serving:
Calories: 243   Fat: 1.0g   Carbs: 27g   Protein: 5.1g

418. Chocolate Custard
Cook Time: 35 minutes
Servings: 8
Ingredients:
- 9 egg yolks, whisked
- 3 cups dark cooking chocolate, finely chopped
- ¾ cup castor sugar
- 1 ½ teaspoons vanilla extract
- 2 cups full fat milk
- Fresh strawberries for garnish
- 1 ½ cups cream

Directions:
Pour 2 cups of water into your instant pot, and place the trivet inside of it. Pour cream, milk, vanilla and sugar into a saucepan. Place the saucepan over medium heat, and simmer until the sugar is dissolved. Remove from heat and add chocolate pieces and stir until the chocolate melts. Gently pour the yolks into the mixture while whisking. Pour the mixture into a heatproof dish and place on top of the trivet. Close the lid on pot, and select the Manual setting on high with a cook time of 30-minutes. When the cook time is completed, release the pressure naturally for 10-minutes. Remove the dish from pot and allow it to sit for awhile. Serve warm and garnish with strawberries.

Nutritional Information per serving:
Calories: 282 Fat: 1.4g Carbs: 37g Protein: 5.3g

419. Bread Pudding
Cook Time: 10 minutes
Servings: 8
Ingredients:
- 8 slices old bread, trim crusts, cut into cubes
- 4 eggs, lightly beaten
- 4 cups warm milk
- 1 cup walnuts, chopped
- 1 teaspoon cinnamon + extra for garnish
- 1 cup golden raisins
- ½ teaspoon salt
- 2 tablespoons butter
- 1 cup, light brown sugar
- Zest of an orange, cut into thin strips
- 1 teaspoon vanilla extract
- 3 cups water

Directions:
Grease heatproof dish with butter, then set it aside. In a mixing bowl, mix bread, walnuts, raisins, and orange zest. In a separate mixing bowl, mix brown sugar, cinnamon, eggs, salt, milk, and vanilla extract. Pour this mixture into the bowl of bread mix. Mix well, then transfer bread mixture into the prepared dish. Cover dish with foil. Pour water into instant pot, and place the trivet in. Set the dish on top of the trivet, and close lid to pot. Set on Manual setting on high with cook time of 10-minutes. When the cooking is completed, release the pressure naturally for 10-minutes. Remove the dish from instant pot and loosen the foil and allow it to cool a bit. Sprinkle with cinnamon for garnish, and serve warm.

Nutritional Information per serving:
Calories: 289 Fat: 2.4g Carbs: 31g Protein: 6.1g

420. Blueberry Custard

Cook Time: 25 minutes **Servings: 4**

Ingredients:
- 4 eggs
- 1 ½ tablespoons confectioners' sugar
- ½ teaspoon nutmeg, ground
- ½ cup blueberries
- 1/3 cup almond flour
- 2 tablespoons honey
- 1 ½ tablespoons butter, melted
- 1 ¼ cups milk
- ½ teaspoon vanilla extract
- ¼ teaspoon salt

Directions:
Add the butter to a baking dish and spread the butter all over the dish. Blend the honey, milk, vanilla, flour, salt, and eggs until smooth. Pour into dish. Sprinkle the blueberries all over mix. Place trivet inside of instant pot, along with 2 cups of water. Place the dish on top of trivet. Close lid and select Manual setting on high with a cook time of 25-minutes. When the cook time is completed, release the pressure naturally for 15-minutes. Chill for a few hours. When ready to serve, run a knife all around the edges of the pan and invert on to a plate. Sprinkle nutmeg and confectioners' sugar for garnish and serve chilled.

Nutritional Information per serving:
Calories: 304   Fat: 2.3g   Carbs: 38g   Protein: 7.2g

421. Purple Pudding

Cook Time: 5 minutes **Servings: 6**

Ingredients:
- 2 cans thick coconut cream, divided
- 5 cups water
- ½ cup brown sugar
- ½ cup seed tapioca
- 1 cup ripe jackfruit, cubed
- 1 cup glutinous rice, shaped into balls
- 1 cup taro root, cubed
- 2 cups ripe plantains, sliced into disks
- 1 ½ cups purple yam, cubed

Directions:
Add the purple yam, glutinous rice, taro root, ripe plantains, ripe jackfruit, brown sugar, tapioca pearls, and water into instant pot. Close the lid and set to Manual setting on high for a cook time of 5-minutes. When the cook time is completed, release the pressure using the quick-release. Add the coconut cream, and allow the residual heat to cook the cream. Serve by ladling pudding into bowls. Serve cold.

Nutritional Information per serving:
Calories: 262   Fat: 1.3g   Carbs: 27g   Protein: 6.5g

422. Mango & Cashew Cake

Cook Time: 35 minutes **Servings:** 8

Ingredients:

- ½ cup powdered sugar for dusting top of cake
- ¼ cup cashew nuts, ground
- ¼ cup mango jam
- ½ cup cashew milk
- 1 teaspoon vanilla essence
- ½ teaspoon baking soda
- ¼ cup coconut butter
- ½ cup almond flour
- 2 cups of water for instant pot
- 1 teaspoon baking powder

Directions:

Lightly grease bundt pan with coconut oil, and dust pan with flour. Set aside. In a mixing bowl, mix coconut butter, almond flour, baking powder, baking soda, vanilla essence, milk, and mango jam. Stir well to combine. Pour the batter into the bundt pan. Add 2 cups of water to your instant pot, add in the trivet, and place the bundt pan on top of trivet. Close the lid to pot, and set to Manual setting on high for a cook time of 35-minutes. When the cook time is completed, release the pressure naturally for 15-minutes. Transfer the bundt cake onto a rack and allow to cool at room temperature. Place on a platter, sprinkle with ground cashews and powdered sugar. Slice and serve at room temperature.

Nutritional Information per serving:

Calories: 293 Fat: 1.2g Carbs: 29g Protein: 6.8g

---

423. Corn Pudding

Cook Time: 2 minutes **Servings:** 4

Ingredients:

- 1 can cream of corn
- ¾ cup rice
- ¼ cup white sugar or 1 tablespoon Truvia
- 3 cups water
- Pinch of salt
- 2 cans thick coconut cream
- ¼ cup freshly toasted coconut flakes, for garnish

Directions:

Add the rice, cream of corn, salt, white sugar, and water into your instant pot. Stir well to blend. Close the lid to pot, and select Manual setting on high for a cook time of 2-minutes. When the cook time is completed, release the pressure using the quick-release. Add in the coconut cream and stir. Ladle into bowls and garnish with coconut flakes. Serve cold.

Nutritional Information per serving:

Calories: 282 Fat: 1.4g Carbs: 24g Protein: 5.1g

---

424. Pumpkin Pie

Cook Time: 35 minutes **Servings:** 8

Ingredients:

Crust:

- ½ cup crushed pecan sandies cookies, about 6 cookies
- 1/3 cup toasted pecans, chopped
- 2 tablespoons butter, melted

Filling:
- ½ teaspoon salt
- ½ cup light brown sugar
- 1 ½ teaspoon pumpkin pie spice
- 2 tablespoons lemon zest
- 1 ½ cups oats
- 1 ½ cups light brown sugar
- 1 ¼ cups almond flour
- ½ cup evaporated milk
- 1 ½ cups pumpkin puree
- 1 egg beaten
- 1 teaspoon cinnamon, ground
- 1 teaspoon nutmeg, ground
- 1 ½ sticks butter

Directions:
Coat a 7-inch spring-form pan with non-stick cooking spray. In a mixing bowl, combine pecans, cookie crumbs, butter (melted), and spread evenly over pan bottom. Set in the freezer for about 10-minutes. In another mixing bowl, add brown sugar, pumpkin pie spice, salt, egg, pumpkin puree, evaporated milk and mix well. Pour mix onto pie crust and cover with foil. Pour 1 cup of water into bottom of instant pot, and set trivet inside. Take an 18-inch long piece of foil and fold it over twice. Carefully place the pan onto the foil strip, and lower in onto the trivet, fold the foil so you can close the instant pot lid. Close the lid, and select the Manual setting on high for a cook time of 35-minutes. When the cook time is completed, release the pressure naturally for 15-minutes. Remove the pan to cool, and remove the foil. When it has cooled, cover the pie with plastic wrap and place in the fridge for at least 4-hours. Serve cold or warm.

Nutritional Information per serving:
Calories: 294   Fat: 1.6g   Carbs: 31g   Protein: 8.3g

425. *Instant Pot Chocolate Fondue*
Cook Time: *1 minute*   **Servings:** *8*
Ingredients:
- 2 cups of water for instant pot
- 3 ½ ounces dark chocolate 70% cocoa, cut into chunks
- 1 teaspoon sugar or ½ teaspoon Truvia
- Fresh fruit of your choice for serving
- 1 teaspoon Amaretto liquor (optional)
- 3 ½ ounces fresh cream

Directions:
Add 2 cups of water into your instant pot, also place the trivet inside of pot. In a small ceramic fondue pot, or any heat-proof container, place large chunks of chocolate into it. Add the sugar along with the liquor. Carefully, place the container on top of trivet, and close the lid to pot. Select Manual setting on high for a cook time of 1-minute. When the cook time is completed, release the pressure using quick-release. Stir the contents of your mixture until smooth. Using an oven mitt remove container from instant pot. Move to fondue stand with flame on medium setting. Serve fondue with small pieces of your favorite fruits.

Nutritional Information per serving:
Calories: 286   Fat: 2.4g   Carbs: 29g   Protein: 4.6g

426. Samoa Cheesecake

Cook Time: 35 minutes **Servings:** 8

Ingredients:

Crust:
- ½ cup crushed chocolate graham cracker cookies
- 2 tablespoons butter, melted

Filling:
- ¼ cup heavy cream
- ¼ cup sour cream
- 2 eggs, room temperature
- 1 ½ teaspoons vanilla extract
- 12-ounces cream cheese, room temperature
- 1 egg yolk, room temperature
- 1 tablespoon almond flour
- ½ cup sugar or 2 tablespoons Truvia

Topping:
- 1 ½ cups sweetened shredded coconut
- 12 chewy caramels, unwrapped
- ¼ cup chopped semisweet chocolate
- 3 tablespoons heavy cream

Directions:

Using a 7-inch spring-form pan, spray it with non-stick cooking spray. Combine butter and graham crackers, in a mixing bowl. Spread the mixture nice and evenly on the bottom of the pan. Store the pan in the freezer for at least 10-minutes. In another mixing bowl, add cream cheese, sugar, blending on medium speed with hand mixer until smooth. Add the flour, sour cream, vanilla, heavy cream, and blend. Beat in the eggs one at a time. Pour the batter into the spring-form pan on top of crust. Now, cover top of pan with foil. Add 1 cup of water to bottom of your instant pot, also place trivet inside instant pot. Construct a foil sling, and carefully lower the pan onto the trivet using the sling. Make sure to fold the sling down, so you can close the lid to your instant pot.

Select Manual mode, setting on high with a cook time of 35-minutes. When the cook time is completed, release the pressure naturally for 15-minutes. Transfer the pan from your instant pot onto a wire rack to cool, remove the foil. Once your cheesecake has cooled, cover it with plastic wrap and place it in the fridge for at least 4-hours or overnight. When the cheesecake is chilled prepare the topping: Preheat oven to 300° Fahrenheit. Gently spread the coconut evenly on parchment-lined baking sheet and toast it for 20-minutes, frequently stirring. Cool coconut on baking sheet. When the coconut has cooled, add the cream and caramels into a microwave-safe bowl, microwave for 2-minutes, mixing every 20-seconds or so. Once smooth, mix in the toasted coconut. Now, spread the topping gently over the cheesecake. Now, melt the chocolate in microwave-safe dish, mixing often, then add it to a Ziploc bag, snip of a little bit of corner of bag. Drizzle over the top of the caramel topping. Serve chilled or at room temperature.

Nutritional Information per serving:
Calories: 332 Fat: 2.7g Carbs: 32g Protein: 7.3g

427. Salted Caramel Cheesecake

Cook Time: 35 minutes
Servings: 8
Ingredients:
For the Crust:
- 2 tablespoons sugar or 1 tablespoon Truvia
- 4 tablespoons butter, melted
- 1 ½ cups finely crushed Ritz, about 1 ½ sleeves

Cheesecake:
- ½ cup light brown sugar
- ¼ sour cream
- 2 eggs
- 16-ounces cream cheese, room temperature
- 1 ½ teaspoons vanilla
- ½ teaspoon salt
- 1 tablespoon almond flour

Toppings:
- ½ cup caramel
- 1 teaspoon flaked sea salt

Directions:
Start by spraying a 7-inch spring-form pan with non-stick cooking spray. Cut a piece of parchment paper and spray again, set aside. In mixing bowl, combine the Ritz crumbs, butter, and sugar. Take the mixture and press it firmly into the bottom and up the sides of prepared pan. Set aside.

With a hand blender mix the cream cheese and sugar until well combined. Add sour cream and mix for 30 more seconds until smooth. Add the flour, salt, and vanilla, scraping sides of the bowl when necessary. Finally, add the eggs and mix until just smooth. Add your cream cheese mixture on top of the prepared crust. To your instant pot add 2 cups of water, and add the trivet inside the instant pot. Create a foil sling that you will use to lower pan onto top of trivet. Make sure to fold down foil, so that you can shut the lid to pot. Set to Manual mode, on high with a cook time of 35-minutes. When the cook time is completed, release the pressure naturally for 15-minutes. Transfer the pan from pot and place on wire rack to cool. Wrap your pan in foil, and place in the fridge overnight. When you are ready to serve the cheesecake, top with caramel sauce and sprinkle top lightly of cake with sea salt. With a butter knife loosen the sides of the cheesecake from the pan. Serve chilled or room temperature.

Nutritional Information per serving:
Calories: 348   Fat: 2.8g   Carbs: 32g   Protein: 7.9g

428. Pumpkin Crème Brulee
Cook Time: 6 minutes **Servings: 6**
Ingredients:
- 6 egg yolks
- 1/3 cup granulated sugar
- 2 tablespoons firmly packed brown sugar
- ¼ cup pumpkin puree
- 2 ½ cups heavy cream
- ¼ teaspoon pumpkin pie spice
- 6 tablespoons fine sugar
- Pinch of salt
- ½ teaspoon cinnamon
- 1 teaspoon vanilla extract

Directions:
Start by adding 1 cup of water into your instant pot, and place a trivet inside of it. Using a large mixing bowl with a pouring spout, whisk egg yolks, granulated sugar, brown sugar, pumpkin puree, and vanilla. Mix cinnamon, pumpkin pie spice, heavy cream, salt and add to small saucepan. Place your pan over medium heat until the cream begins to boil. Whisk constantly pour the warm cream mixture into the egg mixture and continue to whisk until well-blended. Add the mixture to six custard cups that are heat-proof, cover with foil. Place three cups on the trivet.

Place the second trivet on the first on, and place the three remaining custard cups onto it. Close the lid to the pot, and select Manual mode, on high with a cook time of 6-minutes. When the cook time is completed, release the pressure using quick-release. Transfer the cups to a wire rack to cool. Once they have cooled, wrap them in plastic wrap and store them in the fridge overnight. Before serving sprinkle tops of custards, with sugar, move the flame of torch over each one to melt the sugar and form a caramelized topping. Serve room temperature.

Nutritional Information per serving:
Calories: 286   Fat: 1.5g   Carbs: 22g   Protein: 5.2g

429. Peanut Buttercup Cheesecake
Cook Time: 50 minutes **Servings: 8**
Ingredients:
For the Crust:
- 2 tablespoons butter, melted
- 1 cup crushed Oreo cookie crumbs

Filling:
- 12-ounces cream cheese, room temperature
- ½ cup smooth peanut butter
- 2 eggs, room temperature
- ½ cup sugar or 2 tablespoons Truvia
- ¾ cup semisweet chocolate chips
- 1 egg yolk, room temperature
- 1 ½ teaspoon vanilla extract
- 1 tablespoon almond flour
- ¼ cup heavy cream

Topping:
- 1/3 cup heavy cream
- 2/3 cups coarsely cut peanut butter cups
- 6-ounces milk chocolate, finely chopped

Directions:

Begin by preparing a 7-inch spring-form pan, by coating it with non-stick cooking spray. Once finished spraying pan set it aside. Combine Oreo cookie crumbs and melted butter in mixing bowl. Carefully, spread the Oreo mix evenly over the bottom of the pan. Store the pan in your freezer for about 10-minutes. In a mixing bowl, blend cream cheese and sugar on medium speed until well combined. Add in the peanut butter, vanilla, heavy cream and flour, and continue to mix. Mix in the eggs one at a time, while also adding in the chocolate chips. Add the batter into the spring-form pan on top of crust.

Now, cover the top of pan with foil. Add a cup of water into your instant pot, and place trivet inside it. Make a foil sling to use to lower pan onto top of trivet. Make sure to fold over foil, so you can close the lid to pot. Select the Manual mode, on high with a cook time of 50-minutes. Once the cook time is completed, release the pressure naturally for 15-minutes. Transfer your cheesecake onto a wire rack to cool, and remove the foil. Once the cheesecake has cooled cover it in plastic wrap, then store it in the fridge overnight. Once your cheesecake is chilled, prepare the topping: Add half of the chocolate into a mixing bowl. Heat your heavy cream over medium heat in small saucepan, until it begins to boil. Remove cream from heat and pour over chocolate, stirring until chocolate is melted. Add the remaining chocolate and continue to stir until melted. Carefully, spoon the chocolate over your cheesecake. Top the cake with coarsely chopped peanut butter cup chocolates. Keep refrigerated until ready to serve.

Nutritional Information per serving:
Calories: 342   Fat: 2.8g   Carbs: 33g   Protein: 6.9g

---

430. Oreo Cheesecake

Cook Time: 40 minutes   **Servings: 8**

Ingredients:

For the Crust:
- 13 whole Oreo cookies, crushed into crumbs
- 2 tablespoons salted butter, melted

For the Cheesecake:
- 2 large eggs, room temperature
- 9 whole Oreo cookies, coarsely chopped
- 1 tablespoon almond flour
- 16-ounces cream cheese, room temperature
- 2 teaspoons pure vanilla extract
- ¼ cup heavy cream
- ½ cup granulated sugar or 2 tablespoons Truvia

For Topping:
- 9 whole Oreo cookies, coarsely chopped
- 1 cup whipped cream or whipped topping
- Chocolate sauce, optional

Directions:

Take a 7-inch spring-form pan and with non-stick cooking spray. In a mixing bowl, stir the crushed Oreo cookies and melted butter. Press the crumbs into the bottom of the pan, and store the pan in the freezer for 10-minutes.

Blend cream cheese and sugar with a blender until smooth. Add in the eggs one at a time. Add in the heavy cream, flour as well as the vanilla to mix. Gently, fold in the 9 chopped Oreo cookies, and add the batter into the prepared pan. Using a piece of foil, cover the top of the pan. Add 1 cup of water to your instant pot, and place the trivet into pot. Construct a foil sling, this you will use to lower the pan onto the top of the trivet. Fold down the foil, so that you can close the lid of your instant pot. Select the Manual mode, on high with a cook time of 40-minutes. When the cook time is completed, release the pressure naturally for 15-minutes. Transfer the cheesecake onto a wire rack to cool. Once the cheesecake has properly cooled, store it in the fridge overnight. Before serving, top with whipped cream, covered with chopped Oreo cookies, and then drizzle cheesecake with chocolate sauce. Serve chilled.

Nutritional Information per serving:
Calories: 352   Fat: 2.4g   Carbs: 29g   Protein: 6.9g

---

431. *Orange Marble Cheesecake*
Cook Time: 25 minutes   **Servings: 8**
Ingredients:
For the Crust:
- 2 tablespoons butter, melted
- 1 ½ cups crushed Oreo cookie crumbs (12 Oreos)

For the Filling:
- 16-ounces cream cheese, room temperature
- 2 eggs, divided, room temperature
- 1 tablespoon orange zest
- ½ cup sugar or 2 tablespoons Truvia
- ½ cup orange candy melts, melted and cooled
- 1 teaspoon vanilla extract
- 2 tablespoons sour cream
- 16-ounces cream cheese, room temperature

Directions:
Take a 7-inch spring-form pan, and coat inside it with a non-stick cooking spray. Combine Oreo cookie crumbs and butter in a mixing bowl. Carefully, spread the crumbs evenly over the bottom of the pan, store your pan in freezer for 10-minutes. In a mixing bowl add 8-ounces of cream cheese and sugar, combine well. Add in sour cream, and vanilla and mix well. Add one egg at a time and blend mixture well.
In another mixing bowl, add 8-ounces of cream cheese and add ¼ cup sugar and beat until the mixture is nice and smooth. Gradually begin to add in the melted candy melts. Mix in one egg. Stir in the orange zest to mixture. Scatter dollops of vanilla batter on top of the crust alternating with dollops of orange batter. Use a skewer to swirl the orange and vanilla batters to help blend them together.
Add a cup of water to your instant pot, and a trivet inside as well. Make a foil sling for you to use to lower pan onto to the top of trivet. Remember to fold down the foil, so that you can close the pot lid. Set the pot to Manual setting on high with a cook time of 25-minutes. When the cook time is completed, release the pressure naturally for 15-minutes. Transfer the cheesecake and allow it to cool on wire rack. Once your cheesecake is cool, wrap in

plastic wrap and store it in the fridge overnight. When ready to serve decorate with grated orange candy, whipped cream, and Oreo cookie crumbs. Serve room temperature.

Nutritional Information per serving:
Calories: 322   Fat: 1.2g   Carbs: 33g   Protein: 6.8g

---

432. *Key Lime Pie*
Cook Time: 15 minutes   **Servings: 8**
Ingredients:
Graham Cracker Crust:
- 1 tablespoon sugar or 1 ½ tablespoons of Truvia
- 3 tablespoons unsalted butter, melted

Filling:
- 3 tablespoons grated key lime zest
- 1/3 cup light sour cream
- 1 (14-ounce) can sweetened condensed milk

- ¾ cup graham crackers (about five crackers)

- 4 large egg yolks
- ½ cup fresh key lime juice

Directions:
Begin by using a 7-inch spring-form pan and spray it with non-stick cooking spray. Add graham crackers crumbs, sugar and butter to a mixing bowl and mix well. Now, gently press crumb mix onto bottom of pan. Store your pan in the freezer for 10-minutes. In a large mixing bowl, beat egg yolk, and slowly add in sweetened condensed milk. Add in the lime juice and beat until nice and smooth.

Add in the sour cream and zest. Add your batter into the spring-form pan on top of crust. Cover the top of pan with piece of foil. Add a cup of water to your instant pot, and place trivet inside of your instant pot. Make a foil sling that you can use to lower pan onto top of trivet. Fold your foil sling down, so you can close the lid to pot. Set to Manual mode, on high with a cook time of 15-minutes. When the cook time is completed, release the pressure naturally for 15-minutes. Transfer the pie onto a wire rack to cool, and remove the foil. Once your pie has cooled, cover it with plastic wrap and store it in the fridge overnight. Serve with whipped cream on top.

Nutritional Information per serving:
Calories: 342   Fat: 1.5g   Carbs: 24g   Protein: 5.4g

---

433. *Hazelnut Flan*
Cook Time: 11 minutes   **Servings: 8**
Ingredients:
For the Caramel:
- ¾ cup granulated sugar

For the Custard:
- 3 tablespoons Hazelnut syrup
- 1 teaspoon vanilla extract
- ½ cup whipping cream

- ¼ cup water

- 2 cups whole milk
- Pinch of salt
- 1/3 cup granulated sugar

- 3 egg yolks
- 3 whole eggs

Directions:
Add to a medium saucepan, ¾ cup sugar and ¼ cup water, and bring to boil. Cover the pan and allow to boil for 2-minutes. Remove the lid, continue cooking until mix becomes amber in color. Move the pan gently to keep the mixture moving. Pour into 8 ungreased custard cups, that are heat-proof, 6-ounces, coat the bottom of cups. In a bowl, whisk eggs and yolks with 1/3 cup sugar and pinch of salt.

Boil milk, until it begins to bubble, in a small saucepan. Slowly, add the hot milk to the eggs to temper the eggs. Whisk in cream, hazelnut syrup, and vanilla. Now, carefully strain into a large measuring bowl with pour spout. Pour 1 ½ cups of water into your instant pot, and place a trivet inside of it. Pour custard into lined custard cups (ramekins), cover with foil, place on trivet, stack the cups in a second layer. Close the lid to pot, and set to Manual setting on high for a cook time of 6-minutes. When the cooking time is completed, release the pressure using the quick-release. Transfer the cups onto a wire rack to cool. Once cups are cool cover them with plastic wrap and store them in the fridge overnight. To serve, run a knife along the outside of ramekins, holding firmly a plate on top, then flip the whole thing over. Serve topped with whipped cream and chopped hazelnuts. Serve at room temperature.

Nutritional Information per serving:
Calories: 353   Fat: 2.8g   Carbs: 34g   Protein: 7.3g

---

434. *Custard Cream Cheesecake*
Cook Time: 25 minutes   **Servings: 8**
Ingredients:
For the Base:
- 10.6 ounces custard cream biscuits
- 1.4 ounces melted butter

For the Filling:
- 20-ounces full fat cream cheese
- 2 tablespoons Bird's custard powder
- 2 large eggs
- 4.4 ounces double cream
- Few drops almond extract
- 1 teaspoon vanilla extract
- 4 tablespoons sugar or 2 tablespoons Truvia

To Finish (optional)
- 2 teaspoons icing sugar
- 60ml double cream
- 4 extra custard cream biscuits

Directions:
Chop the biscuits into a fine crumb with the use of a food processor. Add melted butter and pulse to mix. Add mix into a 7-inch spring-form pan that has been sprayed with non-stick cooking spray. Firmly, press into base and up the sides to give a nice even layer. Combine all the filling ingredients in a mixing bowl. Add the mix on top of base in pan. Add 1 cup of water to your instant pot, and place trivet inside of it. Make a foil sling for you to use to lower the pan onto the top of your trivet. Fold down the foil sling, so you can close the pot lid. Set to Manual setting on high for a cook time of 25-minutes. When the cook time is completed, release the pressure naturally for 15-minutes. Transfer the pan onto a wire rack to cool. Once pan has cooled, chill it in your fridge overnight. Set on

serving tray, whisk cream to soft peaks with the icing sugar, add pieces of biscuits on top of cake. Serve chilled or at room temperature.

Nutritional Information per serving:
Calories: 346   Fat: 2.6g   Carbs: 32g   Protein: 7.1g

---

435. *Cranberry Baked French Toast*

Cook Time: 30 minutes   **Servings:** 8

Ingredients:
Cranberry Orange Sauce:
- ¼ teaspoon cinnamon, ground
- ¼ teaspoon salt
- ¼ cup fresh orange juice
- 2 ½ cups cranberries, fresh, washed
- ½ cup granulated sugar

French Toast:
- 5 tablespoons butter, melted
- ½ cup sugar or a tablespoon of Truvia
- 2 cups whole milk
- 1 loaf Challah bread, cubed
- ¼ teaspoon salt
- 1 teaspoon vanilla extract
- Orange zest from 1 orange, grated
- 3 eggs, beaten

Directions:
Prepare the cranberries, orange juice, ¼ teaspoon cinnamon, ½ cup sugar, and ¼ teaspoon salt and bring to a boil in small saucepan over medium-high heat. Cook for 5-minutes, stirring often. Remove from heat. Add mixture to a buttered cake pan "7x3", it needs to fit into your instant pot.

In a mixing bowl, whisk melted butter, and ½ cup sugar. Add milk, beaten eggs, orange zest, vanilla, and salt. Add in cubed bread. Allow the mixture to rest until the bread absorbs the milk, stirring occasionally. Carefully, spread bread mixture on top of cranberry sauce in the pan. Take a foil sling and use it to lower your pan on top of trivet inside the instant pot. Add 1 cup of water inside the instant pot. Fold the foil sling over so that you can close the lid. Set to Manual mode, on high for a cook time of 25-minutes. When the cook time is completed, release the pressure naturally for 10-minutes. Remove the pan from instant pot; you may want to place the pan under the broiler for a few moments to brown top. Serve at room temperature.

Nutritional Information per serving:
Calories: 341   Fat: 2.7g   Carbs: 25g   Protein: 5.4g

---

436. *Cinnamon Raisin Bread Pudding with a Caramel Pecan Sauce*

Cook Time: 20 minutes   **Servings:** 8

Ingredients:
- ½ cup packed brown sugar or 2 tablespoons Truvia
- 5 tablespoons butter, melted
- 4 eggs, beaten
- 3 cups whole milk
- ½ cup raisins
- ¼ teaspoon salt

- 7 (3/4 inch) slices cinnamon bread, cubed and toasted

Caramel Pecan Sauce:
- ¾ cup brown sugar
- ¼ cup corn syrup
- 3 tablespoons butter
- 2 tablespoons heavy cream
- 1 teaspoon vanilla extract
- ½ teaspoon cinnamon, ground
- 1 teaspoon vanilla extract
- ½ cup pecans, toasted, coarsely sliced
- ½ teaspoon salt

Directions:
In a large pot whisk together melted butter, brown sugar, beaten eggs, milk, vanilla, cinnamon. Add in the cubed bread and raisins. Allow mixture to rest for about 20-minutes or until the bread absorbs the milk, stirring occasionally.
Add the bread pudding into a buttered 1 ½ quart glass or metal baking dish (needs to fit in your instant pot). Cover the top of dish with foil. Make a foil sling for you to use to lower dish onto top of trivet that is placed inside instant pot. Add 1 ½ cups of water into instant pot. Close and secure the lid to pot and set to Manual mode, on high for a cook time of 20-minutes. When the cooking time is completed, release the pressure naturally for 15-minutes. Transfer the dish into oven that is preheated to 350° Fahrenheit for 10-minutes to crisp up the top. Serve warm or at room temperature.
Prepare the pecan sauce in a saucepan, combine the brown sugar, corn syrup, heavy cream, salt and butter. Cook sauce over medium heat, constantly stirring, until sauce comes to a boil. Reduce heat and simmer until sugar is dissolved, and sauce is smooth. Stir in vanilla and chopped pecans.

Nutritional Information per serving:
Calories: 313   Fat: 1.6g   Carbs: 36g   Protein: 6.7g

---

437. Chocolate Cake
Cook Time: 45 minutes   **Servings: 6**

Ingredients:
- ¼ cup milk
- 1 egg
- ½ teaspoon lemon juice
- ¾ cup almond flour
- 4 tablespoons butter
- ¼ cup water
- ½ cup sugar
- 3 tablespoons cocoa powder
- ¼ teaspoon salt
- ¾ teaspoon baking soda
- ¾ cup almond flour
- ½ teaspoon vanilla extract

Directions:
Whisk together baking soda, salt and flour in a pot. Set aside. In a mixing bowl, cream the butter and sugar with a whisk. Add egg, and beat again well, add water and cocoa and mix well to combine. Add the lemon juice and vanilla and continue to mix. Add the flour mixture and fold in gently. Grease a 6" cake pan with butter and pour the batter into pan. Add 1 cup of water into instant pot, and place trivet inside of it. Make a foil sling for you to use to lower the pan to the top of trivet. Set to Manual mode, on high for 45-minute cook time. When the cook time is completed, release the pressure naturally for 15-minutes. Transfer the pan onto a wire rack to cool. Once it is cool gently invert on serving plate. Serve at room temperature.

Nutritional Information per serving:
Calories: 301 Fat: 2.3g Carbs: 29g Protein: 5.2g

---

438. Borlotti Bean Brownie Cake
Cook Time: 32 minutes   **Servings: 10**
Ingredients:
For Beans:
- 1 ½ cups Borlotti beans, dried and soaked overnight
- 4 cups water

For Cake:
- 4 tablespoons extra virgin olive oil
- 1/3 teaspoon pure almond extract
- 2 teaspoons baking powder
- 2 pinches of salt
- 2 large eggs
- ½ cup raw honey
- ½ cup bitter cocoa powder

For Garnish:
- ¼ cup almonds, slivered

Directions:
Prepare Beans
Add the soaked, rinsed, strained beans and water into your instant pot. Now, close the lid, and set to Manual mode, on high for a cook time of 12-minutes. When the cook time is completed, release the pressure naturally for 10-minutes.

Prepare the Cake
Strain the beans, and add them to a food processor, blend to almost a puree (reserve the cooking liquid for stock). Allow the beans to cool for about 10-minutes. Rinse out the instant pot, add 1 cup of water, and the trivet and set aside. Coat a 4-cup capacity heat-proof bowl with olive oil, a sprinkle of cocoa powder, set aside. Add honey, almond extract, olive oil, eggs, salt and cocoa powder into the processor. Puree the contents at high speed or until they are well combined. Add baking powder and continue to process for another minute. Using a spatula, add the contents of the processor into the heat-proof bowl. Lower the heat-proof bowl into your pot. Close the lid, and set to Manual mode, on high for a cook time of 20-minutes. When the cook time is completed, release the pressure naturally for 10-minutes. Transfer the cake to a wire rack to cool. When ready to serve, sprinkle your cake with sliced almonds for garnish. Serve warm or chilled.

Nutritional Information per serving:
Calories: 311 Fat: 1.2g Carbs: 24g Protein: 6.1g

---

439. Chocolate Fudge Cake
Cook Time: 50 minutes   **Servings: 8**
Ingredients:
- 2 teaspoons of baking powder
- 2 teaspoons vanilla extract
- 1 cup almond flour
- 3 tablespoons dark cocoa powder
- 2 tablespoons olive oil
- ½ cup chocolate almond milk
- ½ cup granulated sugar
- Pinch of salt

Directions:
Add the flour, sugar, baking powder, and pinch of salt in mixing bowl. Stir in the oil, almond milk, and vanilla extract, and whisk until smooth. Add the batter into a greased baking pan that will fit in your instant pot. Add 1 cup of water to instant pot, and place trivet inside it. Cover top of your baking pan with piece of foil. Make a foil sling for you to use to lower the pan to the top of the trivet. Put on the lid to pot and set to Manual mode, on high with a cook time of 50-minutes. When the cook time is completed, release the pressure naturally for 15-minutes. Transfer the cake onto wire rack to cool. Serve chilled. Garnish with chocolate sauce and whipped cream.

Nutritional Information per serving:
Calories: 304   Fat: 1.5g   Carbs: 33g   Protein: 5.2g

---

440. Turtle Pull-Apart Biscuits
Cook Time: 45 minutes   **Servings:** 8
Ingredients:
- 2 tablespoons of whipping cream
- Pinch of salt
- ¼ cup granulated sugar
- 1/3 cup chocolate chips
- ½ cup butter, melted
- 2/3 cup of pecan halves
- 2/3 cup of brown sugar
- 16-ounces of refrigerated buttermilk biscuits, quartered

Directions:
In a small saucepan heat butter and brown sugar over low heat until they have melted. Place the granulated sugar into a Ziploc bag, toss in the biscuit quarters. Place ¼ cup of pecans on the bottom of greased instant pot, then top with 1/3 of biscuits followed by 1/3 of butter mix. Repeat the process to make another 3 layers, with the pecans on the top. Place the lid on the instant pot and set to Manual on high for a cook time of 45-minutes. When the cook time is completed, release the pressure naturally for 15-minutes. Pour the heavy cream into small saucepan and bring to a boil. Remove from heat and add in the chocolate chips, and stir until they have melted. Drizzle the chocolate sauce over the biscuit turtle. Serve warm.

Nutritional Information per serving:
Calories: 316   Fat: 2.5g   Carbs: 36g   Protein: 5.9g

---

441. Lemon Cheesecake
Cook Time: 20 minutes   **Servings:** 8
Ingredients:
- ½ cup coconut flour
- ½ cup walnuts, finely chopped
- ½ cup dates, soaked for 30-minutes
- 1 cup of quick oats
- 1 cup cashews, soaked for 30-minutes
- 1 teaspoon vanilla extract
- Dash of salt
- 1 tablespoon arrowroot powder
- 2 tablespoons lemon juice, fresh
- 2 teaspoons lemon zest, grated
- ¼ cup of coconut palm sugar
- ½ cup vanilla almond milk

Directions:
Soak the dates and cashews in two different bowls with water for 30-minutes. Transfer the soaked dates, oats and walnuts to food processor, and blend until smooth. Add some water if the mix is too dry. Press the crust mix into the bottom of a greased baking pan, then set aside. Drain the cashews and transfer to food processor with half of the soaking water, blend until smooth. Add lemon juice, coconut flour, sugar, lemon zest, milk, vanilla extract and dash of salt, then blend until smooth to make the filling. Add the arrowroot powder and blend again until smooth. Pour the filling over the crust then cover the pan with a piece of foil. Pour 2 cups of water into your instant pot, and place a trivet in it.

Place the cheesecake on top of the trivet, place the lid on the pot, and set to Manual on high with a cook time of 20-minutes. When the cook time has completed, release the pressure naturally for 15-minutes. Remove the cheesecake from pot and allow to sit on wire rack to cool for 30-minutes. Once cool, place the cake into the fridge for 4 hours. Garnish the cake with some fresh berries. Serve chilled.

Nutritional Information per serving:
Calories: 317   Fat: 1.4g   Carbs: 37g   Protein: 6.2g

---

442. *Caramel Macchiato Cake*
Cook Time: *50 minutes*   **Servings:** 8
Ingredients:
- 15-ounces of yellow cake mix
- ½ cup vegetable oil
- Pinch of salt
- 2 tablespoons of butter
- 3 eggs
- ¾ cup of brown sugar
- 1 cup of international delight mix (caramel macchiato)
- 1 ½ cups of boiling water

Directions:
Combine the cake mix with oil, caramel macchiato, and eggs in mixing bowl. Mix until smooth. Pour the batter into a greased baking pan, and cover top of pan with foil. Add 1 cup of water into instant pot, and place trivet in pot. Place the baking pan on top of trivet, and set to Manual on high for a cook time of 50-minutes. When the cook time is completed, release the pressure naturally for 15-minutes. Remove the cake and allow to sit for 30-minutes on wire rack to cool. Serve cake with some warm caramel sauce.

Nutritional Information per serving:
Calories: 321   Fat: 2.5g   Carbs: 36g   Protein: 6.2g

---

443. *Apple Peach Cobbler*
Cook Time: *45-minutes*   **Servings:** 8
Ingredients:
- ¾ cup cornmeal
- 1 cup granulated sugar, divided
- 1 ¼ cups milk
- 1 ½ cups almond flour
- 3 lbs. peaches, sliced
- ¾ cup apple butter
- Pinch of salt
- ¼ cup of bourbon
- ½ cup butter, melted

Directions:
To make the filling, toss ¼ cup of sugar, peach, bourbon, apple butter and pinch of salt into a mixing bowl. Spread the filling on the bottom of the baking pan. Mix the flour with ¾ cup sugar, cornmeal, and pinch of salt in mixing bowl. Add milk, followed by melted butter, mixing continuously. Spread the flour mix over the peach filling. Close the pot lid, and set to Manual on high for a cook time of 45-minutes. When the cook time is completed, release the pressure naturally for 15-minutes. Serve warm.
Nutritional Information per serving:
Calories: 311   Fat: 2.8g   Carbs: 32g   Protein: 6.4g

---

444. Messy Coconut Cake
Cook Time: 40 minutes   **Servings: 8**
Ingredients:
- 1 cup butter, diced
- Pinch of salt
- 28-ounces coconut milk
- 3 ½ ounces coconut flakes
- 1 package of moist cake mix

Directions:
Stir the white cake mix, and coconut milk and flakes, into greased cake pan. Place the diced butter on top, cover pan with foil. Add 1 cup water to instant pot, and place trivet inside. Place the cake pan on top of trivet. Close the lid of pot, and set to Manual setting on high with a cook time of 40-minutes. When the cook time is completed, release the pressure naturally for 15-minutes. Serve cake warm.
Nutritional Information per serving:
Calories: 287   Fat: 1.2g   Carbs: 26g   Protein: 4.2g

---

445. Vanilla Butterscotch
Cook Time: 50 minutes   **Servings: 5 ½ cups**
Ingredients:
- 1 teaspoon vanilla extract
- Pinch of salt
- ¼ cup milk
- 2/3 cup light corn syrup
- 1 cup butter, melted
- 2 cups brown sugar
- 28-ounces of condensed milk, sweetened

Directions:
In a heat-proof bowl that will fit into your instant pot, add butter, condensed milk, sugar, corn syrup, vanilla, and pinch of salt. Add 1 cup of water to your instant pot, and place trivet inside of it. Place the heat-proof bowl on top of trivet, and close the pot lid. Set to Manual setting on low with a cook time of 50-minutes. Once the cook time is complete, release the pressure naturally for 15-minutes. Add the milk gradually whisking while doing this until it is smooth. Enjoy a fondue with butterscotch syrup and your favorite fresh fruit slices. Serve warm.
Nutritional Information per serving:
Calories: 317   Fat: 1.4g   Carbs: 37g   Protein: 4.2g

446. Sticky Caramel Cake
Cook Time: 40 minutes   Servings: 8
Ingredients:
- 1 cup milk
- 1 cup granulated sugar, divided
- 1 cup of almond flour
- ¾ cup of peanut butter
- Pinch of salt
- 1 teaspoon baking powder
- 3 tablespoons cocoa powder
- 18 caramel candy, unwrapped
- 1/3 cup olive oil

Directions:
In large mixing bowl, mix ½ cup of sugar, baking powder, flour, and a pinch of salt. Add the oil, vanilla, peanut butter and milk, whisk until smooth. Spread half of the batter into a greased baking pan, then top with caramel candy followed by the remaining batter. Whisk the remaining sugar, cocoa powder, and boiling water in a small bowl until smooth. Drizzle mix over batter. Add 2 cups of water to instant pot, and place trivet inside of it. Place the cake pan on top of trivet, close the lid to pot, and set to Manual on high for a cook time of 40-minutes. When the cook time is completed, release the pressure naturally for 15-minutes. Remove the cake from instant pot, and allow to cool down a bit. Serve cake warm.

Nutritional Information per serving:
Calories: 319   Fat: 1.7g   Carbs: 31g   Protein: 5.7g

447. Cherry Pie
Cook Time: 15 minutes   Servings: 6
Ingredients:
- 1 ½ tablespoons of butter
- 4 tablespoons of quick cooking tapioca
- 1 cup white sugar or 2 tablespoons of Truvia
- 4 cups of tart cherries, pitted
- 9 inches double pie crust
- Pinch of salt
- ¼ teaspoon of almond extract
- ½ teaspoon vanilla extract

Directions:
In a mixing bowl, mix the cherries, vanilla, almond extract, tapioca, and pinch of salt. Let stand for 15-minutes. Place the bottom crust into the bottom of a greased baking pan, then pour the filling into it. Place the butter in the shape of dots on top of the filling. Cover the filling with the upper crust, then create some holes using a fork. Pour 2 cups of water into your instant pot, and place trivet inside of it. Place the pie pan on top of trivet, and set to Manual on high with a cook time of 15-minutes. When the cook time is completed, release the pressure naturally for 15-minutes. Remove pie pan and set on wire rack to cool. Serve warm or cold.

Nutritional Information per serving:
Calories: 316   Fat: 2.5g   Carbs: 36g   Protein: 5.7g

448. Classic Coconut Pudding

Cook Time: 5 minutes
Servings: 4
Ingredients:

- 1 tablespoon of cocoa powder
- 1/3 cup coconut sugar
- 1 cup coconut milk
- 1 cup Arborio rice
- 2 cups vanilla almond milk
- Pinch of salt
- 2 teaspoons vanilla extract

Directions:
In your instant pot add the coconut milk and almond milk. Set your instant pot on the sauté mode, and bring to a boil. Stir in the rice with a pinch of salt, then place the lid on pot and set on Rice setting on high with a cook time of 5-minutes. When the cook time is completed, release the pressure using the quick-release. Stir in the cocoa powder with vanilla extract. Serve pudding warm.

Nutritional Information per serving:
Calories: 258 Fat: 1.3g Carbs: 23g Protein: 4.2g

449. Buttermilk Banana Bake

Cook Time: 55 minutes
Servings: 8
Ingredients:

- 1 egg white
- 2 eggs
- ¼ cup of butter
- ¼ cup buttermilk
- ½ cup butter
- 1 cup white sugar or 2 tablespoons Truvia
- 1 ¾ cups almond flour
- 3 ripe bananas, cut into chunks
- Pinch of salt
- ½ teaspoon baking soda
- ½ teaspoon vanilla extract
- 1 ½ teaspoons of baking powder

Directions:
In a large mixing bowl, beat the white and brown sugar, and butter until light and fluffy. Add the bananas, eggs, buttermilk, and vanilla beating until smooth. Mix the flour, baking powder, baking soda and a pinch of salt in another bowl. Add this mix to the egg mix and whisk until smooth. Pour the batter into greased baking pan, and cover foil. Add 1 ½ cups of water into your instant pot, and place trivet inside of it. Place the cake pan on top of trivet. Close the pot lid, and set to Manual setting on high for a cook time of 55-minutes. When the cook time is completed, release the pressure naturally for 15-minutes. Remove the cake from instant pot, remove foil, and set on wire rack to cool. Serve warm or cold.

Nutritional Information per serving:
Calories: 294 Fat: 2.3g Carbs: 28g Protein: 6.1g

450. Lemongrass Pudding
Cook Time: 6 minutes
Servings: 8
Ingredients:
- 6-inches of fresh lemongrass, crushed
- 2 teaspoons ginger, fresh, minced
- Pinch of salt
- 4 egg yolks
- 1 cup coconut milk
- 1 cup sugar or 2 tablespoon Truvia
- 1 cup pearl tapioca
- 4 cups coconut milk

Directions:
Stir the lemongrass, coconut milk, tapioca, and ginger in your instant pot. Place the lid on and set to Manual on high for a cook time of 6-minutes. When the cook time is completed, release the pressure using quick-release. Whisk the egg yolks, coconut milk, sugar and a pinch of salt in a mixing bowl. Add the egg mix to the tapioca pudding mix and stir. Press the sauté mode on instant pot, and bring to a boil. Spoon pudding into serving glasses and allow them to cool completely. Chill them in fridge, add pieces of your favorite fruit and chopped nuts as garnish. Serve chilled.

Nutritional Information per serving:
Calories: 264   Fat: 1.3g   Carbs: 28g   Protein: 5.8g

Chapter 13. Collection of Marinades & Sauces Instant Pot Recipes

Sweet Sauces for Hot and Cold Desserts

451. Cherry Cranberry Sauce

Cook Time: 10 minutes
Servings: 2 cups of sauce
Ingredients:
- 1 bag of fresh cranberries
- 1 cinnamon stick
- 1 whole star anise
- 1 tablespoon tangerine zest
- 1 cup white sugar or 2 tablespoons Truvia
- 1 cup cherries, dried
- 3 whole cloves

Directions:
Set your instant pot to sauté mode, add all the ingredients, and cook for 10-minutes, stirring often. When the cook time is completed, allow the sauce to cool down. Remove the star anise, whole cloves and the cinnamon stick from mixture. One sauce has cooled put in a container and keep in the fridge until needed.

Nutritional Information per serving:
Calories: 121   Fat: 1.2g   Carbs: 22g   Protein: 4.8g

452. Sweet Blackberry and Brandy Sauce

Cook Time: 10 minutes
Servings: 2 cups sauce
Ingredients:
- ¼ cup water
- 2 tablespoons cornstarch
- 1 tablespoon brandy
- 1 cup sugar or 2 tablespoons Truvia
- 4 cups blackberries

Directions:
Set your instant pot to sauté mode, and add all the ingredients, except cornstarch and water to pot. Cook for 10-minutes stirring often. Dissolve the cornstarch in the water then add to sauce. Keep sauce on heat until it begins to thicken. Is a great sauce to use on cheesecake.

Nutritional Information per serving:
Calories: 172   Fat: 1.2g   Carbs: 19g   Protein: 4.8g

453. Strawberry Sauce

Cook Time: 15 minutes
Servings: 2 cups sauce
Ingredients:
- 1 pint of fresh strawberries
- 1 teaspoon vanilla extract
- 1/3 of a cup of white sugar or 1 tablespoon Truvia

Directions:
Wash the strawberries, and take off the stalks. Cut the large berries into smaller pieces. In a pan mix the strawberries, sugar and vanilla. Set your instant pot to sauté mode, and cook sauce for 15-minutes. While cooking mash the strawberries. Pour a third of the

sauce into blender and puree it. Add the puree to the rest of the mixture and stir. Allow sauce to cool. Store in fridge.
Nutritional Information per serving:
Calories: 108   Fat: 1.1g   Carbs: 21g   Protein: 4.8g

454. Lemon Dessert Sauce
Cook Time: 3 minutes
Servings: 1 ½ cups sauce
Ingredients:
- Rind of one lemon, grated
- 2 tablespoons butter
- A pinch of salt
- ¼ cup of boiling water
- 4 teaspoons cornstarch
- ½ cup sugar or 1 tablespoon Truvia

Directions:
Set your instant pot to the sauté mode, add the cornstarch, and sugar, mix well. Add the lemon juice, and the boiling water, and stir. Bring the mixture to boil for around 3-minutes. When the cook time is completed, add the lemon rind, butter and salt and stir again.
Nutritional Information per serving:
Calories: 112   Fat: 1.1g   Carbs: 18g   Protein: 3.8g

455. Brandy Sauce
Cook Time: 12 minutes
Servings: 2 cups sauce
Ingredients:
- ¼ cup caster sugar
- 4 tablespoons brandy
- ¼ cup almond flour
- ¼ cup butter

Directions:
Set your instant pot to the sauté mode, add the butter and melt it. Stir in the flour, and cook mixture for about 2-minutes. Bring the mixture to a boil and stir often. Cook for an additional 10-minutes, adding brandy and sugar.
Nutritional Information per serving:
Calories: 102   Fat: 1.2g   Carbs: 22g   Protein: 3.7g

456. Chocolate Sauce
Cook Time: 5 minutes
Servings: 2 cups
Ingredients:
- 1 cup of dark chocolate, 70% cocoa
- 1 cup full-fat milk
- 2 tablespoons double cream
- ¼ cup caster sugar
- ¼ cup butter, diced

Directions:
Break the chocolate up into small pieces, add to instant pot. Set instant pot on the sauté mode, stir often. In a small saucepan over medium-high heat add milk, sugar and cream, stir mixture, as it boils whisk it. Pour the milk mixture into the instant pot with the chocolate and stir to blend well, and cook for 5-minutes. After the cook time is completed, add in the butter and whisk it. This sauce is best served warm.

Nutritional Information per serving:
Calories: 109   Fat: 1.6g   Carbs: 24g   Protein: 3.9g

---

457. Cherry Sauce

Cook Time: 8 minutes
Servings: 1 cup of sauce

Ingredients:
- 2 teaspoons of cornstarch
- 1 tablespoon of lemon juice
- 3 tablespoons of sugar
- ¼ cup water
- 1 lb. cherries, stones removed

Directions:
Set your instant pot to the sauté mode, add the cherries, sugar, water, lemon juice and cornstarch into pot and stir. Cook sauce in pot for 8-minutes stirring often. Keep on the heat until the sauce is thick. This is a great sauce to use with pancakes, crepes and pastries.

Nutritional Information per serving:
Calories: 114   Fat: 1.7g   Carbs: 23g   Protein: 4.8g

---

458. Hot Fudge Sauce

Cook Time: 5 minutes
Servings: 1 cup sauce

Ingredients:
- 1 cup sugar or 1 tablespoon Truvia
- 1/3 cup milk
- 1 tablespoon unsalted butter
- 2 squares unsweetened chocolate squares
- Pinch of salt

Directions:
Set your instant pot to the sauté mode, melt the chocolate with butter. Add the sugar and milk, stir often, cook for about 5-minutes.

Nutritional Information per serving:
Calories: 105   Fat: 1.7g   Carbs: 26g   Protein: 3.8g

---

459. Classic Caramel Sauce

Cook Time: 5 minutes
Servings: 1 cup sauce

Ingredients:
- 1 cup of sugar
- ¼ cup water
- ½ cup corn syrup
- 2 cups of water for the instant pot

Directions:
Add 2 cups water into your instant pot, and place trivet in it. In a heat-proof bowl add sugar, corn syrup and water. Set on Manual on low for a cook time of 5-minutes. When the cook time is completed, release the pressure using the quick-release. Remove the bowl of sauce and stir.

Nutritional Information per serving:
Calories: 103   Fat: 1.8g   Carbs: 20g   Protein: 3.4g

Sauces & Marinades that Compliment Vegetarian Dishes

460. Chicken & Blueberry Pasta Sauce
Cook Time: 5 minutes   **Servings:** 1 cup sauce
Ingredients:
- 3 tablespoons olive oil
- 1 cup of blueberries
- 3 tablespoons lime juice
- 1/3 cup low salt chicken/vegetable broth
- 1 large shallot, sliced
- ¼ teaspoon salt
- 1 teaspoon lime zest
- 1 tablespoon thyme, fresh, chopped
- 1/3 cup of feta cheese

Directions:
Set your instant pot on the sauté mode, add the oil and heat it. Stir and brown, cook for 3-minutes. Add lime juice, feta cheese, broth and stir, cooking for an additional 2-minutes. Pour the sauce over cooked pasta, adding thyme, lime zest, and blueberries. Toss the mixture and serve.

Nutritional Information per serving:
Calories: 154   Fat: 1.6g   Carbs: 26g   Protein: 3.8g

461. Sweet Chocolate Pasta Sauce
Cook Time: 5 minutes   **Servings:** 2 cups
Ingredients:
- 1 cup double cream
- 1 cup chocolate hazelnut spread

For Garnish:
- Raspberries
- Crème Fraiche
- White chocolate shavings
- Chopped hazelnuts

Directions:
Set your instant pot to the sauté mode, add the chocolate and hazelnut spread and cook for 5 minutes. Add the salt and whisk until the sauce feels creamy. Toss the sauce in with your chosen cooked pasta, and garnish with raspberries, white chocolate shavings, crème Fraiche and chopped hazelnuts. You can serve this dish as a starter or a dessert.

Nutritional Information per serving:
Calories: 114   Fat: 1.8g   Carbs: 18g   Protein: 4.3g

462. Strawberry Sauce for Spaghetti
Cook Time: 12 minutes   **Servings:** 2 cups
Ingredients:
- 4-ounces of water reserved from cooking pasta
- 1 cup tomato puree
- 2 tablespoons balsamic vinegar
- 1 lb. strawberries, ripe and cut in half
- 4 tablespoons of olive oil
- Salt and pepper to taste
- Parmesan, grated to serve

Directions:

Set your instant pot to the sauté mode, add the oil and heat. Add half of the strawberries, cooking for about 5-minutes or until juice begins to run free. Add the balsamic vinegar to pot, cooking for another 2-minutes or until reduced by half. Add the reserved water, tomato puree, and the rest of the strawberries and cook for an additional 5-minutes, stirring often. Season to taste and toss the sauce into your spaghetti, top with fresh, grated Parmesan cheese. Serve warm.

Nutritional Information per serving:
Calories: 131   Fat: 1.3g   Carbs: 22g   Protein: 3.3g

---

463. Yogurt Sauce
Cook Time: 5 minutes   **Servings: 2 cups**
Ingredients:

- 2 cups plain yogurt
- 1 tablespoon butter
- 4 crushed garlic cloves
- 1 teaspoon salt
- 2 tablespoons parsley, fresh, chopped
- 3 tablespoons pine nuts

Directions:
Set your pot to the sauté mode, add yogurt into pot. Crush the salt and garlic cloves together in small bowl. Add a small amount of the warm yogurt into bowl and mix into garlic paste. Stir the garlic-yogurt paste into the pot with the rest of the yogurt, cook for 5-minutes, stirring often. Spoon sauce over pasta, and garnish with fresh, chopped parsley and pine nuts. Serve warm.

Nutritional Information per serving:
Calories: 153   Fat: 1.6g   Carbs: 20g   Protein: 3.3g

---

464. Wasabi with Maple Marinade
Cook Time: 2 minutes   **Servings: 1**
Ingredients:

- 1 teaspoon wasabi
- 4 tablespoons of olive oil
- 2 tablespoons maple syrup

Directions:
Set your instant pot to sauté mode, add oil and heat it. Add wasabi and maple syrup and cook for 2-minutes stirring to combine marinade. Chill in fridge until ready to use, this will compliment any fish-based dish.

Nutritional Information per serving:
Calories: 119   Fat: 1.3g   Carbs: 14g   Protein: 5.3g

Marinades & Sauces that Compliment Meat & Chicken Dishes

465. Garlic with Lemon Marinade
Cook Time: 2 minutes　　　　　　　**Servings:** 1
Ingredients:
- 3 tablespoons of olive oil
- 2 tablespoons of lemon juice
- 1 tablespoon lemon zest
- 1 teaspoon garlic, crushed
- Salt and pepper to taste

Directions:
Set your instant pot to sauté mode, add the oil and heat it. Add the rest of the ingredients and cook for 2-minutes, stir to combine. Allow to cool. Keep refrigerated until ready to use marinade.

Nutritional Information per serving:
Calories: 112　Fat: 1.0g　Carbs: 14g　Protein: 3.3g

466. Bourbon Marinade
Cook Time: 2 minutes　　　　　　　**Servings:** 1
Ingredients:
- 1 teaspoon cayenne pepper
- 1 tablespoon sugar or 1 teaspoon Truvia
- 2 tablespoons of bourbon
- 2 tablespoons soy sauce

Directions:
Set instant pot to sauté mode, add in all ingredients and cook for 2-minutes, stirring often. Allow to cool and store in fridge until ready to use marinade.

Nutritional Information per serving:
Calories: 132　Fat: 1.6g　Carbs: 12g　Protein: 4.1g

467. Asian-Inspired Marinade
Cook Time: 2 minutes　　　　　　　**Servings:** 1
Ingredients:
- 2 tablespoons soy sauce
- 2 tablespoons rice wine vinegar
- 2 tablespoons sesame oil
- 2 teaspoons ginger, fresh, grated

Directions:
Set your instant pot to sauté mode, add oil, and heat it. Add remaining ingredients and cook for 2-minutes, stir to combine. Allow to cool and keep in the fridge until ready to use.

Nutritional Information per serving:
Calories: 121　Fat: 1.2g　Carbs: 16g　Protein: 3.3g

468. Spicy Orange Marinade
Cook Time: 2 minutes　　　　　　　**Servings:** 1
Ingredients:

- 3 tablespoons olive oil
- 1 teaspoon red pepper flakes
- 1 tablespoon cilantro, fresh, chopped
- 1 tablespoon orange marmalade
- 2 tablespoons orange juice

Directions:
Set your instant pot to sauté mode, add the oil and heat it. Add the remaining ingredients and cook for 2-minutes, stirring often. Allow to cool. Store in fridge until ready to use.

Nutritional Information per serving:
Calories: 123   Fat: 1.5g   Carbs: 15g   Protein: 4.2g

---

469. *Olive & Lemon Moroccan Sauce*
Cook Time: 5 minutes   **Servings:** 1 ½ cups
Ingredients:
- 1 tablespoon butter
- Salt and pepper to taste
- 1 tablespoon parsley, fresh, chopped
- The juice of 1 lemon
- 1 bay leaf
- 1 stick of cinnamon
- 1 teaspoon coriander, ground
- 1 teaspoon cumin, ground
- 1 cup vegetable soup
- ½ cup green olives, chopped
- 4 garlic cloves, crushed

Directions:
Set your instant pot to the sauté mode, add the garlic cloves and olives into pot, and cook for 1-minute. Add to pot the soup, along with sliced lemon. Also add cinnamon stick, cumin, coriander and bay leaf, stir. Cook for an additional 4-minutes. Remove the bay leaf and cinnamon stick. Stir in the lemon juice and parsley. Add salt and pepper to taste along with butter, and stir. Serve warm.

Nutritional Information per serving:
Calories: 109   Fat: 1.4g   Carbs: 16g   Protein: 4.1g

---

470. *Spicy Peanut Sauce*
Cook Time: 5 minutes   **Servings:** 1 ½ cups sauce
Ingredients:
- 1 cup coconut milk
- ½ cup tamari or soy sauce
- 2 tablespoons brown rice vinegar
- ¼ cup smooth peanut butter
- ¼ cup of water
- 1 tablespoon ginger, fresh, grated
- 1 tablespoon cornstarch
- 2 tablespoons spicy chili sauce

Directions:
Combine all the ingredients and blend in a food processor. Pour the mixture into your instant pot, that you have set to sauté mode. Cook the mix for 5-minutes, stirring often.

Nutritional Information per serving:
Calories: 115   Fat: 1.2g   Carbs: 11g   Protein: 3.3g

471. Spicy Orange Sauce

Cook Time: 4 minutes
Servings: 1 ½ cups sauce

Ingredients:
- Half a cup orange juice
- 2 teaspoons toasted sesame oil
- ¼ cup lemon juice
- ½ cup tamari sauce
- 1/3 cup brown rice vinegar
- ½ cup brown sugar
- 4 garlic cloves, crushed
- A pinch of red pepper flakes

Directions:
In a small bowl mix all the ingredients, except the cornstarch and water. Add the cornstarch and water into another bowl. Add the sauce into your instant pot with the dish you are cooking. Set your instant pot on sauté mode, and cook for 4-minutes. Add the cornstarch mix into pot to thicken sauce.

Nutritional Information per serving:
Calories: 114   Fat: 1.3g   Carbs: 12g   Protein: 3.3g

472. Classic Stir-Fry Sauce

Cook Time: 5 minutes
Servings: 1 ½ cups sauce

Ingredients:
- ¼ cup cold water
- 1 tablespoon cornstarch
- A pinch of red pepper flakes
- 1 tablespoon ginger, ground
- 1 tablespoon garlic, crushed
- 1 tablespoon agave nectar
- 1 tablespoon toasted sesame oil
- 3 tablespoons brown rice vinegar
- ½ cup vegetable soup
- ½ cup tamari or soy sauce

Directions:
Mix all the ingredients in a bowl, except for water and cornstarch. In a separate bowl mix the cornstarch and water. Set your instant pot to the sauté mode, add in the sauce mixture, and cook for 5-minutes, stirring often. Add some of the cornstarch mixture to thicken the sauce. Serve warm.

Nutritional Information per serving:
Calories: 106   Fat: 1.5g   Carbs: 10g   Protein: 4.2g

473. Sorghum Steak Wet Rub

Cook Time: 3 minutes
Servings: 10 cups of wet rub

Ingredients:
- Hot sauce to taste
- Salt and pepper to taste
- 2 ¼ cups balsamic vinegar
- 2 ¼ cups Dijon mustard
- 3 1/3 cups of Worcestershire sauce
- 4 and a half cups tomato sauce
- 6 cups boiling water
- 6 cups raisins
- 3 cups orange juice
- 1 cup sorghum

Directions:

Place the raisins in a bowl of water and allow them to sit for 5-minutes to allow them to plump up. Add the remaining ingredients to food processor and puree until smooth. Set your instant pot to sauté mode, add the puree mixture to instant pot, and cook for 3 minutes. Season to taste with salt, pepper and hot sauce, add in the drained raisins to sauce, stir well. Allow sauce to cool then use the rub on your meat as required.

Nutritional Information per serving:
Calories: 113 Fat: 1.2g Carbs: 10g Protein: 4.1g

---

474. Orange & Nutmeg Poultry Rub
Cook Time: 4 minutes   **Servings:** 1 cup of rub
Ingredients:
- ¼ teaspoon cloves
- ¼ teaspoon nutmeg
- 1 tablespoon black pepper
- 2 tablespoons orange zest
- 2 tablespoons brown sugar
- 2 tablespoons ginger, ground
- 1 cup water

Directions:
Set your instant pot to the sauté mode, add all the rub ingredients to pot, and cook for 4-minutes, stirring often. Allow rub to cool, then store in fridge until ready to use.

Nutritional Information per serving:
Calories: 114 Fat: 1.2g Carbs: 12g Protein: 3.1g

---

475. Creole Rub
Cook Time: 3 minutes   **Servings:** 1 cup rub
Ingredients:
- ¼ cup Cajun seasoning
- 1 tablespoon hot pepper sauce
- 1 ½ tablespoons garlic, crushed
- ½ cup onion, minced
- ½ cup Creole mustard
- ½ cup water

Directions:
Set your instant pot to sauté mode, add all the ingredients into pot, and cook for 3-minutes, stir often. Allow mix to cool before applying it to meat as required.

Nutritional Information per serving:
Calories: 102 Fat: 1.2g Carbs: 13g Protein: 4.2g

---

476. Ketchup with Cola Marinade
Cook Time: 2 minutes   **Servings:** 1 ½ cups marinade
Ingredients:
- 1 garlic clove, crushed
- 1 teaspoon paprika
- 2 teaspoons yellow mustard, dry
- 2 tablespoons olive oil
- 3 tablespoons apple cider vinegar
- 3 tablespoons brown sugar
- 1 cup tomato ketchup
- 1 cup cola

Directions:

Set your instant pot to the sauté mode, add the oil and heat it. Add the rest of the ingredients, and cook for 2-minutes, stirring often. Allow marinade to cool then keep in the fridge until ready to use.

Nutritional Information per serving:
Calories: 103   Fat: 1.6g   Carbs: 17g   Protein: 4.1g

---

477. *Spicy Beer Wings Marinade*
***Cook Time:* 3 minutes   *Servings:* 1 cup of marinade**
Ingredients:
- Half a cup of beer
- 1 tablespoon of olive oil
- 2 whole jalapenos
- 7 garlic cloves, crushed
- 2 whole habaneros
- ½ a teaspoon of paprika
- 1 teaspoon garlic powder
- 2 teaspoons salt

Directions:
Add all the ingredients into food processor, and blend until finely chopped. Set your instant pot to sauté mode, add the mixture into pot, and cook for 3-minutes, while stirring to combine. Allow the mixture to cool. Put mixture in container and place in fridge to chill for a few hours. Remove from fridge add to a plastic lock bag along with chicken wings. Lock the bag and shake it to make sure the wings are coated with marinade sauce. Place the bag in the fridge overnight, shake every couple of hours. Remove your wings from the fridge about 10-minutes before you want to cook them.

Nutritional Information per serving:
Calories: 111   Fat: 1.6g   Carbs: 15g   Protein: 4.2g

---

478. *Coffee Steak Marinade*
***Cook Time:* 5 minutes   *Servings:* 1 ½ cups marinade**
Ingredients:
- A teaspoon of salt
- A teaspoon of black pepper
- A teaspoon of red pepper flakes
- 2 fresh rosemary sprigs
- 3 garlic cloves, chopped
- 4 tablespoons maple syrup
- 1 cup of black coffee, cooled

Directions:
Set your instant pot to the sauté mode, add all the ingredients and cook for 5-minutes, stir often. Allow marinade to cool, place in a container and refrigerate for 2-hours. Marinate steak in mixture for 2 hours in the fridge. After 1 hour turn the steak over during the marinating process. Once steak is fully marinated cook it to taste and serve hot.

Nutritional Information per serving:
Calories: 110   Fat: 1.7g   Carbs: 20g   Protein: 3.3g

479. Blue Cheese Sauce

Cook Time: 5 minutes
Servings: 1 cup sauce
Ingredients:
- 1 cup of blue cheese
- 1 cup of double cream

Directions:
Set your instant pot to the sauté mode, add the ingredients and cook for 5-minutes, stirring often. Serve warm. This sauce is great with beef, pork or chicken dishes.

Nutritional Information per serving:
Calories: 108   Fat: 1.3g   Carbs: 21g   Protein: 5.3g

---

480. Classic Pepper Sauce

Cook Time: 15 minutes
Servings: 2 cups of sauce
Ingredients:
- 2 cups evaporated milk
- 2 tablespoons Worcestershire sauce
- 2 teaspoons black ground pepper
- 2 teaspoons green peppercorns
- 1 tablespoon olive oil

Directions:
Set your instant pot to the sauté mode, and oil and heat it. Add your choice of meat and cook for 5-minutes browning all sides. Remove the meat and set aside. Add sauce ingredients into pot and blend them with the meat juices in pot. Cook for an additional 5-minutes, stirring often. Add the meat back into the pan and continue to sauté for another 5-minutes. Serve hot.

Nutritional Information per serving:
Calories: 117   Fat: 1.5g   Carbs: 16g   Protein: 4.2g

---

481. Chili Sauce with Tomato

Cook Time: 7 minutes
Servings: 2 cups sauce
Ingredients:
- ½ cup water
- Pinch salt and pepper
- 2 tablespoons tomato puree
- 1 cup sugar
- 6 red birds eye chilies, thinly sliced
- 4 red chilies, thinly sliced
- 2 capsicums, peeled and deseeded
- 2 onions, roughly chopped
- 6 large tomatoes, ripe
- 1 tablespoon olive oil

Directions:
Peel all the tomatoes and remove stalks, and slice into quarters. Set your instant pot to the sauté mode, add oil and heat it. Add onions and cook for 2-minutes. Add tomatoes, chili seeds, capsicum and chilies, cook for 5-minutes stirring often. Use a stick blender to make the sauce runny, and stir in the sugar, stir. This sauce works great with red meat dishes.

Nutritional Information per serving:
Calories: 116   Fat: 1.3g   Carbs: 16g   Protein: 4.1g

482. Classic Cream & Garlic Sauce
Cook Time: 5 minutes **Servings: 1 ½ cups sauce**
Ingredients:
- 1 tablespoon corn flour
- ¾ cup of cream
- 1 beef stock cube
- 1 cup water
- 1 tablespoon garlic steak seasoning
- 1 tablespoon of garlic powder
- 4 garlic cloves, crushed
- 1 tablespoon olive oil

Directions:
Set your instant pot to the sauté mode, add oil and heat it. Peel and crush up garlic cloves and add to instant pot, cook for 2-minutes. Add water, and crumble in the stock cube. Add seasoning and garlic powder into pot and stir. Pour in the cream and stir again, cook for an additional 3-minutes. Add in corn flour and stir, this will thicken sauce. This sauce goes great with steak or surf and turf. Serve hot.

Nutritional Information per serving:
Calories: 114   Fat: 1.4g   Carbs: 18g   Protein: 3.3g

483. Marinara Sauce
Cook Time: 15 minutes
Servings: 1 cup sauce
Ingredients:
- ¼ cup oregano, fresh, chopped
- Salt and pepper to taste
- 3 tablespoons of olive oil
- 1 head of roasted garlic
- ½ cup red wine
- 2 (28-ounce) cans of plum tomatoes
- 1 red onion, large, finely chopped

Directions:
Set your instant pot to the sauté setting, add oil and heat it. Add the red onions, and cook for 2-minutes. Add garlic into pot and cook for an additional 3-minutes. Add the wine to pot and mix well. Add half of the oregano, salt and pepper, stir. Add the tomatoes and rest of ingredients into pot. Set the pot to Manual setting on high with a cook time of 10-minutes. When the cook time is competed, release the pressure naturally for 10-minutes. Allow the sauce to cool for 30-minutes. Add sauce to blender and blend until smooth. Leave in fridge overnight. Serve with pasta.

Nutritional Information per serving:
Calories: 219   Fat: 1.6g   Carbs: 21g   Protein: 4.2g

484. Brown Sauce
Cook Time: 5 minutes
Servings: 1 ½ cups sauce
Ingredients:
- ½ cup red wine
- 2 tablespoons butter
- 2 tablespoons almond flour
- 1 cup beef stock

- Salt and black pepper to taste
- ½ teaspoon parsley, dried

Directions:
After you have browned your meat in instant pot, remove it from pot. Set pot on sauté mode, and add the butter and heat it. Add flour and whisk sauce in pot. Add wine and seasonings and whisk. When sauce thickens, pour it over your meat and serve hot.

Nutritional Information per serving:
Calories: 218   Fat: 1.2g   Carbs: 12g   Protein: 3.3g

---

485. Veloute Sauce
Cook Time: 10 minutes   **Servings:** 1 cup sauce
Ingredients:
- 1 cup shallots, chopped finely
- ½ cup white mushrooms, diced
- ½ cup white wine
- Salt and black pepper to taste
- 1 cup of chicken stock
- 2 tablespoons butter
- 1 tablespoon almond flou

Directions:
Set your instant pot to the sauté mode, add the butter and heat it. Add flour and stir. Add the shallots and cook for 2-minutes. Add the mushrooms and cook for an additional 3-minutes, stir. Add the stock, white wine, seasonings, stir and cook for another 5-minutes, stirring often. Serve sauce hot, pour over protein dishes or even just vegetables.

Nutritional Information per serving:
Calories: 218   Fat: 1.5g   Carbs: 19g   Protein: 4.6g

---

486. Tuscan Style Meat Sauce
Cook Time: 28 minutes   **Servings:** 2 cups sauce
Ingredients:
- 1 lb. tomatoes, peeled, and chopped
- 1 tablespoon tomato paste
- ½ cup red wine vinegar
- 4-ounces pork, ground
- 4-ounces beef, ground
- 1 large stalk of celery, minced
- 1 carrot, large, minced
- 1 onion, minced
- 2 tablespoons extra-virgin olive oil
- Salt and pepper to taste

Directions:
Set your instant pot to the sauté mode, add the oil and heat it. Add the pork and beef, and cook for 5-minutes, stirring and browning on all sides. Remove meat from pan and set aside. Add onions, carrots, celery to pot and cook for 3-minutes. Add the wine, tomatoes, seasoning, stir to combine. Add the meat back into pot. Close the lid to pot and set on Manual, on low with a cook time of 20-minutes. When the cook time is completed, release the pressure naturally for 10-minutes. Serve hot over pasta.

Nutritional Information per serving:
Calories: 262   Fat: 2.8g   Carbs: 26g   Protein: 25.3g

487. Indonesian Soy Sauce

Cook Time: 15 minutes
Servings: 1 cup sauce

Ingredients:
- 2/3 cup soy sauce
- 8 bay leaves
- 2/3 cup brown sugar
- 1 cup water

Directions:
Set your instant pot to the sauté mode, and add the ingredients into it, and stir. Blend well to combine, and cook for 5-minutes. Set the pot to Manual setting on low, for a cook time of 10-minutes. When the cook time is completed, release the pressure naturally for 10-minutes. Serve sauce hot or cold.

Nutritional Information per serving:
Calories: 131   Fat: 1.1g   Carbs: 11g   Protein: 3.2g

488. Sweet Coney Island Sauce

Cook Time: 30 minutes
Servings: 1 cup sauce

Ingredients:
- ¼ cup ketchup
- ¼ teaspoon hot pepper sauce
- ¼ teaspoon celery seed
- 1 teaspoon Worcestershire sauce
- 1 tablespoon water
- 2 tablespoons white sugar or 1 tablespoon Truvia
- 2 tablespoons cider vinegar
- 2 tablespoons prepared mustard
- 1 lb. ground beef
- 2 tablespoons olive oil

Directions:
Set your instant pot to sauté mode, add oil and heat it. Add the ground beef, brown on all sides, stir and cook for 10-minutes. Add in the rest of the ingredients and stir. Close lid and set to Manual setting on low for 20-minute cook time. When the cook time is completed, release the pressure naturally for 10-minutes. Serve warm over pasta.

Nutritional Information per serving:
Calories: 223   Fat: 1.7g   Carbs: 24g   Protein: 23.9g

489. Wine Sauce

Cook Time: 15 minutes
Servings: 1 ½ cup sauce

Ingredients:
- 1 cup plain bread crumbs
- 2 tablespoons red wine vinegar
- 1 cup beef stock
- 3 tablespoons parsley, dried
- 2 cloves garlic, minced
- 2 shallots, minced
- 2 yellow onions, minced
- ¼ cup white wine

Directions:
Set to sauté mode, add all the ingredients into pot and stir, cook for 5-minutes. Set to Manual on low for a cook time of 10-minutes. When the cook time is completed, release the pressure naturally for 10-minutes. Serve this wine sauce over boneless pork butt roast.

Nutritional Information per serving:
Calories: 172   Fat: 2.8g   Carbs: 26g   Protein: 4.3g

---

490. Mustard Cream Sauce
Cook Time: 5 minutes   **Servings:** 1 cup sauce
Ingredients:
- 2 tablespoons heavy cream
- 2 tablespoons coarse-grain mustard
- 1 cup chicken stock

Directions:
Set your instant pot to the sauté mode, add the ingredients for sauce and cook for 5-minutes, stirring often. Serve this sauce over cooked steaks. Serve hot.

Nutritional Information per serving:
Calories: 182   Fat: 1.7g   Carbs: 22g   Protein: 4.1g

---

491. Green Pea Sauce
Cook Time: 5 minutes   **Servings:** 1 ½ cups sauce
Ingredients:
- ½ cup canned evaporated milk
- 1 tablespoon olive oil
- 1 medium onion, finely diced
- 2/3 cup frozen peas
- 1 cup vegetable broth
- Salt and pepper to taste

Directions:
Set your instant pot to the sauté mode, add the oil and heat it. Add the onion and cook for 2-minutes, stir. Add the garlic, and stir. Add the peas into pot and stir to thaw. Add the evaporated milk, and vegetable stock. Close the lid to pot and set pot to Manual on low with a cook time of 3-minutes. When the cook time is complete, release the pressure using quick-release. Add salt and pepper to taste and stir. Serve warm over honey-glazed ham.

Nutritional Information per serving:
Calories: 153   Fat: 1.6g   Carbs: 21g   Protein: 4.2g

---

492. Mexican Mole Sauce
Cook Time: 10 minutes   **Servings:** 1 cup sauce
Ingredients:
- 1 (4-ounce) can diced green chile peppers
- 1 (10.75-ounce) can condensed tomato soup
- 1/8 teaspoon of garlic, minced
- 1 teaspoon cilantro, dried
- 1 teaspoon cumin, ground
- 1 tablespoon unsweetened cocoa powder
- ¼ cup onion, finely chopped
- 2 tablespoons olive oil

Directions:
Set your instant pot to the sauté mode, add the oil and heat it. Add the onion, and cook for 2-minutes, stir. Mix in cumin, cilantro, garlic, and cocoa powder. Stir in the tomato soup

and green peppers. Close lid and set to Manual on low with a cook time of 8-minutes. When the cook time is completed, release the pressure using quick-release. Transfer to gravy boat and serve warm over red meat dishes.

Nutritional Information per serving:
Calories: 186   Fat: 1.3g   Carbs: 20g   Protein: 4.2g

---

493. *Thai-Style Peanut Sauce with Honey*
Cook Time: 4 minutes   **Servings:** 1 cup sauce

Ingredients:
- 1 tablespoon ginger, fresh, minced
- 1 teaspoon red pepper flakes, crushed
- 2 teaspoons garlic cloves, minced
- 2 tablespoons sesame oil
- 2 tablespoons extra-virgin olive oil
- 2 tablespoons rice vinegar
- 3 tablespoons soy sauce
- 1 tablespoon crunchy peanut butter
- ¼ cup smooth peanut butter
- ½ cup honey

Directions:
Set your instant pot to the sauté mode, add olive and sesame oil, heat them. Add honey, peanut butter, rice vinegar, soy sauce, ginger, red pepper flakes, stir and cook for 4-minutes. Serve warm over favorite Thai dish.

Nutritional Information per serving:
Calories: 163   Fat: 1.6g   Carbs: 24g   Protein: 6.2g

---

494. *Ginger-Tamarind Sauce*
Cook Time: 20 minutes   **Servings:** 3 cups sauce

Ingredients:
- ½ teaspoon red pepper, ground
- 2 tablespoons coriander powder
- 1 tablespoon tamarind paste
- 2 cups water
- 2 tablespoons ginger, chopped, fresh
- 1 cup onion, chopped
- 1 teaspoon mustard seed
- 1 tablespoon olive oil
- ½ teaspoon chile powder

Directions:
Set your instant pot to sauté mode, add the oil and heat it. Add in the mustard seeds, and cook for 2-minutes. Add in the onion, and ginger, stir and cook for an additional 3-minutes. Stir in the tamarind paste, water and season with chile powder, red pepper, coriander and salt. Close the lid to pot and set to Manual on low for a cook time of 15-minutes. When the cook time is completed, release the pressure naturally for 15-minutes. Stir in ½ pound of fish of choice such as cod fillets, cubed into 1-inch pieces, and set on sauté until the fish is cooked through, stir often. Serve warm.

Nutritional Information per serving:
Calories: 189   Fat: 1.2g   Carbs: 21g   Protein: 3.2g

495. Enchilada Sauce

Cook Time: 13 minutes
Servings: 2 cups sauce
Ingredients:
- Garlic powder to taste
- ¼ cup tomato sauce
- 2 cups water
- ¼ cup chili powder
- 2 tablespoons almond flour
- 2 tablespoons olive oil

Directions:
Set your instant pot to the sauté mode, add the oil and heat it. Stir in the flour and cook for 1-minute. Add in the chili powder and cook for another minute. Add in the water, tomato sauce, seasonings and whisk to remove lumps. Cover with lid and set pot to Manual setting on low with a cook time of 11-minutes. When the cook time is completed, release the pressure naturally for 10-minutes. Serve warm over enchilada dish.

Nutritional Information per serving:
Calories: 173   Fat: 1.2g   Carbs: 21g   Protein: 4.4g

496. Creamy White Wine Sauce

Cook Time: 5 minutes
Servings: 1 cup sauce
Ingredients:
- 1 teaspoon parsley, dried
- 1 teaspoon salt
- 2 tablespoons almond flour
- ¾ cup white wine
- 1 cup heavy whipping cream

Directions:
Set your instant pot to the sauté mode, add the sauce ingredients and stir to combine. Cook the sauce for 5-minutes stirring often, bring to a boil. Serve warm over favorite chicken dish.

Nutritional Information per serving:
Calories: 166   Fat: 1.2g   Carbs: 24g   Protein: 4.4g

497. Sweet & Sour Sauce

Cook Time: 5 minutes
Servings: 2 cups sauce
Ingredients:
- 1 teaspoon cornstarch
- ¼ cup water
- 3 drops red food coloring
- 1 teaspoon garlic powder
- 4 teaspoons soy sauce
- ½ cup ketchup
- 2 teaspoons monosodium glutamate (MSG)
- ½ cup pineapple juice
- 1 cup white sugar or 2 tablespoons Truvia
- 1 cup distilled white vinegar

Directions:
Set your instant pot to the sauté mode, add vinegar and sugar and stir to combine. Add pineapple juice, monosodium glutamate, ketchup, garlic powder, salt, soy sauce, and cook for 5-minutes and stir. Add in the food coloring and mix. In a small cup mix water and

cornstarch, slowly add to mixture in pot until you get desired consistency. Serve warm with favorite pork or chicken dish.
Nutritional Information per serving:
Calories: 206   Fat: 2.6g   Carbs: 29g   Protein: 4.8g

---

498. *Mustard Sauce*
Cook Time: 3 minutes
Servings: 1 cup sauce
Ingredients:
- ¼ cup sour cream
- ¼ cup Dijon mustard
- 2 teaspoons cornstarch
- 1 cup chicken broth

Directions:
Set your instant pot to the sauté mode, add the sauce and cornstarch, whisk and cook for 1-minute. Add in mustard, and sour cream, stirring often, and cooking for an additional 2-minutes. Serve warm over favorite chicken dish.
Nutritional Information per serving:
Calories: 209   Fat: 2.5g   Carbs: 24g   Protein: 3.8g

---

499. *Cranberry Sauce*
Cook Time: 10 minutes
Servings: 1 ½ cups sauce
Ingredients:
- 1 cinnamon stick
- ½ teaspoon salt
- 1 tablespoon apple cider vinegar
- ¼ cup white sugar
- 1/3 cup seedless raspberry jam
- 2/3 cup water
- 1 cup pitted prunes, quartered
- 1 (12-ounce) package of fresh or frozen cranberries

Directions:
Set your instant pot to the sauté mode, combine prunes, water, cranberries, raspberry jam, sugar, salt, vinegar, and cinnamon stick in pot, stir occasionally for 3-minutes. Close lid and set to Manual setting on low with a cook time of 10-minutes. When the cook time is completed, release the pressure naturally for 10-minutes. Allow sauce to cool then transfer to container and place in fridge for at least 3 hours before serving. Serve warm or cold over favorite poultry dish.
Nutritional Information per serving:
Calories: 213   Fat: 2.8g   Carbs: 28g   Protein: 4.7g

---

500. *Rum Sauce*
Cook Time: 5 minutes
Servings: 1 ½ cups sauce
Ingredients:
- 3 tablespoons white or dark rum
- 1 cup milk
- ½ cup sugar or 1 tablespoon Truvia
- 1 tablespoon cornstarch
- 2 tablespoons butter

Directions:

Set your instant pot to the sauté mode, add the sugar and cornstarch and mix. Add in the butter. Pour in the milk and stir often cooking for 5-minutes. Transfer sauce into a bowl and stir in the rum. Serve warm.

Nutritional Information per serving:
Calories: 210   Fat: 2.8g   Carbs: 27g   Protein: 4.5g

Conclusion

I do hope that you have enjoyed reading my recipe book, as much as I have enjoyed writing it. I hope that my recipe collection will offer you some new and healthy options to add to your daily diet.

The best thing that I discovered while writing this book is that your meals do not have to be tasteless and boring to be healthy. Within these pages is a wide selection of recipes that are full of wonderful flavors that will have your tastebuds tingling with delight while at the same time offering you good nutritious meals.

To further reduce your sugar intake, I would suggest replacing any sugars in my recipe collection with the wonderful "Truvia" a calorie-free natural sweetener that comes from the Stevia plant, native to South America. I wish you immense success in adding new and healthier meal choices to your diet—that are not only good for you but taste amazing!

Printed in Great Britain
by Amazon